America

Since 1945

America

Since 1945

Edited by

Robert D. Marcus

and

David Burner

State University of New York

at Stony Brook

St. Martin's Press

New York

PART ONE   1945-1952

"Russia and the Cold War" by Averell Harriman. From *America and Russia in a Changing World* by Averell Harriman. Copyright © 1970, 1971 by W. Averell Harriman. Reprinted by permission of Doubleday & Company, Inc.

"The Cold War: A Revisionist View" by David Horowitz. From *The Free World Colossus* by David Horowitz. Copyright © 1965, 1967, 1971 by David Horowitz. Reprinted with the permission of Hill and Wang, Inc.

"Truman and Domestic Politics: The Election of 1948" by Richard Kirkendall. From *The American Scene: Varieties of American History*, Volume II, edited by Robert D. Marcus and David Burner. Copyright © 1971. By permission of Appleton-Century-Crofts, Educational Division, Meredith Corporation.

"Truman and Foreign Policy: The Korean War" by Walter LaFeber. From *America, Russia, and the Cold War, 1945-1966* by Walter LaFeber. Copyright © 1967 by John Wiley & Sons, Inc. Reprinted by permission.

PART TWO   1952-1959

"Nixon Agonistes: The Checkers Speech" by Garry Wills, on pages 91-93 and 95-114 of Wills' *Nixon Agonistes*. Copyright © 1969, 1970 by Garry Wills. Reprinted by permission of the publisher, Houghton Mifflin Company.

"The Underestimation of Dwight D. Eisenhower" by Murray Kempton. Reprinted by permission of John Cushman Associates, Inc. First published in *Esquire* Magazine. Copyright © 1967 by Murray Kempton.

"Eisenhower Revisited—A Political Genius? A Brilliant Man?" by Richard H. Rovere. © 1971 by The New York Times Company. Reprinted by permission.

A selection reprinted from Chapter 2 of *The Feminine Mystique* by Betty Friedan. By permission of W. W. Norton & Company, Inc. Copyright © 1963 by Betty Friedan.

"The Texture of Poverty" by Michael Harrington. Reprinted with permission of The Macmillan Company from *The Other America* by Michael Harrington. © Michael Harrington 1962, 1969.

PART THREE   THE 1960's

"Kennedy: A Cold Warrior" by David Burner. From *A Giant's Strength: America in the 1960's* by David Burner, Robert D. Marcus, and Thomas R. West. Copyright © 1971 by Holt, Rinehart and Winston, Inc. Reprinted by permission of Holt, Rinehart and Winston, Inc.

"Building the Great Society: The Case of Equal Rights" by James Sundquist. From *Politics and Policy* by James Sundquist. Copyright 1968 by The Brookings Institution, Washington, D.C. Reprinted by permission of The Brookings Institution.

"Lyndon Johnson and Vietnam: 1968" by Townsend Hoopes. Copyright © 1969 by Townsend Hoopes. From *The Limits of Intervention* by Townsend Hoopes, pub-

Preface

The United States since the end of World War II has contained all the makings of a great historical subject. More powerful yet more vulnerable than ever before, this nation has been not only the world's major military and economic power but also increasingly the center of the world's culture. Having completely terminated their role as European provincials, Americans in this new era have often seemed most awkward at the center of the world's stage, and reviews of their performance, in diplomacy as well as in culture, have varied widely. Rarely a complacent people, they have sought eagerly for a perspective on their place in the world.

Keeping in mind this search for a perspective, we have tried to choose articles that deal with—and link together—the most significant political and social events of the past quarter century. In the area of foreign affairs there are many selections, such as Averell Harriman's and David Horowitz's views of the Cold War, Walter LaFeber's discussion of Truman and the Korean war, and Townsend Hoopes' account of the changes in Vietnam policy in 1968. In the domestic realm we have included not only political articles, such as Garry Wills' re-evaluation of Nixon's famous Checkers speech, but also articles that deal with some of the social transformations of the last twenty-five years—selections from Betty Friedan's *The Feminine Mystique,* Michael Harrington's *The Other America,* and Kenneth Keniston's *Youth and Dissent.* Throughout the anthology we have attempted to achieve a good mix of primary and secondary materials, and have included excerpts from such original sources as the *Report to the President's Committee on Civil Rights* in 1947, the Army-McCarthy hearings, and *The Walker Report.*

It is impossible to write anything like a definitive history of the past twenty-five years, but it is possible to look back on the events since 1945 and try to make some sense of them; try to gain some insight into the effects that our immediate past is having on our present.

Robert D. Marcus
David Burner

Contents

PART ONE

1945-1952

In 1945 World War II ended and the atomic age began. It was a year of high drama: of the final defeat of the Axis powers, the establishment of the United Nations, and the beginning of what people hoped would be a great "American century" in which, under our guidance, the world would know a long era of peace and progress. Americans eagerly awaited demobilization, the sweet harvest of victory. Yet they were uneasy. The great leader, Franklin D. Roosevelt, was dead and in his place a modest ex-haberdasher from Missouri. Victory in Europe had left that continent devastated. Victory over Japan had introduced the world to the horror of nuclear weapons. And in America victory raised the question of whether an economy which had been depressed for a decade would not lapse into the same dismal state from which war production had roused it. Moreover, the unusual homefront harmony had suppressed intense conflicts that would break out again in an era of peace.

Many of the hopes and even more of the fears were realized in the next few years. The United Nations survived, the United States remained the greatest world power, and the domestic economy showed little inclination to slip back into depression. But the image of an "American century" rapidly gave way before the reality of a cold war. New Deal reforms were continued but not expanded, as bipartisan forces vigorously pursued the ideological conflict with the Soviet Union. Amid confusion and ill-feeling the nation rearmed, fought an inconclusive war in Asia, created an economy dependent on military spending, and moved irregularly toward a social order which in the 1950's seemed more stable than in fact it was. In reaction to a threatening world, Americans in 1952 closed ranks behind a popular and decidedly unmilitaristic general whom they hoped—correctly as it turned out—would put the sour era of postwar adjustment behind them.

Russia and the Cold War

AVERELL HARRIMAN

From 1926 when he bargained with Leon Trotsky in Moscow over a manganese concession until 1968 when he conferred in Paris with the North Vietnamese, Averell Harriman has probably been our most experienced and influential representative to the Communist world. His reminiscences are important not only for the insights he has acquired about Communist governments over the years, but for what they reveal about developing American foreign policy.

Harriman never conceived of American-Soviet relations as a struggle to the death between hostile forces, one destined to conquer, the other to die. He had contempt for the crusading cold-warrior mentality in international affairs and strongly criticized Eisenhower's Secretary of State, John Foster Dulles, for taking "the position that Communism was evil and that countries were either for us or against us in our struggle with it."

Harriman's opinions are quite typical of American policy makers in the immediate postwar era. He himself called it "a fairly glorious period, perhaps the most creative period in American foreign policy." The idealism he expresses—as in his account of the Marshall Plan—is undoubtedly genuine. Although some critics such as David Horowitz (in the next selection) have suggested that those liberal ideals actually defined the world in a way that made the Cold War inevitable, Harriman contends that Stalin's intransigence led to an unavoidable collapse of the wartime alliance.

There has grown a myth about Yalta that somehow or other Roosevelt and Churchill sold out Eastern Europe to Stalin. That wasn't true at all. I can't imagine why Stalin went to such extreme lengths in breaking the Yalta agreements if it had been true that they were so much to his advantage. It was agreed that the people in these countries were to decide on their own governments through free elections. But Stalin didn't permit it.

One wonders why he broke his agreement on Poland so soon. It's rather hard to guess. Personally, I think one of the reasons was that Bierut, the leading member of the Lublin Polish government—the Communist government—was in Moscow on Stalin's return from Yalta. He may have told Stalin that if he carried out his plan for free elections, Bierut and his comrades couldn't deliver Poland. Stalin had the idea that the Red Army would be accepted as a liberating army. In fact, he told me so. In this regard, perhaps the Communist partisans had reported too optimistically to Moscow. At any rate I think the Kremlin leaders were awfully hurt when they found that the Red Army was

3

looked upon by the Poles, the Romanians, and others as a new invading force.

In addition, there appeared to be two schools of thought in the Kremlin hierarchy—the Politburo itself. One is apt to think of the Communist government as one single brain; it isn't. It is made up of men with sometimes differing views; this was true even under Stalin. I was conscious of the fact that members of Politburo even during the war had different views on different subjects. Let me quickly say that there was free discussion in the Politburo on *new* subjects only. On anything Stalin had decided, that was it. That couldn't be questioned. I think it is fair to say that in these discussions about new matters, Stalin listened, smoked his pipe, and walked up and down the room. Then, when he had heard enough, he said, "This is what we are going to do." If anyone left the room with a shrug of his shoulders, he might find himself on the way to Siberia the next afternoon. That may be somewhat of an exaggeration, but I think it's pretty nearly right.

In any event, I feel sure that there was a difference of opinion as to whether it would be wise for the Soviet Union in the immediate postwar period to soft-pedal Communist expansion for a time and continue to collaborate with the Western Allies to get the value of loans and trade, technical assistance, and other cooperation for the terrific job of reconstruction they faced; or whether they should push ahead and use the extraordinary opportunities in the dislocations in Europe and elsewhere to extend Communist control. Stalin once told me, "Communism breeds in the cesspools of capitalists." In this sense, Europe looked as if it were going to be in a mire.

I was so concerned about this that in early 1945, I sent messages about the need to help Western Europe, urging that the recovery of Europe would require much more than most people thought. I said that UNRRA would not be enough, food would not be enough. We would have to supply working capital and raw materials to get trade going again. Imports would be needed for raw materials for industrial production as well as for reconstruction. Without that, there would be vast unemployment and misery, in which the Communists might well take over.

I believe that Stalin hoped to get to the Atlantic, and that was perhaps the reason why he didn't carry out the Yalta agreements. The prospects for Communist takeover simply looked too good.

He said a number of things on different occasions, some of them contradictory, and it is hard to know what he had in mind. After Teheran he sent President Roosevelt a telegram in which, among other things, he said, "Now it is assured that our people will act together, jointly and in friendship, both at the present time and after the completion of the war." This is only one of the many expressions of that kind which gave some indication that he had in mind postwar cooperation. But that didn't happen. Roosevelt died, and I know that before he died he realized that his hopes had not been fully achieved; he knew Stalin had already broken some of the Yalta agreements. I know that from the telegrams I received from him to deliver to Stalin and also from some of the people who talked to him just before his death.[1] . . .

While I was home, I did spend several weeks in San Francisco during the United Nations Conference. At the request of Ed Stettinius, the Secretary of State, I had three off-the-record talks with editors, columnists, and reporters to give them some background on our growing problems with the Soviet government. I told them we would have real difficulties with the Soviet Union in the postwar period. This came as a great shock to many of them. At one meeting, I explained that our objectives and the Kremlin objectives were irreconcilable; they wanted to communize the world, and we wanted a free world. But I added that we would have to find ways to compose our differences if we were to live in peace on this small planet. Two men were so shocked that they got up and left. Some of the press at that time criticized me for being so unkind to what were then known as "our gallant allies," and some even suggested that I should be recalled as Ambassador. It was one of the few times in my experience that members of the press have broken the confidence of an off-the-record talk.

People ask when and why I became convinced we would have difficulties with the Soviets. This judgment developed over a period of time. . . .

A talk I had with Stalin at Potsdam in July 1945 is illuminating. The first time I saw him at the conference I went up to him and said that it must be very gratifying for him to be in Berlin, after all the struggle and the tragedy. He hesitated a moment and then replied, "Czar Alexander got to Paris." It didn't need much of a clairvoyant to guess what was in his mind.

I don't think there is any doubt that, with the strong Communist Parties both in Italy and in France, he would have extended his domination to the Atlantic, if we had not acted to frustrate it. In all probability, the Communist leaders in those countries had reported to Moscow that they could take over, and I think they would have succeeded if we had not helped Western Europe to recover. Some of Western Europe would have had Communist governments under the control of Moscow. One doesn't know what the rest of Europe would have been like, but perhaps some countries would have been something less independent than Finland and allowed to be cautiously neutral at the grace of Moscow.

But that isn't what happened. I know that some young people

---

1. Mrs. Hoffman wrote me a letter some years later describing her conversation with Roosevelt on March 24, 1945, his last day in Washington:

The President was in his wheel chair as we left the room, and both Mrs. Roosevelt and I walked at his side. He was given a message which I learned later was a cable from you which had been decoded. He read it and became quite angry. He banged his fists on the arms of his wheel chair and said, "Averell is right; we can't do business with Stalin. He has broken every one of the promises he made at Yalta." He was very upset and continued in the same vein on the subject.

These were his exact words. I remembered them and verified them with Mrs. Roosevelt not too long before her death.

think that everything that has been done before them wasn't just right, but we did have a fairly glorious period, perhaps the most creative period in American foreign policy, immediately after the war. It was due to the leadership of President Truman and the effective cooperation of Senator Vandenberg, the Republican Senator from Michigan, who was then Chairman of the Foreign Relations Committee. The undertakings included aid to Greece, which was under Communist attack, and Turkey, which was threatened at that time; the Marshall Plan, which was an extraordinarily ambitious and successful venture in cooperation; and that led to NATO. These things developed one from the other. Public opinion in the West was deeply disturbed by the Czech coup of March 1948 and then the Berlin blockade three months later. . . .

I was involved in the Marshall Plan, in charge of operations in Europe for more than two years. This was a European effort, with United States help. By the way, I should recall that General Marshall's offer of aid was made to all of Europe, including Russia and Eastern Europe. In fact, Molotov came to the meeting of Foreign Ministers of the European countries called in Paris in July 1947 to consider Marshall's offer with a staff of sixty, including senior economists. However, he demanded that each country act independently. He wanted the European nations to reply to the United States along these lines, "Tell us how much money you will give us, and we will divide it on the basis of those who suffered most will get the most. Then each country will look after its own recovery." But Marshall's proposal was that the European countries should cooperate together in a mutual recovery program. Bevin and Bidault, the British and French Foreign Ministers, stood firm for the cooperative concept, and Molotov left in a huff. The Czechs and the Poles had wanted to join the Marshall Plan, but the Kremlin ordered them not to do so.

At that time the Soviets organized the Cominform and declared war on the Marshall Plan, calling it an "American imperialist plot to subjugate Western Europe." Needless to say, that was just exactly the reverse of what we wanted. We wanted a strong, united and independent Europe. Everything that we did was to minimize our role and maximize the cooperative effort of the Europeans. "Self-help and mutual aid" was the slogan. It was amazingly successful—a spirit of cooperation and unity developed within Europe which had never before existed. They abandoned some of the restrictive business and labor practices of the intra-war years and accepted the necessity of an expanding economy as the basis for a rising standard of living. . . .

Now, Western Europe is more vital and dynamic than ever. When De Gaulle was in control, France was, perhaps, a little too nationalistic. But today the Europeans are again moving toward greater integration and closer cooperation. This was part of the objective of the Congress, and certainly of President Truman in initiating the Marshall Plan. . . .

The Berlin blockade in June of 1948 was a startling event and led to the pressure for NATO. You have to remember that never in history has a nation destroyed its armed strength as rapidly as we did after the

Second World War. The demand for bringing the boys home was irresistible. No one was to blame; it was the deep desire of the American people. We thought we had won the war and everyone in the world would want peace. We had the strongest military force in being at the end of the war, but after the Japanese surrendered, it was dissipated. The Russians didn't do that. They strengthened their forces. They developed new weapons. We in Moscow reported to Washington in late 1945 evidence which indicated that Soviet research expenditure was being doubled, that production of certain new weapons and military equipment was continuing at wartime levels, and that combat training for the Red Army was being emphasized.

Although for a time we had a monopoly in nuclear weapons, Stalin ordered the highest priority be given to developing nuclear capability. Much to the surprise of most people at the time, the Soviets exploded their first nuclear device in September 1949.

The Berlin blockade was countered not by direct force. There has been a lot of argument about that at the time and since. People can argue whether Truman's decision was right or wrong—whether to try to drive our forces through and threaten a nuclear attack, or whether to supply Berlin by airlift. In any event, the least provocative of these responses—the airlift—was chosen, and with full British cooperation it was successful. The Soviets lifted the blockade a year later.

We have had difficulty over Berlin ever since, some times more dangerous than others. Of course, one can criticize the arrangements which made Berlin the capital of occupied Germany. Frankly, Ben Cohen and I favored at the time a capital in a new location, where the three zones came together, just north of Magdeburg. I was influenced in part by the appalling way in which the Soviets had stripped Berlin of most everything they could take out, between V-E Day and the Potsdam meeting. The factories, particularly, were emptied of all machinery and machine tools. But these arrangements had been made by the European Advisory Commission in London. They had been accepted by the three Allies and would have been pretty hard to change at Potsdam.

Sometimes I have thought our presence in Berlin was of great value. Other times I have wondered if it was worthwhile. These are things that historians can argue about. But we are there in West Berlin, and the division of Germany continues along the line of the Soviet occupational zone.

Some think that General Eisenhower should have taken Berlin, but if he had done that, our Third Army wouldn't have been in Austria, and Austria, which is a free and independent country, probably would have been occupied largely by the Red Army and might have been turned into a satellite.

These are all questions which one can weigh. It is hard to say what might have been done. If one objective had been gained, something else would have been lost. I think by and large with the Soviet recalcitrance it would have made very little difference.

Some people have even argued that if General Eisenhower had

liberated Prague somehow or other Czechoslovakia would be free today. That's nonsense! The Czech government under President Benes was set up under an agreement in Moscow, negotiated by Benes with Czech party leaders, including the Communists. This government returned to Czechoslovakia from the East, as the Red Army, joined with four or five Czech divisions, advanced. Under the agreement Benes had to take Communists into the government.

I had several talks with Benes when he came to Moscow from London in March 1945 before returning to Czechoslovakia. He told me that he was not too well satisfied with the composition of the new government, but he added, "It might have been worse." Benes was confident he could control the situation in Czechoslovakia as he believed the people would support him. He told me that Stalin had assured him that the Soviets would not interfere in Czech internal affairs.

Unfortunately, Benes was ill in March 1948 when the coup took place. Of course, the Red Army had long since retired. It had withdrawn from Czechoslovakia more than two years earlier. Our troops had also withdrawn long before, so nothing we did in 1945 would have affected the outcome. Whether or not it would have been different if Benes had been well and vigorous, and whether he could have held his own, I don't know. But the Communist coup was successful without the participation of the Red Army, but undoubtedly with Moscow's collusion.

I had long talks with Jan Masaryk in San Francisco in May 1945. He was Benes' Foreign Minister. He told me I must understand that in the United Nations he would have to vote with Molotov. The Soviets were insisting that the Czech government support them in foreign policy. In return, he thought they would have a free hand at home. Unfortunately, it did not work out that way, and Masaryk himself came to a violent end in March 1948.

The Truman period was an exciting period. President Truman was a man of great determination. He was very humble at the start. He said he had not been elected; Roosevelt had been elected, and it was his responsibility to carry out Roosevelt's policies. He did the best he could. Very early he showed that he recognized the unique problems facing the United States in the world, and he had the extraordinary courage to undertake new policies and programs. And I think they were extraordinarily successful.

President Truman proposed in January 1949 the Point Four Program, announcing that since science and technology had developed to such a point that the old enemies of mankind—hunger, misery, poverty, and disease—could be overcome, it was the obligation of the United States and other more technologically advanced nations to help. That concept has moved ahead. There have been some outstanding successes in some ways and in some countries—some disappointments in others. Unfortunately, our development assistance is in rather a low state today —one of the casualties of Vietnam.

There have been lasting constructive results from the Truman period. Germany has revived and has become a strong ally; Japan has revived and is becoming a strong partner. Western Europe is more productive and united than ever. Other countries have made progress as well and are on their way to sustained economic development, for example in Asia, Korea, and Taiwan, and in Latin America, Mexico, Venezuela, and Colombia. There have been disappointments, of course. The developing countries as a whole have not been able to advance as rapidly as had been hoped, and the gap between them and the industrial nations has widened.

China was an enigma. Roosevelt first of all wanted to get the Soviet Union into the war against Japan. There was never any doubt in my mind that Stalin would attack Japan when it suited him. We could not have kept him out. The question was whether that would be soon enough to do us good. Our Chiefs of Staff estimated that it would take eighteen months after the fall of Germany to defeat the Japanese and would require an amphibious landing on the plains of Tokyo. American casualties were estimated to run up near a million with perhaps a couple of hundred thousand killed. This was a grim prospect to President Roosevelt. Yet, if the Russians attacked the Japanese Kwangtung Army in Manchuria, the Japanese strength to defend the home islands would be reduced. President Roosevelt had a deep sense of responsibility to protect American lives, and it was hoped that possibly, with Russia in the war and with American use of Soviet airfields in Siberia, we could bring Japan to surrender without invasion. Therefore, Soviet intervention seemed of vital importance.

It didn't turn out to be important because, unexpectedly, the nuclear bomb became operative and events moved so rapidly. At Yalta, when plans about Soviet entry into the war against Japan were agreed to, the nuclear bomb had not yet been completed, and nobody knew whether it would work. Even five months later at Potsdam, after the first test explosion took place, one of the most distinguished Navy officers bet an apple that it would not go off as a bomb. Of course, after things happen they seem so easy and so obvious that people say, "Why didn't you think of this at the time?"

Apart from Soviet entry into the war, Roosevelt also wanted to get Stalin to accept Chiang Kai-shek's Nationalist government as the government of China. And that, too, was part of the agreements reached at Yalta about the Far East. This was formalized in a treaty negotiated by T. V. Soong, Premier of the Nationalist government, with Stalin six months later. During these negotiations in Moscow I saw T. V. Soong almost every day. He was finally well satisfied, and in fact the world applauded the agreement. . . .

There were certain concessions to the Russians related to the railroads and ports in Manchuria for a thirty-year period, but the important point for Chiang was that the Soviets accepted Chinese sovereignty over the area. Some of us had been concerned when the Russians got into Manchuria they would establish a "Manchurian People's Republic" just as they had the Mongolian People's Republic. The fact that the Soviets accepted Chinese sovereignty was the thing that impressed Chiang.

Curiously, Stalin did not have much respect for Mao Tse-tung. During the war he spoke about him several times, and at one time he called him a "margarine Communist." That created a great deal of puzzlement in Washington. Some didn't know what it means. It would be entirely clear to any dairy farmer what he meant—a fake, not a real product. I gained the impression from several of my talks with Stalin that he was not keen to support Mao Tse-tung in China and that, perhaps, he wanted to see a new group more amenable to Moscow, take over the Chinese Communist Party before he gave his full support.

After the war, in January 1946, he told me that he had "poor contacts with the Communists." He said that the Soviet government's "three representatives in Yenan had been recalled" and that the Soviet influence with the Chinese Communists was not great. I think there is other evidence to that effect. For example, the Red Army not only stripped Manchuria of its industrial machinery for use in the Soviet Union but also blew up facilities such as blast furnaces. However, the Mao Communists were stronger than Stalin thought, and Chiang was weaker. As events developed, Chiang's forces collapsed in 1949, and he was driven out of mainland China.

Some people have said, "We lost China." It just happens that we never owned China. Whatever we had done in China over the years had had only a limited impact. And although it is unfortunate that a government friendly to us did not survive, we could not have involved ourselves in a major war at that time in China. President Truman, in spite of all the initiatives we had taken in other parts of the world, was wise enough to exercise restraint and not become involved in a civil war in mainland China.

So not all the postwar developments were favorable. Some of them did not go as well as we had hoped they might. . . .

President Kennedy handled the Cuban missile crisis with consummate skill and induced Khrushchev to take the offensive missiles out of Cuba. He was able to go on to an agreement with him on a limited test ban. The signing and ratification of the Limited Nuclear Test Ban Treaty marked a high water point in our relations with the Soviet Union. There were of course unsolved critical problems, particularly in regard to Germany and Southeast Asia. But the change in less than a year from the Cuban missile crisis to the test ban was so striking that I believe President Kennedy began to think seriously of a visit to the Soviet Union early in his second term should he be re-elected. But President Kennedy was assassinated three months later.

Within a year new personalities were to take over in Moscow. Khrushchev was removed from office, Brezhnev took his place as Secretary of the Party and Kosygin as Chairman of the Council of Ministers. . . .

QUESTIONS AND ANSWERS

Q—Do you believe that there is anything America could have done to assist Chiang, particularly in the latter period when we did withdraw our support?

A—I don't think so. I went to Chunking to talk with Chiang Kai-shek in January 1946. General Marshall was there at the time. Chiang had grave doubts about coming to an agreement for a coalition with the Communists, and he may have been justified in his fears. I asked him why he did not strengthen his government at once by bringing in the Democratic League, which included the leading Chinese intellectuals. They had recently participated in a Consultative Conference which had attempted to reconcile the contending parties. I also asked him why he didn't get rid of some of his warlords and some of the obviously corrupt people around him. He replied that they were the only ones he could count on for support if he brought the Communists into the government.

Perhaps the outcome might have been better if we had had quite a different approach. Looking at things from Moscow, my idea at the time was that we might better accept temporarily a divided China. If we could have prevented Chiang from sending his best troops into Manchuria where they were chewed up, he would have been far better off. It was hopeless for him to expect to take over the rule of Manchuria when he was having difficulty in controlling even the area where his forces were concentrated—southern China.

I also had grave doubts about the attempts to form a coalition government with the Communists. It seemed to me at the time that Chiang was too weak and the Communists too strong for him to have had much of a chance of survival.

In any event, General Marshall was sent out to attempt to mediate between the Nationalists and the Communists, and he did everything he could under his instructions. Despite General Marshall's patience and skill, the reluctance and suspicion of both sides and the inherent weakness of the Kuomintang made successful mediation impossible. . . .

Q—Mr. Ambassador, would you comment on the motivation of Soviet foreign policy? Do you think the motivation is primarily that of power politics and national power concerns, or of Communist ideology, or are they both equally determining factors?

A—It is a combination of both. Stalin had both. He was a Russian imperialist with ambitions similar to the Czars. He was also utterly determined to promote world Communist revolution with the oracle in Moscow. Since Stalin's death the world situation has changed, but the Kremlin still has both motivations. . . .

Q—If you could relive history, what changes would you make in the United States foreign policy during the wartime conferences and what effect that might have had on the future?

A—Well, I don't think much would have been different. You can argue about a lot of different things. People blame Eisenhower for not going to Berlin, but there had been a decision made in which the occupational zones of Germany were set. It was considered important that we should not meet and clash with the Russians, that we should decide in advance the zones each would occupy to avoid that possibility. The agreed zones were considered to be very favorable by our chiefs of staff at the time they were decided upon. They thought the Russians would be much further into Germany than they got and that we would not have gotten as far as we did. It didn't work out that way. I am not critical of them for this, as no one could have foreseen the military events.

Now if we had tried to do what Churchill proposed after V-E Day—stand on the Elbe until there was a political settlement about Eastern Europe—I don't think it would have done any good, and we would then have been held responsible for the cold war. Furthermore, our military plans required a redeployment of our forces in Europe to the Pacific. Churchill wanted to force a political settlement about the areas occupied by the Red Army before we withdrew from the Elbe. But even if we had gotten an agreement and free elections had been held, the governments elected would, in all probability, not have lasted. There was, in fact, a free election in Hungary in 1945 in which the Smallholders party (the small peasants' party) got over 50 per cent of the votes and the Communists only about 18 per cent. The government established after this election lasted only a short time, and the Communists—supported by the Red Army—took over and squeezed out the others.

There was no way we could have prevented any of these events in Eastern Europe without going to war with the Russians. There were a few military people who considered that. This wasn't De Gaulle, but a few French and American officers talked about going in and cleaning them up while we had such superiority in air power. It is perfectly absurd to think the American people would have stood for it, even if the President wanted to do it, which he didn't.

I think it was very important that Roosevelt and Churchill made the effort to come to an agreement with Stalin. One achievement was the establishment of the United Nations. With all the disappointments, it has been effective in many activities during the twenty-five years of its life, although handicapped by the differences that exist between the great powers. The fact that Stalin broke the agreements about Eastern Europe exposed his perfidy and aggressive designs. This aroused the suspicion of the West and eventually led to steps for mutual defense.

There is a group of historians who are now attempting to rewrite the history of that time. Arthur M. Schlesinger, Jr., has pointed out that such attempts to rewrite history have happened frequently in the past. These revisionists are creating myths about what happened and what our objectives were. Some of them take facts out of context and try to build up a case for imagined objectives. Some conveniently overlook Stalin's failure to cooperate, his violation of specific agreements and aggressive actions. Of course, I am not talking about those thoughtful analysts who, with the advantage of hindsight, point out more clearly the significance of events and perhaps mistakes than was possible at the time.

The military alternatives were perhaps more obvious than the political. At the time some people wanted us to go to Vienna, up the Ljubljana Gap, and get there before the Russians, instead of landing in the south of France as we did. Yet as things have turned out, Austria is free today anyway.

Churchill was always very much worried about attempting to cross the Channel. It turned out successfully. It would have been disastrous for the British if it hadn't. Churchill wanted to go at Hitler from the south—"the soft underbelly," as he called it. He didn't want to take the risk of crossing the Channel. Stalin, after having berated and even insulted us for two years for not establishing a second front in Europe by crossing the Channel, said to me after we had successfully landed, "The history of war has never witnessed such a grandiose operation." He added neither Napoleon nor Hitler had dared attempt it. Later, after he had received detailed reports, he spoke to me again about crossing the Channel, as "an unheard of achievement in the history of warfare." The number of men and the vast amount of equipment which had been thrown into France impressed him greatly. He added "the world had never seen an individual operation of such magnitude— an unbelievable accomplishment." He was unconcerned by the fact that he had previously minimized its difficulties and had accused us of cowardice in not having undertaken it before.

Undoubtedly mistakes were made, and undoubtedly many things might have been improved. Your question is an interesting one, and I have thought a lot about it. But the facts are that, although militarily unprepared, we fought a war successfully on two fronts. With our allies in Europe, we completely defeated Hitler, and almost alone we defeated Japan in the Pacific. That was an extraordinary achievement— and particularly as it was done in less than four years. As far as our relations with the Soviet Union since the end of the war are concerned, I doubt whether any different wartime military or political decisions would have had much effect.

The Cold War:
A Revisionist View

DAVID HOROWITZ

David Horowitz is one of the "revisionists" whom Averell Harriman criticizes for "creating myths about what happened [in the Cold War] and what our objectives were." The revisionist position, expressed repeatedly during the 1960's, holds that Stalin was basically cautious rather than aggressive in his actions immediately after the war; that the United States government, aiming to preserve American access to a world trading empire, overlooked legitimate Russian security needs; and that, possessing preponderant power in the world, America refused to cooperate with Russia, forcing the Kremlin into a hostile posture in Eastern Europe to protect itself from future military threats.

Only a small proportion of American diplomatic historians have totally accepted this analysis of American foreign policy, but it has influenced virtually every student in the field. Its central point, that its power allowed the United States wider options than Russia ever had, seems hard to question. Some theorists also maintain that American and Soviet social and economic policies would eventually have converged, and that such abrasive conflict between the two ideologies need not have occurred at all. Yet, we know so little of what Stalin was thinking and he gave so many contradictory signals that almost any interpretation is possible. The present is often a dubious guide to the past and while Vietnam has made Cold War revisionism seem particularly relevant, the question remains one for close historical inquiry.

. . . [C]ertain important facts . . . have been largely overlooked by most Western accounts of the cold war's origins. . . . [A]s of 23 April 1945 the Russians found themselves faced with a new and unfriendly American leadership prepared to abandon the wartime coalition and to employ overt pressures against their former allies as soon as the war was actually over. In addition, the Russians could not fail to realize quickly that this new American leadership did not intend to offer aid to the Soviet reconstruction programme, and that they would even go so far as to actively resist attempts to take, in reparations, the materials which the Soviets considered necessary to their task of rebuilding.

During this and the immediately preceding period, moreover, the Russian rulers witnessed an expansion of American power on a prodigious scale.[1] As a result of American victory in the war and the terms of

---

1. Some aspects of this power expansion certainly had an immediate and important post-war impact on Soviet thinking: "In July 1945 President Truman . . . declared emphatically that the United States would not take one inch of additional territory as a result of the part she had played in winning the victory. An uproar

14

the peace, the new areas of American dominance were 7,000 miles distant from her borders and included the strongest Asiatic power, Japan, and the source of power of the potentially strongest European nation, Germany. Since 1942, America had displaced Britain as ruler of the seas, including "that most British of all waters," the east Mediterranean. In 1946, US troops were still stationed in fifty-six countries and on every continent. By 1949, America was said to have a lien on some four hundred world-wide naval and air bases. This meant, "that any empire linked to its motherland by water exists on American sufferance, as it did last century on British sufferance—a fact that need never be expressed to have a profound influence on its policies." Pacts to standardize arms tied virtually the whole of North and South America to the United States. (The same arrangement was soon made with Western Europe.) This meant that it was nearly impossible for the attached nations either to enter or to stay out of war without the consent of the United States.

Partly as a consequence of the war and partly as a consequence of American initiatives, American economic penetration of the world reached tremendous proportions in the post-war period.[2] To mention but one area, America came to own concessions "on nearly half the wealth of the Middle East," the vital land bridge of three continents. By grants and loans, "the economic veins of a large part of the world [became] connected to America's pumping industrial and agricultural heart." Many of the countries depended on America not only for aid, without which they would be worse off, but "for naked survival." "By a decision on whatever grounds to reduce or cut off the flow, America could stop factories, cause riots and upheaval, break governments."[3]

While United States leaders exercised tactical prudence in this period (thus avoiding unnecessary reactions to their dominance) they were by no means inhibited about capitalizing on the power at their disposal, when they felt the necessity to do so. A case in point was the Italian election of 1948. This was the first post-war election in Italy and the Communist–Socialist bloc was given an "even chance" by Western observers to win a 51 per cent majority. When the votes were in, the

---

arose in the Congress, and from American Army and Navy leaders. They protested that the United States must retain as her exclusive property all the strategic bases in the Pacific which American forces had captured. The President thereupon let it be known that he had not meant precisely what he had said. . . . The effect of these incidents was much more far-reaching than has generally been recognized. Many of these Pacific bases lay within a short distance of the Soviet Union's Siberian provinces. The United States' claim for permanent possession could only create deep-rooted suspicion on the part of the Soviet Government" (Sumner Welles, *Where Are We Heading?*, 1946, p. 365).

2. America's large economic expansion continued throughout the cold war. In 1950 total direct foreign assets of American corporations amounted to $11.8 billion. "By 1963 this had grown to $40.6 billion, or 244 per cent, in thirteen years" (*Monthly Review*, January 1965. Figures from *Survey of Current Business*, October 1964).

3. The above account is based on Howard K. Smith, *The State of Europe*, 1949, pp. 70-71.

pro-Western Christian Democrats had 53 per cent of the ballots, a stunning victory, while the pro-Communist bloc polled but 30 per cent.

> The most important factor in the turning of the tide [wrote Howard K. Smith] was the frank, open entrance of America into the campaign. . . . The opening salvo was the dramatic joint proposal of America, Britain and France to Russia that Trieste—the former Italian port in the Adriatic, made a 'free city' by the peace treaty with Italy—be returned to Italy. . . . After that event not a day passed without the anti-Communist majority of the press having a new, effective American gesture to put in its headlines. President Truman made Italy a badly needed gift of 29 merchant ships; gold looted from Italy by the Nazis was returned; the first Marshall Aid ships arrived and were unloaded amid ceremony and with a speech by the American Ambassador; the State Department announced that Italians who were known to have voted Communist would be denied that dream of all Italians, emigration to America; the War Department announced that American naval contingents in the Mediterranean would be strengthened; American occupation troops in Trieste held their first full-dress military parade since the war, complete with tanks and big guns; American and British warships anchored off Italian ports during the campaign. . . .4

In March, Secretary of State Marshall bluntly told Italy and all other nations participating in the European Recovery Programme (the Marshall Plan) that "benefits under ERP will come to an abrupt end in any country that votes [sic] Communism into power."5 Given the dollar crisis in Europe, which had hit the Italians particularly hard, this threat alone might have sufficed to swing the elections.

In view of such open United States intervention, the Truman Doctrine's promise that it would be United States policy to support free peoples against external pressures and to "assist free peoples to work out their own destinies in their own away" proved to be an empty one. These events, however, throw light on a far more significant reality than the failure of United States actions to conform to United States ideals. For the open but relatively peaceful manner in which the United States was able to intervene to protect its strategic interests, was a factor of key significance in the development of the early cold war.

The scene of the most interesting and historically important contrast between attempts by the United States and the USSR to extend their respective "security zones" in his period, was Iran. The Iranian incidents, which occupied world attention from November 1945 until May 1946, deserve special attention, because they are generally held up as the first overt instance of the Soviet Union's remorseless post-war expansion.

During the war, all three of the major allies had occupied Iran in order to assure wartime oil supplies to Russia; this seemed a prudent step in view of the Iranian Government's flirtation with the Nazis. After the war, it was agreed that all three should move out simultaneously, but the Russians stayed beyond the deadline. During this time,

---

4. Ibid., pp. 204-6.
5. Kenneth Ingram, *History of the Cold War*, 1955, p. 63.

they fomented a rebellion against the central Iranian Government in the Soviet-occupied areas of northern Iran and set up a friendly "autonomous" government there. By this pressure they were able to induce the central government to grant them oil-exploitation rights in northern Iran. Russian aims were to win oil resources to supplement the production of their own badly damaged Caucasian fields.

The Western powers condemned these actions in the Security Council and, in May, the force of public opinion induced the Russians to withdraw from Iran. Then the central Iranian Government sent troops to break up the autonomous Azerbaijan Government. With this accomplished the Iranian parliament denounced the oil agreement with Russia.

The sequel to these events is not so widely known. As the Russians left, the Americans moved in—not with troops and revolution—"but silently with dollars in support of the *status quo.*" In addition to American funds, the Iranian Government received American advisers, civil and military, and Iran became in effect "an American satellite." If America did not yet have military bases there, she could have them any time she wished.[6]

The effect of this incident on Russian mentality can be easily guessed. The United States had achieved exactly the end that Russia had sought, but there was no way to make a case of it before the United Nations. Moreover, as one Western correspondent pointedly observed, "this 'defense' base that America had for the taking was six thousand miles from America, but on Russia's most sensitive border. Russia could legitimately adopt the question the West put to her: where does security end short of domination of the whole earth?" Thereafter, "Russia fought tooth and nail to close her satellite nations to the 'Iranian method.' "[7]

From this brief review of the scope and use of United States power in the initial post-war period, it can be seen that by early 1947, when the cold war became a public reality, the Russians had real cause for concern about United States intentions and the future employment of United States economic and military muscle. Then the bombshell of the Truman Doctrine was exploded, followed by the economic "counter-offensive" of the Marshall Plan in Europe. It was at this point that the public phase of the cold war was really engaged by the Soviets as they responded to the Truman-Marshall initiatives by subverting the non-Communist governments of Hungary and Czechoslovakia, and by taking swift steps to integrate fully the economies and political structures of the East European countries and to reduce them to satellites in the service of their mobilization against the West. Even as late as 1948-9, the resistance to Sovietization within the East European Communist

6. This account is taken from Smith, op. cit., pp. 407-8.
7. "When Russia extends her security zone abroad, it almost inevitably requires an overthrow of the *status quo,* for the *status quo* of the world is capitalist; which means a lot of noise and ugly scenes. If America extends her zone of influence abroad, for the same reason—that the rest of the world is capitalist—it involves only supporting the *status quo*: no scenes, no noise" (Smith, op. cit., p. 93).

Parties themselves (let alone non-party groups) was so considerable as to require the purging of vast numbers of "Titoists" and nationalist elements.

Putting the sequence of events in its proper perspective in this way, raises the inescapable question of the *casus belli* of the cold war itself: was the Sovietization of East Europe an inevitable development after the Yalta Agreements of February 1945? Or was it rather the product of interacting post-war American policies and Stalinist responses? In other words, would Stalinist strategy, of itself, have led to the attempted Sovietization of East Europe, regardless of the policies of the post-war American leadership?

There are, it should be noted, preliminary grounds for supposing that United States policy was a very important and probably decisive factor in the post-war development of United States–Soviet relations. In the first place, preponderance of power gave the United States a flexibility and range of alternatives that the Russians simply did not have. In the second place, there was a divergence in the highest levels of the United States administration over the options to be taken towards the Soviet Union after the war, and in fact, an established course which had worked in the preceding period was replaced at the end of the war by an untried policy which did not.

What we have subsequently learned about events behind the Stettin–Trieste line in the years 1945-9 not only bears out the above preliminary assumptions but amplifies them. The importance of these facts for assessing United States foreign policy in the period justifies a brief review of the main outlines of what took place.

In the mid 1920s, Stalin's thesis of 'socialism in one country' became the dogma of the revolution and the guiding principle of Soviet foreign policy down through the end of the Second World War. Indeed, the wartime alliance was predicated on this concept. In the words of Isaac Deutscher, "Soviet self-containment was the very premise of joint allied policy, written into the paragraphs and clauses of the Teheran, Yalta, and Potsdam Agreements." The agreements divided spheres of influence between the Allies, allotting all of Eastern and much of Central Europe to Russia, while at the same time stipulating that this was to be the sphere of influence of Russia, not of Communism.[8]

"In retrospect," observes Deutscher, "it appears extraordinarily shortsighted of the great statesmen of the West to have believed that Russia's personality could be thus split and her national-power ambitions separated from her social and political outlook. But the illusion was not merely Roosevelt's and Churchill's. It was shared by Stalin." It may be argued, of course, that Stalin's wartime attitude was deception on his part, his pledges of noninterference in the internal affairs of neighbouring countries "simply dust thrown into the eyes of his allies." But Stalin's deeds at the time lent weight to his vows, and "both Churchill and Roosevelt had solid evidence that Stalin's policy was in fact geared to self-containment."

8. This account is based on Isaac Deutscher, *Russia After Stalin*, 1953, pp. 74ff. Cf. also Deutscher's *Stalin*, 1966.

They saw Stalin acting, not merely speaking, as any nationalist Russian statesman would have done in his place—they saw him divested, as it were, of his communist character. He was approaching the problems of the Russian zone of influence in a manner calculated to satisfy nationalist Russian demands and aspirations and to wreck the chances of communist revolution in those territories.

He prepared to exact and did in fact exact heavy reparations from Hungary, Bulgaria, Rumania, Finland, and Eastern Germany. This, he knew, would make the name of communism as well as that of Russia odious to the peoples of those countries, to whom it did not even occur to distinguish between the two. With a zeal worthy of a better cause he insisted on slicing territories away from Poland, Hungary, and Germany, and on expelling many millions of citizens from their homes.

Stalin's policies in the initial post-war period thus made sense only if he assumed that these countries would remain capitalist, that is, "if he had no design to impose communist governments on them." He expected, of course, that Russia would enjoy a position of diplomatic and economic "preponderance" in neighbouring countries ruled by "friendly" governments, but he also expected them to remain essentially capitalist. "If [Stalin] had been viewing those countries as future provinces of his empire, it would have been the height of folly on his part to insist on levying in the most unrelenting manner heavy reparations and enforcing expulsions."

Stalin had become convinced in the inter-war period that the revolutionary potentialities of foreign Communism were nil. Accordingly, he did what he could to discourage the Communist parties from making bids for power and from jeopardizing his relations with his wartime allies:

. . . He urged the French Communists to take their cue from General de Gaulle at a time when they were the chief driving force behind the French Resistance. He urged the Italian Communists to make peace with the House of Savoy and with the government of Marshal Badoglio, and to vote for the re-enactment of Mussolini's Lateran pacts with the Vatican. He did his best to induce Mao Tse-tung to come to terms with Chiang Kai-shek, because he believed, as he said at Potsdam, that the Kuomintang was the only force capable of ruling China. He angrily remonstrated with Tito because of the latter's revolutionary aspirations, and demanded his consent to the restoration of the monarchy of Yugoslavia.

He stared with incredulity and fear at the rising tides of revolution which threatened to wash away the rock of "socialism in one country," on which he had built his temple. This so-called prophet of Marxism and Leninism appears at this moment as the most conservative statesman in the world.[9]

9. This picture of Stalin as conservative with regard to the world revolution is orthodox among sovietologists: "From the bourgeois world, as from his political entourage in the world of communism, Stalin wanted only one thing: weakness. This was not at all identical with revolution. . . . Stalin did not want other states to be communist. He was concerned only that they should be weak, or that they should at least expend their strength not against him and his regime but against each other. . . ." (Kennan, op. cit., p. 253). On the 1944-5 period see Alperovitz, op. cit., pp. 131-2, 139. cf. also Deutscher's *Stalin*, pp. 506ff.

The subsequent post-war "wrecking" of Stalin's policy of self-containment "partly by forces beyond Stalin's control and partly by Stalin himself," is a complex story of which only a small but significant part is yet known. Of the European countries which became Communist in this period, Yugoslavia was one that had not been allotted to the Soviet sphere of influence during the wartime negotiations, but was to have been a border zone between the British and Russian spheres. Stalin was therefore most interested in keeping the Yugoslav revolutionaries in check lest his relations with the Allies be compromised:

. . . For long he disparaged Tito's partisans and extolled the counter-revolutionary Chetniks of Drazha Mikhailovich as the alleged heroes, of anti-Nazi resistance. The embittered Tito, still one of the most faithful agents of the Stalinist Comintern, implored him: "If you cannot send us assistance, then at least do not hamper us." Stalin, so Tito relates, "stamped with rage" and tried to induce Tito to agree not merely to the restoration of the monarchy but to a possible British occupation of Yugoslavia. . . . Tito's unruly revolutionary moves were to Stalin a "stab in the back of the Soviet Union." [10]

Stalin's rage can be appreciated, for he was beginning to lose control over his own Communist parties, whereas he had always been confident that he could use them "as pawns in his great diplomatic game of chess." The pawns, however, were beginning to show "a life of their own," and Stalin "could not even lay hands on them." Moreover, Stalin "could not afford the odium of an open betrayal" of the revolution. To what extent in each individual case he merely yielded to the will of the pawns, pretending to move them, and to what extent he actually moved them himself, is still not known. Only the "accident" of Yugoslavia's break with Moscow has revealed the information that we have. What is "certain" however,

is that as Stalin began reluctantly to identify himself with the rising forces of foreign communism his Western allies also began to identify him with those forces. The Grand Alliance was giving place to the Great Enmity. Stalin then sought reinsurance against the West; and Communist regimes in the Russian sphere of influence promised to provide it. And then it was without a doubt he who moved the pawns.

From Tito himself comes an even more explicit verification of the shape of this dynamic of forces; for as Deutscher reports, "According to Tito, Stalin finally decided to bring Eastern Europe under close Soviet control in 1947, *at the time when the Truman Doctrine was proclaimed.*" [Emphasis added.]

The impetus to integrate and absorb East Europe at the time of the Truman Doctrine, however, did not stem only from the collapse of the alliance and, with that, Stalin's reasons for holding back these forces. As we have seen, the alliance was already dead by the autumn of 1945. The pressure to fully integrate East Europe in the Soviet system

10. Deutscher, *Russia After Stalin.*

after the Truman Doctrine seems rather to have come from the twofold desire to close East Europe to the "Iranian method" and to facilitate the military defence of the Soviet Union.

To understand this latter tactic, we must add to the picture of American post-war power sketched earlier . . . , America's possession of the atomic bomb. Russian military leaders were likely to be impressed not merely by American possession of this weapon, and by its use against a defeated country, but by the emphasis in Western military theory on the efficacy of strategic air power, the much-touted doctrine of preventive war, and the effort to secure air bases on the perimeter of the Soviet Union.

Soviet responses to the possibility of atomic attack took several forms, including a crash programme to produce nuclear weapons, a huge fighter defence programme, a build-up of land forces to provide "their only possible military reply to the Western nuclear striking power" and maintenance of "strict geographical secrecy over their land areas so as to deny target information to the Strategic Air Command."

Since the main military threat was from manned nuclear bombers, writes P.M.S. Blackett, "the greatest possible depth for air defence was vital. During the Second World War it was found that the efficacy of a fighter defence system increased rapidly with the depth of the defence zone." Therefore, at the political level, "the Soviet Union consolidated its forward military line by the political *coup* in 1948 in Czechoslovakia, and integrated the other satellite countries more closely into the Soviet defence system":

Support for the view that the communist *coup* in Czechoslovakia was not solely due to the desire to spread the borders of the Soviet world, but had at least a strong military foundation, is seen by noting that the USSR did not act similarly in Finland. The military difference is obvious. Czechoslovakia in the Western orbit would have greatly weakened Russia's military strength. Finland's geographical position made it unnecessary to stage a communist *coup* to keep her out of the Western military orbit. However, if Sweden had joined Nato, the Soviet military staff might have pressed for the full integration of Finland.[11]

Thus, the Truman Doctrine of a world divided into two opposing camps proved to be a self-fulfilling prophecy: given the mentality of the Russian leaders, the whole post-war United States policy of facing the Soviets with an "iron fist" and "strong language," while at the same time making it as difficult as possible for them to carry out the work of reconstruction, ensured the "expansion" that the policy, allegedly, had been designed to prevent.

11. P.M.S. Blackett, *Studies of War*, 1962, pp. 151-2.

To Secure These Rights

THE PRESIDENT'S COMMITTEE
ON CIVIL RIGHTS, 1947

The American Negro Revolution is popularly dated from the Supreme Court's 1955 school desegregation decision, the celebrated Brown v. Board of Education. *But the two main features of the civil rights movement, the militancy of black Americans and the activist role of the federal government, have much earlier origins. The first can be traced at least as far back as W. E. B. DuBois' Niagara Movement of 1908, which later became the National Association for the Advancement of Colored People. Changing circumstances and definitions should not obscure the reality that this was an aggressive organization. The second feature—the concern of the federal government for civil rights—was present as early as the Reconstruction and is evident in the New Deal. Under Franklin Roosevelt new executive policies on appointments, regulations governing hiring in the war industries, and welfare programs came into being. Most significantly, the Supreme Court in those years initiated the series of decisions which inevitably led to the Brown case. And the Democratic party, which in the thirties became the party of black Americans, began to recognize its black constituents.*

The President's Committee on Civil Rights, which Harry S Truman appointed at the end of 1946 in response to a revival of lynching, is another high point of these forgotten years of the civil rights revolution. To read their report 25 years after its formulation is to experience the shock of self-recognition. The Committee saw clearly the vulnerability of the southern system of segregation, recognized covert segregation in the North, and predicted that civil rights would go from a southern to an urban and national problem. Most of all, they saw the expanding role of the federal government as a main force for change. Virtually every piece of civil rights policy enacted in the 1960's is foreshadowed in the recommendations of this report: the civil rights acts and federal election laws, a strengthened civil rights section in the Justice Department, a Fair Employment Practices Act, non-discriminatory administration of federal funds as a condition of receiving them, and much besides. The Committee could not, of course, have prophesied the second phase of the civil rights revolution, the direct action that Martin Luther King would initiate. And of course they could not dream of the day when even King's form of protest would seem too moderate and when the nearly complete enactment of their program after only a generation's delay would seem too little too late.

A PROGRAM OF ACTION: THE COMMITTEE'S RECOMMENDATIONS

THE TIME IS NOW

Twice before in American history the nation has found it necessary to review the state of its civil rights. The first time was during the 15 years between 1776 and 1791, from the drafting of the Declaration of Independence through the Articles of Confederation experiment to the writing of the Constitution and the Bill of Rights. It was then that the distinctively American heritage was finally distilled from earlier views of liberty. The second time was when the Union was temporarily sundered over the question of whether it could exist "half-slave" and "half-free."

It is our profound conviction that we have come to a time for a third re-examintion of the situation, and a sustained drive ahead. Our reasons for believing this are those of conscience, of self-interest, and of survival in a threatening world. Or to put it another way, we have a moral reason, an economic reason, and an international reason for believing that the time for action is now.

THE MORAL REASON

We have considered the American heritage of freedom at some length. We need no further justification for a broad and immediate program than the need to reaffirm our faith in the traditional American morality. The pervasive gap between our aims and what we actually do is creating a kind of moral dry rot which eats away at the emotional and rational bases of democratic beliefs. There are times when the difference between what we preach about civil rights and what we practice is shockingly illustrated by individual outrages. There are times when the whole structure of our ideology is made ridiculous by individual instances. And there are certain continuing, quiet, omnipresent practices which do irreparable damage to our beliefs.

As examples of "moral erosion" there are the consequences of suffrage limitations in the South. The fact that Negroes and many whites have not been allowed to vote in some states has actually sapped the morality underlying universal suffrage. Many men in public and private life do not believe that those who have been kept from voting are capable of self rule. They finally convince themselves that disfranchised people do not really have the right to vote.

Wartime segregation in the armed forces is another instance of how a social pattern may wreak moral havoc. Practically all white officers and enlisted men in all branches of service saw Negro military personnel performing only the most menial functions. They saw Negroes recruited for the common defense treated as men apart and distinct from themselves. As a result, men who might otherwise have maintained the equalitarian morality of their forebears were given reason to look down on their fellow citizens. This has been sharply illustrated by the Army study discussed previously, in which white servicemen expressed great surprise at the excellent performance of Negroes who joined them in the firing line. Even now, very few people know of the successful experiment with integrated combat units. Yet it is important in explaining why some Negro troops did not do well; it is proof that equal treatment can produce equal performance.

Thousands upon thousands of small, unseen incidents reinforce the impact of headlined violations like lynchings, and broad social patterns like segregation and inequality of treatment. There is, for example, the matter of "fair play." As part of its training for democratic life, our youth is constantly told to "play fair," to abide by "the rules of the game," and to be "good sports." Yet, how many boys and girls in our country experience such things as Washington's annual marble tournament? Because of the prevailing pattern of segregation, established as a model for youth in the schools and recreation systems, separate tournaments are held for Negro and white boys. Parallel elimination contests are sponsored until only two victors remain. Without a contest between them, the white boy is automatically designated as the local champion and sent to the national tournament, while the Negro lad is relegated to the position of runner-up. What child can achieve any real understanding of fair play, or sportsmanship, of the rules of the game, after he has personally experienced such an example of inequality?

It is impossible to decide who suffers the greatest moral damage from our civil rights transgressions, because all of us are hurt. That is certainly true of those who are victimized. Their belief in the basic truth of the American promise is undermined. But they do have the realization, galling as it sometimes is, of being morally in the right. The damage to those who are responsible for these violations of our moral standards may well be greater. They, too, have been reared to honor the command of "free and equal." And all of us must share in the shame at the growth of hypocrisies like the "automatic" marble champion. All of us must endure the cynicism about democratic values which our failures breed.

The United States can no longer countenance these burdens on its common conscience, these inroads on its moral fiber.

THE ECONOMIC REASON

One of the principal economic problems facing us and the rest of the world is achieving maximum production and continued prosperity. The loss of a huge, potential market for goods is a direct result of the economic discrimination which is practiced against many of our minority groups. A sort of vicious circle is produced. Discrimination depresses the wages and income of minority groups. As a result, their purchasing power is curtailed and markets are reduced. Reduced markets result in reduced production. This cuts down employment, which of course means lower wages and still fewer job opportunities. Rising fear, prejudice, and insecurity aggravate the very discrimination in employment which sets the vicious circle in motion. . . .

Economic discrimination prevents full use of all our resources. During the war, when we were called upon to make an all-out productive effort, we found that we lacked skilled laborers. This shortage might not have been so serious if minorities had not frequently been denied opportunities for training and experience. In the end, it cost large amounts of money and precious time to provide ourselves with trained persons.

Discrimination imposes a direct cost upon our economy through the wasteful duplication of many facilities and services required by the "separate but equal" policy. That the resources of the South are sorely strained by the burden of a double system of schools and other public services has already been indicated. Segregation is also economically wasteful for private business. Public transportation companies must often provide duplicate facilities to serve majority and minority groups separately. Places of public accommodation and recreation reject business when it comes in the form of unwanted persons. Stores reduce their sales by turning away minority customers. Factories must provide separate locker rooms, pay windows, drinking fountains, and washrooms for the different groups.

Discrimination in wage scales and hiring policies forces a higher proportion of some minority groups onto relief rolls than corresponding segments of the majority. A study by the Federal Emergency Relief Administration during the depression of the Thirties revealed that in every region the percentage of Negro families on relief was far greater than white families:

PER CENT OF FAMILIES ON RELIEF
(MAY, 1934)

	Negro	White
Northern cities	52.2	13.3
Border state cities	51.8	10.4
Southern cities	33.7	11.4

Similarly, the rates of disease, crime, and fires are disproportionately great in areas which are economically depressed as compared with wealthier areas. Many of the prominent American minorities are confined—by economic discrimination, by law, by restrictive covenants, and by social pressure—to the most dilapidated, undesirable locations. Property in these locations yields a smaller return in taxes, which is seldom sufficient to meet the inordinately high cost of public services in depressed areas. The majority pays a high price in taxes for the low status of minorities.

To the costs of discrimination must be added the expensive investigations, trials, and property losses which result from civil rights violations. In the aggregate, these attain huge proportions. The 1943

Detroit riot alone resulted in the destruction of two million dollars in property.

Finally, the cost of prejudice cannot be computed in terms of markets, production, and expenditures. Perhaps the most expensive results are the least tangible ones. No nation can afford to have its component groups hostile toward one another without feeling the stress. People who live in a state of tension and suspicion cannot use their energy constructively. The frustrations of their restricted existence are translated into aggression against the dominant group. Myrdal says:

Not only occasional acts of violence, but most laziness, carelessness, unreliability, petty stealing and lying are undoubtedly to be explained as concealed aggression. . . . The truth is that *Negroes generally do not feel they have unqualified moral obligations to white people.* . . . The voluntary withdrawal which has intensified the isolation between the two castes is also an expression of Negro protest under cover.

It is not at all surprising that a people relegated to second-class citizenship should behave as second-class citizens. This is true, in varying degrees, of all of our minorities. What we have lost in money, production, invention, citizenship, and leadership as the price for damaged, thwarted personalities—these are beyond estimate.

The United States can no longer afford this heavy drain upon its human wealth, its national competence.

THE INTERNATIONAL REASON

Our position in the postwar world is so vital to the future that our smallest actions have far-reaching effects. We have come to know that our own security in a highly interdependent world is inextricably tied to the security and well-being of all people and all countries. Our foreign policy is designed to make the United States an enormous, positive influence for peace and progress throughout the world. We have tried to let nothing, not even extreme political differences between ourselves and foreign nations, stand in the way of this goal. But our domestic civil rights shortcomings are a serious obstacle.

In a letter to the Fair Employment Practice Committee on May 8, 1946, the Honorable Dean Acheson, then Acting Secretary of State, stated that:

. . . the existence of discrimination against minority groups in this country has an adverse effect upon our relations with other countries. We are reminded over and over by some foreign newspapers and spokesmen, that our treatment of various minorities leaves much to be desired. While sometimes these pronouncements are exaggerated and unjustified, they all too frequently point with accuracy to some form of discrimination because of race, creed, color, or national origin. Frequently we find it next to impossible to formulate a satisfactory answer to our critics in other countries; the gap between the things we stand for in principle and the facts of a particular situation may be too wide to be bridged. An atmosphere of suspicion and resentment in a country over the way a minority is being treated in the United States is a formidable obstacle to the development of mutual understanding and trust between the two countries. We will have better international relations when these reasons for suspicion and resentment have been removed.

I think it is quite obvious . . . that the existence of discriminations against minority groups in the United States is a handicap in our relations with other countries. The Department of State, therefore, has good reason to hope for the continued and increased effectiveness of public and private efforts to do away with these discriminations.

The people of the United States stem from many lands. Other nations and their citizens are naturally intrigued by what has happened to their American "relatives." Discrimination against, or mistreatment of, any racial, religious or national group in the United States is not only seen as our internal problem. The dignity of a country, a continent, or even a major portion of the world's population, may be outraged by it. A relatively few individuals here may be identified with millions of people elsewhere, and the way in which they are treated may have world-wide repercussions. We have fewer than half a million American Indians; there are 30 million more in the Western Hemisphere. Our Mexican American and Hispano groups are not large; millions in Central and South America consider them kin. We number our citizens of Oriental descent in the hundreds of thousands; their counterparts overseas are numbered in hundreds of millions. Throughout the Pacific, Latin America, Africa, the Near, Middle, and Far East, the treatment which our Negroes receive is taken as a reflection of our attitudes toward all dark-skinned peoples. . . .

We cannot escape the fact that our civil rights record has been an issue in world politics. The world's press and radio are full of it. This Committee has seen a multitude of samples. We and our friends have been, and are, stressing our achievements. Those with competing philosophies have stressed—and are shamelessly distorting—our shortcomings. They have not only tried to create hostility toward us among specific nations, races, and religious groups. They have tried to prove our democracy an empty fraud, and our nation a consistent oppressor of underprivileged people. This may seem ludicrous to Americans, but it is sufficiently important to worry our friends. The following United Press dispatch from London proves that (*Washington Post*, May 25, 1947):

Although the Foreign Office reserved comment on recent lynch activities in the Carolinas, British diplomatic circles said privately today that they have played into the hands of Communist propagandists in Europe. . . .

Diplomatic circles said the two incidents of mob violence would provide excellent propaganda ammunition for Communist agents who have been decrying America's brand of "freedom" and "democracy."

News of the North Carolina kidnapping was prominently displayed by London papers. . . .

The international reason for acting to secure our civil rights now is not to win the approval of our totalitarian critics. We would not expect it if our record were spotless; to them our civil rights record is only a convenient weapon with which to attack us. Certainly we would like to deprive them of that weapon. But we are more concerned with the good opinion of the peoples of the world. Our achievements in building and maintaining a state dedicated to the fundamentals of freedom have already served as a guide for those seeking the best road from chaos to liberty and prosperity. But it is not indelibly written that democracy will encompass the world. We are convinced that our way of life—the free way of life—holds a promise of hope for all people. We have what is perhaps the greatest responsibility ever placed upon a people to keep this promise alive. Only still greater achievements will do it.

The United States is not so strong, the final triumph of the democratic ideal is not so inevitable that we can ignore what the world thinks of us or our record.

THE COMMITTEE'S RECOMMENDATIONS

I. *To strengthen the machinery for the protection of civil rights, the President's Committee recommends:*

1. The reorganization of the Civil Rights Section of the Department of Justice to provide for:

The establishment of regional offices;

A substantial increase in its appropriation and staff to enable it to engage in more extensive research and to act more effectively to prevent civil rights violations;

An increase in investigative action in the absence of complaints;

The greater use of civil sanctions;

Its elevation of the status of a full division in the Department of Justice.

2. The establishment within the FBI of a special unit of investigators trained in civil rights work.

3. The establishment by the state governments of law enforcement agencies comparable to the federal Civil Rights Section.

4. The establishment of a permanent Commission on Civil Rights in the Executive Office of the President, preferably by Act of Congress; and the simultaneous creation of a Joint Standing Committee on Civil Rights in Congress.

5. The establishment by the states of permanent commissions on civil rights to parallel the work of the federal Commission at the state level.

6. The increased professionalization of state and local police forces.

II. *To strengthen the right to safety and security of the person, the President's Committee recommends:*

1. The enactment by Congress of new legislation to supplement Section 51 of Title 18 of the United States Code which would impose the same liability on one person as is now imposed by that statute on two or more conspirators.

2. The amendment of Section 51 to remove the penalty provision which disqualifies persons convicted under the Act from holding public office.

3. The amendment of Section 52 to increase the maximum penalties that may be imposed under it from a $1,000 fine and a one-year prison term to a $5,000 fine and a ten-year prison term, thus bringing its penalty provisions into line with those in Section 51.

4. The enactment by Congress of a new statute, to supplement Section 52, specifically directed against police brutality and related crimes.

5. The enactment by Congress of an antilynching act.

6. The enactment by Congress of a new criminal statute on involuntary servitude, supplementing Sections 443 and 444 of Title 18 of the United States Code.

7. A review of our wartime evacuation and detention experience looking toward the development of a policy which will prevent the abridgment of civil rights of any person or groups because of race or ancestry.

8. Enactment by Congress of legislation establishing a procedure by which claims of evacuees for specific property and business losses resulting from the wartime evacuation can be promptly considered and settled.

III. *To strengthen the right to citizenship and its privileges, the President's Committee recommends:*

1. Action by the states or Congress to end poll taxes as a voting prerequisite.

2. The enactment by Congress of a statute protecting the right of qualified persons to participate in federal primaries and elections against interference by public officers and private persons.

3. The enactment by Congress of a statute protecting the right to qualify for, or participate in, federal or state primaries or elections against discriminatory action by state officers based on race or color, or depending on any other unreasonable classification of persons for voting purposes.

4. The enactment by Congress of legislation establishing local self-government for the District of Columbia; and the amendment of the Constitution to extend suffrage in presidential elections, and representation in Congress to District residents.

5. The granting of suffrage by the States of New Mexico and Arizona to their Indian citizens.

6. The modification of the federal naturalization laws to permit the granting of citizenship without regard to the race, color, or national origin of applicants.

7. The repeal by the states of laws discriminating against aliens who are ineligible for citizenship because of race, color, or national origin.

8. The enactment by Congress of legislation granting citizenship to the people of Guam and American Samoa.

9. The enactment by Congress of legislation, followed by appropriate administrative action, to end immediately all discrimination and segregation based on race, color, creed, or national origin, in the organization and activities of all branches of the Armed Services.

10. The enactment by Congress of legislation providing that no member of the armed forces shall he subject to discrimination of any kind by any public authority or place of public accommodation, recreation, transportation, or other service or business.

IV. *To strengthen the right to freedom of conscience and expression the President's Committee recommends:*

1. The enactment by Congress and the state legislatures of legislation requiring all groups, which attempt to influence public opinion, to disclose the pertinent facts about themselves through systematic registration procedures.

2. Action by Congress and the executive branch clarifying the loyalty obligations of federal employees, and establishing standards and procedures by which the civil rights of public workers may be scrupulously maintained.

V. *To strengthen the right to equality of opportunity, the President's Committee recommends:*

1. In general:

The elimination of segregation, based on race, color, creed, or national origin, from American life.

The conditioning by Congress of all federal grants-in-aid and other forms of federal assistance to public or private agencies for any purpose on the absence of discrimination and segregation based on race, color, creed, or national origin.

2. For employment:

The enactment of a federal Fair Employment Practice Act prohibiting all forms of discrimination in private employment, based on race, color, creed, or national origin.

The enactment by the state of similar laws;

The issuance by the President of a mandate against discrimination in government employment and the creation of adequate machinery to enforce this mandate.

3. For education:

Enactment by the state legislatures of fair educational practice laws for public and private educational institutions, prohibiting discrimination in the admission and treatment of students based on race, color, creed, or national origin.

4. For housing:

The enactment by the states of laws outlawing restrictive covenants;

Renewed court attack, with intervention by the Department of Justice, upon restrictive covenants.

5. For health services:

The enactment by the states of fair health practice statutes forbidding discrimination and segregation based on race, creed, color, or national origin, in the operation of public or private health facilities.

6. For public services:

The enactment by Congress of a law stating that discrimination and segregation, based on race, color, creed, or national origin, in the rendering of all public services by the national government is contrary to public policy;

The enactment by the states of similar laws;

The establishment by act of Congress or executive order of a unit in the federal Bureau of the Budget to review the execution of all government programs, and the expenditures of all government funds, for compliance with the policy of nondiscrimination;

The enactment by Congress of a law prohibiting discrimination or segregation, based on race, color, creed, or national origin, in interstate transportation and all the facilities thereof, to apply against both public officers and the employees of private transportation companies;

The enactment by the states of laws guaranteeing equal access to places of public accommodation, broadly defined, for persons of all races, colors, creeds, and national origins.

7. For the District of Columbia:

The enactment by Congress of legislation to accomplish the following purposes in the District:

Prohibition of discrimination and segregation, based on race, color, creed, or national origin, in all public or publicly-supported hospitals, parks, recreational facilities, housing projects, welfare agencies, penal institutions, and concessions on public property;

The prohibition of segregation in the public school system of the District of Columbia;

The establishment of a fair educational practice program directed against discrimination, based on race, color, creed, or national origin, in the admission of students to private educational institutions;

The establishment of a fair health practice program forbidding discrimination and segregation by public or private agencies, based on race, color, creed, or national origin, with respect to the training of doctors and nurses, the admission of patients to hospitals, clinics, and similar institutions, and the right of doctors and nurses to practice in hospitals;

The outlawing of restrictive covenants;

Guaranteeing equal access to places of public accommodation, broadly defined, to persons of all races, colors, creeds, and national origins.

8. The enactment by Congress of legislation ending the system of segregation in the Panama Canal Zone.

VI. *To rally the American people to the support of a continuing program to strengthen civil rights, the President's Committee recommends:*

A long-term campaign of public education to inform the people of the civil rights to which they are entitled and which they owe to one another.

The most important educational task in this field is to give the public living examples of civil rights in operation. This is the purpose of our recommendations which have gone before. But there still remains the job of driving home to the public the nature of our heritage, the justification of civil rights and the need to end prejudice. This is a task which will require the cooperation of the federal, state, and local governments and of private agencies. We believe that the permanent Commission on Civil Rights should take the leadership in serving as the coordinating body. The activities of the permanent Commission in this field should be expressly authorized by Congress and funds specifically appropriated for them.

Aside from the education of the general public, the government has immediate responsibility for an internal civil rights campaign for its more than two million employees. This might well be an indispensable first step in a large campaign. Moreover, in the armed forces, an opportunity exists to educate men while in service. The armed forces should expand efforts, already under way, to develop genuinely democratic attitudes in officers and enlisted men.

Truman and Domestic Politics: The Election of 1948

RICHARD KIRKENDALL

The election of 1948 will be forever famous as the year the pollsters were wrong, unanimously and erroneously predicting that Thomas E. Dewey would defeat the incumbent president. First edition headlines the morning after election day proclaimed "Dewey Defeats Truman" and brought delight even to some voters who had opposed Truman, for the headlines seemed to protect the integrity of the American voter whose decisions could not be anticipated by the scientific pundits.

Richard S. Kirkendall points out, however, that the real significance of the election lies elsewhere. It was a low-turnout election which maintained "the pattern of partisan attachments prevailing in a preceding period." Truman's victory was owing to his successful identification with the policies of the New Deal: It was in many ways a posthumous political triumph for his predecessor in office. The maintenance of New Deal reforms in the new circumstances of postwar America was hardly a foregone conclusion. The Republican Congress elected in 1946 seemed bent on dismantling the Roosevelt program of social welfare, economic regulation, internationalism, and government support of interests such as labor and agriculture. The combination of a conservative, business-oriented Congress and a Democratic President stabilized New Deal reforms, neither extending nor curtailing them. Some Americans—more in the 1950's—were beginning to turn away from drama in the international arena. They looked at their private existences and opportunities. The great exception was black America whose restlessness had rent the Democratic Party in 1948 but whose ability to command the nation's interest had only begun.

The 1948 election is the delight of romantics. They see a brave man, fighting almost alone against great odds, defying the experts who unanimously predicted his defeat and emerging as the winner in the greatest upset in American political history. While in touch with some of the realities, the interpretation obscures at least as much as it reveals. It exaggerates the significance of Truman's own efforts—he did not wage a lonely campaign—and understates his debts to others. Most important, the romantic view of 1948 pays inadequate attention to the strengths of the Democratic party and the weaknesses of the Republican party and its presidential candidate. The interpretation also neglects Truman's weaknesses, which the election returns also reflected. . . .

Perhaps the most important statement that has been made about 1948 is the classification of it as a "maintaining election." In such an election, according to Angus Campbell, "the pattern of partisan attachments prevailing in the preceding period persists, and the majority party wins the Presidency." In addition, 1948 was a "low turnout" and a "narrow margin" election.

STRENGTHS AND WEAKNESSES OF THE PARTIES

Truman had the strength of the nation's majority party behind him. Roosevelt, or the Great Depression and the New Deal, had provided Truman with the base needed for victory. The Democrats had taken control of Congress in 1931, they had maintained control until 1947, and they had moved into the White House in 1933 and remained there in 1948. *Fortune* reported on the eve of that election year that thirty-nine percent of the people thought of themselves as Democrats while only thirty-three percent regarded themselves as Republicans, and the American Institute of Public Opinion discovered at the same time that fifty-six percent of the partisans and fifty-seven percent of the independents preferred the Democrats to the Republicans and that white and blue collar workers and farmers had much more confidence in the Democrats than in their foes.

Basic Democratic strength did not guarantee a Truman victory, however, for weaknesses in the Democracy were obvious by 1948. The clearest sign was new Republican strength in Congress. The G.O.P. revival, which had begun in 1938, had reached a high in the congressional elections of 1946 and produced Republican control of Congress for the first time since 1930. The Eightieth Congress (1947–48) contained fifty-one Republicans and forty-five Democrats in the Senate and 246 Republicans and only 188 Democrats in the House of Representatives. These figures reflected widespread dissatisfaction with the Truman administration and suggested to many observers that the Republicans would gain control of the White House as well in 1948. One feature of the troubled Democratic picture was evidence that Northern Negroes were returning to the Republican party. They had been enthusiastic supporters of Roosevelt, but Truman seemed an unworthy successor. They also resented the attitudes and behavior of Southern Democrats and the failure of the federal government to establish a permanent Fair Employment Practices Commission and to outlaw lynching.

The once-powerful Democratic coalition seemed to be falling apart. Liberal dissatisfaction with Truman had developed during 1945 and 1946 as New Dealers moved out of the administration and were replaced by more conservative Democrats, as the administration developed its "get tough" policy toward the Soviet Union and as Truman clashed with organized labor. He had, it seemed, betrayed Franklin Roosevelt. In September of 1946, Henry A. Wallace, once Roosevelt's Secretary of Agriculture and Vice President and the most prominent liberal in the administration, publicly criticized the emerging foreign policy, an act that was quickly followed by his dismissal as Truman's Secretary of Commerce. Out of office, he campaigned strenuously and expanded his criticism to include basic features of the American political and economic system.

In 1947, Wallace became a candidate for the Presidency and gained significant support. The new Progressive Citizens of America [P.C.A.], a group that believed liberals and communists could work together, provided support and encouragement for Wallace's crusade against the administration. Members of the Communist party, sharing hostility to the emerging containment policy, also rallied behind Wallace. Since the end of the war, they had been making plans for the formation of a new political party, and late in 1947 communist leaders decided that Wallace should be the new party's presidential candidate. Most members of the P.C.A. agreed, as did the American Labor Party, a few old New Dealers and a few members of the Congress of Industrial Organizations, the National Association for the Advancement of Colored People, and the National Farmers Union. On December 29, 1947, Wallace, convinced that he had widespread support but would be denied the Democratic nomination, announced that he would run on a third-party ticket.

Foreign policy became the focal point of the campaign that Wallace waged. His followers, both communists and non-communists, agreed essentially on this issue. They regarded the containment policy as the imperialistic creature of Wall Street and the military, destined to lead the world into atomic war. They could not agree on some other large questions, most notably the future of capitalism. Unlike the communists, Wallace and his liberal followers believed in the possibility of a dynamic, progressive capitalism, a reformed capitalism, that would supply the material needs of all men. They believed that Roosevelt had moved in the right directions and that his efforts must be resumed. A return to the reliance upon Roosevelt's United Nations would permit a revival of Roosevelt's New Deal.

By early 1948, Wallace seemed to threaten Truman's chances for victory. The polls suggested that at least six percent of the voters favored Wallace, that most of these people had voted for Roosevelt in 1944, and that Wallace had substantial strength in the Far West, especially California, and in the big cities, including Chicago and New York, that had been so important in Roosevelt's victories. In February, voters in a New York City congressional district elected a Wallaceite, Leo Isacson of the American Labor Party, and shortly thereafter Democratic leaders in New York suggested that Truman's chances in the Empire State were very slim.

At the same time, Truman encountered trouble on the right wing of his party. Discontent with the policies of the national party and administration had been growing in the South for more than a decade. Discontented Southerners resented the decline in their influence in the Democratic party and the expansion of the role of the federal government in their lives. Some of the discontent was economic, reflecting a belief among Southern planters and businessmen that their interests were being subordinated to those of the urban working classes and the rural poor. Of growing importance was fear of change in race relations and resentment of efforts by Washington to promote those changes.

In October, 1947, Truman's Committee on Civil Rights issued a list of bold recommendations, and on February 2, 1948, he incorporated some of them into a special message on civil rights that advocated government action in several areas. Leading Southerners, including Governor Fielding Wright of Mississippi, protested loudly against these developments and began to organize in hopes of forcing party leaders to behave more conservatively.

The Southern revolt moved forward and gained strength. Southern governors warned that the South was "aroused" and that Democratic leaders would soon realize that the section was "no longer 'in the bag.' " Polling evidence, which indicated a sharp drop in Southern support for Truman and in Southern approval of his handling of his office, supported the threat. Southerners seemed divided only on the question of the steps to be taken. While some insisted that the South must continue to work within the Democratic party, others proposed a bolt from it. On May 10, a conference in Jackson, Mississippi, stressed opposition to civil rights legislation, called upon the Democrats to repudiate Truman's proposals, and made plans for a meeting in Birmingham after the Democratic convention to decide upon future action. The rebels hoped their threats would restrain the Democrats and encourage them to adopt a weak plank on civil rights and nominate a foe of civil rights legislation. . . .

PREPARATIONS AND PRIMARIES

Two groups were especially important in early preparations for the campaign: several administration officials, headed by Clark Clifford, and the staff of the Democratic National Committee, . . . had begun to make plans for 1948 shortly after the disastrous elections of 1946. Struggling for influence against conservatives such as John Snyder, an old friend of Truman serving as Secretary of the Treasury, they encouraged the President to become militantly liberal, and they achieved their first major victory with the veto of the Taft-Hartley Act in June, 1947. . . .

These committee officials recognized the basic strength of their party and sought ways to exploit it. They realized that their policies were more popular than those of the congressional Republicans and were convinced that the Democrats had lost the 1946 election by default. The thinking of a year was drawn together in a confidential memorandum from Clifford to the President on November 19, 1947, dealing with "The Politics of 1948." It was a tough-minded document with its toughness moderated by the assumptions that the policy that was "politically wise" was also "the best policy for the country" and that "the future of this country and the future of the world" were "linked inextricably" with Truman's reelection. It contained suggestions for more "exposure" for the President, including a "nonpolitical" tour, and advice on ways of dealing with the Wallace threat—liberal appointments, liberal programs, charges of communist control. The "basic premise" was that the Democratic party was "an unhappy alliance of Southern conservatives, Western progressives and Big City labor," and the test of Democratic leadership was "its ability to lead enough members of these three misfit groups to the polls. . . ." Heavy emphasis was placed on the Western vote and ways of getting it for it seemed crucial. Clifford also insisted that the administration must *renew* its "working relationship with progressive and labor leaders."

Two other items were especially significant: the advice on ways of dealing with the second session of the Eightieth Congress and the suggestions on the South, the Negro, and civil rights. Assuming that the congressional Republicans would move "left," the adviser suggested that Truman must remain left of them. He must expect conflict rather than legislation and thus must not bargain and compromise. He must tailor his recommendations for the voter, not the congressman. "The strategy on the Taft-Hartley Bill—refusal to bargain with the Republicans and to accept any compromises—paid big political dividends," Clifford reminded the President. "That strategy should be expanded in the next session to include all the *domestic* issues." (High prices, housing, tax revision, conservation, and civil rights seemed especially important.) In his message on the State of the Union he should present his program to the American people, and he should present it in a simple and clear fashion that would enable them to know what he was asking Congress to do. Thus he would be in a position "to receive credit for whatever they do accomplish while also being in a position to criticize the Congress for being obstructionists in failing to comply with other recommendations."

On civil rights, Clifford assumed not only that Truman must act but that he could act without risk. The situation demanded action, for Negro voters held the balance of power in Illinois and perhaps in New York and Ohio, and the Republicans appeared to be making progress in their efforts to regain Negro support. And he could act, for no policies "initiated by the Truman Administration no matter how 'liberal' could so alienate the South in the next year that it would revolt." The South could be considered "safely Democratic" and could be "safely ignored" in formulating national policy. Anticipating that "Republican strategy at the next session will be to offer an FEPC, an anti-poll tax bill, and an anti-lynching bill," Clifford advised that "the President go as far as he feels he possibly could go in recommending measures to protect the rights of minority groups." The resulting difficulties with the South would be "the lesser of two evils."

Truman accepted many, but not all, of the suggestions, and with the new year the strategy began to unfold. On January 7, he delivered his State of the Union message with its long list of proposals for action in both domestic and foreign affairs and its appeals to many groups of voters. And as this broad message dealt with specific issues in general ways, he supplemented it with a series of special messages. One of these called for the extension and improvement of legislation authorizing rent control and emergency financial aids for housing and for new housing legislation that would establish "an integrated program to assist in obtaining more housing at lower cost, both in the immediate future and for the long run." Another major message called for a ten-point civil rights program that would provide federal protection against lynching, protect the right to vote, prohibit discrimination in interstate transportation facilities, and establish a Fair Employment Practices Commission to prevent unfair discrimination in employment.

Clearly, the administration expected that the civil rights message would create difficulties for both Wallace and the Republicans in the Negro wards. But the Southern reaction was stronger than expected. The administration and the national committee now recognized that the South would not be solid and began to work to limit the scope of the Southern revolt. While refusing to modify the civil rights proposals or withdraw them from Congress, the administration did not introduce a draft of a civil rights bill and delayed action against discrimination in federal employment and against segregation in the armed forces. Advisers most concerned about the loss of Negro votes to Wallace urged action, but those who were worried about the Southern revolt counseled delay and, for the moment, dominated the administration's handling of civil rights.

Most leaders of the labor movement recognized the great importance to it of the Democratic party, the party of F.D.R., and feared the damage that Wallace might do. The years of Democratic rule had been years of progress for the movement and for the wage-earner. The Taft-Hartley Law constituted evidence of what they could expect from the Republicans while Truman's veto demonstrated the value of the Democratic connection. Passage of the law encouraged them to increase their political activity in hopes of defeating congressmen who had voted for it and bringing about the repeal of the law. Support for the administration's new foreign policy was also involved in labor's refusal to support Wallace. The C.I.O., for example, endorsed the Marshall Plan at the same time that it condemned Wallace's candidacy, and the A.F.L. charged that the communists hoped to elect an archreactionary with isolationist leanings and that this "Would play into the hands of Soviet Russia's expansionist policies."

Liberals in the A.D.A. and the New York Liberal Party evaluated the Wallace movement in a similar way and joined in efforts to weaken it. After failing to persuade him that a decision to run would harm the liberal cause, they advised others that a vote for him would help conservative Republicans gain power. Denying that liberals and communists should work together, they joined in the attack upon Wallace's connections and made some of the most sensational and influential presentations of the thesis that the Wallace movement was essentially a communist movement designed chiefly to destroy Truman's foreign policy.

The Russians also helped to weaken Wallace. While he preached the possibility of peaceful coexistence between communists and noncommunists, including Russia and the United States, the communists staged a coup in Czechoslovakia in February, overturning a liberal regime. Wallace bungled badly in his efforts to explain this development while Truman responded with a strong speech condemning Russian aggression, advocating enactment of the European recovery program, universal military training and selective service and denouncing

Wallace. Other Russian and communist actions also challenged Wallace's thesis. Most important of these was the blockade of West Berlin, beginning in June. Truman responded with the dramatic airlifting of supplies to the city. ". . . if foreign Communists had deliberately tried," David A. Shannon suggests, "they could not have done much more than they did to hurt the Wallace campaign." . . .

As these many steps were taken, plans were moving forward for the preconvention tour that had been suggested by Sullivan, Redding, and Clifford. Before it began, Truman took another step that his advisers had suggested: he changed his speaking style. He actually returned to an old style that he had employed frequently in his prepresidential years but only on informal occasions after he moved into the White House. Then he had attempted to develop a formal manner deemed appropriate for the Presidency. It involved efforts to sound like Roosevelt, something that Truman proved incapable of doing. He was, as a consequence, widely regarded as a very poor speaker. Facing this problem squarely, his advisers persuaded him to adopt an informal manner, aided only by notes or an outline, that would permit his own personality to be expressed. He accepted the advice for he recognized that he read speeches poorly. The "new" method was tested publicly at a meeting of the American Society of Newspaper Editors in April; and, as the response was enthusiastic, the method was employed on three other occasions in May and endorsed for the "nonpolitical" tour by train in June.

Taking advantage of an offer of an honorary degree from the University of California, Truman left Washington on June 3, not to return for two weeks. Traveling several days ahead of the train, Oscar Chapman, the Under Secretary of Interior, provided important assistance, talking to local political leaders, mending fences, getting advice on speech topics that should be emphasized in each location, and making other preparations for Truman's visit. The President pushed west to the Pacific Coast, making many speeches in communities from Indiana to Washington, then moved down the coast to Los Angeles and returned through the Southwest and the Middle West, talking from the back platform at every stop. While he emphasized domestic matters, he did not limit his attention to them but talked also about peace and pictured his foreign and military policies and proposals as ways of avoiding war. Hitting matters of major and special interest to the communities he visited, he covered most of the major issues of the day, stressed Democratic accomplishments and Republican failures and paid some attention to the threats from Wallace and Eisenhower. Although he made several formal speeches, most of them employed the new style, and as he progressed, his mistakes diminished, his effectiveness increased and the crowds grew larger.

Thus Truman's preparations for the fall campaign were well advanced by the beginning of the summer. He had not made great gains in the public opinion polls, but they contained several encouraging signs. Approval of his handling of his office was on the rise again, and Wallace was slipping. . . . Truman was ready for the task that lay ahead and had many people working for him in various ways. The Republicans, on the other hand, had not yet selected his opponent.

At the beginning of the year, the Republicans appeared to have several rather strong choices. According to the polls, Thomas E. Dewey was in the lead. But Harold Stassen, Senator Robert A. Taft, Senator Arthur Vandenberg, General Douglas MacArthur, and Governor Earl Warren also had substantial followings.

An experienced public official and politician, Dewey represented a middle ground position in the party. Relatively young, he had been born in Michigan in 1902, the son of a newspaperman, and educated at the University of Michigan and the Columbia Law School. He had become famous as a racket buster in the 1930s and was elected district attorney in New York City in 1937. Failing in bids for the governorship in 1938 and the Republican nomination for the Presidency two years later, he won the gubernatorial election in 1942 and the Republican nomination for the Presidency in 1944. His defeat in Roosevelt's last campaign did not harm his career seriously, and his reelection as Governor of New York by a large margin in 1946 gave him a big boost. His record as governor was efficient, economical, and relatively liberal, and his moderate stand on national issues involved endorsement of much that had been done by the Democratic administrations, a stand that did not make him attractive to the more conservative Republicans. A man of average height with a neatly trimmed moustache, Dewey was weakened by a rather stiff public manner. . . .

From March to May, the Republican contenders competed in a series of presidential primaries. The first was held in New Hampshire on March 9, and there, after only a small amount of campaigning by Dewey and Stassen, Dewey won six of the eight delegates. The next test came in Wisconsin on April 6, and there MacArthur, serving in far-off Japan, was the predicted winner. With Dewey and Stassen campaigning strenuously, Stassen picked up nineteen of the twenty-seven delegates while MacArthur won only eight, thereby killing the MacArthur boom. The Nebraska primary the next week had a long list of names on the ballot, including Taft, Warren, and Vandenberg, as well as Stassen and Dewey, and Taft joined them in the campaign. Again Stassen won, finishing far ahead of Dewey and even farther ahead of Taft and Vandenberg. Clearly, he had replaced Dewey as the front runner. But now Stassen over-reached himself and not only entered the Ohio primary against Taft but campaigned vigorously against him. Stassen failed to achieve a dramatic victory and thus moved into the Oregon primary of May 21 in a weakened position but still the favorite. With both Stassen and Dewey needing victories, both campaigned hard. Stassen stirred controversy with his proposal to outlaw the communist party, and in a radio debate, Dewey challenged this persuasively on civil libertarian grounds and moved on to win fifty-three percent of the vote and all twelve delegates, a victory that strengthened him substantially.

As the Republican convention drew near, Dewey seemed capable of defeating Truman. So did Vandenberg, Stassen, and MacArthur. Dewey, however, led Truman by a slightly larger margin, forty-four to thirty-two percent or twelve percent as compared with the ten percent margins separating the others from the President. Relative to Truman, Dewey, as well as Stassen, had moved from a loser to a winner since the beginning of the year. And they had done so despite the preparations the President had been making and the help he had been receiving.

THE CONVENTIONS

The Republicans met first and revealed that the presidential wing of their party was quite liberal and international in point of view. The G.O.P. came together in Philadelphia on June 21 and, with a significant number of television viewers able for the first time to look in on a national political convention, clashed more than mildly over issues of both domestic and foreign policy. The platform indicated that the faction that dominated the congressional party was not in control of the convention. The platform, which endorsed both the United Nations and the containment policy, was in harmony with the congressional party's record on foreign policy and with its efforts to cut expenditures and taxes, but the platform endorsed many domestic schemes that the Eightieth Congress had refused to pass, including civil rights legislation, inflation control, public housing, an increase in the minimum wage, and aid to displaced persons. The platform committee, however, appeased conservatives by omitting any reference to federal aid to education, by a meaningless compromise on reciprocal trade and by dropping a plan favoring an F.E.P.C. Republicans were making their own efforts to court the South.

The contrast between the efficiency of the Dewey organization and the ineptitude of the Taft forces helped Dewey win the nomination. . . . He fell short by more than 100 votes on the first ballot as Taft, Stassen, Vandenberg, and Warren demonstrated substantial strength. Taft gained on the second ballot, but Dewey gained even more and Stassen slipped back. Stassen then refused Taft's suggestion that he withdraw. Not until Taft and then Warren conceded defeat did Stassen do so. With the opposition out of the way, the convention nominated Dewey unanimously on the third ballot. . . .

Despite the obvious divisions within the party, great optimism now gripped the G.O.P., and the polls endorsed the Republican predictions of victory. The Boston *Globe* poll suggested that even in Massachusetts, which had supported the Democratic presidential candidate in the five preceding elections, Dewey would win by a large margin, and the New York *Herald Tribune* poll made a similar prediction. Gallup indicated that the big cities, which had provided strong support for Democrats since the 1920s, favored Dewey.

A pessimistic band of Democrats followed the Republicans into Philadelphia on July 12. Some of the most prominent men in the party expected to lose with Truman at the head of the ticket and wished that he would step aside, and some labor leaders shared this wish. The efforts to substitute Eisenhower for Truman continued to the eve of the convention when the General made it unmistakably clear that he would not run. Then Leon Henderson, the chairman of the A.D.A., tried to switch the Eisenhower support to Justice Douglas, but his liberalism made him unacceptable to many who had favored Eisenhower. Senator Claude Pepper announced his candidacy, saying he was the only man available who would carry on the tradition of F.D.R., but when the A.D.A. and the C.I.O. withheld support, Pepper took himself out of the race. Jacob Arvey of Chicago and William O'Dwyer of New York City issued a joint statement endorsing Truman. Any chance of dumping him had been killed.

Truman's hold on the convention was not total however. He failed to get the civil rights plank that he advocated, failed to prevent a Southern bolt, failed to receive a unanimous nomination, and failed to obtain his first choice for the vice-presidency. For the most part, the party platform conformed to White House desires.

On such issues as repeal of Taft-Hartley, support for the international control of atomic energy, Marshall Plan appropriations, Reciprocal Trade, and aid for Israel, the final product differed significantly from the Republican platform. On civil rights, however, Truman chose the McGrath strategy. The administration's proposal essentially repeated the party's 1944 plank, one that the Southerners had found at least tolerable, ignored the specific proposals that Truman had made in February, and contained the same ambiguous emphasis upon limits that had been present in McGrath's statements since the civil rights message.

The A.D.A. contingent, led by Andrew J. Biemiller of Wisconsin and Hubert H. Humphrey of Minnesota, disliked the proposal and battled successfully to strengthen the plank. Failing with the platform committee, which was dominated by Truman supporters, the liberals decided to take the issue to the convention floor. Biemiller and Joseph L. Rauh proposed the deletion of the ambiguous sentence about what Congress should do and the substitution of one calling upon the lawmakers "to support our President" in guaranteeing a set of clearly defined civil rights. A candidate for the Senate, Humphrey hesitated to employ his oratorical powers in a fight that might hurt him and the party but agreed to do so after the insertion of a sentence commending Truman "for his courageous stand on the issue of Civil Rights," a sentence that might help Humphrey retain links with the administration and party leaders. Southerners countered with a states' rights substitute that not only rejected recent developments on civil rights but rejected the party's 1944 stand as well, but this substitute was defeated decisively. With Humphrey supplying a stirring speech and a number of big city bosses rallying behind the liberals, the convention endorsed the A.D.A. proposal, an impressive accomplishment for a group that had suffered a disastrous defeat in its efforts to dump the President. The organization's representatives had made the President's stand of February 2 the official position of the party and had done so despite his desires. His representatives at the convention opposed the liberal substitute.

While the change encouraged liberals, it also produced the Southern bolt the administration had feared. Following the acceptance of the civil rights plank, thirty-five delegates from Mississippi and Alabama withdrew from the convention. Most Southerners remained in the convention, but almost all of them now voted against Truman's nomination. They could not veto it. In fact, the Truman forces had worked, again successfully, against Southern efforts to restore the old Democratic rule requiring a two-thirds vote for nomination. But when the roll was called, only thirteeen Southern votes, all of them from North Carolina, were cast for Truman. All of the other Southerners voted for Senator Richard Russell of Georgia, an advocate of settling the civil rights issue within the party. Russell got 263 votes while Truman received 947½, and the Southern mood checked any move to make the nomination unanimous. Although Truman now had the nomination, he could not be fully satisfied with the proceedings. He had not wanted to go as far as the platform went on civil rights, and he would certainly have welcomed a unanimous endorsement. But as a politician with a quarter-century of experience, he understood and sympathized with the behavior of Southerners who voted against both his civil rights proposal and his nomination. "I would have done the same thing myself if I were in their place and came from their states," he explained to two members of his administration. . . .

Despite his failures, Truman now had the nomination and fully intended to make something out of it. The first step was to come to the convention and deliver an inspiring acceptance speech. He gave the kind of fighting, optimistic speech that his advisers recommended and drafted, the type he had delivered on his western trips a month before.

The advocates of such a step made their case in a memorandum written a few days after the Republican convention. The memo suggested that the election could "only be won by bold and daring steps, calculated to reverse the powerful trend now running against us" and that calling a special session would be the "boldest and most popular step the President could possibly take. . . ." It would focus attention on the "rotten record" of the Congress, force Dewey and Warren to defend that record, "keep a steady glare of publicity on the Neanderthal men of the Republican party," split that party on domestic issues, and "give President Truman a chance to follow through on the fighting start he made on his Western tour." Although opposed at first; Truman accepted the counsel of boldness, convinced that the party needed a dramatic move. Contrasting the record of the Eightieth Congress with the Republican platform, he suggested that the special session would be a test. Predicting that the Republicans would fail the test, he concluded his speech with an appeal for help in the election. "The country can't afford another Republican Congress."

The speech produced the enthusiastic reaction from Democrats outside the South that Truman and his advisers had sought. Southerners lacked enthusiasm, however, and some of them assembled in Birmingham on July 17 for a convention or "conference" of their own. The most important men present were the leading Democrats of Mississippi, the conservative faction of the Alabama Democracy, and Governor Thurmond. Men of less importance came from a number of other states. While most of the Southern political leaders stayed away, those who came decided without any dissenting voices that Thurmond should run for the presidency with Wright as his running mate. . . .

On July 23, politics returned to Philadelphia for the fourth significant convention of the year. It was the first convention of the new party, which now formally adopted the name "Progressive." The meeting was large and colorful. More than 3,000 delegates participated; most of them young people, many of them women, many black, very few were professional politicians. The delegates did very little drinking for a political gathering, and an unusually large amount of singing. Banjoes and guitars rather than a band provided the music; the songs were folk songs, and Pete Seeger sang many of them. An open-air rally at Shibe Park highlighted the gathering.

The delegates discussed issues as well as sang songs. They did not debate candidates, for long before the meeting they had agreed that Wallace would be nominated for the presidency and his running mate would be Glen Taylor, a singing cowboy who had been elected to the Senate by the Idaho Democrats in 1944. Wallace and Taylor were nominated by acclamation. The platform, on the other hand, was discussed at great length, although the basic work on it had also been done earlier. The main ideas had been expressed in Wallace's declaration of candidacy and his subsequent campaign speeches. They emphasized "Peace, Freedom, and Abundance" and included cooperation between Russia and the United States, the removal from power of the war-producing elite, opposition to the Marshall Plan and to American intervention in Greece, Turkey and China, the repudiation of universal military training, the repeal of the draft law, the end of the military buildup, the destruction of the stockpile of atomic bombs, the breaking up of monopolies, better housing, lower food prices, and the abolition of segregation. Although communists played a large role in drafting the platform, the ideas it contained were not exclusively or essentially communist ideas. Communist enthusiasm was limited to the planks of foreign and military policies, but that was enough to secure endorsement of Wallace by the Communist party. . . .

THE FALL CAMPAIGNS

Truman faced a difficult task as the fall campaigns approached. If the polls were accurate, Dewey needed only to hold the support that he had already acquired and hope that most of the Wallace people resisted the temptation to vote for the "lesser evil." The President had a tougher assignment. In addition to maintaining the loyalty of those who favored him, he had to convert both the uncertain and some of those who at present seemed devoted to his opponents. He was, however, well prepared, and as President he had power in his hands that he could use.

On July 26, the day the congressmen assembled for the special session, Truman employed one of his powers in a very significant way. He issued two executive orders on civil rights, one dealing with the armed forces, the other with civilian employment in the federal government. The administration had decided early in the year to move on these problems by administrative action rather than by legislation. The Southern revolt, however, as well as opposition from the Army, encouraged delay. But Negro leaders demanded action. A. Philip Randolph, for one, threatened to advise young Negroes not to register for the draft if the Army remained a segregated institution. And the Republican platform expressed opposition to "the idea of racial segregation in the armed services of the United States." Finally, the Democratic civil rights plank, which included promises of "equal opportunity of employment" and "equal treatment in the service and defense of our Nation," increased the pressure. Truman accepted the advice of liberals; Clifford, Ewing, and Philleo Nash, a member of the White House staff, drafted the order; and when confusion arose as to the purpose of the one on the armed forces, Truman stated in a press conference on July 29 that it was intended to end segregation. After McGrath met with Randolph to provide further assurances, he brought his civil disobedience campaign to a close. . . .

The liberal strategy dominated Truman's campaign even though the earlier tests of it had produced the Southern revolt and had not destroyed the Wallace threat. Obviously, no other group had been able to suggest a strategy that made greater sense to Truman. Actually, of course, the civil rights plank prevented him from switching to an emphasis on the cultivation of the South, even if he had desired to do so. And the suggestion of a strenuous swing around the country had obvious appeal to him, especially now that he had new confidence in his effectiveness as a campaigner.

From Labor Day to Election Day, Truman stumped the country. He began in Michigan, crossed the continent from Pennsylvania to California, and returned to Washington via Texas and Oklahoma, all of this in September. During October, he concentrated on the populous Middle West and East, although he did make a quick trip into the South, stopping only at Miami and Raleigh. He covered more than 20,000 miles and gave more than 250 speeches, most of them informal and many of them delivered from the rear platform of his train. It was the longest and hardest campaign of his career, but, despite his sixty-four years, he had all of the strength and energy that the ordeal demanded.

The speeches had a significant conservative dimension: they sought to preserve the New Deal as well as maintain Democratic control of the national government. Employing hard-hitting and frequently folksy and entertaining language, referring to particular features of a community and to the political leaders of the area, and emphasizing issues of especially strong interest there, the President focused attention on the Eightieth Congress rather than on Dewey, and upon domestic issues, such as housing, high prices, resource development, social security, health insurance, and Taft-Hartley. His speeches pictured politics as dominated by a struggle between the "people," represented by the Democrats, and the "special interests," represented by the Republicans, while at the same time viewing the people as composed of groups with special interests. The President identified himself and his party with Roosevelt's

New Deal, pictured the Republicans as a threat to it and interpreted the New Deal as beneficial to the interests of his listeners.

Although Truman emphasized Congress, he did not ignore Dewey. He attacked and ridiculed the challenger's emphasis upon unity, interpreting Republican unity as, for example, "unity in giving tax relief to the rich at the expense of the poor," insisting that "some things are worth fighting for" and listing several worthy foes—"isolationists and reactionaries, the profiteers and the privileged class." He also attacked Dewey's neglect of issues, maintaining that the American people wanted "to hear more than platitudes" and that as long as Dewey was afraid to tell where he stood he would "lose more votes than he gains."

The campaign paid somewhat greater attention to farmers than had been planned. The liberal advisers, while not overlooking this group, had emphasized the cities. But after the campaign got under way, an issue that could be exploited was discovered. It was the failure of Congress to provide grain storage bins. Linking this with Stassen's suggestion that the Republicans favored lower farm prices, Truman charged that his opponents wanted to sabotage the price support program, and, with farm prices dropping and farmers suffering from a shortage of bins, he presented the Republicans as a threat to the farm prosperity that the Democrats had produced.

Truman followed the liberals' advice on the South, visiting there only briefly and emphasizing economics. [But he] did not pay as much attention to civil rights as his liberal advisers advocated. In fact, he devoted only one speech to it; but that was a major one in Harlem. His advisers had recommended a speech there, assuring him that it "would have a powerful effect on Negro voters throughout the United States." He was especially pleased with this part of his campaign. The crowds were large and enthusiastic. In a speech that had been drafted with great care by Philleo Nash, the President discussed the Civil Rights Committee and his efforts to implement its recommendations, and promised to keep moving toward the goal of equal rights and equal opportunities "with every ounce of strength and determination that I have."

Truman's advisers urged him to make two arguments against a vote for the Progressive party. He should stress the role of the communists in it and point out that a vote for Wallace would hurt the party of effective liberalism—the Democratic party—and "play into the hands of the Republican forces of reaction." In a major speech in Los Angeles on September 23, Truman hit both themes and concluded: "This is the hour for the liberal forces of America to unite. We have hopes to fulfill and goals to attain. Together we can rout the forces of reaction once again."

Concern about Wallace also affected Truman's handling of the foreign policy issue during the campaign. Although it did not receive as much attention as domestic policy, it was not ignored, and efforts were made to portray the Republican party as the party of high tariffs and isolationism, and the Democrats as the party of international cooperation and peace. While Truman campaigned, he worried about the possibility that the Berlin crisis would lead to war, and about the charge, made most frequently by Wallace, that he was not seriously working for peace. Thus, he accepted a suggestion from his advisers that he should send Chief Justice Vinson to Russia in October for discussions with Stalin. Secretary of State Marshall, however, talked Truman out of this. The press learned of the plan and publicized it, and the Republicans criticized the President for it. As soon as it became public, he issued a statement explaining the episode, but his advisers, deeply troubled about the affair, pressed him to discuss it in a campaign speech and worked out a response to the criticism. Addressing the American Legion Convention in Miami on October 18, Truman maintained that his purpose had been "to ask Premier Stalin's cooperation in dispelling the present poisonous atmosphere of distrust which now surrounds the negotiations between the Western Powers and the Soviet Union," and he insisted that he was determined "to utilize every opportunity to work for peace." . . .

Also in the foreign policy area, Truman dealt with Republican charges that communists had dangerously infiltrated the Roosevelt–Truman administrations. His advisers believed that the "Communist issue" was a major one demanding a speech that would have "the widest possible radio audience." They urged him to discuss it in the Middle West, for there the voters were not sharply divided on the issue and they were especially upset by the congressional investigations.

Speaking in Oklahoma City to a nationwide radio audience on September 28, Truman presented his party as the effective foe of communism and charged that the Republicans were "unwittingly the ally of the Communists in this country." In support of his claim about the Democrats, he pointed to the "strong foreign policy" which he had developed and which "checked" the "Communist tide," to the domestic programs of the Roosevelt–Truman administrations which prevented the communists from making "any progress whatever in this country," and to his loyalty program which made sure "that Communists and other disloyal persons are not employed by the Federal Government."

This hard-hitting campaign was not a lonely venture. Truman travelled on a crowded train, filled with advisers and aides, members of the Secret Service and newsmen. His wife and daughter made the trips and were frequently introduced to the crowds. Politicians climbed aboard the presidential special, many of them remaining for short trips, and representatives of the Democratic National Committee and organized labor also frequently rode the train. Politicians now seemed eager rather than reluctant to be associated with the President and to have him refer to them in his speeches. . . .

Many Democrats supplemented Truman's meager efforts in the South. The national committee, convinced that Truman must carry the South to win, worked at this; Congressman Rayburn and Senator Barkley [the vice-presidential nominee] campaigned strenuously there, and Brannan and other administration officials also spoke in the South. Prominent Southerners, such as Senators George of Georgia and Pepper of Florida, Governors Folsom of Alabama and Estes Kefauver of Tennessee openly supported Truman, while others worked more quietly behind the scenes. Loyal Democrats, especially representatives of the liberal wing of the party, worked to prevent further bolts, to obtain a place for Truman on the ballot, as the Democratic candidate if possible or as an independent if necessary, and to keep their states in the Democratic column at a time when some Southern conservatives, while remaining in the party, refused to work for Truman or to punish those who endorsed his foes.

Others helped Truman get and hold labor and liberal votes. Almost all labor leaders formally or informally endorsed him, although John L. Lewis was a major exception. Many had reservations about Truman as President and strong doubts that he could win, but they liked his record, with the Taft-Hartley veto, and his platform. The unions gave greater attention to congressional elections, hoping that either Dewey or Truman would face a strong pro-labor bloc in Congress that would repeal the new labor law.

In many places, unions performed functions that had been performed by Democratic organizations in their stronger days, and at times labor organizations and party organizations combined their efforts. Dewey, on the other hand, obtained almost no help and received much criticism from organized labor.

While Truman and his allies made these giant efforts, Dewey waged a relatively dull campaign. After the Republican convention, he and his advisers decided to discard the aggressive methods he had employed in 1944 and in this year's battle for the nomination, and to pitch the campaign on a high level. Several considerations influenced this decision. One was the belief that he had made a mistake in 1944. Another was the divided character of his party. He hoped that lofty generalizations would alienate neither the right nor the left wings. The high-level approach would conceal the divisions within the party and unite all members behind him. Also involved was a rather low estimate of the impact of campaigns or a tendency to believe that the voters reached decisions by summer. And perhaps nothing was more important than Dewey's confidence that he would win. When, late in the campaign, he became troubled by Truman's slashing attacks and feared they might be effective, his advisers talked him out of changing his approach, arguing that his campaign was going well and no one believed the President.

Dewey did not feel compelled to work as hard as Truman. He did not begin as early but called instead upon Stassen to campaign on Labor Day, an assignment he handled rather ineffectively; and after Dewey hit the campaign trail, he started his days later than Truman did and brought them to a close earlier. He did not cover nearly as many miles, and, to an even greater degree than Truman, he confined his attention to the East, the Middle West and the Far West. He did not make as many speeches, and a higher percentage of those he made were the formal type that imposed fewer demands upon his memory, his sense of humor and his ability to identify with the public.

Although he was fearful that the Democrats would gain control of the Senate and he devoted an unusually large amount of time to the congressional races, Dewey did not tackle Truman's criticism of the Eightieth Congress. Perhaps he agreed with some of Truman's charges for Dewey's point of view was rather close to the President's on many issues, both domestic and foreign, and he did endorse much of Truman's program. Perhaps he should have made a greater effort to persuade the farmers that his party would not destroy the New Deal farm program. He surely recognized that the Republican record created some difficulties for him in the big cities and that militant defense of it would not guarantee victory. On the other hand, he could not join in the criticism for that would help the Democrats and weaken his chances of getting a Congress with which he could work. So he tended to remain silent or praise Congress mildly and infrequently. And this meant that he ignored weaknesses in the Democratic record, such as Democratic failure to pass Truman's domestic proposals when the Democrats controlled Congress, or did not attack them vigorously. It also meant that he seldom praised Republican accomplishments, such as crucial Republican support for the European Recovery Program. But would praise for Republican support for Truman's foreign policy help Dewey more than Truman? Dewey, in short, suffered from certain Republican weaknesses and Democratic strengths that, despite his confidence, he at least dimly perceived.

Dewey seldom subjected Truman to the type of slashing attack that the latter made upon the Republicans. The G.O.P. candidate did suggest that more should be done to help the Nationalist Chinese but did not hit this very hard. On this issue, Republicans were torn between a belief that China deserved more help, including military aid, and doubts concerning the Chinese situation and fears of deep involvement in China's problems. Dewey also tapped the issue of communists in government, but did so infrequently and usually in a quite restrained way. And he did not fully exploit the Vinson episode. Nor did he remind the voters that the man who was calling the Taft-Hartley law a "slave-labor law" had urged as recently as 1946 that striking railroad workers should be drafted and that the man who spoke of Wall Street domination of the Republican party employed many men from Wall Street in his own administration.

Dewey did not depend, of course, upon only his own efforts to combat Truman's campaign. He had the help of most of the nation's press. Sixty-five percent of the dailies favored him while only fifteen percent favored Truman.

Dewey did not receive as much help from the Dixiecrats and the Progressives as had been expected. Thurmond limited his campaign almost exclusively to the South, and there he had to contend with the opposition of most of the press and most of the politicians and to campaign with but little financial support. He and his allies battled fiercely with the Truman Democrats over control of the Democratic party name and machinery but succeeded in capturing them in only four states: Alabama, Louisiana, Mississippi, and South Carolina. Elsewhere, the movement was clearly a third-party effort that had to contend against the Southerner's allegiance to the Democratic label. . . .

Wallace campaigned much more extensively than Thurmond but

could not check the decline in the Progressive party. His campaign sur-
passed Truman's in miles covered as he visited every part of the country
and spent much more time in the South than Truman did. Unlike orthodox campaigns, the Progressives charged admission to their rallies
and took up collections. They continued to provide a Broadway touch
and to sing, with Paul Robeson and Pete Seeger lending their voices to
the Progressive cause. . . .

The polls revealed that Wallace lost ground during the campaign.
They also suggested that Truman had been the most effective campaigner. He alone, of the four presidential candidates, gained support
during the fall. He narrowed the gap separating him from Dewey as the
latter, as well as Wallace, fell back. Nevertheless, the pollsters remained
confident that the Republican would win although in a rather close
election.

Placing a higher value on campaigns than the pollsters did, Truman
really did not believe their prediction, and his advisers were encouraged
by their analyses of the political situation and by their evaluation of his
campaign, although few of them were as confident as he was. Beyond the
Truman camp, few informed observers expected a Truman victory.
They were not swayed by the large crowds that Truman drew or the
other signs that encouraged Democrats.

THE OUTCOME AND THE EXPLANATION

To the great surprise of almost everyone, Truman won! He received more than twenty-four million votes, or 49.5 percent of the total,
while Dewey received fewer than twenty-two million, or forty-five percent. Wallace and Thurmond trailed far behind, dividing slightly more
than 2.3 million votes almost equally. In the electoral college, Truman's
performance was more impressive, Wallace's more dismal. The Democratic candidate gained 303 electoral votes, or fifty-seven percent of
them, while Dewey's total was 189 and Thurmond obtained all of the
others (thirty-nine percent).

How had Truman accomplished his surprising victory? Basically,
the answer is that he had taken advantage of the strength of his party,
much of which had been developed by Franklin Roosevelt. Two major
factors were involved: both party strength and rather effective campaigning. Truman had battled so strenuously that many observers gave
him all of the credit. While they provided a distorted view, so do those
who treat the campaign as insignificant.

The question that has been raised, however, produces distortions
if one stops with it. Much of the strength of the question actually rests
upon the failures of the pollsters to understand the political situation.
Had they been more perceptive, then the victory would not have been
so surprising, and more attention would have been paid to the size of
the victory and less to the fact of victory. A focus on Truman's victory
alone draws attention to strengths only, which were a factor in the situation, but ignores weaknesses in Truman and his coalition. They were
also important.

Those who give Truman exclusive credit ignore the contributions of other people in 1948, including Clark Clifford and other Truman advisers. They also ignore the importance of the strength that the party had developed. Truman's advisers understood that element of the situation, devised a strategy to exploit it, and helped Truman implement the strategy. The election results confirmed the wisdom of their analysis. Of the twenty-eight states that voted for Truman, all but five had supported Roosevelt each time he ran; and of the five, three had voted for Roosevelt three times and two had supported him twice.

Truman maintained most but not all of the strength that the Democratic party had developed by the 1940s. He returned five states to the Democratic column after they had deserted it in 1940 or 1944, but this accomplishment was more than matched by the loss of eight states that had supported Roosevelt in every election year and of four that had supported him in each of his last three elections. Truman also failed to carry Michigan although it had supported Roosevelt in every year but 1940. The strategy had worked well enough but not perfectly.

A swing to Truman had taken place during the fall. In September, Dewey had been in the lead, but Truman had caught up by mid-October and moved into the lead in the final weeks. The pollsters missed this swing for they made errors in sampling and interviewing, stopped collecting data too early, and did not know how to predict the voting behavior of the large number who remained undecided in early October and even of those who stated a preference. In the final weeks, Truman lost the support of some, but most of them decided not to vote, and gained the support of many who either moved away from Dewey and Wallace or reached a decision they had been unable to make earlier. The net result of a large number of shifts favored Truman. . . .

In the campaign, Truman had successfully identified himself with the New Deal and persuaded a sufficient number of people that he was a sincere fighter for policies and programs that had benefited them. His stand on foreign policy was less important to the people who voted for him. They saw him as a New Dealer, as a friend of the worker, the farmer, the Negro, and the "common man," and as the champion of programs that were in their interest and would protect the prosperity that many of them had come to enjoy in recent years. His stand on domestic issues was the most important factor; his personal qualities as they related to those issues were not insignificant.

Much of Truman's strength was in the cities, although they were not as strong for him as they had been for Roosevelt. Truman's plurality in the twelve largest cities fell nearly 750,000 below Roosevelt's 1944 plurality, and he failed to carry several highly urban states—Maryland, Delaware, New Jersey, Pennsylvania, New York, Connecticut, and Michigan—that had supported Roosevelt all or most of the time. But Truman did win in the biggest cities; two highly urban states—Ohio and Wisconsin—returned to the Democratic fold after deserting it in 1944, and four other states with cities among the top twelve—Massachusetts, Missouri, Illinois, and California—and also densely populated Rhode Island remained Democratic as it had been in the Roosevelt period. Almost everywhere, Truman defeated Dewey in the densely populated areas; and in them, the late swing to Truman by those who had planned to vote for Dewey or Wallace or who had been undecided was very substantial. . . .

While weaker in the South and East than Roosevelt had been, even in his poorest race in 1944, the President partially compensated for these losses by gains in the Far West and the Middle West. Farmers throughout the nation provided substantial support for Truman. For many, 1948 meant a return to their way of behaving in the 1930s. Then they had resented Republican handling of farm policy and looked upon Roosevelt's New Deal for agriculture as their salvation. But in 1940, they turned away from F.D.R. for a variety of reasons, including dislike for his foreign policy. But now Truman, aided by Brannan, the Eightieth Congress, a drop in farm prices, and a shortage of storage facilities, had revived old loyalties. Once again, farmers had concluded that the Democratic party served their economic interests and that those interests should guide their behavior in the polling booths. The Republican party seemed to threaten the economic gains they had made since 1932.

Dewey had received more electoral votes than he had in his first bid for the Presidency. . . . [His] popular vote, however, fell short of his 1944 total by more than 36,000. With the voters, he suffered from both personal weaknesses and weaknesses in his party. The upper income groups, the better educated, the professional and managerial classes, and the older people tended to prefer him to Truman while white collar workers, middle-income people, and Protestants divided their votes about equally between the two leading candidates. Dewey had a substantial bloc of loyal Republicans upon whom he could depend, and they had a strong tendency to go to the polls. But not even the desire for a change that some voters felt was enough to compensate for the minority status of the Republican party and its identification with big business in the eyes of many. And Dewey's personality and his campaign certainly failed to fill the gap. Although he was regarded as experienced, capable, and intelligent by many, many more found him unattractive. He seemed patronizing, cold, complacent, and smug. And his campaign was regarded as filled with weaknesses, including neglect of the issues. Even many Republicans found him inadequate as a person and a campaigner. Most important, he had been unable to maintain the support of many of the Democrats and independents who had thought seriously of voting for him, and he had been unable to capture many of the votes of those who were undecided and of those who became disenchanted with Truman or Wallace as time passed. These groups tended to switch to Truman or stay at home.

In the popular vote, however, Dewey had not fallen far behind Truman. Nineteen forty-eight was a narrow-margin election. Roosevelt's margin had reached as high as 24.5 percent, had dropped no lower than 7.5 and had averaged 14.75. Truman's, on the other hand, was but 4.5, the lowest since 1916 when Wilson's was three percent. . . .

The election revealed that Truman as well as Dewey had weaknesses as a party leader. In addition to being a narrow-margin election, 1948 was also a low-turnout election. Fewer than 49-million people voted. This total was less than 750,000 above 1944, a war year; and it was more than a million below 1940 despite the growth in population from slightly above 130 million in 1940 to more than 150 million in 1950. (In 1952, more than sixty-one million voters would go to the polls.) Clearly, many people found Truman as well as Dewey uninspiring. . . .

Angus Campbell regards the "extraordinarily low turnout" as the "most striking feature" of the election and refers to 1948 as "the prototype of the low-stimulus presidential election." With only 51.5 percent of the total citizenry voting, it was, he points out, "the smallest presidential vote since the establishment of the two-party system, except for the two elections immediately following the advent of women's suffrage." Nothing had "aroused strong public interest in the choice of alternatives" and thus "the turnout was low. . . ."

Dewey and Truman had been unable to draw large numbers to the polls, and they had also failed to change the political faith of many voters. Campbell points out that "partisanship of the vote was determined largely by the established party loyalties of the voters." According to the work of his Survey Research Center, seventy-four percent of the Democratic vote for President came from Democratic party "identifiers" and seventy-one percent of Dewey's vote came from Republican identifiers while only six percent of the vote for each candidate came from those who identified with the opposing party.

The election was not a "realigning election." Popular feelings associated with politics were not so strong that the basic partisan commitments of a portion of the electorate changed and a new party balance was created. The 1930s had been such a period, and Truman benefited and Dewey suffered from the party realignment that had taken place then.

The election of 1948 was a maintaining election. Truman and his aides had maintained Democratic control of the White House. He had accomplished this despite his weaknesses, and he had not worked alone. Many people had helped him, including some perceptive political analysts on the White House staff. Beyond Truman and his closest advisers, many other people made contributions to his victory: the leaders of the Democratic National Committee, strong campaigners like Brannan and Barkley, loyal party members working openly or behind the scenes against party rebels, the A.D.A., organized labor, strong candidates for other offices, among others. The participation of many people in the campaign demonstrated that the party still possessed much of the strength and vitality it had developed in the age of Roosevelt. And one of its greatest strengths was the approach to domestic issues with which the party had become identified then, an approach that emphasized the use of the powers of the national government to deal with the nation's social and economic problems. This point of view had been endorsed by the voters. Dewey lacked the personal qualities needed to compensate for the weaknesses of his party, and he helped Truman by waging a dull, uninspiring campaign that failed to swing the independent voters and the discontented Democrats behind him.

While Truman received much help, he also helped himself. Although his campaign was not a lonely affair, neither was it ineffective. He played rather skillfully and very strenuously the role that his advisers had suggested. He demonstrated that he was a political man of strengths as well as weaknesses. Recognizing that his situation contained advantages as well as disadvantages—above all, basic Democratic strength —he exploited those advantages and helped his party maintain control of the Presidency for four more years. Although he failed to rally a spectacular number of voters behind him or to convert a substantial bloc to his political faith, he and his aides attracted enough support to accomplish their immediate objective.

Truman and Foreign Policy: The Korean War

WALTER LA FEBER

Doubts about whether the United States should ever have intervened in Vietnam have inevitably encouraged reconsideration of our earlier intervention in Korea. There are certain—perhaps superficial—similarities between the two situations. Both were unpopular wars, demoralizing to the troops, misunderstood at home, and fought with a mixture of technical brilliance and gross miscalculation. When in Korea the aggressive American drive northward brought on the subsequent Chinese intervention, American officials, political and military, were caught as unprepared as they were later to be for the Tet offensive of early 1968. Exactly whom we were fighting—apart from the abstraction of communism—was almost as mysterious in Korea as in Vietnam. And the political repercussions of Korea—the McCarthy era at home—continue to haunt those who uneasily await the final reaction to Vietnam.

Unpopular as it was, the Korean war was relatively short and quickly forgotten. Americans were satisfied that they had taught the Communists a lesson—no longer would attempts to absorb (or snatch) territory go unchallenged. Only with the rise of Cold-War revisionism in the 1960s was the Korean conflict evaluated afresh. Walter LaFeber, whose careful study of the Cold War has probably gained a wider acceptance than any other work of revisionism, considers the Korean war in the context of a global design for an American-sponsored world order. He suggests that long-range objectives involving Europe, all of Asia, and the Pacific shaped American policy in Korea. The Communist adventure in Korea thus provided an opportunity for American policy-makers to define international power relations for a number of years thereafter.

In June 1950, Korea was a Cold War-wracked country which lacked everything except authoritarian governments, illiteracy, cholera epidemics, and poverty. For nearly a century, it had been a pawn in Far Eastern power plays. In 1905, Japan, after using force to stop a Russian thrust, had established a protectorate over Korea and in 1910 annexed that country. When the Japanese surrendered Korea in 1945, it became a testing ground in the renewed battle between Russia and the United States. After setting up dependent but Korean-led governments in zones seized from the Japanese, Russia and the United States evacuated their occupation armies in 1948 and 1949, respectively. In March 1949, North Korea and the Soviets signed an agreement for economic cooperation. Russian military advisers and aid strengthened a formidable 100,000-man army. American military advisers also remained in the south, but President Truman encountered difficulty sending large amounts of aid to Syngman Rhee's government. At the end of June 1950, about $60 million of an allotted $110 million in economic aid had been shipped. Military assistance had scarcely begun. As at the turn of the century, Korea was a prize in the struggle between Russia and countries to the West; and, as in 1904, China, although now a very different China, stood apart from the conflict. Mao's regime devoted itself to internal reconstruction and drawing up plans for a probable invasion of Formosa sometime during 1950.

Mao had little cause to linger over Korean problems; South Korea itself posed no threat to his new government or, apparently, to the remainder of the Communist bloc. MacArthur and Acheson had defined Korea as beyond the perimeter of American military defenses, although not outside the realm of United Nations responsibility. It seemed possible, moreover, that without either Chinese or Russian overt pressure, the South Korean government might crumble. South Korea suffered under Rhee's authoritarian government until the State Department publicly protested his disregard of constitutional rights in early 1950. In an election in May, President Rhee's party collected only forty-eight seats as opposed to one hundred and twenty seats for the other parties; this defeat occurred despite Rhee's arrest of thirty political opponents in "anti-communist" raids just before the election was held. The Korean President pieced together a coalition government that began what promised to be a precarious, perhaps short, struggle to hold power.

On June 7 the northern government of Kim Il Sung attempted to exploit Rhee's problems by initiating an all-out campaign for peaceful reunification of the country through general elections. Rhee attempted to stop the news of this offer from circulating in the South. With that encouragement, the northern government reiterated the proposal on June 19 and intensified its political offensive.

This North Korean initiative apparently fitted within a general strategy which Stalin was designing to counter two threats. In mid-May, Truman announced that discussions on a Japanese peace treaty would receive high priority. The negotiations would particularly consider Japanese independence and the establishment of American military bases on Japan's soil under long-term agreements. The talks, American officials observed, would not be burdened with Russian representation. For Stalin this announcement opened the unhappy prospect of unity between the two greatest industrial nations in the Pacific, perhaps even the extension of a NATO-like organization on the Asian periphery of the Soviet Union. The Sino-Soviet pact in February had singled out Japan as a potential threat to Asian Communism, and this had been followed by the Soviet press accusing Truman with attempting to "draw the Asiatic and Pacific countries into aggressive military blocs, to entangle those countries in the chains of some 'little' Marshall Plan for Asia." On May 30, the Japanese Communist party climaxed weeks of demonstrations with attacks on United States military personnel in Tokyo. If North Korea could unify the country, peacefully or otherwise, the threat of a militarized, western-oriented Japan would be blunted, perhaps neutralized.

The second threat might well have caused Stalin even more concern. Mao's success had not created but probably encouraged revolutions throughout Asia, particularly in Indochina, the Philippines, and Indonesia. The possibility that some of these revolutions might triumph, perhaps following the pattern set by Mao, could weaken Stalin's two-camp premise and loosen his direction over the world Communist bloc. Stalin's view of world matters had become so rigid that he could not accept the nationalist content of these revolts without wrecking his own doctrines and tempering his grip on Soviet and satellite affairs. Malenkov had added to these troubles with his November speech, but by the spring of 1950 (that is, after the Chinese had shown their obstinacy in the Sino-Soviet negotiations and the revolutionary situation had intensified in Asia), Malenkov came back into line. In a speech in March, he no longer talked about the "friendly" nations surrounding Russia, but about a Europe, and especially Germany, which "fascist and revanchist forces," led by the United States, planned to turn into "a military-strategic bridgehead of American aggression." A speech by Molotov the same month was equally aggressive. Stalin had confined the domestic debate; a short and successful war by a Russian-controlled North Korea could intimidate Japan and check the expansive aims and reputation of Mao. On June 25, large numbers of North Korean troops moved across the 38th parallel which divided the country. They followed Soviet-built tanks which had been shipped to Korea during the previous two months.

Attending to family business in Independence, Missouri, when the attack occurred, Truman immediately returned to Washington. He and Acheson assumed the invasion was Russian-directed, perhaps the beginning of an extensive Sino-Soviet thrust. Their initial reaction, however, was carefully measured. They ordered MacArthur in Tokyo to dispatch supplies to the South Korean troops. Then, moving to contain the action, Truman ordered the American Seventh Fleet to sail between China and Formosa, and sent additional assistance to counter-revolutionary forces in the Philippines and Indochina. In a hurriedly called session of the United Nations Security Council, an American resolution branding the North Koreans as aggressors, demanding a cessation of hostilities, and requesting a withdrawal behind the 38th parallel, passed 9–0 with Yugoslavia abstaining. The Soviet Union was not represented, for Yakov Malik continued his boycott to protest the exclusion of Red China. Two days later, as the military situation worsened, Truman ordered American air and naval units into action. That same day, the 27th, the United Nations passed a resolution recommending that its members aid South Korea in restoring peace. This passed 74–1, with Yugoslavia opposing and Egypt and India abstaining. Malik still had not appeared; the rapidity and extent of Truman's reaction had taken the Soviets by surprise.

The day after American units had been committed, the President conferred with Congressional leaders for the first time to inform them of his action. The only strong objection was voiced by Senator Taft who approved of Truman's action but disliked the sending of Americans to war without consulting Congress. Neither then nor later did the President discuss Taft's objection with the full Congress. Two days later, on June 30, Truman made the final commitment. The South Korean army of 65,000 men had suffered heavy losses in the first week of fighting. The President decided that only American ground units could stop the southward flood. In sending these troops Truman emphasized that the United States aimed only "to restore peace there and . . . restore the border." Supporting air attacks were similarly to be limited to the area around the 38th parallel.

Throughout the first week of the war the President carefully refrained from publicly linking the Russians to the attack. He hoped thereby to enable them to stop the aggression without loss of public face. On June 27 Truman dispatched a note to Moscow assuring Stalin that American objectives were limited; the President expressed the hope that the Soviets would help in quickly restoring the *status quo ante bellum*. Truman's immense concern about potential Russian involvement motivated the American statement on June 30 that the United Nations wanted only to restore the parallel as the dividing line, and also resulted in Truman countermanding Air Force directives of July 6 which ordered high-level photo reconnaissance over Russian ports. The Soviets initially responded to Truman's overtures by accusing South Korean forces of invading North Korea. Within ten days this view underwent considerable change. The war was a "civil war among the Koreans," Deputy Minister of Foreign Affairs Andrei Gromyko claimed on July 4. Under these circumstances, Gromyko concluded, the Soviet Union could take no action.

Privately in June and publicly during the late summer, the Truman Administration became less restrained in defining the Soviet role. "In Korea the Russians presented a check which was drawn on the bank account of collective security," Acheson claimed. "The Russians thought the check would bounce. . . . But to their great surprise, the teller paid it." The terms "collective security" and "U.N. action" became the catchwords which supposedly explained and justified Truman's decisions in late June. Both terms were misleading. The United States had no collective security pact in the Pacific in 1950. If the Japanese occupation served as an example of how collective security worked in the abstract, the American exclusion of Australia and Great Britain from control of Japan between 1945 and 1950 twisted collective security to mean unilateralism. As Acheson used the term "collective security," it meant the United States would both define the extent of the "collective" and unilaterally, if necessary, furnish the "security." Nor is there any indication that the President consulted his European or Asian allies before committing American air and naval units on the 27th. This was not the first nor would it be the last time the United States would take unilateral action in an explosive situation without consulting its Western European partners.

As for the sudden American concern to bolster the United Nations, this had not been apparent when the United States acted unilaterally or with some Western powers to establish the Truman Doctrine, the Rio Pact, the Marshall Plan, and NATO. American actions in Korea were consistent with this history, for the United States used the June 27th resolution to establish a military command in Korea that took orders not from the United Nations but from Washington. "The entire control of my command and everything I did came from our own Chiefs of Staff," MacArthur later recalled. "Even the reports which were normally made by me to the United Nations were subject to censorship by our State and Defense Departments. I had no direct connection with the United Nations whatsoever." Sixteen nations finally contributed to "United Nations" forces, but the United States provided 50 percent of the ground forces (with South Korea providing most of the remainder), 86 percent of the naval power, and 93 percent of the air power. In October during the Truman-MacArthur conference at Wake Island, a dozen American officials prepared plans for the reconstruction of *all* Korea without consulting anyone, not even the United Nations or Syngman Rhee.

The American attitude toward the United Nations was exemplified on November 3, 1950 when American delegate John Foster Dulles successfully pushed through the General Assembly a "Uniting for Peace" proposal giving the Assembly the right to make recommendations to United Nations members for collective security measures, including the use of force, if the use of the veto stopped the Security Council from taking action. The resolution also established a permanent "Peace Observation Commission" to report on trouble spots around the world and, finally, invited members to contribute troops that could be used in a United Nations force. This resolution transfigured the United Nations. The organization no longer rested on agreements among the great powers, without which neither the United Nations nor world peace could be viable. Instead power was thrown into a body where Costa Rica had voting power equal to that of the United States or the Soviet Union. Weakening the Soviet veto, the United States also weakened its own. Assuming, however, that it could control the General Assembly, the Administration had taken a calculated risk; it had, to paraphrase Acheson, issued a blank check on the future. After a decade of increased neutralist feelings among the multiplying underdeveloped nations, that check would appear increasingly rubberized.

The United States suffered 142,000 casualties in Korea not for the sake of "collective security" or the United Nations, but because the Executive branch of the government decided that the invasion signaled a direct threat to American interests in both Asia and Europe. Europe, indeed, remained uppermost in the minds of high State Department officials. As the fighting raged in Korea, Acheson devoted increasing amounts of time to the European situation. The State Department had long defined Europe as having first importance. Acheson, moreover, had gotten burned politically and diplomatically when the Korean attack raised questions about his January 12th speech which termed the Communist threat in Asia one of "subversion and penetration," and not "military." This was a rare, probably traumatic, departure from his usual reliance upon military "positions of strength," and he moved quickly to improve the military balance in Europe. . . .

[Meanwhile,] American forces were advancing to greater victories in Korea. What magnifying effects a series of battle losses would have on Republican power and McCarthyism, Democrats did not wish to contemplate. General MacArthur had apparently removed this possibility on September 15 with a brilliant landing at Inchon, back of the North Korean lines, while simultaneously launching a counterattack from the shallow perimeter at Pusan. Within two weeks the United Nations forces joined to cut off large sections of North Korean troops. The Administration's political goals developed accordingly. In late June, Truman reported that the main objective was the restoration of the 38th parallel; on September 1, he told the nation that the Koreans "have a right to be free, independent, and united"; ten days later he approved a National Security Council recommendation that MacArthur should drive the North Koreans north of the 38th and, if encountering no Chinese or Russian troops, to move north of the parallel and prepare for occupation; on September 27, Truman ordered MacArthur north of the parallel; and on October 7, the General Assembly cooperated by endorsing Truman's order 47-5. That day the lead troops of the United States First Cavalry Division crossed into North Korea.

All eyes now turned to China. Throughout July and August, the new Communist government had made little response to the conflict. Recovering from famine, a quarter century of war, and having as her top diplomatic objective the conquest of Formosa, China did not pose an immediate threat to the United Nations forces. In late August, Foreign Minister Chou En-lai made his first important move. At the United Nations, American delegate Warren Austin asked for the open door "within all parts of Korea," and later in the month, Secretary of Navy Francis Matthews applauded "a war to compel co-operation for peace." At this point, Chou reminded the world that "Korea is China's neighbor" and urged that the neighbor's problems be settled "peacefully." Mass anti-American rallies began to appear in Chinese cities. Ten days after the Inchon landing Peking warned India, which had become China's main link with the Western world, that it would not "sit back with folded hands and let the Americans come to the border." After the first remnants of the North Korean troops retreated behind the 38th, Chou formally told India in a dramatic midnight meeting on October 2 that China would attack if United Nations troops moved into North Korea. The United States discounted this threat, believing that it was aimed at influencing upcoming votes on the conflict in the United Nations. MacArthur responded by issuing an ultimatum for the complete surrender of North Korea. On October 7, as the first American troops crossed the border, Chinese troop concentrations on the Manchurian border just across the Yalu River from Korea increased from 180,000 to 320,000. On October 16, a few Chinese "volunteers" crossed the Yalu.

The Truman Administration remained convinced that China would not intervene. Emphasizing, as he had in earlier speeches, that China's immediate concern was with Russian penetration in the north, Acheson commented on national television on September 10, 1950, "I should think it would be sheer madness" for the Chinese to intervene, "and I see no advantage to them in doing it." Acheson later admitted that until late September, American intelligence considered Chinese intervention improbable. On October 9, the danger reached the boiling point when two American F-80 jets strafed a Soviet airfield only a few miles from Vladivostok, a major Russian city close to the Korean border. After the Soviets strongly protested, the United States apologized. Vexed that such a crisis could arise, and angered that he had to back down before Soviet protests just a month before national elections, Truman cancelled a trip to Independence, where he was to watch his sister installed as Worthy Matron in the Order of Eastern Star, and flew to Wake Island to check on MacArthur's policies. In the heavily-censored text of that meeting, little was implied about Russia, but the General assured the President, "We are no longer fearful of [Chinese] intervention. We no longer stand hat in hand." The Chinese, he informed Truman, possessed no air force. They might move 50,000 or 60,000 men across the Yalu, but if these troops attempted to move farther south without air cover, "there would be the greatest slaughter."

Eleven days later, on October 26, the first Chinese prisoner was captured, "so that you began to know, at that point," Acheson later commented, "that something was happening." This realization, however, made little apparent impact on American policies during the next four weeks. On November 21, advanced elements of American troops peered at Chinese sentries stationed several hundred yards across the Yalu. Three days later, MacArthur grandly announced the launching of the end-the-war offensive. At this point the United States government was still not certain whether, in Acheson's words, the Chinese "were committed to a full-scale offensive effort." Two days later, on November 26, the Chinese moved across the river in mass, trapping and destroying large numbers of United Nations troops, including 20,000 Americans and Koreans at the Chosin Reservoir; this outfit finally escaped with 4400 battle casualties and 7000 noncombat casualties, mostly severe cases of frostbite. Three weeks later the retreating United Nations forces once again fought below the 38th parallel, and now it was Chou En-lai who proclaimed his nation's intention of reunifying Korea. "They really fooled us when it comes right down to it; didn't they?" Senator Leverett Saltonstall once asked Acheson. "Yes, sir," the Secretary of State replied.

Throughout September and October the United States had continually assured Peking that Americans never wanted to fight Chinese or threaten in any way China's vital interests. All the Administration wanted, the Secretary of State remarked on November 29, was to "repel the aggressors and restore to the people of Korea their independence." The Chinese retaliated precisely because they interpreted "independence" and Austin's request for "full access" to all Korea to mean the stationing of American power on China's doorstep. From there the United States could exert pressure on both Mao's internal and external policies. China's intense hatred for the West, a hate nurtured by the just-concluded century of western exploitation of China, and Mao's determination to restore Chinese supremacy in Asia made impossible the acceptance of such an American presence. Although historically accustomed to hairsplitting on points of diplomacy, the Chinese failed to see the difference between American presence on the Yalu and American danger to Chinese industries and politics just across the Yalu.

Soviet thinking during November and December was more inscrutable than usual, but Stalin seems to have agreed with the Chinese that the United States could not be allowed to conquer all of Korea. Chinese intervention was a preferred preventive because it would not involve Russian men or large Soviet resources. Stalin meanwhile attempted to use the Chinese successes to pressure the West into reversing German rearmament policies.

In Washington, Administration officials were thoroughly frightened, and Truman's response to the intervention was considerably more explicit than Stalin's. The President reiterated that the United States had no "aggressive intentions toward China," and believed that the Chinese people opposed this sending of troops by their leaders. (This remark was in line with Truman's general theory that Communism anywhere never had popular support.) Because these people could not be heard, the President continued, the aggression must be crushed or "we can expect it to spread throughout Asia and Europe to this hemisphere." As in late June, however, Truman's response was measured. He countermanded MacArthur's order to bomb Chinese troops and supplies in Manchuria. The President finally allowed only the Korean halves of the bridges crossing the Yalu to be bombed, a compromise that infuriated Mac-Arthur and told the Chinese exactly how restrained American retaliation to their intervention would be. In a news conference of November 30, Truman showed signs of losing this restraint. He intimated that the United States would use all the power it possessed to contain the Chinese, and he explicitly did not exclude using atomic bombs. This remark brought [British] Prime Minister Attlee flying to the United States on December 4.

Attlee was not without responsibility for the crises; his government had participated in the decision to send United Nations troops to the Yalu. He now worried that in the newly expanded war Truman would not be able to control the military, and particularly wondered at the spectacle of Truman flying 5000 miles to Wake Island to meet Mac-Arthur who had flown 1900. ("I thought it a curious relationship between a Government and a general," Attlee commented later.) The Prime Minister received Truman's assurances that the United States was not planning to use the bomb. The two men then undertook a full, candid, and most revealing evaluation of the Asian tinderbox.

Both agreed that a general war must be averted and that the United Nations forces should not evacuate Korea unless forced out militarily. Then basic differences emerged. Attlee argued that China's admission to the United Nations could bring her into regular consultations leading to a cease-fire. Acheson doubted that in their present advantageous military position the Chinese would want a cease-fire; if they did and negotiations resulted, Mao would next demand a United Nations seat and concessions on Formosa. The United States had refused to discusss these two items before the intervention and Acheson now was in no mood to reward aggressors. Attlee countered that a cease-fire would make explicit the divisions between China and Russia: "I want them [the Chinese] to become a counterpoise to Russia in the Far East," Attlee argued. If "we just treat the Chinese as Soviet satellites, we are playing the Russian game."

Truman now hardened his earlier view of the Chinese. They were "Russian satellites," and if they succeeded in Korea "it would be Indo-China, then Hong Kong, then Malaya." Acheson interposed that he did not think it mattered whether China was a satellite or not, for she would act like Russia anyway. He believed the invasion into Korea "had design," and, like Truman, adopted the domino theory to warn that any compromise with the Chinese would have a "serious" effect on the Japanese and Philippine islands. Acheson recalled a "saying among State Department officials that with communistic regimes you could not bank good will; they balanced their books every night." Therefore, he argued, the West must develop great military power to stop "this sort of thing from happening in the future." Acheson and Truman also reminded Attlee that the United States could not be "internationalist" in Europe and "isolationist" in Asia; domestic political pressures made that impossible.

At that point Attlee questioned the basic American premise, the fundamental belief that underlay United States policy in Europe as well as Asia. He emphasized that the United Nations must be kept together even if this meant alienating important segments of American public opinion. Whatever the United States and Great Britain did would have to be done through the United Nations, Attlee argued, and this could not be accomplished by the efforts and votes of only the United States and the United Kingdom, "important as we are." Truman and Acheson disagreed; they believed the two nations were "important" enough. By controlling the United Nations forces and now, apparently, the United Nations itself through the "Uniting for Peace" resolution, American officials believed they could keep the American people united, prevent a bigger war in Asia, follow an "internationalist" policy in both Europe and Asia, punish China for moving into Korea by excluding her from the United Nations and Formosa, build up great military power throughout the world, and through it all keep the other United Nations members in agreement with American policies. It was a tall order, so demanding and inflexible that it fixed the American position on China for the next fifteen years.

American intelligence estimates reinforced Truman's and Acheson's views. A December 13 report stated that the Soviet Union hoped to use the war to move American power away from Korea and Formosa, establish China as the dominant power in the Far East and seat her in the United Nations, eliminate American power in Japan, and prevent German rearmament. The Administration expected little help from the United Nations in thwarting these Soviet drives. The most the United Nations could do was brand the Chinese as aggressors, which it did on February 1, 1951 by a vote of 44–7 with 9 abstentions. As the United Nations debated, its forces retreated from the South Korean capital of Seoul.

Although the military situation steadily eroded, not even the other nations in the Western Hemisphere would offer much assistance. The Latin Americans dutifully voted with the United States on resolutions in the United Nations and the Organization of American States, but in the early spring of 1951, when Truman personally appealed to Latin American Foreign Ministers to "establish the principle of sharing our burdens fairly," only Colombia responded with troops. Several other nations sent materiel, but Latin America as a whole failed to see the relevance of Korea to their own economic deprivation and political instability. Later in 1951 a shocked Administration attempted to woo its southern neighbors by extending to them the Mutual Security Program of military aid. Eight nations took the money in 1952 to protect themselves against Communist aggression; this both giver and receiver interpreted to mean preservation of the *status quo*. No other Latin American nation, however, sent men to Korea.

The United States would have to depend primarily upon its own resources in defending what Niebuhr had called "our far-flung lines." In December and January, the President requested emergency powers to expedite war mobilization. Closely following the guidelines suggested in NSC-68, he submitted a $50 billion defense budget; this contrasted with the $13.5 billion budget of six months before. The Administration doubled the number of air groups to ninety-five and obtained new bases in Morocco, Libya, and Saudi Arabia. Army personnel increased 50 percent to 3.5 million men. Truman thereby placed the nation on the Cold War footing on which it would remain, with few exceptions, during the 1950s and 1960s.

The President also embarked the United States upon another costly and momentous journey by committing it to developing and protecting the Western Pacific and Southeast Asia. The riches of the area made it a formidable prize: Burma, Thailand, and Indochina provided rice for much of Asia; Southeast Asia produced nearly 90 percent of the world's natural rubber, 60 percent of the world's tin, and the bulk of Asia's oil. Movements toward independence threw the area into turmoil immediately after the war, but with several exceptions (particularly Vietnam and the Philippines where an Un-Filipino Activities Committee tried to aid the Army in ferreting out the "Huk" rebels), a semblance of order appeared by 1950. Attempted Communist uprisings had been contained in most countries by nationalist elements.

Throughout Asia these anticolonial, nationalist movements had triumphed either peacefully or after short struggles. Vietnam was a tragic exception. There Ho Chi Minh had conducted anti-Japanese underground operations during the war and emerged in 1946 as the leading Communist and nationalist leader. Roosevelt had pressured the French to evacuate Indochina in early 1945. De Gaulle resisted that pressure until the Truman Administration reversed the American policy in order to obtain French cooperation in Europe. After a year of uneasy truce with the French, who were determined to reclaim their control over Indochina, full-scale war broke out in December 1946. The French army moved back into Vietnam carrying large numbers of American lend-lease weapons to eradicate Ho's forces. The Soviets, like the United States, refused to recognize Ho's Republic of Vietnam. Typically distrusting such revolutionaries, Stalin, like Truman, concentrated on European problems in 1946 and early 1947. By 1948 Ho was turning to the Communist Chinese for aid. He had not easily reached this decision, for the Indochinese had historically feared and distrusted their giant neighbor. On January 18, 1950, China recognized Ho's government. The Soviets followed thirteen days later.

After an intensive policy review, the United States fully committed itself to the French cause. On February 6, four and one-half months before the Korean war began, the United States recognized the Bao Dai government which had been established by the French. On June 12, an American military advisory mission prepared to aid the French forces. As early as May, Truman discussed large-scale aid for Bao Dai, and after the Korean conflict, began to pump in aid at the rate of half a billion dollars per year. When French General de Lattre de Tassigny visited Washington in September 1951, the State Department endorsed French war aims and methods.

Although involving itself in the French struggle long before June 1950, the Korean war provided a convenient background as the United States began explaining its commitments in Vietnam. A State Department pamphlet of 1951 defined United States interests as the "much-needed rice, rubber, and tin," but added, "perhaps even more important would be the psychological effect of the fall of Indochina. It would be taken by many as a sign that the force of communism is irresistible and would lead to an attitude of defeatism." The statement concluded that "Communist forces there must be decisively conquered down to the last pocket of resistance," to accomplish this, large amounts of American aid had been given. "Without this aid," the analysis concluded, ". . . it is doubtful whether [Bao Dai and the French] could hold their ground against the Communists."

After mid-1950, Congress began its first systematic aid program to Southeast Asia. The Administration coupled with this economic approach a program for overall military security. The linchpin would necessarily be Japan, the most highly industrialized Asian nation and the only one capable of providing a counterpoise to the Chinese. For three years Truman had failed to write the peace treaty which would cement an independent Japan to the West. The Soviets naturally opposed the pact Truman had in mind, but another intra-Administration dispute between the Defense and State Departments also retarded progress. Defense feared a pact would weaken its hold on Japanese military bases, but State argued that healthy political relations demanded a new agreement.

In March 1950, John Foster Dulles assumed control of the negotiations and almost single-handedly drove the treaty through to a successful conclusion in September 1951. It was a bravura performance. He silenced Defense Department critics by giving them a separate security pact assuring American bases in Japan. Russia was simply excluded from the early, decisive negotiations while Dulles talked only with Japan. When the Soviets finally were asked to participate, Dulles interpreted their proposal as an attempt to dominate the area around Japan; he read out the Russian resolution, one participant later recalled, demonstrated its effect on a map, "took this map dramatically and held it up like this . . . and then threw it on the floor with the utmost contempt. And that made a tremendous impression."

After shrewd parliamentary maneuvering by Dulles, who led the American delegation, and Acheson, who chaired the conference, the treaty was signed by fifty-one nations at a San Francisco conference on September 8, 1951. Russia was not one of the signatories. The treaty restored Japanese sovereignty over the home islands, but not over the Ryukyus (which included the large American base at Okinawa) or the Bonin Islands; these remained in American hands. The agreement allowed Japanese rearmament and "the stationing or retention of foreign armed forces on Japanese territory." In the security pact signed the same day, Japan allowed the stationing of American troops and planes on her soil, but not those of any third power.

The Administration hoped that the treaty would serve as the basis for a long-lasting anti-Communist alliance. For this reason Dulles rode roughshod over demands from American allies and neutrals in Asia who demanded reparations from Japan for her occupation of those countries during World War II. Dulles retained vivid memories of how the Versailles Peace Conference in 1919, in which he had participated as a young economic adviser, had blundered by fastening unreasonably high reparations on Germany. Now, he warned, he would brook no "Carthaginian peace" which would "lead to bitter animosity and in the end drive Japan into the orbit of Russia." Many allies in the Pacific area also urged reparations in order to weaken Japanese war potential; their memories of 1941–1945 matched the vividness of Dulles' recollection of 1919. Dulles solved this problem by negotiating a series of mutual defense treaties to insure the Philippines, Australia, and New Zealand against both reemerging Asian giants, Japan and China. Thirty months before, Acheson had assured Senator Lodge that other than NATO, the Administration contemplated no further regional arrangements. On September 1, 1951 the United States signed with Australia and New Zealand the so-called ANZUS treaty, pledging the security of these two nations and establishing a foreign ministers council for regular consultation.

Because Australia and New Zealand belonged to the British Commonwealth, Great Britain was conspicuous by its absence from ANZUS. As early as March 1914, Winston Churchill, then First Lord of the Admiralty, predicted that with British resources increasingly devoted to Europe, the "white men" in the Pacific would soon have to seek American protection. Thirty-seven years later the British were not as understanding. Angered because Dulles had informed it neither of prior arrangements on the Japanese treaty nor of the discussions of ANZUS, the London government argued that ANZUS derogated British prestige and left the vital British areas of Hong Kong, Malaya, and Burma outside its defensive perimeter. Dulles granted these arguments, but countered that if Britain came in, the French and Dutch would also and thereby transform ANZUS in the eyes of suspicious Asians into a colonial alliance. This argument effectively reduced British influence in the Pacific. "All roads in the Commonwealth lead to Washington," a Canadian official observed.

These negotiations in late 1950 and 1951 determined the geographical extent of the American commitment in the Pacific. During the spring of 1951, with drama and flourishes seldom seen in American history, the military extent of that commitment was decided. In late January, United Nations forces opened a successful drive back to the 38th parallel. As the battle stalemated along the former boundary line, State Department and Pentagon officials cautiously explored the possibility of negotiations with the Chinese on March 20. Three days later General MacArthur issued a personal statement urging that the Red military commanders "confer in the field" with him on surrender; China is "doomed to imminent military collapse," the General proclaimed. Not for the first time had MacArthur undercut his superiors in Washington.

As early as July 1950, he had shown reluctance to accept Truman's decision that Chiang Kai-shek should be contained on Formosa rather than unleashed on the mainland or allowed to ship troops to Korea. A month later, MacArthur sent a message to the annual convention of the Veterans of Foreign Wars, which labeled as "appeasement" any policy that would restrain Chiang. Truman angrily demanded that this message be recalled, and MacArthur complied although it had already been published. The Wake Island conference muted these differences, but the published minutes are embarrassing in their revelation of MacArthur's incredible condescension and Truman's tittering insecurity. Once the President was back in Washington, this insecurity disappeared. After MacArthur again recommended a naval blockade of China, air attacks to level Chinese military and industrial installations, and the use of 30,000 Formosan troops in Korea, Truman patiently explained on January 13 "the political factors" involved in the "world-wide threat" of the Soviet Union which made containment of the Korean war necessary. When MacArthur issued his March 23rd ultimatum, Truman's patience, never inexhaustible, evaporated.

Only the method and timing of relieving the General remained to be decided. On April 5, Representative Joe Martin, the leading Republican in the House, read a letter from MacArthur which charged that "here we fight Europe's war with arms while the diplomats there still fight it with words." "We must win," the letter emphasized. "There is no substitute for victory." The Joint Chiefs of Staff agreed with Truman that MacArthur would have to be relieved immediately; reports from the field indicated that the General was losing the confidence of his men and had already lost confidence in himself. On April 11, the President recalled MacArthur.

Truman knew the political dynamite in the decision. Less than two weeks earlier he had agreed with top advisors that an all-out speaking campaign would have to be undertaken by Cabinet-level officers because the Administration's " 'story' was not reaching the American public." The American people preferred quick victory to containment. This preference was dramatically demonstrated when the General returned to the greatest popular reception in American history. Senator McCarthy expressed the feelings toward Truman of not a few Americans when with characteristic restraint he told a press conference, "The son of a bitch ought to be impeached." Congress warmly received MacArthur's speech before a joint session, then in April and May settled down to investigate the case of the President versus the General.

In a battle of MacArthur versus Truman, the long-range issues tended to be overshadowed by the personalities involved. In Mac-Arthur's case this was not an advantage. Having last set foot in the United States fourteen years before, the General seemed unable or unwilling to grasp the political and social as well as the diplomatic views of his country. He revealed much describing the power he wielded in Japan between 1945 and 1950: "I had not only the normal executive authorities such as our own President has in this country, but I had legislative authority. I could by fiat issue directives." Although he had repeatedly advocated policies which contained the most somber worldwide ramifications, he now admitted having only a "superficial knowledge" of NATO and European affairs.

His basic message was curiously close to Truman's and Niebuhr's in 1948: because Communism posed a threat to all civilization, "you have got to hold every place." Or again, "What I advocate is that we defend every place, and I say that we have the capacity to do it. If you say that we haven't you admit defeat." Like Acheson, he insisted on not putting military power and politics into the intellectual equivalent of a cream separator; in time of war, however, MacArthur demanded the reversal of Acheson's priority: once involved in war, the General argued, the military commander must be supreme over all military and political affairs in his theater, "or otherwise you will have the system that the Soviet once employed of the political commissar, who would run the military as well as the politics of the country." Such a remark cut across the grain of traditional American policies of subordinating military to civilian officials unless the nation was involved in total war. This Mac-Arthur assumed to be the case. When he heard the suggestion of Assistant Secretary of State Dean Rusk that war in Korea must not become a "general conflagration," MacArthur branded it "the concept of appeasement, the concept that when you use force, you can limit the force."

The General believed that by controlling the sea and air no one could "successfully launch an effort against us," but the United States could "largely neutralize China's capability to wage aggressive war and thus save Asia from the engulfment otherwise facing it." He expressed contempt for the Chinese Communists. "Never, in our day, will atomic weapons be turned out of China. They cannot turn out the ordinary weapons." Nor was there threat of Soviet intervention. Time, however, was short. If, as MacArthur once told Forrestal, Europe was a "dying system," and the Pacific would "determine the course of history in the next ten thousand years," victory must be won immediately. The "dreadful slaughter" had to end, MacArthur pleaded; American blood as well as dust is settling in Korea, and the "blood, to some extent" rests "on me." But now, he concluded emotionally, "There is no policy —there is nothing, I tell you, no plan, or anything."

The Administration had a plan, and Acheson outlined it in his testimony after MacArthur finished. Korea must be viewed as part of a "collective security system," Acheson argued. When so viewed two things readily became apparent. First, all-out war in Korea would suck in Russian force to aid Stalin's "largest and most important satellite." "I cannot accept the assumption that the Soviet Union will go its way regardless of what we do," the Secretary of State declared. If Russia did intervene, there could be "explosive possibilities not only for the Far East, but for the rest of the world as well." Unlike MacArthur, Acheson insisted on keeping the European picture uppermost in dealing with Korea. (Truman once added a variant on this: expansion of the war could "destroy the unity of the free nations," the President declared. "We cannot go it alone in Asia and go it with company in Europe.") Second, if Europe and the prevention of Russian entry in force did comprise the main objectives, American forces were not engaged in a "dreadful slaughter," or as Acheson remarked, "a pointless and inconclusive struggle," but had "scored a powerful victory" by dealing "Communist imperialist aims in Asia a severe setback" in preventing the armed conquest of all Korea.

MacArthur lost the argument. He lost it so decisively, moreover, that while negotiations to conclude a stalemated war fitfully began in Korea during the summer of 1951, Acheson accelerated the military buildup of Europe.

PART TWO

1952-1959

The age of Eisenhower—that era of placidity and order that has already become an object of nostalgia—was shorter than we remember. Eisenhower became President, the Korean war ended, and Joseph Stalin died —all in 1953. But Joseph McCarthy was still a power in the land and the economy sagged immediately after Korea, so that placidity scarcely developed before about 1954. And by 1957 and 1958, beneath the Eisenhower consensus, anxiety stirred over Russian spacecrafts, colonial revolutions, civil-rights disorder, and muckraking journalism—all harbingers of the decade to come.

This short and welcome respite from the strains of war did not bring long-term social stability. In the interchangeable suburbs, Americans were learning new styles of living, new attitudes toward money and family behavior. An economy increasingly based on consumer credit undermined old habits. Meanwhile, the great flux was obscured by public assurances of rooted values and by political stalemate. Yet the decade of the 1950's moved rapidly toward a rendezvous with the new world it was creating. Blacks were increasingly angry; the right wing more sour and disillusioned; the dispirited and invisible poor rising into view of the liberal middle class; adolescents in high school and college finding their own voices (and musical sounds).

Before the decade's end, a fresh spirit of criticism was abroad. The Supreme Court had spoken in a historic school segregation case, and blacks had already discovered the techniques that could force change. Martin Luther King demonstrated their resolve to an uneasy nation at Montgomery in 1955. In John Kennedy, liberals had found a practical hero and the Right a vulnerable enemy. An era of muckraking, which began late in the decade with the writings of C. Wright Mills, John Kenneth Galbraith, Michael Harrington, and others, revealed areas of national shame and failure. The nation would soon come to noisy confrontation over the changes the 1950's had quietly wrought.

Nixon Agonistes:
The Checkers Speech

GARRY WILLS

Nixon-watching, like Johnson-watching and Kennedy-watching, has become a minor national pastime. Men who get to be President usually are highly complex people, and political success at any level often requires a certain amount of evasion, what Richard Nixon himself has called being "devious . . . in the best sense." However understandable evasiveness may be, it is ironic that a large amount of the unflattering reputation for deviousness that has accompanied Nixon throughout his political career comes from his famous "Checkers" speech of 1952— a talk given in defense against charges that the candidate had spent campaign funds on personal needs. ("Checkers" was the Nixons' cocker spaniel, an irrelevant animal Nixon dragged into the speech along with his wife's "cloth" coat.) As Garry Wills shows, this was in many ways the most open moment of Nixon's career, an occasion when he was forced to tear aside the veil of privacy which has been his primary way of handling the ferocious demands of public life. Unlike Lyndon Johnson, Richard Nixon is not comfortable before the crowds.

The Checkers speech ushered in the age of television politics. Estes Kefauver, investigating criminals in 1950, had made himself a household name in a series of nationally televised hearings, but he had not tailored the medium to his ends. Nixon was the first politician to realize the immense possibilities of television and to exploit every subtle popular response the new medium could evoke. Intellectuals have always held the Checkers speech in bad odor, seeing in it a disgusting exhibition of bathos and an unvarnished attempt to manipulate public emotions. But Wills details the tensions and political infighting which surged around the vice-presidential candidate during the week preceding the speech. He argues persuasively that the Checkers speech was both Nixon's only chance to save his career and also a direct confrontation with the presidential candidate, Dwight D. Eisenhower.

One other thing I probably should tell you, because if I don't they'll probably be saying this about me too, we did get something—a gift—after the election. A man down in Texas heard Pat on the radio mention the fact that our two youngsters would like to have a dog. And, believe it or not, the day before we left on this campaign trip we got a message from Union Station in Baltimore saying that they had a package for us. We went down to get it. You know what it was? It was a little cocker spaniel dog in a crate that he sent all the way from Texas. Black and white spotted. And our little girl— Tricia, the six-year-old—named it Checkers. And you know the kids love that dog and I just want to say this right now, that regardless of what they say about it, we're going to keep it.—The Checkers Speech

Riding in the staff bus during Nixon's 1968 campaign, I talked with one of his speech writers about the convention in Miami. Nixon's wooing of Strom Thurmond had been much criticized. But Nixon's man now said the acceptance speech eclipsed everything that went before: "That was so clearly the major event of the convention—a brilliant job. To talk about that convention is, simply, to talk about that speech. What did *you* think of it?" I answered that it reminded me of the Checkers speech. The comment seemed to horrify my interlocutor; and Professor Martin Anderson, traveling with Nixon as an adviser on urban matters, turned around in the seat before us to object: "People forget that the Checkers speech was a political master stroke, an act of political genius!" But I had not forgotten: that was, I assured him, my point.

Professor Anderson's defensiveness was understandable. Nixon has often been sneered at, over the years, for his television speech in the campaign of 1952. The very term "Checkers speech," reducing the whole broadcast to its saccharine doggy-passage, is a judgment in itself. But that broadcast saved Nixon's career, and made history. By the beginning of the 1968 campaign, sixteen years later, it was a journalistic commonplace that Nixon did not appear to advantage on television. His wan first TV encounter with John Kennedy had dimmed the public's earlier impression. But Nixon only risked that debate with Kennedy because he had such a record of success on the TV screen: in the history of that medium, his 1952 speech was probably a greater milestone than the presidential debate that came eight years later. Nixon first demonstrated the political uses and impact of television. In one half hour Nixon converted himself from a liability, breathing his last, to one of the few people who could add to Eisenhower's preternatural appeal— who could gild the lily. For the first time, people saw a living political drama on their TV sets—a man fighting for his whole career and future —and they judged him under that strain. It was an even greater achievement than it seemed. He had only a short time to prepare for it. The show, forced on him, was meant as a form of political euthanasia. He came into the studio still reeling from distractions and new demoralizing blows.

Nixon, naturally, puts the Checkers speech, along with the whole "fund crisis," among the six crises he survived with credit. It belongs there. He probably displayed more sheer nerve in that crisis than in any of the others. As a freshman in Congress, he did not stand to lose so much by the Hiss investigation. He had, moreover, an unsuspected hoard of evidence in that encounter; and he was backed by dedicated men like Father Cronin, while backing another dedicated man, Whittaker Chambers. In the crises he deals with after 1952, he was a Vice-President, in some way speaking for the nation, buoyed by its resources, defending it as much as himself; never totally without dignity. But at the time when he went onto the TV screen in 1952, he was hunted and alone. Nine years later he would write of that ordeal, "This speech was to be the most important of my life. I felt now that it was my battle alone. I had been deserted by so many I had thought were friends but who panicked in battle when the first shot was fired." It was, without exaggeration, "the most searing personal crisis of my life." It was also the experience that took the glitter out of politics for Mrs. Nixon. . . .

The first news story broke on Thursday, September 18. There had been warnings in the Nixon camp all the four preceding days. A newsman in Washington asked Nixon about the fund on Sunday. Monday, three other reporters checked facts with Dana Smith, the administrator of the fund. By Wednesday, Jim Bassett, Nixon's press secretary, heard something was brewing from his old reporter friends. The candidate had just begun his first major tour—a whistlestop north through California; when the train stopped for water around midnight, a worried staff man waited with more rumors. Thursday, it broke: the New York *Post* had a story with the headline, SECRET RICH MEN'S TRUST FUND KEEPS NIXON IN STYLE FAR BEYOND HIS SALARY. The story did not justify that sensational summary, and neither did subsequent investigation. The fund was public, independently audited, earmarked for campaign expenses, and collected in small donations over two years by known Nixon campaign backers. It was neither illegal nor unethical. And the press soon discovered that the Democratic nominee, Adlai Stevenson, had similar funds, only larger in their amount and looser in their administration. Why, then, was so much made of Nixon's fund, and so little of Stevenson's?

Nixon's official explanation, at the time, was his standard charge: the commies were behind it all. By Friday morning, the day after the charge was published, there were hecklers at his train stops to shout "Tell us about the sixteen thousand!" At a town called Marysville, he did tell them. His own version of that speech, included in his book, is more moderate than some others; but even his excerpts seem gamy enough: "You folks know the work that I did investigating Communists in the United States. Ever since I have done that work the Communists and the left-wingers have been fighting me with every possible smear. When I received the nomination for the Vice Presidency I was warned that if I continued to attack the Communists in this government they would continue to smear me. And believe me, you can expect that they will continue to do so. They started it yesterday. They have tried to say that I had taken $16,000 for my personal use." The *they* is conveniently vague throughout. They—i.e., the New York *Post* and other papers—published the charge. Go far enough back up the paragraph, through intervening "theys," and you find that the antecedent is, more immediately, "the Communists in this Government," and, in the first place, "Communists and [broad sweep here] left-wingers." The explanation is beautifully lucid and inclusive (if a little unspecific about the machinery that makes the nation's press perform the communists' bidding): since the publicizing or nonpublicizing of fund scandals is at the disposal of communists, who were (naturally) supporting Adlai Stevenson, the Stevenson fund got (naturally) no publicity like that accorded to Nixon.

Behind this funny explanation, there are scattered but clear indications, in his book, of the true story, a sad one. At one point Nixon asks why his own statement of the "basic facts" about the fund received so little attention from the press. His answer ignores the conspiratorial explanation given eight pages earlier, and supplies four reasons, two of them technical (denials never get as big a play as accusations in the press, news travels east to west and he was in California), and two more substantive: reporters are mainly Democrats (though Nixon admits that publishers are mainly Republicans, which makes for some balance), and "the big-name, influential Washington reporters cover the presidential candidates while the less-known reporters are assigned to the vice presidential candidates." The last reason, the real one, looks like another point of newspaper mechanics—the mere logistics of press assignment; until we ask why that should matter. The answer, in Nixon's own words, is that his own press release "got lost in the welter of news and speculation over whether General Eisenhower would or would not choose to find a new running mate." *That* was the news on Eisenhower's train— because Ike's advisers were known to be searching for a way to dump Nixon, and Ike was a man who at this stage followed his advisers almost blindly. In short, the Nixon fund was a big story because Eisenhower, by his silence and hints and uneasiness, made it one. For no other reason.

It was natural for Eisenhower to acquiesce in a staff decision to drop Nixon. That staff had presented him with Nixon in the first place. (Ike's knowledge of his running mate was very slim—he thought, for instance, he was forty-two rather than thirty-nine.) The General had, in fact, learned of Nixon's choice at exactly the same time Nixon did. When Herb Brownell asked Ike what he thought of Nixon, the presidential nominee expressed surprise that the decision was his to make. He said he would leave the matter to Brownell, provided the latter consulted "the collective judgment of the leaders of the party" (the top man, in military politics, protects himself by putting a subordinate in charge of the operation, under staff scrutiny). So Brownell called a meeting of the party's leaders, and went through the form of considering Taft and others. But then Dewey got up, to speak for the winning camp. Nixon he said, and Nixon it was. That decision made, Brownell went to the phone, dialed Nixon, and had him listen in while, on another phone, he told Eisenhower that the choice had been made.

As the fund story broke, Nixon wondered where Ike stood. Thursday went by, and Friday. No word from the General—to the public, or to Nixon. But the Establishment was at work: the very thing that had made Nixon good "for balance" made him unpalatable in himself, seen through Establishment eyes. He was there to draw in the yokels. If there was any doubt about his ability to do that, no one would feel compunction at his loss: Ike was too valuable a property to be risked with anyone who might hurt him. This was the attitude on Eisenhower's train, and it spread to Nixon's as newsmen jumped over from the main tour to watch the death throes in the smaller one. The machinery of execution made itself visible Saturday morning, when the New York *Herald Tribune*—the voice of the Eastern Establishment—asked for Nixon's resignation from the ticket. It was, Nixon realized, an order. The same voice that had summoned him was now dismissing him. A waiting game had been played for three days to see if he would go without having to be ordered, and Nixon had not gone. The Saturday editorial (written Friday), following so close on the *Post*'s revelation, appearing before Nixon had conferred with Eisenhower, was the first of several "hints" that he was not wanted. Despite his studied deference toward Eisenhower, Nixon makes it clear he was not dense: "The publishers and other top officials of the *Tribune* had very close relations with Eisenhower and" (for which read, *I mean*) "with some of his most influential supporters. I assumed that the *Tribune* would not have taken this position editorially unless it also represented the thinking of the people around Eisenhower. And, as I thought more about it, it occurred to me" (the little light bulb above a cartoon character's head—Nixon must play this role straight) "that this might well be read as" (*obviously had to be*) "the view of Eisenhower himself, for I had not heard from him since the trouble began two days before."

At ten o'clock Friday night a reporter told him the next day's *Herald Tribune* would ask him to resign. Nixon, who had not heard this, was stunned. He summoned his closest advisers, Chotiner and Bill Rogers (who would, after more of Nixon's crises, at last be his Secretary of State). These two had received the editorial an hour and a half earlier, but they were not going to tell him about it till morning—afraid he would lose sleep if he saw it (a judgment events confirmed). He asked for the editorial and read: "The proper course of Senator Nixon in the circumstances is to make a formal offer of withdrawal from the ticket." So that was it. Nixon is quite candid here: "I knew now the fat was in the fire. That sounded like the official word from Eisenhower himself." He spent four hours discussing his options with Chotiner and Rogers. Then, at two in the morning, he told his wife, and went through the whole discussion again with her.

The next day, Saturday, three days after the story broke, with newsmen plaguing him for his decision, he had to brace himself for defiance of the Establishment. It was an all-day job. He asked Chotiner and Rogers to get the ultimatum spelled out, if they could, from Ike's inner circle—Chotiner tried to reach Dewey, Rogers called Fred Seaton. They got no direct answer. But the indirect command was growing more insistent; sharper and sharper "hints" were thrown to the public (and, by this roundabout path, to Nixon). Sherman Adams had summoned a man all the way from Hawaii to join the Eisenhower train, and the man was all too obviously a second-string Nixon: Bill Knowland, tough anticommunist and Californian. Eisenhower had finally spoken too, off the record. The newsmen on his train had taken a poll that came out forty-to-two for dumping Nixon; news of this was passed along to Ike's press secretary (Dewey's press man in the last campaign, Jim Hagerty), along with the newsmen's opinion that Ike might be stalling to arrange a whitewash job for Nixon. Ike did not like such talk; it questioned not only Nixon's honesty, but his. He invited the newsmen into his compartment for a talk off the record—but the main part of it was soon made public. "I don't care if you fellows are forty-to-two against me, but I'm taking my time on this. Nothing's decided, contrary to your idea that this is all a setup for a whitewash of Nixon. Nixon has got to be clean as a hound's tooth." Again, Nixon got the point: "Our little group was somewhat[!] dismayed by reports of Eisenhower's attitude.

I must admit it made me feel like the little boy caught with jam on his face."

By Saturday night, then, the issue was clear: knuckle under, or defy the closest thing modern America has had to a political saint. Nixon, here as in all his crises, claims the decision was made on purely selfless grounds: he was thinking of Ike's own welfare—switching men in mid-campaign might make the General unpopular. (This is like worrying that the Milky Way might go out.) Not that Nixon is insincere in his claim. Politicians are very deft at persuading themselves that the world's best interests just happen to coincide with the advancement of their own careers. He says he put the question to his four advisers (Chotiner, Rogers, Bassett, and Congressman Pat Hillings) this way: "Forget about me. If my staying on the ticket would lead to Eisenhower's defeat, I would never forgive myself. If my getting off the ticket is necessary to assure his victory, it would be worth it, as far as any personal embarrassment to me is concerned. Looking at it this way—should I take the initiative and resign from the ticket at this time?"

But Nixon does not feel obliged to present his friends as men crippled by nobility. Chotiner, for instance, plays straight man here, saying all the "natural" things Nixon is too lofty for: "How stupid can they be? If these damned amateurs around Eisenhower just had the sense they were born with they would recognize that this is a purely political attack . . . This whole story has been blown up out of all proportion because of the delay and indecision of the amateurs around Eisenhower." Not even good old Murray, though, blunt fellow as he is, can be described in this book as attacking the Big Man himself—just the little men around him. When Nixon's friends start criticizing Eisenhower, the veil of anonymity must be lowered over them: "But now, some were beginning to blame Eisenhower, for not making a decision one way or the other." Nixon himself would never dream of questioning his leader: "What had happened during the past week had not shaken my faith in Eisenhower. If, as some of my associates thought, he appeared to be indecisive, I put the blame not on him but on his lack of experience in political warfare and on the fact that he was relying on several equally inexperienced associates. I could see his dilemma."

The decision to be made at this session was simple: obey the order relayed by the *Herald Tribune,* or risk disobedience. But, after a full day of campaigning through Oregon, he sat up with his inner circle, in Portland, debating the matter till three in the morning. Then, left alone, he went over the whole thing in his mind for two more hours. By five o'clock Sunday morning, he had set himself on a course he meant never to abandon: he would not resign. Sunday brought blow on blow meant to shake that resolution. First, there was a long telegram from Harold Stassen, still trying to clear some path for himself. He recommended, for Nixon's own good ("it will strengthen you and aid your career"), that a resignation be sent right off to Ike. Then, that afternoon, Dewey called to give Nixon the decision of "all the fellows here in New York." Dewey had a plan for breaking the stalemate caused by Nixon's refusal to resign and Eisenhower's refusal to back him: Nixon must plead his cause before the people. If the response was big enough, he could stay. And when Dewey said big enough, he meant the impossible—near-unanimity. Nixon reports the ultimatum this way: "You will probably get over a million replies, and that will give you three or four days to think it over. At the end of that time, if it is sixty percent for you and forty percent against you, say you are getting out, as that is not enough of a majority. If it is ninety to ten, stay on." It is no wonder Nixon—or, rather, "some of the members of my staff"—felt wary of this offer: "They feared a concerted campaign might be put under way to stack the replies against me." The whole plan was stacked against him. It started with the presumption that Nixon was through, and with feigned generosity gave him a chance to climb back onto the ticket. If Nixon took the offer and (as was expected) lost, then he must abide by the consequences. It was a brilliant way of forcing resignation on a man who was determined not to resign.

Nixon said he would consider it. Chotiner got in touch with Party Chairman Arthur Summerfield, to find out how the broadcast would be handled. Summerfield said they had offers from some TV sponsors to give Nixon one of their spots. Chotiner naturally protested: Nixon could hardly go on the air to defend himself against the charge of being a messenger boy for California businessmen, and explain this on time given him by some large corporation! He told Summerfield the National Committee would have to buy the time, if they expected any show at all. (Money had already been set aside for two half-hour appearances by the vice-presidential candidate. But now Summerfield was in the unfortunate position of not knowing who would be the candidate: if he gave one of the periods to Nixon, and Nixon failed, that left only one spot for his successor. At $75,000 a throw, these were not shows to be granted easily.)

Nixon had to deliver a scheduled speech that night (Sunday) at the Portland Temple Club. He was still considering the TV broadcast when he came back to his hotel. He knew this contest was not what it appeared—Nixon against the press, or the Democrats, or the people. It was Nixon against Ike—a contest that, as Stevenson would learn twice over, no one can expect to win. Candidates simply do not get 90 percent victories in America—and Nixon was being told to produce that figure or get lost. He was asked to do it in circumstances that told against him. Eisenhower had been presented by his managers as the voice of a purgative honesty meant to remedy corruption. The very fact that this arbiter of morals was silent, that Nixon was sent out to argue on his own, was an implied judgment on him. He would be guilty until proved innocent, and he could not call on the one character witness who, in this set of circumstances, mattered.

Meanwhile, the Eisenhower camp had received no answer to its "offer." Now was the time to turn the screw. No escape was to be left him. The phone rang in Portland. Ike. For the first and last time during the crisis. Giving the ultimatum all his personal weight: "I think you ought to go on a nationwide television program and tell them everything there is to tell, everything you can remember since the day you

entered public life. Tell them about any money you have ever received."
The public self-revelation for which Nixon would be blamed in later
years was being forced on him, against all his own inclinations, personal
and political. By temperament and conditioning, Nixon is reserved,
with Quaker insistence on the right of privacy. Nixon's mother, a
woman of tremendous self-control, later said of the Checkers speech:
"At the point when he gave that itemized account of his personal expenditures, I didn't think I could take it."

Nixon asked Eisenhower if he meant to endorse him. The response
was put in a particularly galling way: "If I issue a statement now backing you up, in effect people will accuse me of condoning wrongdoing."
Ike knew, and Nixon knew he knew, that the results of a vast survey of
Nixon's affairs would be available in a matter of hours. This study had
been going on for three days; Sherman Adams, at the outset of the
scandal, called Paul Hoffman, one of the architects of Eisenhower's
candidacy, and ordered a thorough inquest into Nixon's finances. Hoffman went to the best. He put Price Waterhouse to work checking
Nixon's accounts, and the law firm of Gibson, Dunn and Crutcher went
over all legal aspects of the matter. Fifty lawyers and accountants worked
on a round-the-clock basis. The results of this scrutiny were being com-
piled Sunday night. No wrongdoing would be found. The objective
moral evidence would soon be in Eisenhower's hands. But he refused
to make his own judgment based on this evidence. He wanted the people, who could not know as much as he did, to decide whether Nixon
was honest, and he would follow them. The people, meanwhile, were
waiting to hear Ike's decision so they could follow *him*. Nixon was
caught between two juries, each of which was waiting for the other to
reach a verdict before it would move.

He tried to strike a bargain: if Eisenhower was satisfied with the
TV broadcast, would he *at that point* make a decision to endorse
Nixon? (If he did not, then a victory scored on the TV screen would
be subject to attrition, as lingering or renewed doubts worked on a
situation inexplicably unresolved.) But Ike was not making bargains:
he said he would need three or four days (the same period Dewey had
mentioned) for the popular reaction to be accurately gauged—during
which time, Nixon would presumably be stalled in Los Angeles waiting
for the response, his campaign tour all too noticeably suspended. Nixon
finally blew: "There comes a time when you have to piss or get off the
pot!" But Seraphim piss not, neither Cherubim. The great Cherub sat
blithely there, enthroned on his high pot. Nixon sculpts and prettifies
the unyielding refusal: "One of Eisenhower's most notable characteristics is that he is not a man to be rushed on important decisions."

There was nothing he could do now but go ahead with the show.
And if so, the sooner the better. Chotiner was back on the phone getting
clearance for the $75,000. Sherman Adams and Arthur Summerfield
finally yielded that point around midnight. The press corps had been
alerted, an hour before, that there would be an announcement. It was
one o'clock in the morning when Nixon came down; newsmen thought
this must be it—his resignation. He deliberately built up suspense by

saying he was breaking off—tense pause—his campaign tour. To make a statement over television. Two days from now. Tuesday night. He let them think it might still be his resignation he would announce. The more interest he could generate in the next two days, the bigger his audience on Tuesday night.

That was Monday morning. He got little sleep before he boarded a plane for Los Angeles that afternoon; during the flight, he drafted the first of a series of outlines for his talk. In Los Angeles, he got the reports from Price Waterhouse and Gibson, Dunn in time to put their findings in presentable summary. After midnight, he called his old English and history teachers at Whittier College, with a request that they find some suitable Lincoln quotes for the speech. They phoned two quotes to him by ten o'clock that morning—one witty and one maudlin (he used the latter). Nixon walked the streets with Bill Rogers, discussing approaches he might take. He was keyed up, and thought he just might bring it off.

And then the last blow fell. Tuesday, after a mere four hours of sleep, he kept at his outline resolution, as is his way. He did not go to El Capitan Theater to check the TV set or props or lighting; he wanted every minute for his preparation—it was a pattern familiar to those who have watched Nixon key himself up for a crisis by mood-setting spiritual exercises. And then, with less than an hour before he must leave for the studio, the cruel blow came, shattering his schedule, his carefully programmed psychological countdown. It was Dewey on the phone again, with a last demand: "There has been a meeting of all of Eisenhower's top advisers. They have asked me to tell you that it is their opinion that at the conclusion of the broadcast tonight you should submit your resignation to Eisenhower." The Establishment was taking no chances that its scheme might misfire. Nixon asked if that was the word from the General's own mouth. Dewey answered that the men he spoke of would not have commissioned him to make such a call at such an hour unless they were speaking for the master. (But, as usual, Ike was protected: afterward he could write, "Just before the broadcast Governor Dewey telephoned him from New York reporting the conviction of some of my supporters there"—two can play at that "some of the staff" game—"that he should resign, which the young Senator later said he had feared represented my views." Poor Senator, so fearful, so young, so avuncularly cared for in this retrospective benediction. Those who have called Nixon a master of duplicity should contrast his account of the fund crisis with the smoothed-over version in Eisenhower's book, which does not even mention the "hound's tooth" remark.)

Nixon stalled on the line to Dewey, stalled and wriggled. He said it was too late to change his prepared speech. Dewey said he could, of course, deliver his personal defense and accounting; all he had to do was tack on, at the end, a formal resignation offered to Ike. Nixon said he had to leave for the studio. Dewey: "Can I say you have accepted?" Nixon: "You will have to watch the show to see—and tell them I know something about politics too!"

Nixon had a half hour to tell his staff of this new lightning bolt, get their reaction, shower, shave, dress for the show, making meanwhile his own decision—and trying to collect his wits and memory over the notes for his talk. It had been five days full of pressure, sleeplessness, betrayal, ultimatums—climaxed with the most unsettling demand of all, made when he was at a poise of tension and could be knocked off balance so easily. A whole series of crises. Thursday: answer the charges? Friday: dodge newsmen, or face them; rely on the formal answer or return to the defense again and again; stall or throw oneself upon Ike's mercy? Saturday: heed the *Trib* and resign? Sunday: do the TV show? Monday: what to say on the show? And now, at the last minute, Tuesday: defy Dewey (and, through him, Ike)? Already the strain had shown in Nixon. Sunday in Portland, when Hillings brought a wire from Nixon's mother with the Quaker understated promise of prayers WE ARE THINK-ING OF YOU, Nixon broke down and cried. "I thought I had better leave the room," Hillings said, "and give him time to compose himself." Chotiner, busy calling party people to get money for the show, remembered "I was more worried about Dick's state of mind than about the Party. He was edgy and irritable."

Even the inner circle could not tell for sure whether Nixon would stand up to the pressure, or give in while he spoke. After reporting Dewey's call, he was silent, his mind working desperately at the problem. During the twenty-five-minute ride to the studio, he went over his notes (on debater-type cards). He had withdrawn to his last ditch, to make an entirely lone stand there. The one thing he demanded in studio arrangements was that even Chotiner and Rogers be kept out. Only his wife would be present, within camera range, visible to Nixon. It is as if he were dramatizing, to himself more than others, the isolation he stood in at this dying moment of defiance.

One of the criticisms made of Nixon's television speech is that the hoarse voice and hurt face, hovering on the edge of tears, were either histrionic or (if unfeigned) disproportionate and "tasteless." But no one who knows the full story can suspect Nixon of acting, or blame him for the tension he felt and conveyed—it would be like blaming a recently flayed man for "indecent exposure." Nixon was deserted, in more ways than he could tell. And he was fighting back with more nerve than anybody knew. Besides concentrating fiercely on his appeal to the audience, which had to succeed if anything else were to follow, he was reaching out across their heads to touch swords in a secret duel with Ike.

And Eisenhower understood. Stewart Alsop, in his useful little book *Nixon and Rockefeller,* quotes from an interview with one who watched Eisenhower's reactions throughout the TV show. The General had to give a speech in Cleveland as soon as Nixon went off the air; the audience for that talk was watching a large screen in the auditorium, while Eisenhower and thirty of his people clustered by the TV set in a backstage office. Even this entourage, predominantly opposed to Nixon, was touched as the show progressed; some wept openly. But Eisenhower was calm, tapping a yellow pad with his pencil, ready to jot down comments on the speech. He took no notes while the talk was in progress, though the tapping stopped twice. Nixon, forced to act like a criminal who must clear himself, deftly made his actions look like those of a man with nothing to fear. And he issued a challenge: the *other* candidates must have something to fear, unless they followed his example. He devoted much of his half hour to this challenge, dictating terms to his accusers. (It is this part of the speech—moving onto the offensive—that so pleased Chotiner.)

Now I'm going to suggest some courses of conduct.

First of all, you have read in the papers about other funds. Now, Mr. Stevenson, apparently, had a couple—one of them in which a group of business people paid and helped to supplement the salaries of state employees. Here is where the money went directly into their pockets.

I think what Mr. Stevenson should do is come before the American people, as I have, and give the names of the people who have contributed to that fund, and give the names of the people who put this money into their pockets at the same time they were receiving money from their state government, and see what favors, if any, they gave out for that.

I don't condemn Mr. Stevenson for what he did. But, until the facts are in there, a doubt will be raised.

As far as Mr. Sparkman is concerned, I would suggest the same thing. He's had his wife on the payroll. I don't condemn him for that. But I think he should come before the American people and indicate what outside sources of income he has had.

I would suggest that under the circumstances both Mr. Sparkman and Mr. Stevenson should come before the American people, as I have, and make a complete statement as to their financial history. If they don't it will be an admission that they have something to hide. And I think you will agree with me.

Because, remember, a man who's to be President and a man who's to be Vice President must have the confidence of all the people. That's why I'm doing what I'm doing, and that's what I suggest that Mr. Stevenson and Mr. Sparkman, since they are under attack, should be doing.

Eisenhower stopped tapping with his pencil—jabbed it, instead, down into the yellow pad—when Nixon said any candidate who did not reveal his finances must have something to hide. Of course, Nixon did not mention Eisenhower, and his phrase about other candidates joining him "since they are under attack" left a loophole for the General. But the overall force of the passage could not be missed. All candidates, he was arguing, should act as he had. That meant *Eisenhower,* too—as Ike realized, and events were to prove. After this all the candidates did make their statements.

There were reasons why it was inconvenient for Eisenhower to make his books public—e.g., the special tax decision on earnings of his *Crusade in Europe.* Besides, as Alsop delicately puts it, "the military rarely get into the habit of making charitable contributions . . ." More important, Nixon was turning the tables on Ike. Eisenhower had brought him to this revelation. Nixon would force the same hard medicine down his mentor's throat.

Yet an even defter stroke followed. Dewey had been vague on how the speech should be judged. He told Nixon to have telegrams addressed to Los Angeles, and measure the talk's impact by their content. This arrangement, besides tying Nixon down for several days, still left the matter with Eisenhower. The real decision would be made by the General, assessing news reaction. Nixon would be left to play games with his switchboard and his mail, unable to vindicate himself if Eisenhower decided the show had not cleared him.

But when it came time for Nixon to mention the sending of telegrams, he said: "I am submitting to *the Republican National Committee* tonight, through this television broadcast, the decision *it is theirs to make* . . . Wire and write *the Republican National Committee* whether you think I should stay or whether I should get off; and whatever *their decision* is, I will abide by it." (Italics added.) The General stabbed again, pencil into pad, a sword struck down as he fenced that image on the screen, and lost. Nixon has always been a party man; his strength lay there. Karl Mundt and Robert Humphreys, manning the Washington headquarters of the National Committee while Chairman Arthur Summerfield traveled with Ike, had routinely issued statements backing Nixon from the very first day of his troubles. Now, by a cool disarming maneuver, Nixon was taking the matter away from the Eastern Establishment and putting it in the hands of men sympathetic to the regulars, to grassroots workers—people who respond in a partisan way to partisan attacks upon one of their own, people most vulnerable to the planned schmaltz and hominess of the Checkers reference, people with small debts of their own and Republican cloth coats. If the decision was theirs to make, then—the real point of the broadcast as Nixon had reshaped it—*it was not Ike's.* It is no wonder that, while others in Cleveland wept, the man who had directed OVERLORD, the largest military operation in the world's history, the *General,* made an angry stab. He knew enough about maneuver to see he was outflanked. Alsop's informant said: "Before that, I'd always liked and admired Ike, of course, but I'd often wondered how smart he really was. After that, I knew Ike got what Dick was getting at right away."

The importance of that decision, redirecting the appeal to the National Committee, explains Nixon's breakdown when he saw he had gone off the air. Under the pressure of the performance, undertaken without rehearsal, using sketchy notes, he had done something rare for him—missed the countdown toward sign-off by a minute or two: "Time had run out. I was cut off just as I intended to say where the National Committee was located and where the telegrams and letters should be sent." He had based everything on this point; he needed every wire that would reach Washington. What if the telegrams were diffused ineffectually about the country, sent to him, to Ike, to TV channels and local campaign offices? He needed a crushing weight of response all directed to one point, and now (he thought) he would not get it. (The wires in fact did go everywhere, but in such breathtaking numbers that all doubt was swept before them.) He threw his cards to the floor in a spasm, told Pat he had failed; when Chotiner came into the studio, elated by the skilled performance, Nixon just shook his head and claimed, "I was an utter flop." Outside the theater, as his car pulled away, an Irish setter friskily rocked alongside barking: Nixon turned,

Bill Rogers would remember, and twisted out a bitter, "At least I won the dog vote tonight." The end, he thought, of the Checkers speech. He was touching bottom. That night he would finally, after all his earlier resistance, resign.

But it took more kicks and blows to bring him to it. During the first hours after his broadcast, others were jubilant and support poured in; but no call came from the General (a wire had been sent off, but was stuck in the traffic-jam of them at Nixon's hotel switchboard—no one called from the Cleveland camp to give Nixon its message). The first notice he had of the telegram came over the news wires—and it brought word of still another ultimatum. Eisenhower did not often lose wars of attrition. They were his kind of battle.

The crowd waiting for Ike in Cleveland was hoarse with shouts and praise for the TV show they had witnessed. Eisenhower's own first comment was to Chairman Summerfield, about the $75,000: "Well, Arthur, you got your money's worth." Hagerty came back from the auditorium and told Eisenhower he could not deliver his prepared talk on inflation with this crowd. He would have to speak to the Nixon issue. The General knew. He had already chosen his strategy. He fashioned its main lines on the yellow pad, and tried it on his advisers. First, a sop to the crowd: "I like courage . . . Tonight I saw an example of courage . . . I have never seen anyone come through in such a fashion as Senator Nixon did tonight . . . When I get in a fight, I would rather have a courageous and honest man by my side than a whole boxcar full of pussyfooters."

All the praise was a cover, though. Eisenhower was a master of the basics—supply, firepower, and retention of position. After praising Nixon for courage, Ike added that he had not made his mind up on the main subject—whether Nixon would remain on the ticket: "It is obvious that I have to have something more than one single presentation, necessarily limited to thirty minutes, the time allowed Senator Nixon." But if Eisenhower, who had chosen him as his running mate, who had access to the research of the lawyers and accountants, to the advice of top politicians in the party, could not make up his mind after watching the TV show, then how could anyone in the public do so? There is only one explanation for this performance: Ike was determined not to let Nixon take the decision out of his hands. "I am not going to be swayed by my idea of what will get most votes . . . I am going to say: Do I myself believe this man is the kind of man America would like to have for its Vice President?" That is, at one minute he will not be swayed by what the people want and would vote for, and the next minute he is accepting the sacred pledge of finding out what the public wants and will vote for!

Then Eisenhower read them his telegram to Nixon, which shows the real thrust of his remarks: "While technically no decision rests with me, you and I know the realities of the situation require a pronouncement which the public considers decisive." (Or: Get your National Committee support, and see how far it carries you without me.) "My personal decision is going to be based on personal conclusions." (Or: I won't judge you by reaction to your talk—which is what he had promised he *would* do.) "I would most appreciate it if you can fly to see me at once." (Or: Here, Rover.) "Tomorrow evening I will be at Wheeling, W. Va." (Or: Tomorrow *you* will be at Wheeling, W. Va.) Not only was Eisenhower reasserting the personal jurisdiction Nixon had challenged; he wanted a public dramatization of the lines of authority. Having cleared himself with the public, Nixon must appear before a superior tribunal, summoned there to make his defense again, in greater detail, while judgment was pointedly suspended.

Nixon could not submit; yet, once the demand was made public, he could not go further in public defiance, either. He gave in. Rose Woods took down his dictated telegram of resignation.

But he would get in one last blow of his own. The wire was not directed toward Eisenhower, as Dewey had insisted it should be. He addressed it to the National Committee! As Rose Woods went out of the room to send the message, Chotiner followed her and tore off the top sheet of her pad. Rose said she could not have sent it anyway. Nixon is, by his own admission, subject to sharp lapses and lowering of his guard in the emotional depletion that follows on conflict. In four of his book's six crises he finds an example of that pattern: and the example for the fund crisis is his telegram to the National Committee. His loss of grip began the minute the show went off the air and he threw his cards to the floor. " 'What more can he possibly want from me?' I asked . . . I didn't believe I could take any more of the suspense and tension of the past week." Chotiner went to work on him, however, and persuaded him that he could avoid both of the unpalatable things being forced on him—resignation, or compliance with Eisenhower's summons. If he just resumed his interrupted campaign-schedule (next step, Missoula, Montana), the General would have to back down. The wave of public response was already seismic. Nixon reports Chotiner's counsel this way: "Chotiner, particularly, insisted that I not allow myself to be put in the position of going to Eisenhower like a little boy to be taken to the woodshed, properly punished, and then restored to a place of dignity." At this point, there was a call from Ike's camp. Arthur Summerfield, pleased that things had turned out well, was asking for Chotiner—who soon dashed his spirits. Murray said Nixon had just dictated his resignation; he admitted, when Summerfield gasped, that the telegram was torn up—"but I'm not so sure how long it's going to stay torn." Summerfield said things could be smoothed over when Dick reached Wheeling. But Dick was not going to Wheeling: "We're flying to Missoula tonight." Summerfield wanted to know how to head off this disaster—so Chotiner set terms: Nixon will not come unless he is sure of a welcoming endorsement, without further inquisition. This was, of course, a demand that Eisenhower back down on the stated purpose of the summons, which was to go into greater detail than thirty minutes would allow.

Eisenhower, realistic about cutting his losses, saw when this news reached him that the idea of further investigation could not be sustained. He let Summerfield give Nixon's camp the proper assurances.

But Nixon would still be answering a humiliating public call. Just before the plane took off for Missoula, Bert Andrews, who had worked with Nixon all through the Hiss affair, called from the Eisenhower press room in Cleveland: Ike would have no choice now but to receive Nixon warmly; Nixon would have to lose a little face in order to avoid flouting the General's summons. Nixon agreed, and let his staff arrange a flight to Wheeling after the stop at Missoula. Ike was at the airport, to throw his arm around him and call him "my boy"—looking gracious, kind, generous, as if supporting an embattled man rather than picking up strength from a victorious one. The only thing that could resolve the crisis—Ike's blue-eyed smile of benediction—had been bestowed.

But they did not forget the night when they touched swords. There would never be any trust between them. And Nixon had begun a tutelage that would gall him and breed resentment through years of friction and slights.

The Army-McCarthy Hearings

America's painful adjustment to the Cold War will be forever memorialized by the era to which Joseph McCarthy gave his name. When people do not understand what is happening or what is required of them, when their best instincts and their worst fears are somehow tangled together, then men like Joseph McCarthy have their chance. In the early 1950's there was such a thing as subversion; the problem of disloyalty was real if limited; some spies were discovered in government (although not by Senator McCarthy). But a limited security problem in the hands of an oily demagogue proved to have virtually unlimited political use. McCarthy became a prime agent in the Republican drive to oust the Democrats from a 20-year hold on the federal government. Through accusation or insinuation he retired men from public careers and damaged the reputation of many innocent men in private lives.

Buoyed by these successes, McCarthy took on establishment institutions such as the church and—the case before you—the army.

McCarthy should have selected his victims with more care. Six months after his bout with the army he had been censured by his colleagues in the Senate and his national influence was over. McCarthy had believed that he represented a massive national sentiment which could do battle with every constituted power; and many commentators and politicians, liberal and conservative, had taken him at his word. They were all wrong: when powerful men decided to stop him, he was quickly demolished, and with few political aftereffects.

The Army-McCarthy hearings were on television for 188 hours during their 36-day run from April 22 to June 16, 1954. In David T. Bazelon's description it was "in a fabulously exact sense, the greatest political show on earth." Amid the welter of names, the confusion of charges and countercharges, the points of order and other interruptions, millions of viewers nevertheless got the message. As the Checkers speech showed the way television could save a political career, these hearings showed how it could pitilessly destroy one. The show was unforgettable. McCarthy's sarcasm and disparaging tone of voice lost their customary effectiveness; he went from fame to an alcoholic's death. His flinty adversary, Joseph E. Welch, whose capacity for wit as well as for righteous indignation had thrilled 20 million viewers, was able in his retirement to play a star role as a movie lawyer. The age of television politics was upon us.

Cast of principal characters:

Robert T. Stevens   Secretary of the Army

Senator Joseph R. McCarthy U.S. Senator, Wisconsin (Rep.)
            Chairman, Senate subcommittee

John G. Adams	Counselor for the Army
Joseph N. Welch	Special Counsel for the Army
Senator Karl E. Mundt	U.S. Senator, Kansas (Rep.) Chairman of hearings
Ray H. Jenkins	Chief Counsel, Senate subcommittee
John L. McClellan	U.S. Senator, Arkansas (Dem.) Subcommittee member
Stuart Symington	U.S. Senator, Missouri (Dem.) Subcommittee member
Pvt. G. David Schine	U.S. Army private and former McCarthy aide
Roy M. Cohn	Chief Counsel for Sen. McCarthy

MC CARTHY

The average American can do very little insofar as digging Communists, espionage agents, out of our government—is concerned. They must depend upon those of us whom they send down here to man the watchtowers of the nation. The thing that the American people can do is to be vigilant day and night to make sure they don't have Communists teaching the sons and daughters of America. Now, I realize that the minute anyone tries to get a Communist out of a college, out of a university, there'll be raised the phony cry that you're interfering with academic freedom. I would like to emphasize that there is no academic freedom where a Communist is concerned. He is not a free agent. He has no freedom of thought, no freedom of expression. He must take his orders from Moscow, or he will no longer be a member of the Communist Party. I may say, Mr. Jenkins, I don't care how much of a screwball or a crackpot any professor or teacher may be as long as he or she is a free agent. But once, once you have this United States, from the Atlantic to the Pacific, covered with a network, a network of professors and teachers who are getting their orders from Moscow, from an organization that wants to destroy this nation, that wants to corrupt the minds of youth, then, Mr. Jenkins, we're rapidly losing the battle. The thing that I think we must remember is that this is a war which a brutalitarian force has won to a greater extent than any brutalitarian force has won a war in the history of the world before. For example, uh, Christianity, which has been in existence for two thousand years has not converted, convinced nearly as many people as this Communist brutalitarianism has enslaved in 106 years—and they're not going to stop. I know that many of my good friends seem, uh, to feel this is sort of a game you can play. Uh, that you can talk about Communism as though it's, uh, something, uh, 10,000 miles away. Mr. Jenkins, in answer to your question, let me say it's right here with us now. If we, unless we make sure there's no infiltration of our government, then just as certain as you sit there in the period of our lives, you will see a Red World. Mr. Jenkins, anyone who has followed the Communist conspiracy even remotely, and who can add two and two, will tell you that there is no remote possibility of this war which we're in today, and it's a war, a war which we've been losing—no remote possibility of this ending except by victory or by death for this civilization.

MUNDT
The Committee will please come to order. [*Gavel.*]

SYMINGTON
I suggest that in the interest of these Hearings, the charges are often forgotten. The charges were, did Senator McCarthy and two members of his staff use improper pressure for Mr. David Schine with the Army? The countercharge was that there was blackmail on the part of the Army and the use of Mr. Schine as a hostage. Uh, those are the charges that have been made.

STEVENS
Gentlemen of the Committee: In order that we may all be quite clear as just why this hearing has come about, it is necessary for me to refer at the outset, to Private D., G. David Schine, a former consultant to this Committee. I have been informed, one, from mid-July of last year until March first of this year, David Schine was discussed between one branch or other of the Department of the Army and Senator McCarthy or members of his staff in more than sixty-five telephone calls. Two, this matter was discussed at approximately nineteen meetings between Army personnel and Senator McCarthy or members of his staff. Three, requests made on Schine's behalf ranged from several for a direct commission before he was inducted into the Army to many for special assignments, relief from routine duty such as K.P., extra time off, and special visitor privileges. I may say that during my tenure as Secretary of the Army, there is no record that matches this persistent, tireless effort to obtain special consideration and privileges for this man. The Schine case is only an example of the wrongful seeking of privilege, of the perversion of power—it has been a distraction that has kept many men from the performance of tasks far more important to the welfare of this country than the convenience of a single army private.

ADAMS
I said, let's talk about Schine. And that started a chain of events that, aah, an experience similar to none which I have had in my life. Aah, Mr. Cohn became extremely agitated, and uh, uh, became extremely abusive. The thing that he was so violent about was the fact that the Army was not, uh, was not agreeing to an assignment for Schine. I said

to Cohn that I'd like to give him some advice. I pointed out to him that the national interest required that Schine be treated just like every other soldier. Uh—

JENKINS

Well, what was his reply to that, Mr. Adams?

ADAMS

He exploded at that, and he said that if the national interest was the thing we were interested in, he'd give us a little bit. I knew that, ah, 90 per cent of all inductees ultimately face overseas duty, and I knew that one day we were going to face that problem with Mr. Cohn as to Schine. I asked him what would happen if Schine got overseas duty.

JENKINS

You mean you were breaking the news gently, Mr. Adams?

ADAMS

Yes sir, that's right. I asked him what would happen if Schine got overseas duty, and he responded with vigor and force, "Stevens is through as Secretary of the Army." I said, "Oh, Roy," something to this effect, "Oh, Roy, now don't say that." I said, "Come on. Really, what is going to happen if Schine gets overseas duty?" And he responded with even more force, *"we'll wreck the Army."* This was the subject, uh—Schine.

JENKINS

Well, now, do we get it that you deny, you affirm it, or you say you've got no recollection of it? Now let's get it straight.

COHN

I'm telling you, sir. Uhh—number one, I have a pretty good recollection. Number two, I remember that day. Number three, I do not remember saying any of those things, the way Mr. Adams has them. And number four, I checked with the only other person who was there on that occasion, and he says my recollection is correct that I did not make those statements.

JENKINS

And as I get it now, you're saying that you have no recollection of it?

COHN

No, sir. I say I do not recall having said that.

JENKINS

Well, that's, that's what, that's what you're anxious for your answer to be—now you don't recall having said it?

COHN

No, sir.

JENKINS

But you don't deny it?

COHN

Sir, I'm saying I'm sure I did not say it. I am sure—

JENKINS

All right, now you're saying you did not say it, Mr. Cohn.

COHN

Yes, sir. I say I am sure I did not make that statement, and I am sure that Mr. Adams and anybody else with any sense, and Mr. Adams has a lot of sense, could not ever believe that I was threatening to wreck the Army, or that I could wreck the Army. I say, sir, the statement is ridiculous.

JENKINS

I'm talking about Stevens being through as Secretary of the Army.

COHN

That's equally ridiculous, sir.

JENKINS

And untrue.

COHN

Yes, sir. Equally ridiculous and untrue.

STEVENS

Senator McCarthy said that one of the few things that he had trouble with Mr. Cohn about was David Schine. He said that Roy thinks that Dave ought to be a General and operate from a penthouse on the Waldorf Astoria, or words to that effect.

SMITH

Mr. Cohn telephoned me on the afternoon of July 31st. He stated that Mr. David Schine of the Committee staff was about to be drafted, and that he, Mr. Cohn, and Senator McCarthy felt that he should have a direct commission for which they considered him qualified by education. I phoned General Hull about 4:30 on July 31st. He informed me that Mr. Schine's qualifications did not justify his direct commissioning in any of these branches. General Hull said that the opportunity to qualify for officer candidate training was open to Mr. Schine, as it was to any other citizen drafted into the Armed Forces, and that the Secretary of the Army who was aware of all the facts in the case had directed that the treatment accorded and the opportunities afforded Mr. Schine after his entry into the military service should be the same as for any other American citizen, no more and no less.

Mr. Cohn came to my office at 11:20 A.M. on August 1st, 1953. I told him the substance of General Hull's reply to my inquiries. I asked if Mr. Schine had had ROTC. Mr. Cohn replied that Mr. Schine had had no ROTC training, and that there appeared to be no chance of a commission in one of the other branches, except at the expense of a protracted term of service. Mr. Cohn then asked if the CIA could not arrange to have Mr. Schine commissioned, as he had investigative experience. I replied that the CIA drew a few commissioned personnel by detail from the Armed Services, but gave them additional training and required a longer tour of duty. However, I offered to telephone Mr. Allen Dulles, director of Central Intelligence, to ask about the possibilities. Mr. Cohn said that I need not do this. The CIA, he said, was too juicy a subject for future investigation, and it would not be right to ask them to get Mr. Schine commissioned and then investigate the organization later.

Very sincerely, Walter B. Smith.

JENKINS

State whether or not on either of those occasions you felt that Mr. Cohn was being too persistent or was trying to high-pressure anyone—

SMITH

Not me, sir.

JENKINS

Now, Mr. Secretary, that was not a part of your pattern to hold this boy Schine as a sort of a hostage and use him as a bait for the purpose of evading this investigation, was it?

STEVENS

Certainly not. And if he was a hostage so have hundreds of thousands, if not millions, of young Americans been hostages when they were doing their duty in service for their country.

MC CLELLAN

The implication is here—and you just well face it, sir. The implication is here that you were trying to buy off this Committee from investigating the Army.

. . . .

ADAMS

This is a letter signed Dwight D. Eisenhower, addressed to the Honorable Secretary of Defense, Washington, D.C.:

Dear Mr. Secretary:

It is essential to the successful working of our system that the persons intrusted with power in any one of the three great branches of government shall not encroach upon the authority confided to the others. The ultimate responsibility for the conduct of the executive branch rests with the President.

However, throughout our history, the President has withheld information whenever he found that what was sought was confidential or its disclosure would be incompatible with the public interest, or jeopardize the safety of the nation. Because it is essential to efficient and effective administration that employees of the executive branch be in a position to be completely candid in advising with each other on official matters, and because it is not in the public interest that any of their conversations or communications or any documents or reproductions concerning such advice be disclosed, you will instruct employees of your department that in all of their appearances before the Subcommittee of the Senate Committee on Government Operations regarding the inquiry now before it, they are not to testify to any such conversations or communications or to produce any such documents or reproductions.

I direct this action so as to maintain the proper separation of powers between the executive and legislative branches of the government in accordance with my responsibilities and duties under the Constitution. This separation is vital to preclude the exercise of arbitrary power by any branch of the government.

Sincerely, Dwight D. Eisenhower."

MUNDT

Thank you. The Chair will recognize Senator McCarthy or Mr. Cohn.

MC CARTHY

Mr. Chairman, I, must admit that I'm somewhat at a loss as to know how to—what to do at this moment. One of the subjects of this inquiry is to find out who was responsible for succeeding in calling off the hearing of Communist infiltration in government. At this point I find out there's no way of ever getting at the truth. The iron curtain is pulled down so we can't tell what happened. There's no reason why anyone should be afraid of the facts. The question is, how far, how far can, I'm not talking about the present occupant of the White House, but we got a tremendously important question here, Mr. Chairman. That is, how far can the President go? Uh, who all can he order not to testify? Then any president, we don't know who will be president, 1956, 1960, 1964, any president—[*Committee room laughter, McCarthy chuckles.*] I won't repeat that. [*McCarthy chuckles again.*] Any president can, by an executive order, keep the facts from the American people, and as I say, I think that—I don't believe that this is the result of President Eisenhower's own personal thinking. I am sure if he knew what this was all about, that he would not sign an order saying that you cannot tell the Senate Committee what went on when they cooked up those charges against Mr. Cohn, Mr. Carr, and myself.

Someone for his own benefit should contact the President immediately and point out to him perhaps, that he and I and many of us campaigned and promised the American people we would no longer involve, engage in government by secrecy, white-wash, and cover up; and I think that these facts should be brought to the President because the American people will not stand for this.

Let's go through, let's lay all the facts upon the table, and we can't lay the facts upon the table if we're going to draw an iron curtain—and we're half way through the hearings, so, Mr. Chairman, I would like to ask for an executive session, a meeting in the Committee so I will know to what extent the Committee is going to honor this order or any other like it. May I say, Mr. Chairman, I feel that the Senate must determine that we're entitled to all of this information, and what Mr. Jenkins says here as Counsel, what you say as Chairman can be quoted as precedent in the future when we decide just how far the President can go in a secrecy order. May I say that I think if the witness asserts a type of Fifth Amendment privilege here—

ADAMS

I'm not asserting Fifth Amendment privilege, Senator—

MC CARTHY

Uh—some presidential privilege—I think the Chair should allow him to do it rather than to get into this, uh, question which will take us months to decide. Ultimately, may I finish, Mr. Chairman, I think this is infinitely more important than anything we bring out at this hearing. It's a question of just what a President can do. Now I disagree as the Chair knows with the Truman blackout order of 1948. I think that Eisenhower had been badly advised. I think there's only one person can claim a privilege, whether it's a Fifth Amendment privilege, whether it's a presidential privilege, or any other—

ADAMS

Mr. Chairman, just a moment, sir . . .

MC CARTHY

May I—may I finish—

ADAMS

I don't like the Senator from Wisconsin inferring that I'm claiming the Fifth Amendment privilege because I'm not, and I'm not claiming any privilege on this memorandum. This is an instruction from the President of the United States and I consider myself bound by it, sir.

MC CARTHY

Mr. Chairman, Mr. Chairman, may I say that I think it's very important that we follow the time-worn rule of law, that no one can exert a privilege except the witness. I don't care whether it's a Fifth Amendment privilege, whether it's this new privilege that we have today, or what it is. . . .

Mr. Stevens, I am getting awfully weary of this attempt to get a few simple facts from you as though we're pulling teeth. We've spent just a vast amount of time here trying to get answers to some simple questions.

The question is this. You made a statement this morning under oath. You say, "I wish to make it perfectly plain that the decisions and the acts on the part of the Army concerning the controversy presently being heard by the Senate Subcommittee were the decisions and the acts of the Department of the Army alone." Now do you still stand by that statement?

STEVENS

I do.

MC CARTHY

Do you say that John Adams was not telling the truth when he said that the decision was made in the Justice Department, with White House aides present, with the Attorney General present, the Deputy Attorney present, the Ambassador to the U. N. present. Now I'm sure that any man who can add two and two, Mr. Secretary, will agree that that completely contradicts your statement that all decisions were the decisions of the Department of the Army alone. I wonder if you want your, your sworn testimony this morning to stand as it is or not?

STEVENS

I want it to stand.

MC CARTHY

Mr. Secretary, here is the testimony of Mr. Browder, and I take this from a report, dated, eh, let's see. Just a minute—

STEVENS

Does that mean I am a Communist, Senator?

MC CARTHY

That's awfully funny, isn't it, Mr. Secretary? That's terribly funny. I've made it very clear to you at all times that I felt that you are anti-Communist. I've also made it very clear to you that I thought that you were very naïvely and unintelligently anti-Communist. You know that, Mr. Secretary?

JACKSON

I'm a little confused here. This is a copy of a letter that's being introduced, and I'd like to know how it arrived here at the Committee. Where it came from? How did it get here?

JENKINS

It was handed to me just now, by Senator McCarthy. It purports to be a letter written October 26th, 1951, to the Federal Bureau of Investigation and signed by J. Edgar Hoover, the Director. It is addressed to Major General Boling, Assistant Chief of Staff, G2, Department of the Army, Washington, D.C.

JACKSON

Well, I understand that it could readily be identified whether this was a matter that was subpoenaed from the Army files or whether the Army voluntarily gave it to—

WELCH

Mr. Chairman.

MUNDT

Mr. Welch.

WELCH

I respectfully suggest that that be done. I am a lawyer, and, uh, the appearance of what purports to be a copy of a letter from J. Edgar Hoover in 1951 addressed to some Colonel, is that right sir?

JENKINS

Major General.

WELCH

Major General. The mere fact that we have an impressive looking, purported copy of such a letter doesn't impress an old-time lawyer. I would like to have Mr. J. Edgar Hoover say that he wrote the letter and mailed it. Then we'd know what we're dealing with.

MC CARTHY

Mr. Chairman.

MUNDT

Senator McCarthy.

MC CARTHY

The original, uh—I want to question the Secretary as to whether or not the original of this and other letters like it are in the file. I want to make it very clear that I have gotten neither this letter or anything else from the FBI.

WELCH

Well, where did it come from then? Mr. Chairman, I—I assure you the —this purported copy did not come from the Army files nor did the Senator for a moment suggest it did.

MC CARTHY

Just—just a minute. Now, let me see.

MUNDT

Mr. McCarthy.

MC CARTHY

Now, Mr. Chairman, if Mr. Welch is going to say there's not a copy of this in the Army files, he should be sworn because that statement is untrue as far as I know.

WELCH

I did not say that, Senator. I said that this purported copy did not come from the Army files, and you know I'm quite right sir, and I have an absorbing curiosity to know how in the dickens you got hold of it. [*Laughter.*]

MC CARTHY

I will, I will read—may I say, Mr. Chair—

MUNDT

The Chair has the floor.

MC CARTHY

May I say, Mr. Chair—

MUNDT

The Chair has the floor. I'll have to advise you again, Mr. Welch, that all investigative agencies in this town operate on the rule that they don't have to disclose the source of their information. Your absorbing curiosity will have to be satisfied some other way, I'm afraid.

WELCH

And by Mr. J. Edgar Hoover.

MC CARTHY

Can I cut in here?

MUNDT

Senator McCarthy.

MC CARTHY

I'd just like to question Mr. Stevens. Mr. Stevens, would you look at that letter, and tell us, number one, whether or not you've ever seen it or were ever notified of its contents?

STEVENS

I'd like to—if I'm—

MC CARTHY

I think you should read the letter.

STEVENS

I'd like to have the advice of counsel if I may as to whether or not I'm at liberty to discuss a letter from Mr. J. Edgar Hoover. [*Letter is passed to Stevens.*]

MC CARTHY

You're at liberty to read it.

STEVENS

I think it's very bad policy to discuss this thing without Mr. Hoover's knowing about it. [*Welch glances over the letter.*]

MC CARTHY
Would you like to read it first?

WELCH
And, may I add, Mr. Chairman, I have the letter in my hand and it's headed "Personal and Confidential, Via Liaison," which seem to be to be rather severe words of a confidential nature. I think Mr. Stevens is quite right in saying that this is a matter that ought to be released by J. Edgar Hoover before we deal with it in this room.

COLLIER
Mr. Hoover has examined the document and has advised me that he never wrote any such letter. And because the document constitutes an unauthorized use of information which is classified as confidential, it is my opinion that it should not be made public. Sincerely yours, Herbert Brownell, Jr., Attorney General.

WELCH
Now, Mr. Collier, as I understand your testimony, this document that I hold in my hand is a carbon copy of precisely nothing. Is that right?

COLLIER
I will say that Mr. Hoover informed me that it is not a carbon copy of a memorandum prepared or sent by the FBI.

WELCH
Let's have it straight from the shoulder. So far as you know, it's a carbon copy of precisely nothing?

COLLIER
So far as I know, it is, yes. But that, again, is a—

WELCH
And so far as you know, this document in this courtroom sprung yesterday by Senator McCarthy is a perfect phony. Is that right?

COLLIER
No sir. I, uh—uh, that is your conclusion. I will not uphold such a conclusion.

WELCH
Well, you've just told us that it's—

MC CARTHY
Mr. Chairman.

MUNDT
Would you care to make a point of order?

MC CARTHY

Yes, Mr. Chairman. I think that, uh, the Chair should insist upon certain rules of honesty on the part of the Counsel for Mr. Stevens, Mr. Adams. Mr. Chairman, this has been referred to as a phony by Mr. Welch. That's one of the most serious reflections upon the integrity of the Chairman that we've had so far, and I've had many reflections upon my integrity.

MUNDT

The Chair has not read the letter, and Mr. Welch has not read the letter, so I suppose we labor under some difficulties.

WELCH

We do. I have higher standards as to my own conduct in respect to these documents than the Senator and his staff have. I do not think it is proper for Mr. Collier to read it and he had declined to read it. I do not think it would be proper for Welch to read it and he has declined to read it, and I await with much interest the Senator's explanation of how it reached his hands and when he read it.

JENKINS

Now, Senator McCarthy, you are bound to be aware of the fact that some attack has been made upon that letter.

MC CARTHY

Just let me make it very clear, Mr. Jenkins and Mr. Chairman, that I will not under any circumstances reveal the source of any information which I get as Chairman of the Committee. Now, one of the reasons that I have been successful, I believe to some extent in exposing the, uh —Communism is because the people who give me information from within the government know that their confidence will not be violated. There is no way on earth that any committee, any force can get me to violate the confidence of those people.

· · · ·

WELCH

Mr. Cohn, what is the exact number of Communists or subversives that are loose today in these defense plants?

COHN

Uh, yes, sir, I'm going to try to particularize for you, if I can.

WELCH

I'm in a hurry. I don't want the sun to go down while they're still in there if we can get them out.

COHN

I'm afraid we won't be able to work that fast.

WELCH

Well, I've got a suggestion about it, sir. How many are there?

COHN

I believe the figure is approximately 130.

WELCH

Approximately one three oh.

COHN

Those are people, Mr. Welch—

WELCH

I don't care. You've told us who they are. And how many plants are there?

COHN

How many plants?

WELCH

How many plants.

COHN

Yes, sir. Just one minute, sir. I see sixteen offhand.

WELCH

Sixteen plants. Are you alarmed at that situation, Mr. Cohn?

COHN

Yes, sir, I am.

WELCH

Nothing could be more alarming, could it?

COHN

It's certainly a very alarming thing.

WELCH

Will you not, before the sun goes down, give those names to the FBI and at least have those men put under surveillance?

COHN

Sir, if there is need for surveillance in case of espionage or anything like that, I can well assure you Mr. John Edgar Hoover and his men know a lot better than I, and I might respectfully suggest, sir, than probably a lot of us, just who should be put under surveillance. I do not purpose to tell the FBI how to run its job.

WELCH

And they do it. And they do it, don't they Mr. Cohn?

COHN

When the need arises, of course.

WELCH

Then they've got the whole 130 have they, Mr. Cohn?

COHN

I am sure of it, sir, and a lot more.

WELCH

Then what's all the excitement about if J. Edgar Hoover is on the job, chasing those 130 Communists.

COHN

Mr. Welch, all the excitement—

WELCH

Well, then, as a second line of defense, let's send the 130 names to the Department of Defense tonight. Would you mind doing that?

COHN

Whatever the Committee directs on that, sir, I will—

WELCH

I wish the Committee would direct that all the names be sent both to the FBI and to the Department of Defense with extreme suddenness.

SYMINGTON

Mr. Chairman, I so move.

MC CARTHY

Mr. Chairman, in view of . . .

MUNDT

Do you have a point of order?

MC CARTHY

Uh—not exactly, Mr. Chairman, but in view of Mr. Welch's request that, uh, the information be given if we know of anyone who might be performing any work for the Communist Party, I think we should tell him that he has in his law firm a young man named Fisher whom he recommended incidentally to do the work on this Committee, who has been, for a number of years, a member of an organization which is named, oh years and years ago, as the legal bulwark for the Communist Party, an organization which always springs to the defense, uh, of anyone who, uh, dares to expose Communists. Uh, I certainly assume that Mr. Welch did not know of this, uh, uh, young man at the time he recommended him as the assistant counsel for this Committee, but he has such terror and such a great desire to know where anyone is located. You may be serving the Communist cause, Mr. Welch, and I thought we should just call to your attention the fact that your Mr. Fisher, who is still in your law firm today, whom you asked to have down here looking over the secret and classified material, is a member of an organization, not named by me, but named by, uh, various committees named by the Attorney General, as I recall. Uh, he belonged to it long after it had been exposed, as the legal arm of the Communist Party. Knowing that, Mr. Welch, I just felt that I had a duty to, uh, respond here to your urgent request that before sundown that if we know of anyone serving the Communist cause we let the agency know. We're now letting you know your man did belong to this organization for either three or four years. Belonged to it long after he was out of law school. And I have hesitated bringing that up, but I have been rather bored with your phony requests to Mr. Cohn here, that he personally get every Communist out of Government before sundown. Therefore, we will give you the information about the young man in your organization. Now, I'm not asking you at this time to explain why you tried to foist him on this Committee. That you did, the Committee knows.

Uh, whether you knew that he was a member of that Communist organization or not, I don't know. I assume you did not, Mr. Welch, because I get the impression that while you are quite an actor, you play for a laugh, I don't think you have any conception of the danger of the Communist Party. I don't think you yourself would ever knowingly aid the Communist cause. I think you're unknowingly siding with it when you try to burlesque this hearing in which we're attempting to bring out the facts.

WELCH

Mr. Chairman.

MUNDT

The Chair may say that he has no recognition or no memory of Mr. Welch recommending either Mr. Fisher or anybody else as counsel for this Committee.

MC CARTHY

I refer to the record, Mr. Chairman on the, to the news story on that.

WELCH

Mr. Chairman. Under the circumstances, I must myself have something approaching a personal privilege.

MUNDT

You may have—

WELCH

Senator McCarthy, I did not know, Senator. Senator, sometimes you say may I have your attention.

MC CARTHY

I'm listening.

WELCH

May I have your attention.

MC CARTHY

I can listen with one ear. [*Laughs.*]

WELCH

Now this time, sir, I want you to listen with both. Senator McCarthy, I think until this moment—

MC CARTHY

Good. Just a minute. Jim, Jim, will you get the news story to the effect that this man belonged to the—to this Communist front organization—

WELCH

I will tell you that he belonged to it.

MC CARTHY

Jim, will you get the citation, one of the citations showing that this was the legal arm of the Communist Party, and the length of time that he belonged, and the fact that he was recommended by Mr. Welch.

WELCH

Senator, you won't need anything in the record when I finish telling you this. Until this moment, Senator, I think I never really gauged your cruelty or your recklessness. Fred Fisher is a young man who went to the Harvard Law School and came into my firm and is starting what looks to be a brilliant career with us. When I decided to work for this Committee, I asked Jim St. Clair, who sits on my right, to be my first assistant. I said to Jim, "Pick somebody in the firm to work under you that you would like." He chose Fred Fisher and they came down on an afternoon plane. That night, when we had taken a little stab at trying to see what the case was about, Fred Fisher and Jim St. Clair and I went to dinner together. I then said to these two young men, "Boys, I don't know anything about you, except I've always liked you, but if there's anything funny in the life of either one of you that would hurt anybody in this case you speak up quick." And Fred Fisher said, "Mr. Welch, when I was in the law school, and for a period of months after, I belonged to the Lawyers' Guild," as you have suggested, Senator.

He went on to say, "I am Secretary of the Young Republican's League in Newton with the son of the Massachusetts governor, and I have the respect and admiration of my community, and I'm sure I have the respect and admiration of the twenty-five lawyers or so in Hale & Dorr." And I said, "Fred, I just don't think I'm going to ask you to work on the case. If I do, one of these days that will come out, and go over national television and it will just hurt like the dickens." And so, Senator, I asked him to go back to Boston. Little did I dream you could be so reckless and so cruel as to do an injury to that lad. It is true, he is still with Hale & Dorr. It is true that he will continue to be with Hale & Dorr. It is, I regret to say, equally true that I fear he shall always bear a scar needlessly inflicted by you. If it were in my power to forgive you for your reckless cruelty, I would do so. I like to think I'm a gentle man, but your forgiveness will have to come from someone other than me.

MC CARTHY

Mr. Chairman. Mr. Chairman. May I say that Mr. Welch talks about this being cruel and reckless. He was just baiting. He has been baiting Mr. Cohn here for hours, requesting that Mr. Cohn before sundown get out of any department of the government anyone who is serving the Communist cause. Now, I just give this man's record and I want to say, Mr. Welch, that it had been labeled long before he became a member, as early as 1944—

WELCH

Senator, may we not drop this? We know he belonged to the Lawyers' Guild. And Mr. Cohn nods his head at me. I did you, I think, no personal injury, Mr. Cohn.

COHN

No, sir.

WELCH

I meant to do you no personal injury, and if I did, I beg your pardon. Let us not assassinate this lad further. Senator. You've done enough. Have you no sense of decency, sir, at long last? Have you left no sense of decency?

MC CARTHY

I know this hurts you, Mr. Welch.

WELCH

I'll say it hurts.

MC CARTHY

Mr. Chairman, as a point of personal privilege, I'd like to finish this.

WELCH

Senator, I think it hurts you too, sir.

MC CARTHY

I'd like to finish this. I know Mr. Cohn would rather not have me go into this. Uh, I intend to, however, and Mr. Welch talks about any sense of decency. It seems that Mr. Welch is pained so deeply he thinks it's improper for me to give the record, the Communist-front record of a man whom he wanted to foist upon this Committee. But it doesn't pain him at all, there's no pain in his chest—about the attempt to destroy the reputation and the, take the jobs away from the young men who are working on my Committee; and Mr. Welch, if, if I have said anything here which is untrue, then tell me. I have heard you and everyone else talk so much about laying the truth upon the table. But when I heard—the completely phony—Mr. Welch, I've been listening now for a long time, saying, now before sundown you must get these people out of government. So I just want you to have it very clear, very clear that you were not so serious about that when you tried to recommend this man for this Committee.

MUNDT

The chair would like to say again that we do not believe Mr. Welch recommended Mr. Fisher as counsel for this Committee; because he has through his office, all the recommendations that had been made, and I do not recall any of them coming from Mr. Welch, and that would include Mr. Fisher.

MC CARTHY

Well, let me ask Mr. Welch. You brought him down, did you not? To act as your assistant?

WELCH

Mr. McCarthy, I will not discuss this further with you. You have sat within six feet of me and could ask, could have asked me about Fred Fisher. You have seen fit to bring it out and if there is a God in heaven, it will do neither you nor your cause any good. I will not discuss it further. I will not ask Mr. Cohn any more questions. You, Mr. Chairman, may, if you will, call the next witness. [*Applause from committee room.*]

The Underestimation
of Dwight D. Eisenhower

MURRAY KEMPTON

Dwight Eisenhower was surely among the most beloved of American Presidents. Yet his case is unusual for he was clearly a man loved for what he was rather than for what he did in the White House. And voter affection for the former General did not apparently extend to his adopted party: for six of his eight years in office, Eisenhower faced a Congress in which the Republicans constituted a minority. As Rexford Tugwell has pointed out, he was "the least partisan President" since George Washington. He stood above the political battle—where the people apparently wanted him to stand. And of course this rendered the battle beneath—the world of such men as Vice President Richard Nixon and Senate Majority leader Lyndon Johnson—that much less interesting. Depression and war had meant a generation of political excitement and conflict. After 1952 the pendulum swung, and Americans enjoyed respite from turbulence, sat back, and left things to Ike.

Eisenhower's accomplishments as President were limited but real. He stabilized the Cold War around a potentially disastrous strategy of "massive retaliation" which he had no intention of invoking except in speeches. And he stabilized the New Deal, neither extending it nor cutting it back, therefore making it part of the mainstream of American politics. And he did cool off the sour tensions accumulating over a generation of political stress. What he did not do, the problems that he simply kept in the cooler, nevertheless began to emerge during his second administration. A long list of national needs (that were to define the accomplishments and the failures of the tumultuous sixties) was already pressing for action when Dwight Eisenhower bid his farewell with a prescient warning about the "military-industrial complex" that had grown over-mighty during his own administration. Whether Eisenhower's record deserved the criticism it drew from liberals during the 1950's or whether his presidency merits the encomiums that they are bestowing on him in the war-weary present is the question posed in these readings by Murray Kempton and Richard H. Rovere.

He was a far more complex and devious man than most people realized, and in the best sense of those words.—Richard Nixon, *Six Crises*

The full moment of revelation about the great captains may be possible only for one of the casualties they leave behind them. Richard Nixon was writing in hospital: just once, the resentment whose suppression is the great discipline of his life breaks through and is taken back with that saving clause about the best sense of the word, of course. Yea, though He slay me yet must I depend on Him.

Dwight Eisenhower was as indifferent as Calvin Coolidge, as absolute as Abraham Lincoln, more contained than John Kennedy, more serpentine than Lyndon Johnson, as hard to work for as Andrew Johnson. Historians seem to accept most of these qualities as necessary for greatness; certainly none of them diminish it. But, then, most are accounted sinister by the great mass of civilians, and to confuse civilians and to keep them off his back is the soldier's art. Eisenhower, who understood everything, seems to have decided very early that life is nothing unless it is convenient; to show the living flesh of greatness to one's contemporaries means to show one's face in combat and to be argued about; the only convenient greatness is to appear as a monument.

The most precise description of Eisenhower was rendered in another connection by Edward Lear:

> On the top of the Crumpetty Tree
>   The Quangle Wangle sat,
> But his face you could not see,
>   On account of his Beaver Hat
> For his Hat was a hundred and
>   two feet wide,
>   With ribbons and bibbons on
>   every side
> And bells, and buttons, and loops,
>   and lace.
> So that nobody ever could see the face
>   Of the Quangle Wangle Quee.

Innocence was Eisenhower's beaver hat, and the ribbons grew longer and more numerous until his true lines were almost invisible. It took a very long watch indeed to catch the smallest glimpse.

"He told Nixon and others, including myself, that he was well aware that somebody had to do the hard-hitting infighting,[1] and he had no objections to it as long as no one expected *him* to do it," Sherman Adams says.

It was the purpose of his existence never to be seen in what he did. When he fired Sherman Adams, his chief of staff, as a political liability in 1958, Adams thought it was Nixon's doing. While he was coldly measuring the gain or loss from dropping Nixon as his 1952 Vice-Presidential candidate, Nixon thought it was Tom Dewey's doing.

When this gesture proved insufficient, Eisenhower accommodated to what was inevitable, if transient, and even offered himself up as battle trophy for Goldwater's brief triumph at the San Francisco convention. It was a situation where, the surreptitiously neat having failed, the heroically messy could hardly succeed. The useless employment of further resources would have been an affront to that superb sense of economy which made Eisenhower a soldier successful just being so immune to notions of glory and to pleasurable anticipations of bleeding.

"He is the most immoral man I have ever known," one of Nelson

---

1. *Definable to the Democrats as the dirty work.*

Rockefeller's captains said not long ago. He was probably wrong; there is always the danger of going overboard in moments when the watcher thinks he has found Eisenhower out. To be absolutely immoral is a perilous excess; being moderate in all things means, after all, being moderate in the expenditure of morality.

No thought was to be uttered undisguised; the face had as many ranges, indeed as many roles as there are sins to commit, because it was an instrument for hinting without ever quite saying. Even the syntax was an instrument. When things were at their stickiest in the Formosa Strait, James Hagerty, his Press Secretary, told the President that the best course would be to refuse to answer any questions at all on the subject if it came up at his press conference.

" 'Don't worry, Jim,' I told him as we went out the door. 'If that question comes up, I'll just confuse them.' "

Those press conferences, his highest achievements as craftsman in masks, seem certain to be half the sport and half the despair of historians; they will give up, one has to assume, and settle for the judgment that he was a man hopelessly confused, it being so difficult to confess that anyone, across so many years, could still so superbly confuse you. The mask he contrived for his comfort has already become the reputation. Generals like MacArthur and Montgomery, as proud of their intelligence as he was appalled by their weakness for theatre, seem to have thought him stupid, as he certainly thought them a little dippy. The other Presidents already evoked most often for comparison with him are General Grant and James Buchanan. But still there abides the mystery of why he never left the country ruined by his laziness, as Buchanan did, or himself ruined by his friends, as Grant did.

The difference in both cases was partly Eisenhower's intelligence, partly his appreciation of those occasions when self-indulgence can produce worse inconveniences, partly that chilliness of his nature which protected him from ever indulging others.

"I could understand it if he played golf all the time with old Army friends, but no man is less loyal to his old friends than Eisenhower," John Kennedy observed when he was a Senator. "He is a terribly cold man. All his golfing pals are rich men he has met since 1945."

"In the evenings when he had no official engagements or on weekends," says Adams, "the President liked to spend his time with old friends whose faces were often seen at Gettysburg—Bill Robinson, the entertaining George Allen, Cliff Roberts, Pete Jones, Bob Woodruff, Al Gruenther, Slats Slater, Freeman Gosden ['Amos' of the famous radio team of Amos and Andy], Sig Larmon."

These Sigs and Petes and Slatses could hardly have been more stimulating than his old Army comrades—of whose intelligence he *does* seem to have entertained the lowest opinion—and, when one member of a salon is granted special distinction as "entertaining," his fellow inmates must be dreary indeed.

But the Sigs and Petes had one substantial advantage; they earned his affection as Casanova made *his* conquests: they were men who paid.

Once, Eisenhower remembers, he had a few days' rest in Scotland on a state trip; and someone, thinking he might be lonely, suggested that he call a few friends to fly over for golf and bridge.

"The idea," he says, "struck me as intriguing, in certain respects the brighest I had heard during the entire trip. Forgetting the time differential, I picked up the telephone and within minutes was talking to Bill Robinson in New York. My call got him out of bed; in New York it was two o'clock in the morning. Without a moment's hesitation he accepted my invitation and a few hours later he and 'Pete' Jones were on their way. I was indeed fortunate to have friends who were such light sleepers."

He lived among strangers; his protective coloration was the appearance of being amiable and innocent. Very seldom does he give himself away: once he said that, when he was President of Columbia, he never went for a walk at night without carrying his service revolver with him. There is surprising hauteur in this image of the most eminent neighbor at large in Morningside Heights; but there is also the grandeur of a man whose dedication it was never to experience a moment on confrontation without the proper weight of means; to him all life was a matter of logistics.

He is revealed best, if only occasionally, in the vast and dreary acreage of his memoirs of the White House years. There he could feel safe in an occasional lapse of guard. For one thing, political history is the opiate of Democrats and he had spent eight years grandly erasing any suggestion from the minds of anyone else that anything he might ever say could be remotely interesting. He had concealed his marvelous intelligence from admirer and critic alike; by now, there was little danger of its being noticed even if confessed; he could be as secure in his memoirs as in his private diary.

The Eisenhower who emerges here intermittently free from his habitual veils is the President most superbly equipped for truly consequential decision we may ever have had, a mind neither rash nor hesitant, free of the slightest concern for how things might look, indifferent to any sentiment, as calm when he was demonstrating the wisdom of leaving a bad situation alone as when he was moving to meet it on those occasions when he absolutely had to.

Of course, we think: That is the way he wants us to see him; he is still trying to fool us; but he won't get away with it this time. And so he has fooled us again, for the Eisenhower who tells us that he never makes an important mistake is telling us for the first time about the real Eisenhower.

There is the sound of trumpets, the fog of rhetoric, then for just a moment the focus of the cold intelligence.

The President-elect goes to Korea.

We used light airplanes to fly along the front and were impressed by the rapidity with which wounded were being brought back for treatment; evacuation was almost completely by helicopter since there were no landing fields for conventional planes in the mountains. Except for sporadic artillery fire and sniping there was little action at the moment, *but in view of the strength of the positions the enemy had developed, it was obvious that any frontal attack would present great difficulties.*

All else would be conversation; one look had decided Eisenhower to fold the war.

Iraq's monarchy has been overthrown, Lebanon's government is collapsing, the British are otherwise committed; President Eisenhower will have to send the Marines.

The basic mission of United States forces in Lebanon was not primarily to fight. Every effort was made to have our landing be as much of a garrison move as possible. In my address I had been careful to use the term 'stationed in' Lebanon. . . . If it had been prudent, I would have preferred that the first battalion ashore disembark at a dock rather than across the beaches. However, the attitude of the Lebanese army was at that moment unknown, and it was obviously wise to disembark in deployed formation ready for any emergency. As it turned out, there was no resistance; the Lebanese along the beaches welcomed our troops. The geographic objectives of the landings included only the city of Beirut and the adjoining airfield.

And, thereunder, he appends this note of explanation:

The decision to occupy only the airfield and capital was a political one which I adhered to over the recommendations of some of the military. If the Lebanese army were unable to subdue the rebels when we had secured their capital and protected their government, I felt, we were backing up a government with so little popular support that we probably should not be there.

There was French Indochina, now of course Vietnam, and this cold intelligence looks upon the French with all the remote distance it would always feel from the romantic poetry of war:

The President is told that the French propose to put 10,000 troops in Dien Bien Phu.

. . . I said, "You cannot do this."

"This will bring the enemy into the open," he said. "We cannot find them in the jungle, and this will draw them out where we can then win."

"The French know military history," I said. "They are smart enough to know the outcome of becoming firmly emplaced and then besieged in an exposed position with poor means of supply and reinforcements."

Never thereafter could he contemplate the war in Indochina except in the frozen tones of a War College report on a maneuver by officers who can henceforth abandon all hope of promotion. The French, he instructs Foster Dulles, have committed the classic military blunder. In Geneva, Dulles is said to have hinted that the United States might use the atom bomb to save the French; there is no evidence that he would have dared transmit that suggestion to a President who plainly would not have trusted him with a stick of dynamite to blow up a fishpond.

Dulles, unhopefully, does transmit a French plea for United States bomber support of the Dien Bien Phu garrison; Eisenhower does not even seem to have noticed it. He had already made up his mind about that:

There were grave doubts in my mind about the effectiveness of such air strikes on deployed troops where good cover was plentiful. Employment of air strikes alone to support French troops in the jungle would create a double jeopardy: *it would comprise an act of war and would also entail the risk of having intervened and lost.*

Sitting with Under Secretary of State Bedell Smith, "I remarked that, if the United States were, unilaterally, to permit its forces to be drawn into conflict in Indochina, and in a succession of Asian wars, the end result would be to drain off our resources and to weaken our overall defensive position."

The French went down; Eisenhower blamed them and the British, who, of course, blamed Dulles.

Then, in his utmost refinement, there is the Eisenhower who supervised the C.I.A.'s U-2 reconnaissance flights over the Soviet Union:

A final important characteristic of the plane was its fragile construction. This led to the assumption (insisted upon by the C.I.A. and the Joint Chiefs) that in the event of mishap the plane would virtually distintegrate. It would be impossible, if things should go wrong, they said, for the Soviets to come into possession of the equipment intact—or, unfortunately, of a live pilot. This was a cruel assumption, but I was assured that the young pilots undertaking these missions were doing so with their eyes wide open and motivated by a high degree of patriotism, a swashbuckling bravado, and certain material inducements.[2]

Then Francis Powers' U-2 was shot down, and Eisenhower, of course, ordered the announcement of the "previously designed 'cover story.' "

Upon which, "Mr. Khrushchev, appearing before the Supreme Soviet once more, announced what to me was unbelievable. The uninjured pilot of our reconnaissance plane, along with much of his equipment intact, was in Soviet hands."

The State Department was still lamely adhering to the cover story. That seemed totally irrational to Eisenhower, who at once ordered a

2. One of the confusions making difficult the full appreciation of Eisenhower's subtlety is the condition that he seems to explain himself in anticlimactic series. For example: "As president of Columbia, I became deeply interested in the educational, financial and public relations aspects of the job." Normally one would expect a college president to be more interested in education than in public relations, and the succession seems anticlimactic. But, with a little thought, one understands that Eisenhower knew he was at Columbia as a public-relations man. In the same way, normal rhetoric would assign the climactic role in the readiness of a soldier to sacrifice his life to "high degree of patriotism"; Eisenhower, with perfect understanding, gives the emphasis to "certain material inducements."

full confession, altering its draft "to eliminate any phrase that seemed to me to be defensive in tone.

"In the diplomatic field," he explained, "it was routine practice to deny responsibility for an embarrassing occurrence when there is even a one percent chance of being believed, but when the world can entertain not the slightest doubt of the facts, there is no point in trying to evade the issue."

And there we have, in Dwight Eisenhower of all unexpected persons, the model of that perfect statesman of Voltaire's ironic dream, the one who could learn nothing from Machiavelli except to denounce Machiavelli.

The precepts are plain to see:

1) Always pretend to be stupid; then when you have to show yourself smart, the display has the additional effect of surprise.

2) Taking the blame is a function of servants. When the orange is squeezed, throw it away.

3) When a situation is hopeless, never listen to counsels of hope. Fold the enterprise.

4) Do nothing unless you know exactly what you will do if it turns out to have been the wrong thing. Walk not one inch forward onto ground which has not been painfully tested by someone else.

5) Never forget the conversation you had with Zhukov about how the Russian army clears minefields. "We march through them," Zhukov had said. It is a useful instruction if applied with the proper economy. Keep Nixon and Dulles around for marching through minefields.

6) Always give an enemy an exit.

7) Never give an ally his head.

8) Assume that your enemies are just as sensible as you are. ("Personally I had always discounted the probability of the Soviets doing anything as 'reaction.' Communists do little on impulse; rather their aggressive moves are invariably the result of deliberate decision.")

9) Lie whenever it seems useful, but stop lying the moment ninety-nine percent of the audience ceases to believe you.

10) Respond only when there is some gain besides honor in meeting the challenge or some serious loss from disregarding it. For example, when Eisenhower was the first candidate for President in memory who indicated that he was unable to pronounce the word "injunction" when discussing the labor problem, I suggested to one of his admirers that he seemed extraordinarily dumb.

"If he's so dumb," was the reply, "why is he such a good bridge player?"

Like all defenses of Dwight Eisenhower, it seemed silly at first; but, with thought one understood its force. Eisenhower spent the Twenties as an officer in garrison; his friends were civilians in towns like Leavenworth, Kansas. He learned to play bridge well because his pay did not cover losing money to civilians. He is equipped to respond to any challenge which seems to him sensible.

He was the great tortoise upon whose back the world sat for eight years. We laughed at him; we talked wistfully about moving; and all the while we never knew the cunning beneath the shell.

I talked to him just once. He was in Denver, getting ready for the 1952 campaign when he would have to run with Republicans like Senator Jenner who had called General Marshall, the chief agent of Eisenhower's promotion, "a living lie." I had thought that anyone so innocent as Eisenhower would be embarrassed by this comradeship and proposed to ask what he thought about what Jenner had said. It seemed cruel to spring any such trap to anyone this innocent, so I told Hagerty that I intended to ask the question.

The time came and I asked, "General, what do you think of those people who call General Marshall a living lie?"

He leaped to his feet and contrived the purpling of his face. How dare anyone say that about the greatest man who walks in America? He shook his finger in marvelous counterfeit of the palsy of outrage.

He would die for General Marshall. He could barely stand to be in the room with anyone who would utter such a profanation. The moment passed when the enlisted man in garrison endures his ordeal as example to the rest of the troops; and suddenly I realized that, in his magnificent rage at me, he had been careful not to mention Senator Jenner at all.

Afterward Hagerty took me over and the General offered the sunshine of his smile; there was not the slightest indication that he was thinking that there was anything for him to forgive or me either. It had simply been the appointed ceremony. I was too dumb to understand him then. It would be ten years before I looked at his picture and realized that the smile was always a grin.

Eisenhower Revisited– A Political Genius? A Brilliant Man?

RICHARD H. ROVERE

It has been slightly more than a decade since Robert Frost greeted the dawn of a "next Augustan age . . . of poetry and power" and Dwight D. Eisenhower, ex-President, left Washington for Gettysburg—still an immensely popular figure who, had the law permitted and the spirit and the flesh been willing, could easily have been the man taking the oath of office on January 20, 1961, thus deferring the Augustan age for at least four more years. Eisenhower was held in high esteem for the rest of his life, but throughout most of the sixties those amateurs who sit in more or less professional judgment on Presidents—other politicians, historians, journalists—came more and more into agreement that his eight years in the White House had been a period of meager accomplishment and lackadaisical leadership. The greatest failure, the consensus seemed to be, was one of anticipation. What a prescient statesman could have foreseen in the fifties, the argument runs, was that the ship of state was headed for a sea of troubles, and this the 34th President conspicuously failed to perceive. He lacked foresight and imagination and thus bore considerable responsibility for the difficulties of the three men who succeeded him in the sixties.

Many of those who judged him most harshly until only a few years ago are now having second and third thoughts about the man and his Presidency—thoughts that should ring most agreeably in the ears of those whose faith had never never wavered. Such nay-sayers on the left as Murray Kempton and I. F. Stone are finding virtues in him they failed to detect while he served, and others are making claims for him that not even his partisans made when he sought office or held it. Garry Wills, the eminent Nixonologist, advises us in "Nixon Agonistes" that Eisenhower was "a political genius." Walter Cronkite, who first knew Eisenhower in France during the war and saw him often in subsequent years, recently said that he never thought highly of Eisenhower "either as a general or a President" but that in the post-White House years he discovered that Eisenhower was in actuality a "brilliant" man—indeed, "more brilliant than many brilliant men I have met."

A political genius? A brilliant man? Who ever said or thought that about Eisenhower in his own time? Certainly not Eisenhower himself. It was not that he was lacking in vanity; he had his share, but there is no evidence that he ever thought of himself as possessing a great talent for politics or a towering intellect, and the aspect of his "genius" that Wills calls "realism" would have deterred him from this kind of self-appraisal. He was, and we can be sure that he knew he was, no slouch politically (had he been below average in this respect, he would not have risen in the Army), and he was certainly not lacking in intelligence. But his real strengths lay elsewhere, and the Wills and Cronkite superlatives seem, one has to say, silly.

In the case of Garry Wills, the judgment supports a theory. Wills maintains that Eisenhower all along saw Richard Nixon in the light in which Wills today sees him. In Cronkite's case, the delayed but nonetheless dazzling illumination appeared in the course of many meetings he had with Eisenhower while taping some television interviews in the mid-sixties. He asserts his discovery of the ex-President's "brilliance" but does not tell us how it was made manifest.

For my part, I think the revisionist phenomenon as a whole can be rather easily accounted for—though I do not wish to suggest that new judgments are erroneous simply because they are new or, at least, as I see it, obvious in their origins. Seen from 1971, the most important single thing about Dwight D. Eisenhower was that, through luck or good management or some combination of both, *we did not go to war* while he was President. To be sure, we came close on occasion, and his Secretary of State practiced a brand of cold-war diplomacy in which what was called "brinkmanship" at the time—risking war, including nuclear war—was an indispensable strategy. It can also be argued that Dulles's and Eisenhower's Indochina policy made Kennedy's and Johnson's and Nixon's all but inevitable and that, had Eisenhower held office for a third term, he would have found himself at war in Vietnam. The contrary can also be argued, but it does not matter, we were at war when he came to office, and six months later we were out of it, and we did not enter another war during his tenure. Eight years of Eisenhower: seven and a half years of peace. Ten years of Kennedy, Johnson, Nixon: almost ten solid years of war.

What else is there to celebrate about the Eisenhower years? I can think of a few things, but they are of far less consequence and, moreover, they are not blessings of the sort that can be appreciated only in hindsight—unless one chooses to include among them such engineering projects as the St. Lawrence Seaway and the interstate highway system. Though I have myself altered some of my views about Eisenhower over the years, I have felt since 1958 or thereabouts that the country benefited from his first term but would have been better off if he had not had a second. I think I can defend this view in 1971. By 1953 we had made our point in Korea—the expulsion of the invading armies—and it was time for a settlement. It required a Republican President (not necessarily Eisenhower, though of course it helped that he was a successful military man) to end that war on terms short of the "victory" for which Gen. Douglas MacArthur said there was "no substitute." As Harry Truman was to say, he or any other Democrat would have been "lynched" for agreeing to the settlement Eisenhower so cheerfully accepted. It also required a Republican in the White House (though, again, not necessarily Eisenhower) to bring about the downfall of Senator Joe McCarthy.

Eisenhower, to be sure, never took the initiative against McCarthy. He declined to "get into the gutter" with the demagogue, and he tolerated, for a while, a certain amount of high-level appeasement. But the fact remains that 15 months after Eisenhower took office McCarthy was done for. With an active, militant President, the job might have been done somewhat sooner and with less loss of dignity all around. However, a Republican President did not have to be an activist to draw McCarthy's fire. Though nominally a Republican, McCarthy was bound by the nature of his mission in American political life to attack any administration, and when in time he attacked his own party's steward-ship of affairs, resistance was bound to be offered. It tends now to be forgotten that McCarthy scored most of his triumphs when the Demo-crats controlled both the White House and Congress, and he would probably have been more difficult to deal with had they remained in control. It has always seemed to me that the election of Adlai Stevenson in 1952, however desirable it might have been in certain respects, would have prolonged both the Korean war and McCarthyism, and I have reason to think that, in later years, Stevenson believed this, too. The country was bitterly divided in 1952, and 20 years of Democratic governance was one of the causes of disunity.

Putting Eisenhower in the White House seemed a way of promoting national unity, which, though hardly the highest of political values, is not one to be disregarded. But by 1956 Eisenhower had achieved just about all that it was in his power to achieve. The war was over, Mc-Carthy was a spent force and the President had, at the Geneva Summit Conference of 1955, helped negotiate a limited but nonetheless helpful *détente* in the cold war.

The second term was anticlimax almost all the way. It was also rather melancholy and at times squalid. The President was not a well man. The Democrats, growing in power in the Congress and knowing that no one would ever again ride Eisenhower's coattails, were openly seeking to embarrass him and passing bills he felt he had to veto. In midterm, he lost the two men he had relied on most heavily. John Foster Dulles left office and soon died, and Sherman Adams, who was general manager at the White House, had to retire because of a clear conflict of interest. Eisenhower began on his own to practice some of Dulles's peripatetic diplomacy, but it didn't work. In 1960, he started for another summit meeting, in Paris, but Nikita Khrushchev refused to make the final ascent because of the unpleasantness over the U-2 affair. Eisenhower set out for Japan, but for security reasons (rioting anti-American students, etc.) was advised to turn around and go home.

There is more to being a President than entering or ending wars—and more than instituting or failing to institute political and social change. Style and character are important and closely related aspects of leadership. Eisenhowever came to us as a hero—not in the old sense of a man who had displayed great valor but in the newer sense of having been an organizer of victory. His style, though, was anything but heroic. It was in part fatherly, in larger part avuncular. He was not an exhorter —except now and then in campaigns—and as a counselor his perform-ance was as a rule inadequate. He had difficulties with language, par-ticularly when he extemporized. Readers of press-conference texts found his syntax all but impenetrable and often concluded that his thinking was as muddled as the verbatim transcripts. Actually, he was seldom as unclear as he appeared to be when encountered in cold type. Those who listened and watched as he talked were rarely in doubt as to what he was saying. Inflection and expression conveyed much of what seemed missing or mixed up in print. But he was never, to put it mildly, eloquent, never a forceful persuader. He never influenced, or sought to influence, American thought.

Eulogizing Eisenhower in April, 1969, President Nixon said of his late mentor: "For more than a quarter of a century, he spoke with a moral authority seldom equaled in American public life." Nixon did not explain how, when or where the impact of this "moral authority" was felt. Eisenhower was an upright man, a believer in the Protestant ethic he seemed to embody. But the man he twice defeated was no less honorable, and Stevenson had a moral vision that seemed somewhat broader, deeper and less simplistic than Eisenhower's. Do any survivors recall the Eisenhower years as a period notable for elevated standards of morality in public life or elsewhere? In our public life, there were two issues full of "moral" content—McCarthyism and race. On neither did the President personally exercise any of the kind of authority Nixon attributed to him. He was not a McCarthyite or a racist, but he conspicuously failed to engage his personal prestige or that of his office in the struggles against demagogy and racial injustice.

A President can also provide leadership by improving the quality of public life—the quality of the people he appoints and associates himself with, the quality of the acts he and they perform, the quality of the ideas his administration espouses. If in the future, the brief Presidency of Eisenhower's successor is well regarded, it will be largely because of his quest for "excellence." Kennedy brought many first-rate people to Washington, and if one of the lessons they taught us is that first-rate people can sometimes mess things up as badly as third-raters or fourth-raters, it is nevertheless true that some of them performed brilliantly and should continue to serve the Republic for some years to come. No such praise, so far as I am aware, accrues to Eisenhower—except in the case of one institution, the Supreme Court.

He appointed a Chief Justice and four Associate Justices, and all but one of the five (Charles Whittaker, who sat only briefly) served with high distinction. In this respect, Eisenhower's record may be as good as any in history. There was about it, though, a kind of inadvertent quality—as if some architect had achieved splendor while seeking only mediocrity. The President was surprised and in some cases hugely disappointed by the performance of the institution he had created.

In the executive branch, mediocrity was the rule. The one Cabinet member of stature was John Foster Dulles, an imposing man in many ways but also a stiff, self-righteous Calvinist who intensified the cold war as an ideological conflict and sometimes seemed bent on making it a theological one as well—making, as he put it, "the moral force of Christendom . . . felt in the conduct of nations." Nevertheless, Dulles was a man of some intellectual prowess, and nothing of the sort could be said for anyone else in the upper echelons. Eisenhower's measure of expertise in any field was that of the Bitch Goddess: success, usually financial success. Especially in the early days, it was a businessman's administration—to a degree that bred misgivings even in the mind of the first Senator Robert Taft of Ohio, who made no bones about being a spokesman for business but said, when he heard of the first appointments, "I don't know of any reasons why success in business should mean success in public service. . . . Anyone who thinks he can just transfer business methods to government is going to have to learn that it isn't so." Eisenhower's appointments were uninspired and uninspiring; one cannot think of any major office holder whose example might have led any young man or young woman to feel that public life might be a high calling. On the White House staff, there were from time to time highly gifted younger men—Maxwell Rabb, Emmet Hughes, Malcolm Moos—but for the most part they lacked power and visibility, though Moos exerted an influence of a kind when he wrote the line about the "military-industrial complex" into Eisenhower's farewell address.

Still and all, who in 1971 wouldn't exchange a trainload of mediocrities, incompetents and even pickpockets for a speedy end to the war in Vietnam and to the rancor and discord it has created? There may be some survivors of the better-dead-than-Red set, but even a number of these, one suspects, no longer see the conflict in Vietnam as one that compels a choice between extinction and the surrender of American independence. There was peace under Eisenhower, and the question of historical interest to those of us who survived the ensuing decade is whether this indisputable fact is to be ascribed to his stewardship or to luck or to some combination of both. I lean toward the combination theory, with perhaps a heavier emphasis on luck than others might care to make.

The opportunities for military involvement during his tenure were fully as numerous as those of the Kennedy, Johnson and Nixon years. In Asia, there were Korea, the Formosa Strait and Indochina; in Europe, Germany and Hungary; in the Middle East, Suez and Lebanon, and in our own hemisphere, Cuba. In some of these troubled areas, intervention was seriously contemplated; in others, it seemed out of the question from the start. In the Suez crisis of 1956, our policy from the onset was to stay out militarily: we made our disapproval so clear to the British and the French that we were not consulted in the planning stages. Nor was there ever much likelihood of our doing anything about Hungary, which erupted just after Suez in the closing days of the Presidential campaign; the Dulles line on Eastern Europe was always that we stood ready to help in the task of "liberation," but it was never much more than a line, and in moments of crisis behind the Iron Curtain—except when there was trouble in Berlin—we looked the other way. In 1958 in Lebanon, we did, at the request of its beleaguered President, land combat-ready Marine and Army units, but there was no combat and the troops spent their time girl-watching on the beaches they had stormed.

But elsewhere the risks were large. Even before his inauguration, Eisenhower went to Korea in search of peace, and in a matter of months a welcome (though far from satisfactory) settlement was made. Politically, in this country, the credit was all his, and if the whole truth is ever known—it will probably never be—it might turn out that he deserves it all. From what is currently known, his principal strategy seems to have been nuclear blackmail—a threat conveyed to our adversaries that if they dragged their feet much longer in the truce talks while pressing on with the war, this country would not consider itself bound to a reliance on conventional weapons. (Eisenhower was never opposed to the use of atomic weapons on moral grounds. He regarded them simply as explosives, suitable for some demolition jobs and not for others. His later assertions about general war's being "unthinkable" in the atomic age were based not on a moral judgment but a military one. He saw no point in a war no one would survive. But tactical "nukes" were another matter.) Maybe that did it, and maybe not. The truth could only come from the other side, and about all we now have on any other factor is Khrushchev's memory of Chou En-lai later explaining that the Chinese losses in Korea had become militarily insupportable. In any case, with all due respect for and gratitude to Eisenhower, one is compelled to wonder what would have happened—what could have happened—if the Communists had said that they weren't afraid of our bombs and intended to carry on with the war. Did he have a fallback position? If so, was it credible? Or did he, as seems so out of character, stake everything on a wildly dangerous threat of holocaust? These are questions that await answers that may never come. We know only that the war was terminated the following summer.

In Formosa we have what is perhaps the clearest case of prudent management during the Eisenhower Presidency. The danger was that we would be suckered into at least an air and sea war against Communist China, which was, as it still is, insisting on the rightness of its claim to sovereignty over Formosa and all the islands between it and the mainland. Eisenhower was, in 1954 and 1955, under enormous pressure from his own military and diplomatic advisers, among them Dulles, from Congressional Republicans and from many prominent Americans who had supported his candidacy (Henry Luce, for example) to give Chiang Kai-shek every form of assistance he asked for and to help in the defense of every rock in the Formosa Strait—not only to help keep the Generalissimo in his fortress but to aid in preparations for a return to the mainland by the Nationalist armies that had been driven out half a decade earlier. Eisenhower quite clearly had no taste for the entire enterprise. He knew that Chiang alone could never dislodge the Communists, no matter how much materiel we gave him, and he knew, too, that Mao Tse-tung's forces, no matter how many shells they lobbed at the close-in islands, were unequipped for an amphibious invasion of Formosa. So he jollied Chiang with hardware and money and high-level visitors, meanwhile protecting himself with a Congressional resolution and a treaty that pledged direct military assistance to Chiang only if we—not he—determined that Peking's maneuvers in the Formosa Strait were unmistakably preparatory to an assault on Formosa itself.

Had Admiral Radford, then Chairman of the Joint Chiefs, been in control, he might have made that fateful determination a dozen times over. Eisenhower read the cables and studied the maps and found no occasion for invoking those parts of the agreements that could have led to war. His methods were in certain ways dubious—there were questions about the constitutionality of the treaty and the resolution—but at least in the perspective of the present he found a way of averting a war that could have been far costlier than the one we have been in for most of the last decade. There can be little doubt that this was his will and his doing, for, as far as Communist China was concerned, he was the only "dove" in his administration.

Indochina—as always, it is the most complicated of matters. Eisenhower did not get involved militarily, but he may, by his patronage of his Secretary of State and by other words and acts, have made subsequent intervention all but unavoidable. It was Eisenhower who articulated the "domino theory" for Southeast Asia, and we know from his memoirs that on several occasions he seriously considered intervention and was deterred not primarily by political or moral considerations but by military and, to some extent, diplomatic ones. An obvious restraint was our lack of troops and weapons suitable for fighting the kind of war he quite correctly judged it to be. He gave thought to the use of nuclear weapons, and two carriers whose planes had nuclear bombs were in the Tonkin Gulf. But, as Earl Ravenal writes in Foreign Affairs, he "could not identify an appropriate enemy or target to fit the massive nuclear response [and] narrowly declined to intervene."

He considered using ground troops to aid the French but stipulated that under no circumstances would he go it alone—that is, without Asian and European allies. Dulles looked for suitable allies but found none. Had Eisenhower found either the appropriate targets for nuclear retaliation or willing partners in intervention, he might still have come up with an excuse for staying out, for nonintervention seemed almost always his preference; his distaste for war was general and a consistent factor in his reasoning. But it was indisputably under Eisenhower that we made heavy commitments to the powers that were and were to be in Saigon, and it was with Eisenhower's blessing that Dulles set up the Southeast Asia Treaty Organization, at once a political joke and a political disaster.

During his time, Eisenhower was not called upon to make good on any of Dulles's commitments in the region. I think it quite conceivable, however, that had he held office in the early sixties he might have found himself a prisoner of his own past and of then-current events and have followed pretty much the course of his successors. One advantage he had over his successors, though, was confidence in his own military judgment, and this might have saved him, us and the Vietnamese from the horrors that were soon to come.

Eisenhower's two terms fell between the two great Berlin crises—the one brought on by the blockade of the Western Sector in 1948 and the one brought on by the Berlin Wall 10 years ago. There was continuous tension over Germany throughout the fifties, but the dangers of war lessened as NATO, whose supreme command he had left to seek the

Presidency, grew in strength and as circumspection seemed increasingly to prevail in the Kremlin. These were the early days of the world of two nuclear superpowers, and the "balance of terror" would probably have held under any leadership save that of a madman. Though in Europe Dulles made a good many enemies for himself and for his Government, his European diplomacy was always more traditional and more prudent, as witness the Austrian treaty, than his diplomacy elsewhere in the world, and it would, I think, be rather difficult to fault Eisenhower for his handling of American policy in Germany.

In his memoirs, Eisenhower wrote of the Bay of Pigs as a "fiasco" for which "indecision and untimely counterorders" were "apparently responsible." He did not elaborate. But whatever he meant by Kennedy's "indecision," the original conclusion that we should sponsor an invasion came out of the Eisenhower, not the Kennedy, Administration. As he acknowledged, his military and intelligence people had, with his encouragement, armed and trained the forces in exile and, as we learned in the aftermath, completion of the scheme was urged on the new President by such holdovers as Allen Dulles of the C.I.A. and Gen. Lyman Lemnitzer, Chairman of the Joint Chiefs of Staff. Kennedy took responsibility for the bad show of which Eisenhower was the original producer. Eisenhower was lucky enough to be out of office when the rehearsals were over and the performers were ready for the opening. We can only conjecture as to whether he would have called off the whole business or gone about it in some other way. But he surely bears some responsibility for the policy and for the crucial failure of intelligence which led the executors of the policy to believe that the Cuban people would welcome the invaders as liberators and would take up arms to join them.

I have been somewhat surprised in thinking and writing about the Eisenhower years a decade later to discover that we know a good deal less about the Eisenhower Administration than about most recent ones. The historians haven't got around to it yet, and the few memoirists it produced haven't revealed very much except about themselves. Eisenhower's two large volumes were put together mainly with scissors and paste. Richard Nixon's "Six Crises" is all about Richard Nixon. Sherman Adams's "First-Hand Report" is not first-hand at all but second- and third-hand—dealing extensively with large events, such as Indochina and Formosa, about which he knew little and, despite his closeness to the President, was seldom if ever consulted. Robert Murphy's "Diplomat Among Warriors" is a stiff-necked but instructive work, only part of which bears on the Eisenhower period. Emmet Hughes's "Ordeal of Power" is a thoughtful, critical work, but Hughes's experience was limited to two brief tours in the White House as a speechwriter and political consultant. A few journalists—notably Robert J. Donovan in "Eisenhower: The Inside Story"—produced creditable works, more useful on the whole than the memoirs, but the literature by and large is thin.

"The President of the United States," Alfred Kazin wrote in reviewing the first volume of Eisenhower's memoirs, "had to look up the public record that most of us more or less knew in order to find out what happened during his Adminstration." This, I think, comes close to the heart of the matter about Eisenhower. For eight years as President, he presided in the most literal dictionary sense—he occupied the seat of authority. But he exercised authority only when there was no other choice. He headed an administration but he rarely administered. In foreign affairs, he stepped in only on certain European questions and when, as Commander in Chief, he was required to make command decisions. In domestic affairs his temperament was in line with his economics—laissez-faire. Whenever possible, he let the Government run itself—and it was possible a good part of the time.

In fairness, though, it must be recalled that Eisenhower never offered himself as an activist. He never pledged innovation or any sort of basic reform. One cannot quite contend that he was the product of a political "draft," but, at least as much as any chief executive in this century, he had the office thrust upon him. His style was well known to those who engineered his nomination and to those who elected and reelected him. Whatever else may be said in dispraise, he did not betray his trust. He construed it rather narrowly, but in doing so he embodied a long tradition and a specifically Republican tradition.

His command decisions seem, in retrospect, to have been generally wise. He was clear about the hazards of intervention in Asia. However, he deputized Dulles to contract military alliances all over the place—confident, perhaps, that in crises he could prevail as he had in Korea. He deputized much to the other Dulles, Allen, too—and it was under him that the C.I.A. became a force in world affairs and undertook such missions as the overturn of Governments in Iran and Guatemala. Eisenhower was anything but an empire builder—he was by almost any definition an anti-imperialist—but it was while he presided that this country began, if not to acquire new holdings overseas, to use its power in an imperial manner far beyond the Americas.

Domestically, he and we marked time. In the first few years, this was more or less defensible. The country might not have sustained him if he had tried to remake it. Once the Korean war was over and McCarthy's fangs had been drawn, complacency was the dominant American mood, and very few Americans were aware of the large structural faults in many of our institutions. In 1954, the Supreme Court ruled that if we were to be true to ourselves and our pretensions, racism had to be deinstitutionalized, but this was about the only blow to complacency until, in the second term, sputnik went aloft and made some Americans wonder about our educational system. With hindsight, we can see that practically all the problems that bedeviled us in the sixties had been worsening in the fifties. It can be said, to be sure, that nearly all of them predated the fifties by decades, even centuries, and that Eisenhower was no more to blame in such matters than most of his predecessors. And this is only just. He was not a cause of any of our present domestic disorders. Neither, though, did he perceive them or heed the prophets of his time—and there were several—who did perceive them.

What Eisenhower clearly lacked—and this was due as much to the education and experience that had been his lot as a servant of his country as to any deficiency of mind or spirit—was the kind of knowledge of the American condition he might have gained if his background had been in politics rather than in the military. He went through most of the fifties and on into the sixties with an image of this country formed in Kansas *circa* 1910. Nowhere is this so dismayingly clear as in the closing words of the second volume of his memoirs, which was published in a dreadful year for this country, 1965—after his successor had met violent death in Dallas, at a time when violence increasingly characterized our race relations, when the generation gap was widening alongside the credibility gap, when our sons were marching by the tens of thousands into the Vietnam quagmire. In that year, he could bring himself to this apostrophe:

I have unshakable faith that the ideals and the way of life that Western civilization has cherished . . . will flourish everywhere to the infinite benefit of mankind . . . At home . . . our level of education constantly rises . . . opportunity for the properly ambitious boy or girl increases daily. Prospects for the good life were never better, provided only that each continues to feel that he, himself, must earn and deserve these advantages.

Imbued with sense and spirit we will select future leaders [who will] keep a firm, sure hand on the rudder of this splendid ship of state, guiding her through future generations to the great destiny for which she was created.

A good man? Of course. A "brilliant" man? Hardly. "A political genius"? If so, the evidence remains concealed. A good President? Better than average, perhaps, and very useful in his early years. But by and large not what the times required.

The Feminine Mystique

BETTY FRIEDAN

*Women have always been a majority treated like a minority: discrimi-
nated against in politics, in schools, and on the job, condescended to
in nearly every social relationship, scoffed at for almost every aspiration.
It is true that certain benefits have accompanied this second-class citizenship. Millions of women enjoyed the advantage of being discounted
as a force in society, took the pleasures of prosperity and apparently
paid few of the tangible costs in meaningless work or early death. But
women as a group have suffered from a remarkably consistent discrimination, and throughout the industrialized countries they have
fought back, winning a place for themselves in the economic, cultural,
and political worlds.*

*But something went wrong in the United States in the twentieth
century; while women in other countries increasingly found satisfying
careers outside the home, American women seemed to be retreating.
More of them worked, but at less demanding or rewarding jobs. And
they had more children than their peers in other countries. Safely
ensconced in the growing suburbs after World War II, apparently
uninterested in politics or a career, they seemed calm and safe—the
envy, one assumed, of the world. But they had one problem. "The
Problem," Betty Friedan called it, "that has no name": more and more
of them were miserable. The bored housewife syndrome became a national parlor game, broadcast through the mass media, discussed in
countless living rooms and doubtless in as many bedrooms. Betty
Friedan brought the problem into the open in her influential* The
Feminine Mystique *(1963), a book that heralded a new assertiveness
on the part of American women such as had not been seen since the
women's suffrage movement.*

*In part, this new militancy reflects the general climate of political
activism in the 1960's; in part it grows from new opportunities open
to women. But clearly much of it is a direct and understandable response to the peculiar circumstances of the postwar era, whose attitude
toward woman's role Betty Friedan has captured in vigorous polemic.*

In the early 1960's *McCall's* has been the fastest growing of the women's
magazines. Its contents are a fairly accurate representation of the image
of the American woman presented, and in part created, by the large-
circulation magazines. Here are the complete editorial contents of a
typical issue of *McCall's* (July, 1960):

1. A lead article on "increasing baldness in women," caused by too
much brushing and dyeing.
2. A long poem in primer-size type about a child, called "A Boy
Is A Boy."

3. A short story about how a teenager who doesn't go to college gets a man away from a bright college girl.

4. A short story about the minute sensations of a baby throwing his bottle out of the crib.

5. The first of a two-part intimate "up-to-date" account by the Duke of Windsor on "How the Duchess and I now live and spend our time. The influence of clothes on me and vice versa."

6. A short story about a nineteen-year-old girl sent to a charm school to learn how to bat her eyelashes and lose at tennis. ("You're nineteen, and by normal American standards, I now am entitled to have you taken off my hands, legally and financially, by some beardless youth who will spirit you away to a one-and-a-half-room apartment in the Village while he learns the chicanery of selling bonds. And no beardless youth is going to do that as long as you volley to his backhand.")

7. The story of a honeymoon couple commuting between separate bedrooms after an argument over gambling at Las Vegas.

8. An article on "how to overcome an inferiority complex."

9. A story called "Wedding Day."

10. The story of a teenager's mother who learns how to dance rock-and-roll.

11. Six pages of glamorous pictures of models in maternity clothes.

12. Four glamorous pages on "reduce the way the models do."

13. An article on airline delays.

14. Patterns for home sewing.

15. Patterns with which to make "Folding Screens—Bewitching Magic."

16. An article called "An Encyclopedic Approach to Finding a Second Husband."

17. A "barbecue bonanza," dedicated "to the Great American Mister who stands, chef's cap on head, fork in hand, on terrace or back porch, in patio or backyard anywhere in the land, watching his roast turning on the spit. And to his wife without whom (sometimes) the barbecue could never be the smashing summer success it undoubtedly is . . ."

There were also the regular front-of-the-book "service" columns on new drug and medicine developments, child-care facts, columns by Clare Luce and by Eleanor Roosevelt, and "Pots and Pans," a column of readers' letters.

The image of woman that emerges from this big, pretty magazine is young and frivolous, almost childlike; fluffy and feminine; passive; gaily content in a world of bedroom and kitchen, sex, babies, and home. The magazine surely does not leave out sex; the only passion, the only pursuit, the only goal a woman is permitted is the pursuit of a man. It is crammed full of food, clothing, cosmetics, furniture, and the physical bodies of young women, but where is the world of thought and ideas, the life of the mind and spirit? In the magazine image, women do no work except housework and work to keep their bodies beautiful and to get and keep a man.

This was the image of the American woman in the year Castro led a revolution in Cuba and men were trained to travel into outer space; the year that the African continent brought forth new nations, and a plane whose speed is greater than the speed of sound broke up a Summit Conference; the year artists picketed a great museum in protest against the hegemony of abstract art; physicists explored the concept of anti-matter; astronomers, because of new radio telescopes, had to alter their concepts of the expanding universe; biologists made a breakthrough in the fundamental chemistry of life; and Negro youth in Southern schools forced the United States, for the first time since the Civil War, to face a moment of democratic truth. But this magazine, published for over 5,000,000 American women, almost all of whom have been through high school and nearly half to college, contained almost no mention of the world beyond the home. In the second half of the twentieth century in America, woman's world was confined to her own body and beauty, the charming of man, the bearing of babies, and the physical care and serving of husband, children, and home. And this was no anomaly of a single issue of a single women's magazine.

I sat one night at a meeting of magazine writers, mostly men, who work for all kinds of magazines, including women's magazines. The main speaker was a leader of the desegregation battle. Before he spoke, another man outlined the needs of the large women's magazine he edited:

Our readers are housewives, full time. They're not interested in the broad public issues of the day. They are not interested in national or international affairs. They are only interested in the family and the home. They aren't interested in politics, unless it's related to an immediate need in the home, like the price of coffee. Humor? Has to be gentle, they don't get satire. Travel? We have almost completely dropped it. Education? That's a problem. Their own education level is going up. They've generally all had a high-school education and many, college. They're tremendously interested in education for their children—fourth-grade arithmetic. You just can't write about ideas or broad issues of the day for women. That's why we're publishing 90 per cent service now and 10 per cent general interest.

Another editor agreed, adding plaintively: "Can't you give us something else besides 'there's death in your medicine cabinet'? Can't any of you dream up a new crisis for women? We're always interested in sex, of course."

At this point, the writers and editors spent an hour listening to Thurgood Marshall on the inside story of the desegregation battle, and its possible effect on the presidential election. "Too bad I can't run that story," one editor said. "But you just can't link it to woman's world."

As I listened to them, a German phrase echoed in my mind— "*Kinder, Kuche, Kirche,*" the slogan by which the Nazis decreed that

women must once again be confined to their biological role. But this
was not Nazi Germany. This was America. The whole world lies open
to American women. Why, then, does the image deny the world? Why
does it limit women to "one position, one role, one occupation"? Not
long ago, women dreamed and fought for equality, their own place in
the world. What happened to their dreams; when did women decide to
give up the world and go back home?

A geologist brings up a core of mud from the bottom of the ocean
and sees layers of sediment as sharp as a razor blade deposited over
the years—clues to changes in the geological evolution of the earth so
vast that they would go unnoticed during the lifespan of a single man.
I sat for many days in the New York Public Library, going back through
bound volumes of American women's magazines for the last twenty
years. I found a change in the image of the American woman, and in
the boundaries of the woman's world, as sharp and puzzling as the
changes revealed in cores of ocean sediment.

In 1939, the heroines of women's magazine stories were not always
young, but in a certain sense they were younger than their fictional
counterparts today. They were young in the same way that the American
hero has always been young: they were New Women, creating with a
gay determined spirit a new identity for women—a life of their own.
There was an aura about them of becoming, of moving into a future
that was going to be different from the past. The majority of heroines
in the four major women's magazines (then *Ladies' Home Journal,
McCall's, Good Housekeeping, Woman's Home Companion*) were career women—happily, proudly, adventurously, attractively career women
—who loved and were loved by men. And the spirit, courage, independence, determination—the strength of character they showed in their
work as nurses, teachers, artists, actresses, copywriters, saleswomen—
were part of their charm. There was a definite aura that their individuality was something to be admired, not unattractive to men, that
men were drawn to them as much for their spirit and character as for
their looks.

These were the mass women's magazines—in their heyday. The
stories were conventional: girl-meets-boy or girl-gets-boy. But very often
this was not the major theme of the story. These heroines were usually
marching toward some goal or vision of their own, struggling with some
problem of work or the world, when they found their man. And this
New Woman, less fluffily feminine, so independent and determined to
find a new life of her own, was the heroine of a different kind of love
story. She was less aggressive in pursuit of a man. Her passionate involvement with the world, her own sense of herself as an individual,
her self-reliance, gave a different flavor to her relationship with the
man. The heroine and hero of one of these stories meet and fall in love
at an ad agency where they both work. "I don't want to put you in a
garden behind a wall," the hero says. "I want you to walk with me
hand in hand, and together we could accomplish whatever we wanted
to" ("A Dream to Share," *Redbook,* January, 1939).

These New Women were almost never housewives; in fact, the stories usually ended before they had children. They were young because the future was open. But they seemed, in another sense, much older, more mature than the childlike, kittenish young housewife heroines today. One, for example, is a nurse ("Mother-in-Law," *Ladies' Home Journal,* June, 1939). "She was, he thought, very lovely. She hadn't an ounce of picture book prettiness, but there was strength in her hands, pride in her carriage and nobility in the lift of her chin, in her blue eyes. She had been on her own ever since she left training, nine years ago. She had earned her way, she need consider nothing but her heart."

One heroine runs away from home when her mother insists she must make her debut instead of going on an expedition as a geologist. Her passionate determination to live her own life does not keep this New Woman from loving a man, but it makes her rebel from her parents; just as the young hero often must leave home to grow up. "You've got more courage than any girl I ever saw. You have what it takes," says the boy who helps her get away ("Have a Good Time, Dear," *Ladies' Home Journal,* May 1939).

Often, there was a conflict between some commitment to her work and the man. But the moral, in 1939, was that if she kept her commitment to herself, she did not lose the man, if he was the right man. A young widow ("Between the Dark and the Daylight," *Ladies' Home Journal,* February, 1939) sits in her office, debating whether to stay and correct the important mistake she has made on the job, or keep her date with a man. She thinks back on her marriage, her baby, her husband's death . . . "the time afterward which held the struggle for clear judgment, not being afraid of new and better jobs, of having confidence in one's decisions." How can the boss expect her to give up her date! But she stays on the job. "They'd put their life's blood into this campaign. She couldn't let him down." She finds her man, too—the boss!

These stories may not have been great literature. But the identity of their heroines seemed to say something about the housewives who, then as now, read the women's magazines. These magazines were not written for career women. The New Woman heroines were the ideal of yesterday's housewives; they reflected the dreams, mirrored the yearning for identity and the sense of possibility that existed for women then. And if women could not have these dreams for themselves, they wanted their daughters to have them. They wanted their daughters to be more than housewives, to go out in the world that had been denied them.

It is like remembering a long-forgotten dream, to recapture the memory of what a career meant to women before "career woman" became a dirty word in America. Jobs meant money, of course, at the end of the depression. But the readers of these magazines were not the women who got the jobs; career meant more than job. It seemed to mean doing something, being somebody yourself, not just existing in and through others.

I found the last clear note of the passionate search for individual

identity that a career seems to have symbolized in the pre-1950 decades
in a story called "Sarah and the Seaplane," (*Ladies' Home Journal*,
February, 1949). Sarah, who for nineteen years has played the part of
docile daughter, is secretly learning to fly. She misses her flying lesson
to accompany her mother on a round of social calls. An elderly doctor
houseguest says: "My dear Sarah, every day, all the time, you are committing suicide. It's a greater crime than not pleasing others, not doing
justice to yourself." Sensing some secret, he asks if she is in love. "She
found it difficult to answer. In love? In love with the good-natured,
the beautiful Henry [the flying teacher]? In love with the flashing water
and the lift of wings at the instant of freedom, and the vision of the
smiling, limitless world? 'Yes,' she answered, 'I think I am.' "

The next morning, Sarah solos. Henry "stepped away, slamming
the cabin door shut, and swung the ship about for her. She was alone.
There was a heady moment when everything she had learned left her,
when she had to adjust herself to be alone, entirely alone in the familiar
cabin. Then she drew a deep breath and suddenly a wonderful sense
of competence made her sit erect and smiling. She was alone! She was
answerable to herself alone, and she was sufficient.

"'I can do it!' she told herself aloud. . . . The wind blew back
from the floats in glittering streaks, and then effortlessly the ship lifted
itself free and soared." Even her mother can't stop her now from getting
her flying license. She is not "afraid of discovering my own way of life."
In bed that night she smiles sleepily, remembering how Henry had
said, "You're my girl."

"Henry's girl! She smiled. No, she was not Henry's girl. She was
Sarah. And that was sufficient. And with such a late start it would be
some time before she got to know herself. Half in a dream now, she
wondered if at the end of that time she would need someone else and
who it would be."

And then suddenly the image blurs. The New Woman, soaring
free, hesitates in midflight, shivers in all that blue sunlight and rushes
back to the cozy walls of home. In the same year that Sarah soloed, the
Ladies' Home Journal printed the prototype of the innumerable paeans
to "Ocupation: Housewife" that started to appear in the women's magazines, paeans that resounded throughout the fifties. They usually begin
with a woman complaining that when she has to write "housewife" on
the census blank, she gets an inferiority complex. ("When I write it
I realize that here I am, a middle-aged woman, with a university education, and I've never made anything out of my life. I'm just a housewife.") Then the author of the paean, who somehow never is a
housewife (in this case, Dorothy Thompson, newspaper woman, foreign
correspondent, famous columnist, in *Ladies' Home Journal*, March,
1949), roars with laughter. The trouble with you, she scolds, is you
don't realize you are expert in a dozen careers, simultaneously. "You
might write: business manager, cook, nurse, chauffeur, dressmaker, interior decorator, accountant, caterer, teacher, private secretary—or just
put down philanthropist. . . . All your life you have been giving away
your energies, your skills, your talents, your services, for love." But

still, the housewife complains, I'm nearly fifty and I've never done what I hoped to do in my youth—music—I've wasted my college education.

Ho-ho, laughs Miss Thompson, aren't your children musical because of you, and all those struggling years while your husband was finishing his great work, didn't you keep a charming home on $3,000 a year, and make all your children's clothes and your own, and paper the living room yourself, and watch the markets like a hawk for bargains? And in time off, didn't you type and proofread your husband's manuscripts, plan festivals to make up the church deficit, play piano duets with the children to make practicing more fun, read their books in high-school to follow their study? "But all this vicarious living—through others," the housewife sighs. "As vicarious as Napoleon Bonaparte," Miss Thompson scoffs, "or a Queen. I simply refuse to share your self-pity. You are one of the most successful women I know."

As for not earning any money, the argument goes, let the housewife compute the cost of her services. Women can save more money by their managerial talents inside the home than they can bring into it by outside work. As for woman's spirit being broken by the boredom of household tasks, maybe the genius of some women has been thwarted, but "a world full of feminine genius, but poor in children, would come rapidly to an end. . . . Great men have great mothers."

And the American housewife is reminded that Catholic countries in the Middle Ages "elevated the gentle and inconspicuous Mary into the Queen of Heaven, and built their loveliest cathedrals to 'Notre Dame—Our Lady.' . . . The homemaker, the nurturer, the creator of children's environment is the constant recreator of culture, civilization, and virtue. Assuming that she is doing well that great managerial task and creative activity, let her write her occupation proudly: 'housewife.' "

In 1949, the *Ladies' Home Journal* also ran Margaret Mead's *Male and Female*. All the magazines were echoing Farnham and Lundberg's *Modern Woman: The Lost Sex,* which came out in 1942, with its warning that careers and higher education were leading to the "masculinization of women with enormously dangerous consequences to the home, the children dependent on it and to the ability of the woman, as well as her husband, to obtain sexual gratification."

And so the feminine mystique began to spread through the land, grafted onto old prejudices and comfortable conventions which so easily give the past a stranglehold on the future. Behind the new mystique were concepts and theories deceptive in their sophistication and their assumption of accepted truth. These theories were supposedly so complex that they were inaccessible to all but a few initiates, and therefore irrefutable. It will be necessary to break through this wall of mystery and look more closely at these complex concepts, these accepted truths, to understand fully what has happened to American women.

The feminine mystique says that the highest value and the only commitment for women is the fulfillment of their own femininity. It says that the great mistake of Western culture, through most of its history, has been the undervaluation of this femininity. It says this femininity is so mysterious and intuitive and close to the creation and origin of life that man-made science may never be able to understand it. But however special and different, it is in no way inferior to the nature of man; it may even in certain respects be superior. The mistake, says the mystique, the root of women's troubles in the past is that women envied men, women tried to be like men, instead of accepting their own nature, which can find fulfillment only in sexual passivity, male domination, and nurturing maternal love.

But the new image this mystique gives to American women is the old image: "Occupation: housewife." The new mystique makes the housewife-mothers, who never had a chance to be anything else, the model for all women; it presupposes that history has reached a final and glorious end in the here and now, as far as women are concerned. Beneath the sophisticated trappings, it simply makes certain concrete, finite, domestic aspects of feminine existence—as it was lived by women whose lives were confined, by necessity, to cooking, cleaning, washing, bearing children—into a religion, a pattern by which all women must now live or deny their femininity.

Fulfillment as a woman had only one definition for American women after 1949—the housewife-mother. As swiftly as in a dream, the image of the American woman as a changing, growing individual in a changing world was shattered. Her solo flight to find her own identity was forgotten in the rush for the security of togetherness. Her limitless world shrunk to the cozy walls of home.

The transformation, reflected in the pages of the women's magazines, was sharply visible in 1949 and progressive through the fifties. "Femininity Begins at Home," "It's a Man's World Maybe," "Have Babies While You're Young," "How to Snare a Male," "Should I Stop Work When We Marry?" "Are You Training Your Daughter to be a Wife?" "Careers at Home," "Do Women Have to Talk So Much?" "Why GI's Prefer Those German Girls," "What Women Can Learn from Mother Eve," "Really a Man's World, Politics," "How to Hold On to a Happy Marriage," "Don't Be Afraid to Marry Young," "The Doctor Talks about Breast-Feeding," "Our Baby Was Born at Home," "Cooking to Me is Poetry," "The Business of Running a Home."

By the end of 1949, only one out of three heroines in the women's magazines was a career woman—and she was shown in the act of renouncing her career and discovering that what she really wanted to be was a housewife. In 1958, and again in 1959, I went through issue after issue of the three major women's magazines (the fourth, *Woman's Home Companion,* had died) without finding a single heroine who had a career, a commitment to any work, art, profession, or mission in the world, other than "Occupation: housewife." Only one in a hundred heroines had a job; even the young unmarried heroines no longer worked except at snaring a husband.

These new happy housewife heroines seem strangely younger than the spirited career girls of the thirties and forties. They seem to get younger all the time—in looks, and a childlike kind of dependence. They have no vision of the future, except to have a baby. The only active growing figure in their world is the child. The housewife heroines are forever young, because their own image *ends* in childbirth. Like Peter Pan, they must remain young, while their children grow up with the world. They must keep on having babies, because the feminine mystique says there is no other way for a woman to be a heroine. Here is a typical specimen from a story called "The Sandwich Maker" (*Ladies' Home Journal,* April, 1959). She took home economics in college, learned how to cook, never held a job, and still plays the child bride, though she now has three children of her own. Her problem is money. "Oh, nothing boring, like taxes or reciprocal trade agreements, or foreign aid programs. I leave all that economic jazz to my constitutionally elected representative in Washington, heaven help him."

The problem is her $42.10 allowance. She hates having to ask her husband for money every time she needs a pair of shoes, but he won't trust her with a charge account. "Oh, how I yearned for a little money of my own! Not much, really. A few hundred a year would have done it. Just enough to meet a friend for lunch occasionally, to indulge in extravagantly colored stockings, a few small items, without having to appeal to Charley. But, alas, Charley was right. I had never earned a dollar in my life, and had no idea how money was made. So all I did for a long time was brood, as I continued with my cooking, cleaning, cooking, washing, ironing, cooking."

At last the solution comes—she will take orders for sandwiches from other men at her husband's plant. She earns $52.50 a week, except that she forgets to count costs, and she doesn't remember what a gross is so she has to hide 8,640 sandwich bags behind the furnace. Charley says she's making the sandwiches too fancy. She explains: "If it's only ham on rye, then I'm just a sandwich maker, and I'm not interested. But the extras, the special touches—well, they make it sort of creative." So she chops, wraps, peels, seals, spreads bread, starting at dawn and never finished, for $9.00 net, until she is disgusted by the smell of food, and finally staggers downstairs after a sleepless night to slice a salami for the eight gaping lunch boxes. "It was too much. Charley came down just then, and after one quick look at me, ran for a glass of water." She realizes that she is going to have another baby.

"Charley's first coherent words were 'I'll cancel your lunch orders. You're a mother. That's your job. You don't have to earn money, too.' It was all so beautifully simple! 'Yes, boss,' I murmured obediently, frankly relieved." That night he brings her home a checkbook; he will trust her with a joint account. So she decides just to keep quiet about the 8,640 sandwich bags. Anyhow, she'll have used them up, making sandwiches for four children to take to school, by the time the youngest is ready for college.

The road from Sarah and the seaplane to the sandwich maker was traveled in only ten years. In those ten years, the image of American woman seems to have suffered a schizophrenic split. And the split in the image goes much further than the savage obliteration of career from women's dreams.

In an earlier time, the image of woman was also split in two—the good, pure woman on the pedestal, and the whore of the desires of the flesh. The split in the new image opens a different fissure—the feminine woman, whose goodness includes the desires of the flesh, and the career woman whose evil includes every desire of the separate self. The new feminine morality story is the exorcising of the forbidden career dream, the heroine's victory over Mephistopheles: the devil, first in the form of a career woman, who threatens to take away the heroine's husband or child, and finally, the devil inside the heroine herself, the dream of independence, the discontent of spirit, and even the feeling of a separate identity that must be exorcised to win or keep the love of husband and child.

In a story in *Redbook* ("A Man Who Acted Like a Husband," November, 1957) the child-bride heroine, "a little freckle-faced brunette" whose nickname is "Junior," is visited by her old college roommate. The roommate Kay is "a man's girl, really, with a good head for business . . . she wore her polished mahogany hair in a high chignon, speared with two chopstick affairs." Kay is not only divorced, but she has also left her child with his grandmother while she works in television. This career-woman-devil tempts Junior with the lure of a job to keep her from breast-feeding her baby. She even restrains the young mother from going to her baby when he cries at 2 A.M. But she gets her comeuppance when George, the husband, discovers the crying baby uncovered, in a freezing wind from an open window, with blood running down its cheek. Kay, reformed and repentant, plays hookey from her job to go get her own child and start life anew. And Junior, gloating at the 2 A.M. feeding—"I'm glad, glad, glad I'm just a housewife" starts to dream about the baby, growing up to be a housewife, too.

With the career woman out of the way, the housewife with interests in the community becomes the devil to be exorcised. Even PTA takes on a suspect connotation, not to mention interest in some international cause (see "Almost a Love Affair," *McCall's,* November, 1955). The housewife who simply has a mind of her own is the next to go. The heroine of "I Didn't Want to Tell You" (*McCall's,* January, 1958) is shown balancing the checkbook by herself and arguing with her husband about a small domestic detail. It develops that she is losing her husband to a "helpless little widow" whose main appeal is that she can't "think straight" about an insurance policy or mortgage. The betrayed wife says: "She must have sex appeal and what weapon has a wife against that?" But her best friend tells her: "You're making this too simple. You're forgetting how helpless Tania can be, and how grateful to the man who helps her . . ."

"I couldn't be a clinging vine if I tried," the wife says. "I had a better than average job after I left college and I was always a pretty independent person. I'm not a helpless little woman and I can't pretend to be." But she learns, that night. She hears a noise that might be a burglar; even though she knows it's only a mouse, she calls helplessly to her husband, and wins him back. As he comforts her pretended panic, she murmurs that, of course, he was right in their argument that morning. "She lay still in the soft bed, smiling sweet, secret satisfaction, scarcely touched with guilt."

The end of the road, in an almost literal sense, is the disappearance of the heroine altogether, as a separate self and the subject of her own story. The end of the road is togetherness, where the woman has no independent self to hide even in guilt; she exists only for and through her husband and children.

Coined by the publishers of *McCall's* in 1954, the concept "togetherness" was seized upon avidly as a movement of spiritual significance by advertisers, ministers, newspaper editors. For a time, it was elevated into virtually a national purpose. But very quickly there was sharp social criticism, and bitter jokes about "togetherness" as a substitute for larger human goals—for men. Women were taken to task for making their husbands do housework, instead of letting them pioneer in the nation and the world. Why, it was asked, should men with the capacities of statesmen, anthropologists, physicists, poets, have to wash dishes and diaper babies on weekday evenings or Saturday mornings when they might use those extra hours to fulfill larger commitments to their society?

Significantly, critics resented only that men were being asked to share "woman's world." Few questioned the boundaries of this world for women. No one seemed to remember that women were once thought to have the capacity and vision of statesmen, poets, and physicists. Few saw the big lie of togetherness for women.

Consider the Easter 1954 issue of *McCall's* which announced the new era of togetherness, sounding the requiem for the days when women fought for and won political equality, and the women's magazines "helped you to carve out large areas of living formerly forbidden to your sex." The new way of life in which "men and women in ever-increasing numbers are marrying at an earlier age, having children at an earlier age, rearing larger families and gaining their deepest satisfaction" from their own homes, is one which "men, women and children are achieving together . . . not as women alone, or men alone, isolated from one another, but as a family, sharing a common experience."

The picture essay detailing that way of life is called "a man's place is in the home." It describes, as the new image and ideal, a New Jersey couple with three children in a gray-shingle split-level house. Ed and Carol have "centered their lives almost completely around their children and their home." They are shown shopping at the supermarket, carpentering, dressing the children, making breakfast together. "Then Ed joins the members of his car pool and heads for the office."

Ed, the husband, chooses the color scheme for the house and makes the major decorating decisions. The chores Ed likes are listed: putter around the house, make things, paint, select furniture, rugs and draperies, dry dishes, read to the children and put them to bed, work in the garden, feed and dress and bathe the children, attend PTA meetings, cook, buy clothes for his wife, buy groceries.

Ed doesn't like these chores: dusting, vacuuming, finishing jobs he's started, hanging draperies, washing pots and pans and dishes, picking up after the children, shoveling snow or mowing the lawn, changing diapers, taking the baby-sitter home, doing the laundry, ironing. Ed, of course, does not do these chores.

For the sake of every member of the family, the family needs a head. This means Father, not Mother. . . . Children of both sexes need to learn, recognize and respect the abilities and functions of each sex. . . . He is not just a substitute mother, even though he's ready and willing to do his share of bathing, feeding, comforting, playing. He is a link with the outside world he works in. If in that world he is interested, courageous, tolerant, constructive, he will pass on these values to his children.

There were many agonized editorial sessions, in those days at *McCall's*. "Suddenly, everybody was looking for this spiritual significance in togetherness, expecting us to make some mysterious religious movement out of the life everyone had been leading for the last five years—crawling into the home, turning their backs on the world—but we never could find a way of showing it that wasn't a monstrosity of dullness," a former *McCall's* editor reminisces. "It always boiled down to, goody, goody, goody, Daddy is out there in the garden barbecuing. We put men in the fashion pictures and the food pictures, and even the perfume pictures. But we were stifled by it editorially.

"We had articles by psychiatrists that we couldn't use because they would have blown it wide open: all those couples propping their whole weight on their kids but what else could you do with togetherness but child care? We were pathetically grateful to find anything else where we could show father photographed with mother. Sometimes, we used to wonder what would happen to women, with men taking over the decorating, child care, cooking, all the things that used to be hers alone. But we couldn't show women getting out of the home and having a career. The irony is, what we meant to do was to stop editing for women as women, and edit for the men and women together. We wanted to edit for people, not women."

But forbidden to join man in the world, can women be people? Forbidden independence, they finally are swallowed in an image of such passive dependence that they want men to make the decisions, even in the home. The frantic illusion that togetherness can impart a spiritual content to the dullness of domestic routine, the need for a religious movement to make up for the lack of identity, betrays the measure of women's loss and the emptiness of the image. Could making men share the housework compensate women for their loss of the world? Could vacuuming the living-room floor together give the housewife some mysterious new purpose in life?

In 1956, at the peak of togetherness, the bored editors of *McCall's* ran a little article called "The Mother Who Ran Away." To their amazement, it brought the highest readership of any article they had ever run. "It was our moment of truth," said a former editor. "We suddenly realized that all those women at home with their three and a half children were miserably unhappy."

But by then the new image of American woman, "Occupation:

housewife," had hardened into a mystique, unquestioned and permitting no questions, shaping the very reality is distorted.

By the time I started writing for women's magazines, in the fifties, it was simply taken for granted by editors, and accepted as an immutable fact of life by writers, that women were not interested in politics, life outside the United States, national issues, art, science, ideas, adventure, education, or even their own communities, except where they could be sold through their emotions as wives and mothers.

Politics, for women, became Mamie's clothes and the Nixons' home life. Out of conscience, a sense of duty, the *Ladies' Home Journal* might run a series like "Political Pilgrim's Progress," showing women trying to improve their children's schools and playgrounds. But even approaching politics through mother love did not really interest women, it was thought in the trade. Everyone knew those readership percentages. An editor of *Redbook* ingeniously tried to bring the bomb down to the feminine level by showing the emotions of a wife whose husband sailed into a contaminated area.

"Women can't take an idea, an issue, pure," men who edited the mass women's magazines agreed. "It had to be translated in terms they can understand as women." This was so well understood by those who wrote for women's magazines that a natural childbirth expert submitted an article to a leading woman's magazine called "How to Have a Baby in a Atom Bomb Shelter." "The article was not well written," an editor told me, "or we might have bought it." According to the mystique, women, in their mysterious femininity, might be interested in the concrete biological details of having a baby in a bomb shelter, but never in the abstract idea of the bomb's power to destroy the human race.

Such a belief, of course, becomes a self-fulfilling prophecy. In 1960, a perceptive social psychologist showed me some sad statistics which seemed to prove unmistakably that American women under thirty-five are not interested in politics. "They may have the vote, but they don't dream about running for office," he told me. "If you write a political piece, they won't read it. You have to translate it into issues they can understand—romance, pregnancy, nursing, home furnishings, clothes. Run an article on the economy, or the race question, civil rights, and you'd think that women had never heard of them."

Maybe they hadn't heard of them. Ideas are not like instincts of the blood that spring into the mind intact. They are communicated by education, by the printed word. The new young housewives, who leave high school or college to marry, do not read books, the psychological surveys say. They only read magazines. Magazines today assume women are not interested in ideas. But going back to the bound volumes in the library, I found in the thirties and forties that the mass-circulation magazines like *Ladies' Home Journal* carried hundreds of articles about the world outside the home. "The first inside story of American diplomatic relations preceding declared war"; "Can the U.S. Have Peace After This War?" by Walter Lippmann; "Stalin at Midnight," by Harold Stassen; "General Stilwell Reports on China"; articles about the last days of Czechoslovakia by Vincent Sheean; the persecution of Jews in Germany; the New Deal; Carl Sandburg's account of Lincoln's assassination; Faulkner's stories of Mississippi, and Margaret Sanger's battle for birth control.

In the 1950's they printed virtually no articles except those that serviced women as housewives, or described women as housewives, or permitted a purely feminine identification like the Duchess of Windsor or Princess Margaret. "If we get an article about a woman who does anything adventurous, out of the way, something by herself, you know, we figure she must be terribly aggressive, neurotic," a *Ladies' Home Journal* editor told me. Margaret Sanger would never get in today.

In 1960, I saw statistics that showed that women under thirty-five could not identify with a spirited heroine of a story who worked in an ad agency and persuaded the boy to stay and fight for his principles in the big city instead of running home to the security of a family business. Nor could these new young housewives identify with a young minister, acting on his belief in defiance of convention. But they had no trouble at all identifying with a young man paralyzed at eighteen. ("I regained consciousness to discover that I could not move or even speak. I could wiggle only one finger of one hand." With help from faith and a psychiatrist, "I am now finding reasons to live as fully as possible.")

Does it say something about the new housewife readers that, as any editor can testify, they can identify completely with the victims of blindness, deafness, physical maiming, cerebral palsy, paralysis, cancer, or approaching death? Such articles about people who cannot see or speak or move have been an enduring staple of the women's magazines in the era of "Occupation: housewife." They are told with infinitely realistic detail over and over again, replacing the articles about the nation, the world, ideas, issues, art and science; replacing the stories about adventurous spirited women. And whether the victim is man, woman or child, whether the living death is incurable cancer or creeping paralysis, the housewife reader can identify. . . .

A baked potato is not as big as the world, and vacuuming the living room floor—with or without makeup—is not work that takes enough thought or energy to challenge any woman's full capacity. Women are human beings, not stuffed dolls, not animals. Down through the ages man has known that he was set apart from other animals by his mind's power to have an idea, a vision, and shape the future to it. He shares a need for food and sex with other animals, but when he loves, he loves as a man, and when he discovers and creates and shapes a future different from his past, he is a man, a human being.

This is the real mystery: why did so many American women, with the ability and education to discover and create, go back home again, to look for "something more" in housework and rearing children? For, paradoxically, in the same fifteen years in which the spirited New Woman was replaced by the Happy Housewife, the boundaries of the human world have widened, the pace of world change has quickened, and the very nature of human reality has become increasingly free from biological and material necessity. Does the mystique keep American woman from growing with the world? Does it force her to deny reality, as a woman in a mental hospital must deny reality to believe she is a queen? Does it doom women to be displaced persons, if not virtual schizophrenics, in our complex, changing world?

It is more than a strange paradox that as all professions are finally open to women in America, "career woman" has become a dirty word; that as higher education becomes available to any woman with the capacity for it, education for women has become so suspect that more and more drop out of high school and college to marry and have babies; that as so many roles in modern society become theirs for the taking, women so insistently confine themselves to one role. Why, with the removal of all the legal, political, economic, and educational barriers that once kept woman from being man's equal, a person in her own right, an individual free to develop her own potential, should she accept this new image which insists she is not a person but a "woman," by definition barred from the freedom of human existence and a voice in human destiny?

The feminine mystique is so powerful that women grow up no longer knowing that they have the desires and capacities the mystique forbids. But such a mystique does not fasten itself on a whole nation in a few short years, reversing the trends of a century, without cause. What gives the mystique its power? Why did women go home again?

The Texture of Poverty

MICHAEL HARRINGTON

The poor, Michael Harrington urges us, "need an American Dickens to record the smell and texture and quality of their lives." Yet his own brilliant mixture of reporting and social analysis served the essential purpose of encouraging a compassionate view of the poor, which meant first forcing people to see them. The book remains curiously stirring— what we might expect from a novel, but not from a book which constantly quotes the findings of empirical social science.

The Other America, from which this excerpt by Harrington is taken, was one of several muckraking social-science works that forced a new perspective on poverty in modern America. John Kenneth Galbraith in The Affluent Society had pointed to the persistence of poverty amid affluence and questioned whether economic growth alone would eradicate it. Robert Lampman and Gabriel Kolko demonstrated that the New Deal had not significantly changed the distribution of wealth. All these writers cleave the path for a new liberal program that, ironically, undermined the claims of older liberals that the New Deal had reformed the economy in the interest of poorer Americans.

Harrington's book continues to be the most vital of the many polemics that muckraked American society in the late fifties and the sixties. It was an important book because it helped launch a war on poverty which, for all its shortcomings, has made a real difference. For one thing the poor are no longer so invisible or politically powerless. They make themselves known despite official efforts to eliminate the word "poverty" from the national vocabulary. This is not to say that they may never become "invisible" again: The job that Harrington did in the early sixties (like Dickens' a century before) will clearly need constant redoing.

I

There are perennial reasons that make the other America an invisible land.

Poverty is often off the beaten track. It always has been. The ordinary tourist never left the main highway, and today he rides interstate turnpikes. He does not go into the valleys of Pennsylvania where the towns look like movie sets of Wales in the thirties. He does not see the company houses in rows, the rutted roads (the poor always have bad roads whether they live in the city, in towns, or on farms), and everything is black and dirty. And even if he were to pass through such a place by accident, the tourist would not meet the unemployed men in the bar or the women coming home from a runaway sweatshop.

Then, too, beauty and myths are perennial masks of poverty. The traveler comes to the Appalachians in the lovely season. He sees the hills, the streams, the foliage—but not the poor. Or perhaps he looks at a run-down mountain house and, remembering Rousseau rather than seeing with his eyes, decides that "those people" are truly fortunate to be living the way they are and that they are lucky to be exempt from the strains and tensions of the middle class. The only problem is that "those people," the quaint inhabitants of those hills, are undereducated, underprivileged, lack medical care, and are in the process of being forced from the land into a life in the cities, where they are misfits.

These are normal and obvious causes of the invisibility of the poor. They operated a generation ago; they will be functioning a generation hence. It is more important to understand that the very development of American society is creating a new kind of blindness about poverty. The poor are increasingly slipping out of the very experience and consciousness of the nation.

If the middle class never did like ugliness and poverty, it was at least aware of them. "Across the tracks" was not a very long way to go. There were forays into the slums at Christmas time; there were charitable organizations that brought contact with the poor. Occasionally, almost everyone passed through the Negro ghetto or the blocks of tenements, if only to get downtown to work or to entertainment.

Now the American city has been transformed. The poor still inhabit the miserable housing in the central area, but they are increasingly isolated from contact with, or sight of, anybody else. Middle-class women coming in from Suburbia on a rare trip may catch the merest glimpse of the other America on the way to an evening at the theater, but their children are segregated in suburban schools. The business or professional man may drive along the fringes of slums in a car or bus, but it is not an important experience to him. The failures, the unskilled, the disabled, the aged, and the minorities are right there, across the tracks, where they have always been. But hardly anyone else is.

In short, the very development of the American city has removed poverty from the living, emotional experience of millions upon millions of middle-class Americans. Living out in the suburbs it is easy to assume that ours is, indeed, an affluent society.

This new segregation of poverty is compounded by a well-meaning ignorance. A good many concerned and sympathetic Americans are aware that there is much discussion of urban renewal. Suddenly, driving through the city, they notice that a familiar slum has been torn down and that there are towering, modern buildings where once there had been tenements or hovels. There is a warm feeling of satisfaction, of pride in the way things are working out: the poor, it is obvious, are being taken care of.

The irony in this . . . is that the truth is nearly the exact opposite to the impression. The total impact of the various housing programs in postwar America has been to squeeze more and more people into existing slums. More often than not, the modern apartment in a towering building rents at $40 a room or more. For, during the past decade and a half, there has been more subsidization of middle- and upper-income housing than there has been of housing for the poor.

Clothes make the poor invisible too: America has the best-dressed poverty the world has ever known. For a variety of reasons, the benefits of mass production have been spread much more evenly in this area than in many others. It is much easier in the United States to be decently dressed than it is to be decently housed, fed, or doctored. Even people with terribly depressed incomes can look prosperous.

This is an extremely important factor in defining our emotional and existential ignorance of poverty. In Detroit the existence of social classes became much more difficult to discern the day the companies put lockers in the plants. From that moment on, one did not see men in work clothes on the way to the factory, but citizens in slacks and white shirts. This process has been magnified with the poor throughout the country. There are tens of thousands of Americans in the big cities who are wearing shoes, perhaps even a stylishly cut suit or dress, and yet are hungry. It is not a matter of planning, though it almost seems as if the affluent society had given out costumes to the poor so that they would not offend the rest of society with the sight of rags.

Then, many of the poor are the wrong age to be seen. A good number of them (over 8,000,000) are sixty-five years of age or better; an even larger number are under eighteen. The aged members of the other America are often sick, and they cannot move. Another group of them live out their lives in loneliness and frustration: they sit in rented rooms, or else they stay close to a house in a neighborhood that has completely changed from the old days. Indeed, one of the worst aspects of poverty among the aged is that these people are out of sight and out of mind, and alone.

The young are somewhat more visible, yet they too stay close to their neighborhoods. Sometimes they advertise their poverty through a lurid tabloid story about a gang killing. But generally they do not disturb the quiet streets of the middle class.

And finally, the poor are politically invisible. It is one of the cruelest ironies of social life in advanced countries that the dispossessed at the bottom of society are unable to speak for themselves. The people of the other America do not, by far and large, belong to unions, to fraternal organizations, or to political parties. They are without lobbies of their own; they put forward no legislative program. As a group, they are atomized. They have no face; they have no voice. . . .

II

Out of the thirties came the welfare state. Its creation had been stimulated by mass impoverishment and misery, yet it helped the poor least of all. Laws like unemployment compensation, the Wagner Act, the various farm programs, all these were designed for the middle third in the cities, for the organized workers, and for the upper third in the country, for the big market farmers. If a man works in an extremely low-paying job, he may not even be covered by social security or other welfare programs. If he receives unemployment compensation, the payment is scaled down according to his low earnings.

One of the major laws that was designed to cover everyone, rich and poor, was social security. But even here the other Americans suffered discrimination. Over the years social security payments have not even provided a subsistence level of life. The middle third have been able to supplement the Federal pension through private plans negotiated by unions, through joining medical insurance schemes like Blue Cross, and so on. The poor have not been able to do so. They lead a bitter life, and then have to pay for that fact in old age.

Indeed, the paradox that the welfare state benefits those least who need help most is but a single instance of a persistent irony in the other America. Even when the money finally trickles down, even when a school is built in a poor neighborhood, for instance, the poor are still deprived. Their entire environment, their life, their values, do not prepare them to take advantage of the new opportunity. The parents are anxious for the children to go to work; the pupils are pent up, waiting for the moment when their education has complied with the law.

Today's poor, in short, missed the political and social gains of the thirties. They are, as Galbraith rightly points out, the first minority poor in history, the first poor not to be seen, the first poor whom the politicians could leave alone.

The first step toward the new poverty was taken when millions of people proved immune to progress. When that happened, the failure was not individual and personal, but a social product. But once the historic accident takes place, it begins to become a personal fate.

The new poor of the other America saw the rest of society move ahead. They went on living in depressed areas, and often they tended to become depressed human beings. In some of the West Virginia towns, for instance, an entire community will become shabby and defeated. The young and the adventurous go to the city, leaving behind those who cannot move and those who lack the will to do so. The entire area becomes permeated with failure, and that is one more reason the big corporations shy away.

Indeed, one of the most important things about the new poverty is that it cannot be defined in simple, statistical terms. Throughout this book a crucial term is used: aspiration. If a group has internal vitality, a will—if it has aspiration—it may live in dilapidated housing, it may eat an inadequate diet, and it may suffer poverty, but it is not impoverished. So it was in those ethnic slums of the immigrants that played such a dramatic role in the unfolding of the American dream. The people found themselves in slums, but they were not slum dwellers.

But the new poverty is constructed so as to destroy aspiration; it is a system designed to be impervious to hope. The other America does not contain the adventurous seeking a new life and land. It is populated by the failures, by those driven from the land and bewildered by the city, by old people suddenly confronted with the torments of loneliness and poverty, and by minorities facing a wall of prejudice.

In the past, when poverty was general in the unskilled and semiskilled work force, the poor were all mixed together. The bright and the dull, those who were going to escape into the great society and those who were to stay behind, all of them lived on the same street. When the middle third rose, this community was destroyed. And the entire invisible land of the other Americans became a ghetto, a modern poor farm for the rejects of society and of the economy.

It is a blow to reform and the political hopes of the poor that the middle class no longer understands that poverty exists. But, perhaps more important, the poor are losing their links with the great world. If statistics and sociology can measure a feeling as delicate as loneliness (and some of the attempts to do so will be cited later on), the other America is becoming increasingly populated by those who do not belong to anybody or anything. They are no longer participants in an ethnic culture from the old country; they are less and less religious; they do not belong to unions or clubs. They are not seen, and because of that they themselves cannot see. Their horizon has become more and more restricted; they see one another, and that means they see little reason to hope.

Galbraith was one of the first writers to begin to describe the newness of contemporary poverty, and that is to his credit. Yet because even he underestimates the problem, it is important to put his definition into perspective.

For Galbraith, there are two main components of the new poverty: case poverty and insular poverty. Case poverty is the plight of those who suffer from some physical or mental disability that is personal and individual and excludes them from the general advance. Insular poverty exists in areas like the Appalachians or the West Virginia coal fields, where an entire section of the country becomes economically obsolete.

Physical and mental disabilities are, to be sure, an important part of poverty in America. The poor are sick in body and in spirit. But this is not an isolated fact about them, an individual "case," a stroke of bad luck. Disease, alcoholism, low IQ's, these express a whole way of life. They are, in the main, the effects of an environment, not the biographies of unlucky individuals. Because of this, the new poverty is something that cannot be dealt with by first aid. If there is to be a lasting assault on the shame of the other America, it must seek to root out of this society an entire environment, and not just the relief of individuals.

But perhaps the idea of "insular" poverty is even more dangerous. To speak of "islands" of the poor (or, in the more popular term, of "pockets of poverty") is to imply that one is confronted by a serious, but relatively minor, problem. This is hardly a description of a misery that extends to 40,000,000 or 50,000,000 people in the United States. They have remained impoverished in spite of increasing productivity and the creation of a welfare state. That fact alone should suggest the dimensions of a serious and basic situation.

And yet, even given these disagreements with Galbraith, his achievement is considerable. He was one of the first to understand that there are enough poor people in the United States to constitute a subculture of misery, but not enough of them to challenge the conscience and the imagination of the nation.

Finally, one might summarize the newness of contemporary poverty by saying: These are the people who are immune to progress. But then the facts are even more cruel. The other Americans are the victims of the very inventions and machines that have provided a higher living standard for the rest of the society. They are upside-down in the economy, and for them greater productivity often means worse jobs; agricultural advance becomes hunger.

In the optimistic theory, technology is an undisguised blessing. A general increase in productivity, the argument goes, generates a higher standard of living for the whole people. And indeed, this has been true for the middle and upper thirds of American society, the people who made such striking gains in the last two decades. It tends to overstate the automatic character of the process, to omit the role of human struggle. (The CIO was organized by men in conflict, not by economic trends.) Yet it states a certain truth—for those who are lucky enough to participate in it.

But the poor, if they were given to theory, might argue the exact opposite. They might say: Progress is misery.

As the society became more technological, more skilled, those who learn to work the machines, who get the expanding education, move up. Those who miss out at the very start find themselves at a new disadvantage. A generation ago in American life, the majority of the working people did not have high-school educations. But at that time industry was organized on a lower level of skill and competence. And there was a sort of continuum in the shop: the youth who left school at sixteen could begin as a laborer, and gradually pick up skill as he went along.

Today the situation is quite different. The good jobs require much more academic preparation, much more skill from the very outset. Those who lack a high-school education tend to be condemned to the economic underworld—to low-paying service industries, to backward factories, to sweeping and janitorial duties. If the fathers and mothers of the contemporary poor were penalized a generation ago for their lack of schooling, their children will suffer all the more. The very rise in productivity that created more money and better working conditions for the rest of the society can be a menace to the poor.

But then this technological revolution might have an even more disastrous consequence: it could increase the ranks of the poor as well as intensify the disabilities of poverty. At this point it is too early to make any final judgment, yet there are obvious danger signals. There are millions of Americans who live just the other side of poverty. When a recession comes, they are pushed onto the relief rolls. (Welfare payments in New York respond almost immediately to any economic decline.) If automation continues to inflict more and more penalties on the unskilled and the semiskilled, it could have the impact of permanently increasing the population of the other America.

Even more explosive is the possibility that people who participated in the gains of the thirties and the forties will be pulled back down into poverty. Today the mass-production industries where unionization made such a difference are contracting. Jobs are being destroyed. In the process, workers who had achieved a certain level of wages, who had won working conditions in the shop, are suddenly confronted with impoverishment. This is particularly true for anyone over forty years of age and for members of minority groups. Once their job is abolished, their chances of ever getting similar work are very slim.

It is too early to say whether or not this phenomenon is temporary, or whether it represents a massive retrogression that will swell the numbers of the poor. To a large extent, the answer to this question will be determined by the political response of the United States in the sixties. If serious and massive action is not undertaken, it may be necessary for statisticians to add some old-fashioned, pre-welfare-state poverty to the misery of the other America.

Poverty in the 1960's is invisible and it is new, and both these factors make it more tenacious. It is more isolated and politically powerless than ever before. It is laced with ironies, not the least of which is that many of the poor view progress upside-down, as a menace and a threat to their lives. And if the nation does not measure up to the challenge of automation, poverty in the 1960's might be on the increase.

There are mighty historical and economic forces that keep the poor down; and there are human beings who help out in this grim business, many of them unwittingly. There are sociological and political reasons why poverty is not seen; and there are misconceptions and prejudices that literally blind the eyes. The latter must be understood if anyone is to make the necessary act of intellect and will so that the poor can be noticed.

Here is the most familiar version of social blindness: "The poor are that way because they are afraid of work. And anyway they all have big cars. If they were like me (or my father or my grandfather), they could pay their own way. But they prefer to live on the dole and cheat the taxpayers."

This theory, usually thought of as a virtuous and moral statement, is one of the means of making it impossible for the poor ever to pay their way. There are, one must assume, citizens of the other America who choose impoverishment out of fear of work (though, writing it down, I really do not believe it). But the real explanation of why the poor are where they are is that they made the mistake of being born to the wrong parents, in the wrong section of the country, in the wrong industry, or in the wrong racial or ethnic group. Once that mistake has been made, they could have been paragons of will and morality, but most of them would never even have had a chance to get out of the other America.

There are two important ways of saying this: The poor are caught in a vicious circle; or, The poor live in a culture of poverty.

In a sense, one might define the contemporary poor in the United States as those who, for reasons beyond their control, cannot help themselves. All the most decisive factors making for opportunity and advance are against them. They are born going downward, and most of them stay down. They are victims whose lives are endlessly blown round and round the other America.

Here is one of the most familiar forms of the vicious circle of poverty. The poor get sick more than anyone else in the society. That is because they live in slums, jammed together under unhygienic conditions; they have inadequate diets, and cannot get decent medical care. When they become sick, they are sick longer than any other group in the society. Because they are sick more often and longer than anyone else, they lose wages and work, and find it difficult to hold a steady job. And because of this, they cannot pay for good housing, for a nutritious diet, for doctors. At any given point in the circle, particularly when there is a major illness, their prospect is to move to an even lower level and to begin the cycle, round and round, toward even more suffering.

This is only one example of the vicious circle. Each group in the other America has its own particular version of the experience, and these will be detailed throughout this book. But the pattern, whatever its variations, is basic to the other America.

The individual cannot usually break out of this vicious circle. Neither can the group, for it lacks the social energy and political strength to turn its misery into a cause. Only the larger society, with its help and resources, can really make it possible for these people to help themselves. Yet those who could make the difference too often refuse to act because of their ignorant, smug moralisms. They view the effects of poverty—above all, the warping of the will and spirit that is a consequence of being poor—as choices. Understanding the vicious circle is an important step in breaking down this prejudice.

There is an even richer way of describing this same, general idea: Poverty in the United States is a culture, an institution, a way of life.

There is a famous anecdote about Ernest Hemingway and F. Scott Fitzgerald. Fitzgerald is reported to have remarked to Hemingway, "The rich are different." And Hemingway replied, "Yes, they have money." Fitzgerald had much the better of the exchange. He understood that being rich was not a simple fact, like a large bank account, but a way of looking at reality, a series of attitudes, a special type of life. If this is true of the rich, it is ten times truer of the poor. Everything about them, from the condition of their teeth to the way in which they love, is suffused and permeated by the fact of their poverty. And this is sometimes a hard idea for a Hemingway-like middle-class America to comprehend.

The family structure of the poor, for instance, is different from that of the rest of the society. There are more homes without a father, there are less marriage, more early pregnancy and if Kinsey's statistical findings can be used, markedly different attitudes toward sex. As a result of this, to take but one consequence of the fact, hundreds of thousands, and perhaps millions, of children in the other America never know stability and "normal" affection.

Or perhaps the policeman is an even better example. For the middle class, the police protect property, give directions, and help old ladies. For the urban poor, the police are those who arrest you. In almost any slum there is a vast conspiracy against the forces of law and order. If someone approaches asking for a person, no one there will have heard of him, even if he lives next door. The outsider is "cop," bill collector, investigator (and, in the Negro ghetto, most dramatically, he is "the Man").

While writing this book, I was arrested for participation in a civil-rights demonstration. A brief experience of a night in a cell made an abstraction personal and immediate: the city jail is one of the basic institutions of the other America. Almost everyone whom I encountered in the "tank" was poor: skid-row whites, Negroes, Puerto Ricans. Their poverty was an incitement to arrest in the first place. (A policeman will be much more careful with a well-dressed, obviously educated man who might have political connections than he will with someone who is poor.) They did not have money for bail or for lawyers. And, perhaps most important, they waited their arraignment with stolidity, in a mood of passive acceptance. They expected the worst, and they probably got it.

There is, in short, a language of the poor, a psychology of the poor, a world view of the poor. To be impoverished is to be an internal alien, to grow up in a culture that is radically different from the one that dominates the society. The poor can be described statistically; they can be analyzed as a group. But they need a novelist as well as a sociologist if we are to see them. They need an American Dickens to record the smell and texture and quality of their lives. The cycles and trends, the massive forces, must be seen as affecting persons who talk and think differently.

I am not that novelist. Yet in this book I have attempted to describe the faces behind the statistics, to tell a little of the "thickness" of personal life in the other America. Of necessity, I have begun with large groups: the dispossessed workers, the minorities, the farm poor, and the aged. Then, there are three cases of less massive types of poverty, including the only single humorous component in the other America. And finally, there are the slums, and the psychology of the poor.

Throughout, I work on an assumption that cannot be proved by Government figures or even documented by impressions of the other America. It is an ethical proposition, and it can be simply stated: In a nation with a technology that could provide every citizen with a decent life, it is an outrage and a scandal that there should be such social misery. Only if one begins with this assumption is it possible to pierce through the invisibility of 40,000,000 to 50,000,000 human beings and to see the other America. We must perceive passionately, if this blindness is to be lifted from us. . . .

III

There are few people in the United States who accept Rousseau's image of the "noble savage," of primitive, untutored man as being more natural than, and superior to, his civilized descendants. Such an idea could hardly survive in a society that has made technological progress one of its most central values. There are occasional daydreams about "getting away from it all," of going to an idyllic countryside, but these are usually passing fancies.

Yet, there is a really important remnant of Rousseau's myth. It is the conviction that, as far as emotional disturbance and mental disease go, the poor are noble savages and the rich are the prime victims of tension and conflict.

There are the literature of the harried executive, the tales of suburban neurosis, the theme of the danger of wealth and leisure. It is not so much that anyone says that the poor are healthy in spirit because they are deprived of material things. Rather, the poor are just forgotten, as usual. The novels and the popular sociology are written by the middle class about the middle class, and there is more than a little strain of self-pity. The result is an image in which personal maladjustment flourishes at the top of the society, the price the well-off pay for their power. As you go down the income scale, this theory implies, life becomes more tedious and humdrum, if less upset. (However, it should be noted that the white-collar strata have the chronicler of their quiet desperation in Paddy Chayevsky.)

The truth is almost exactly opposite to the myth. The poor are subject to more mental illness than anyone else in the society, and their disturbances tend to be more serious than those of any other class. This conclusion has emerged from a series of studies made over the past few decades. There is still considerable controversy and disagreement with regard to the reasons behind this situation. But the fact itself would seem to be beyond dispute.

Indeed, if there is any point in American society where one can see poverty as a culture, as a way of life, it is here. There is, in a sense, a personality of poverty, a type of human being produced by the grinding, wearing life of the slums. The other Americans feel differently than the rest of the nation. They tend to be hopeless and passive, yet prone to bursts of violence; they are lonely and isolated, often rigid and hostile. To be poor is not simply to be deprived of the material things of this world. It is to enter a fatal, futile universe, an America within America with a twisted spirit.

Perhaps the most classic (but still controversial) study of this subject is the book *Social Class and Mental Illness* by August B. Hollingshead and F. C. Redlich. Published in 1958, it summarizes a careful research project in New Haven, Connecticut. It is an academic, scholarly work, yet its statistics are the description of an abyss.

Hollingshead and Redlich divided New Haven into five social classes. At the top (Class I) were the rich, usually aristocrats of family as well as of money. Next came the executives and professionals more newly arrived to prestige and power. Then, the middle class, and beneath them, the workers with decent paying jobs. Class V, the bottom class, was made up of the poor. About half of its members were semi-skilled, about half unskilled. The men had less than six years of education, the women less than eight.

As it turned out, this five-level breakdown was more revealing than the usual three-class image of American society (upper, middle, and lower). For it showed a sharp break between Class V at the bottom and Class IV just above it. In a dramatic psychological sense, the skilled unionized worker lived much, much closer to the middle class than he did to the world of the poor. Between Class IV and Class V, Hollingshead and Redlich found a chasm. This represents the gulf between working America, which may be up against it from time to time but which has a certain sense of security and dignity, and the other America of the poor.

Perhaps the most shocking and decisive statistic that Hollingshead and Redlich found was the one that tabulated the rate of treated psychiatric illness per 100,000 people in New Haven. These are their results:

Classes I and II	556 per 100,000
Class III	538
Class IV	642
Class V	1,659

From the top of society down to the organized workers, there are differences, but relatively small ones. But suddenly, when one crosses the line from Class IV to Class V, there is a huge leap, with the poor showing a rate of treated psychiatric illness of almost three times the magnitude of any other class.

But the mental suffering of the poor in these figures is not simply expressed in gross numbers. It is a matter of quality as well. In Classes I and II, 65 percent of the treated psychiatric illness is for neurotic problems, and only 35 percent for the much graver disturbances of psychoses. But at the bottom, in Class V, 90 percent of the treated illness is for psychosis, and only 10 percent for neurosis. In short, not only the rate but also the intensity of mental illness is much greater for the poor.

One of the standard professional criticisms of Hollingshead and Redlich is that their figures are for treated illness (those who actually got to a doctor or clinic) and do not indicate the "true prevalence" of mental illness in the population. Whatever merits this argument has in relation to other parts of the study, it points up that these particular figures are an understatement of the problem. The higher up the class scale one is, the more likely that there will be recognition of mental illness as a problem and that help will be sought. At the bottom of society, referral to psychiatric treatment usually comes from the courts. Thus, if anything, there is even more mental illness among the poor than the figures of Hollingshead and Redlich indicate.

The one place where this criticism might have some validity is with regard to the intensity of emotional disturbance. Only 10 percent of the poor who received treatment are neurotics, yet the poor neurotic is the least likely person in the society to show up for treatment. He can function, if only in an impaired and maimed way. If there were something done about this situation, it is quite possible that one would find more neurosis in the other America at the same time as one discovered more mental illness generally.

However, it is not necessary to juggle with statistics and explanations in order to corroborate the main drift of the New Haven figures. During the fifties the Cornell University Department of Psychiatry undertook an ambitious study of "Midtown," a residential area in New York City. The research dealt with a population of 170,000 from every social class, 99 percent of them white. (By leaving out the Negroes, there probably was a tendency to underestimate the problem of poverty generally, and the particular disabilities of a discriminated minority in particular.) The goal of the study was to discover "true prevalence," and there was interviewing in depth.

The Cornell scholars developed a measure of "mental health risk." They used a model of three classes, and consequently their figures are not so dramatic as those tabulated in New Haven. Yet they bear out the essential point: the lowest class had a mental health risk almost 40 percent greater than the highest class. Once again the world of poverty was given definition as a spiritual and emotional reality.

The huge brute fact of emotional illness in the other America is fairly well substantiated. The reasons behind the fact are the subject of considerable controversy. There is no neat and simple summary that can be given at the present time, yet some of the analyses are provocative for an understanding of the culture of poverty even if they must be taken tentatively.

One of the most interesting speculations came from the Cornell study of "Midtown" in New York City. The researchers developed a series of "stress factors" that might be related to an individual's mental health risk. In childhood, these were poor mental health on the part of the parents, poor physical health for the parents, economic deprivation, broken homes, a negative attitude on the part of the child toward his parents, a quarrelsome home, and sharp disagreements with parents during adolescence. In adult life, the stress factors were poor health, work worries, money worries, a lack of neighbors and friends, marital worries, and parental worries.

The Cornell team then tested to see if there was any relationship between these factors and mental health. They discovered a marked correlation. The person who had been subjected to thirteen of these stress factors was three times more likely to be mentally disturbed than the person who had felt none of them. Indeed, the researchers were led to conclude that the sheer number of stress factors was more important than the quality of stresses. Those who had experienced any three factors were of a higher mental risk than those who had experienced two.

If the Cornell conclusions are validated in further research, they will constitute an important revision of some widely held ideas about mental health. The Freudian theory has emphasized the earliest years and the decisive trauma in the development of mental illness (for example, the death of a parent). This new theory would suggest a more cumulative conception of mental illness: as stress piles upon stress over a period of time, there is a greater tendency toward disturbance. It would be an important supplement to the Freudian ideas.

But if this theory is right, there is a fairly obvious reason for the emotional torment of the other America. The stress factors listed by the Cornell study are the very stuff of the life of the poor: physical illness, broken homes, worries about work and money, and all the rest. The slum, with its vibrant, dense life hammers away at the individual. And because of the sheer, grinding, dirty experience of being poor, the personality, the spirit, is impaired. It is as if human beings dilapidate along with the tenements in which they live.

However, some scholars have attempted to soften the grimness of this picture with a theory about "drift." The poor, they argue, have a high percentage of disturbed people, not because of the conditions of life in the urban and rural slums, but because this is the group that gets all the outcasts of society from the rest of the classes. If this thesis were true, then one would expect to find failures from the higher classes as a significant group in the culture of the poor.

Hollingshead and Redlich tested this theory in New Haven and did not find any confirmation for it. The mentally impaired poor had been, for the most part, born poor. Their sickness was a product of poverty, instead of their poverty being a product of sickness. Similarly, in the Midtown study, no evidence was turned up to indicate that the disturbed poor were the rejects from other classes. There are some exceptions to this rule: alcoholics, as noted before, often tend to fall from a high position into the bitterest poverty. Still, current research points to a direct relationship between the experience of poverty and emotional disturbance.

And yet, an ironic point turned up in the Midtown research. It was discovered that a certain kind of neurosis was useful to a minority of poor people. The obsessive-compulsive neurotic often got ahead; his very sickness was a means of advancement out of the other America and into the great world. And yet, this might only prepare for a later crisis. On the lower and middle rungs of business society, hard work, attention to detail, and the like are enough to guarantee individual progress. But if such a person moves across the line, and is placed in a position where he must make decisions, there is the very real possibility of breakdown.

IV

Someone in trouble, someone in sorrow, a fight between neighbors, a coffin carried from a house, were things that coloured their lives and shook down fiery blossoms where they walked.—Sean O'Casey

The feelings, the emotions, the attitudes of the poor are different. But different from what? In this question there is an important problem of dealing with the chaotic in the world of poverty.

The definition makers, the social scientists, and the moralists come from the middle class. Their values do not include "a fight between neighbors" as a "fiery blossom." Yet that is the fact in the other America. (O'Casey was talking about Ireland; he might as well have been describing any slum in the United States.) Before going on and exploring the emotional torment of the poor, it would be well to understand this point.

Take the gangs. They are violent, and by middle-class standards they are antisocial and disturbed. But within a slum, violence and disturbance are often norms, everyday facts of life. From the inside of the other America, joining a "bopping" gang may well not seem like deviant behavior. It could be a necessity for dealing with a hostile world. (Once, in a slum school in St. Louis, a teacher stopped a fight between two little girls. "Nice girls don't fight," she told them. "Yeah," one of them replied, "you should have seen my old lady at the tavern last night.")

Indeed, one of the most depressing pieces of research I have ever read touches on this point. H. Warren Dunham carefully studied forty catatonic schizophrenics in Chicago in the early forties. He found that none of them had belonged to gangs or had engaged in the kind of activity the middle class regards as abnormal. They had, as a matter of fact, tried to live up to the standards of the larger society, rather than conforming to the values of the slum. "The catatonic young man can be described as a good boy and one who has all the desirable traits which all the social agencies would like to inculcate in the young men of the community."

The middle class does not understand the narrowness of its judgments. And worse, it acts upon them as if they were universal and accepted by everyone. In New Haven, Hollingshead and Redlich found two girls with an almost identical problem. Both of them were extremely promiscuous, so much so that they eventually had a run-in with the police. When the girl from Class I was arrested, she was provided with bail at once, newspaper stories were quashed, and she was taken care of through private psychotherapy. The girl from Class V was sentenced to reform school. She was paroled in two years, but was soon arrested again and sent to the state reformatory.

James Baldwin made a brilliant and perceptive application of this point to the problem of the Negro in a speech I heard not long ago. The white, he said, cannot imagine what it is like to be Negro: the danger, the lack of horizon, the necessity of always being on guard and watching. For that matter, Baldwin went on, the Negro problem is really the white problem. It is not the Negro who sets dark skin and kinky hair aside as something fearful, but the white. And the resolution of the racial agony in America requires a deep introspection on the part of the whites. They must discover themselves even more than the Negro.

This is true of all the juvenile delinquents, all the disturbed people, in the other America. One can put it baldly: their sickness is often a means of relating to a diseased environment. Until this is understood, the emotionally disturbed poor person will probably go on hurting himself until he becomes a police case. When he is finally given treatment, it will be at public expense, and it will be inferior to that given the rich. (In New Haven, according to Hollingshead and Redlich, the poor are five times more likely to get organic therapy—including shock treatment—rather than protracted, individual professional care.)

For that matter, some of the researchers in the field believe that sheer ignorance is one of the main causes of the high rate of disturbance among the poor. In the slum, conduct that would shock a middle-class neighborhood and lead to treatment is often considered normal. Even if someone is constantly and violently drunk, or beats his wife brutally, people will say of such a person, "Well, he's a little odd." Higher up on the class scale an individual with such a problem would probably realize that something was wrong (or his family would). He will have the knowledge and the money to get help.

One of the researchers in the field who puts great stress on the "basic universals" of the Freudian pattern (mother figure, father figure, siblings) looks upon this factor of ignorance as crucial. He is Dr. Lawrence Kubie. For Dr. Kubie, the fundamental determinants of mental health and illness are the same in every social class. But culture and income and education account for whether the individual will handle his problem; whether he understands himself as sick; whether he seeks help, and so on. This theory leaves the basic assumptions of traditional psychoanalysis intact, but, like any attempt to deal with the poor, it recognizes that something is different.

For the rich, then, and perhaps even for the better-paid worker, breakdowns, neurosis, and psychosis appear as illness and are increasingly treated as such. But the poor do not simply suffer these disturbances; they suffer them blindly. To them it does not appear that they are mentally sick; to them it appears that they are trapped in a fate.

PART THREE

The 1960's

When John F. Kennedy was inaugurated in 1961, the youngest man
ever to be elected President replaced the oldest man ever to serve in the
office. The generation that came of age in the era of World War I was
giving way to a breed shaped by World War II—men like Richard
Nixon, Robert McNamara, William Westmoreland, Norman Mailer,
Barry Goldwater. Kennedy's young administration stirred the nation far
beyond what any of his policies would have suggested. A new generation may not always have fresh perspectives, but it is bound to have a
new style, and even that is exciting.

But that generation paced a hard path. Assassinations, disorders, disastrous foreign adventures, and an accidental President obscured its record before its policies had a chance to bear fruit. Many of Kennedy's ideas resulted in legislation only after his death when Lyndon Johnson pushed his program for a "Great Society" through Congress. By then a generation even younger than the Kennedy administration had burst upon the national political scene, before anyone had even adjusted to the hard brilliance of the men who swept in early in the decade. The 1960's were years of extraordinary self-consciousness. The awareness of self was so sharp—my people, my generation, my "thing"—that the nation became almost ungovernable in traditional ways. Everyone had to be met directly (the process of "confrontation"), had to be self-directed (black power, women's liberation, student power), yet had to fit into a more crowded and interdependent nation (computerized data banks, tax records, the desire for law and order).

Americans—to their credit—have never been an easy people to govern. This old, near anarchic virtue asserted itself more strongly than ever in the 1960's, and strongest of all among the newest generation. The decade ended with accomplishments that would have astonished men of a generation before: the abolition of legal segregation, widespread government-financed medical and educational services, the longest economic boom in our history, men on the moon. Yet it also finished amidst potential chaos with the legitimacy of nearly every major institution—political parties, churches, universities, corporations, the government itself—deeply eroded.

The year 1968 was the climax of this history, a turning point that did not turn. The youngest generation fell back in disarray, the men who depended for inspiration largely on the New Deal vanished from the national scene, and an administration that described itself as conservative came to power. But whatever they called themselves, the new Nixon bureaucrats were another group of the hard young men—now growing old—who had come out of World War II; on many issues their conservatism reached farther forward than had the Kennedy liberalism of 1960—to which they often turned for their rhetoric.

Kennedy: A Cold Warrior

DAVID BURNER

John Fitzgerald Kennedy was one of the most attractive men ever to be President of the United States. He was, Norman Mailer once wrote, "our leading man." His confidence that he could "get the nation moving again," his handsome and stylish wife, photogenic children, and appealing and able associates touched chords in American society which his predecessor, for all the love and respect he generated, could not (and would not have wished to) reach. Kennedy was as passionately loved and hated as any president in our history. And especially, he was the hero of the new men—in the professions, the universities, business and government—who were reaching positions of leadership in the American scene, a new generation "born in this century."

David Burner's discussion of Kennedy and his presidential term recognizes this élan and its vital—if intangible—effect on American culture. Nevertheless, Burner's account of Kennedy is no part of the hagiography that began to appear after his assassination. While the writer has an admiration for Kennedy, this is clearly a "revisionist" account of his administration, sharply aware of its failings as well as its successes. A president who both stalled and spurred civil rights, who both eased and intensified the Cold War, who tended to allow events to move to a crisis but then responded superbly to the emergency, JFK will never be easy to evaluate.

John F. Kennedy came to the office of President as a spokesman for the Cold War at its most sophisticated point. The nation had acquired, during a decade of atomic diplomacy, an intelligence and temperament that enabled it to live with some coolness amidst the continuing strategies and extraordinary technological complex of nuclear confrontation. The language of that intelligence was Kennedy's: he could speak crisply about the dangers of a missile gap, the need for innovation in nuclear weaponry, the advantages of flexible response over massive retaliation. He combined a fascination for military technology with a feeling for military dash and elitism; a naval hero who had survived a bizarre shipwreck, a reader of James Bond novels, he was intrigued by the knowledge that we had it within our ability to fly a specially trained army from New Jersey to Asia in two days, and he admired the Green Berets, telling them to wear their insignia proudly.

The flaws in the temperament of the Cold War strategists are easy to define. In our recent rediscovery of high political emotion, we have learned to condemn past administrations for bringing to desperately human facts little more than the calculations of a computerized intelligence. But that temperament had its special strengths of nerve and patience; and in its quickness to perceive complications, its analytical dislike of ideological formulas, it carried the seeds of its own liquidation. Kennedy was both in person and in time a figure central to that paradox; the Cold War as an assured attitude of mind would not long survive his presidency. Like other technicians of the conflict, from George F. Kennan and Dean Acheson onwards, the President did not want to talk the anti-Communist ideology of the Right—that would be too simplistic and would distract us from the details of power and the diversities in local situation with which our strategies had to cope. Yet if we were to forbear obsessions about the existence of a monolithic international communism and instead think of peasant revolutions and emergent nationalism and tension among Communist states, then we were obliged to prepare for a time when the world quasi war would no longer be necessary, and at that instant to effect quick disengagements. But Kennedy would not himself live to preside over a policy finally twisted and broken with self-contradiction, as it pursues in Vietnam a conflict that its own habit of careful calculation puts into question; and a conflict for which it cannot allow itself a satisfyingly belligerent and chauvinistic rhetoric, for it does not believe in such rhetoric.

Kennedy's unconscious part in all this was to an extent a matter of his sophistication in rhetoric, his insistence during the 1960 campaign, for example, that the developing split between China and Russia should dominate our view of communism. After Kennedy, critics could no longer condemn the mentality of the Cold War for its simplicity; they would need to rebut the complex and highly qualified understanding it had reached. Kennedy had something else to do with the psychology of the decade. He contributed to the youth movement that by the later sixties succeeded in making a major statement against the structures of American power. His appeals to idealism and to sacrifice struck a responsive chord, and beyond these intangibles his administration attracted young people into lives of public service. Kennedy also gave cover and encouragement to the civil rights workers in the South, the early activists of liberation and communalism. Yet even in all this the bite of mind that he brought to nuclear diplomacy was also the verve of his domestic politics. The call to arms was cool and tempered: Kennedy once told a group of White House reporters that he had little faith anything he could do would solve America's problems. He seemed to believe in human depravity.

Though many of John Kennedy's beliefs grew out of the 1950s, his personal manner had set him far apart from other politicians of that decade: he disdained the cronyism of the Senate, the cant of national politicians, and the naïveté of the professional liberals. Toward such things he showed an aristocrat's aloofness, even an arrogance born of having money, brains, good looks, the right education, a war hero's record, a beautiful wife, and a father ambitious for his son. Kennedy's temperament, detached from some accepted values and without illusions, was quite compatible with a manipulation of the electorate. When he first entered presidential politics in 1956 as a candidate for the vice-presidency, he let his adviser Ted Sorenson circulate a memorandum arguing that a Catholic candidate would strengthen rather than harm a national ticket. In 1959 he told a group of Pennsylvanians that if he went into the convention with many delegates and then were denied the nomination, the Democratic party would risk alienating Catholics and losing the election. Such incidents foreshadowed the opportunistic way Kennedy would use his Catholicism in the 1960 campaign, and they created a lasting impression of Kennedy as a man in a hurry.

Kennedy's coolness of manner protected his integrity. Never possessed of a political street personality, he winced at the thought of displaying his emotions. His critical mistake at the 1956 Democratic Convention, where he sought the vice-presidency, was in not visiting Hubert Humphrey to win favor—or so one account has it. The chosen candidate, Estes Kefauver, indulged in a tearful meeting with the sentimental Humphrey that would have been foreign to Kennedy's temper. Senator Kennedy, who had lost potential votes by declaring against high price supports for farmers, barely missed the vice-presidential nomination in 1956, and perhaps he did not try very hard. But it was a lucky thing: a place on the losing ticket would have spoiled his perfect record at the polls, and he was free to win a record-breaking reelection victory from Massachusetts voters in 1958.

Kennedy's record in the House and Senate had been marred by his failure to speak out against the demagogic Senator Joseph McCarthy—a failure especially to be noted in the author of *Profiles in Courage;* he missed the important censure vote because of sickness and did not arrange to pair with some member opposed to censure. He did not lead in introducing new legislation. Yet he was an independent man, usually given to an honest expression of his political views. He supported the St. Lawrence Seaway, despite its unpopularity in Massachusetts; though a decorated veteran, he condemned the powerful American Legion on the floor of the House; an Irishman, he was the only Democratic congressman in his state not to request a pardon for James Michael Curley, the former governor and congressman popular among the Irish in Massachusetts and then serving a term in prison. Kennedy had about him an air of freshness and unpredictability. He was both Irish and a Harvard graduate; he was wealthy, yet was presumed a political underdog because of his religion. His coolness of manner even hinted at a new type of popular hero.

The success of Senator Kennedy and other congressional Democrats in the elections of 1958—a crucial moment in the realignment of forces that was to change the politics of the era—gave political expression to an awareness of things wrong with American society. Older conservatives such as Senators William Knowland, John Bricker, and William Jenner disappeared from national life, and many of the new faces of the sixties first appeared in the Congress that met the following year. The Russian space achievement in sending two sputniks across the sky in 1957 had particularly shocked the country. American scientific education became a major campaign issue for Democrats, and was intensified by the crowding of the enormous postwar generation into inadequate school facilities across the nation. Publicists pointed to still more failures in American society: the coexistence of poverty and affluence; alleged corporate control over American foreign policy; uninhabitable suburbs under-supplied with libraries, parks, and privacy; and a conformity that threatened boredom and demoralization among the very class of technicians and businessmen who might have supplied America with new initiatives. While not all of these were politically effective issues, they contributed to a growing unease.

Most of all, the sluggish economy injured Republican candidates. The Eisenhower administration had discovered the means to prevent depression, but it seemed powerless to avoid repeated recessions, to stem inflation, or even to achieve a national economic growth rate at levels then prevailing in Western Europe or the Soviet Union. That failure came at a bad time. For a rise in productivity for each man-hour created surplus labor that demanded an economy expansive enough to supply it with jobs, while accumulating social needs and programs in health, welfare, and education required a richer economy yielding tax receipts adequate to finance them.

Though Democrats, including Senator Kennedy, blamed the inaction on Treasury Secretary George Humphrey's strong influence with Eisenhower, the cause cut deeper, for the peculiar way the economy had solved some of its older problems had generated new ones. Trusts had settled down into a permanent state to which economists gave the ugly name "oligopoly"; large firms were attempting to run their sectors of the economy not for the venturesome efforts of competition but for the comforts of profits at high prices. Much of the labor problem had been solved by wage increases to a unionized elite of protected workers, often in the same enterprises that were also organized into oligopoly. Gains in wages for the protected workers were passed on to consumers in the form of a general rise in prices. The situation of the unemployed meanwhile remained static because surplus capital was being consumed in the form of inflation long before it turned to new production and new jobs. Investments in plants and equipment shrank; late in the decade investments in the United States for these crucial items were one-eighth those of European countries in proportion to population.

The Eisenhower administration was too firmly grounded in the business community to press for serious changes in economic policy. Undoubtedly, it sincerely desired to stem price increases, but it could make no move at all when business, particularly the steel industry, resisted. The conditions of the late 1950s pose curious questions about the history of fiscal and economic policy. It is a standard assumption that the forces of business and the political Right have tended to favor economic opportunity over social justice. Yet the 1950s present the spectacle of a business-dominated government that seems to have restrained economic growth, while the liberal forces of the late fifties and the early sixties made growth their major domestic objective. Although such influences as simple hostility to the new economics also shaped its thinking, the business community—and its allies in the Republican party —took far longer than most economists, politicians, and publicists to recover from the trauma of the Great Depression.

While unemployment rates went as high as 7.5 percent, their political impact on organized labor, an elite working in heavy industry and participating in Eisenhower prosperity, was remarkably small. But conservative business groups politicized labor in the 1958 elections by placing the open or nonunion shop ("right to work" law) on the ballot in several states. And nonorganized workers were not going to continue being thankful for the absence of outright depression when a sharp recession in 1957–1958 was followed by a weak recovery of only twenty-five months, retarded afresh by a lengthy steel strike, and that in turn coasting into new recession in 1960–1961.

Disadvantaged groups in America suffered most from these economic slackenings. Negroes were flooding into urban ghettos, Indians and Mexicans were lost in self-perpetuating poverty, and growing numbers of elderly men and women were living out useless lives in decaying rooms or becoming medical indigents in hospitals that lacked not simply adequate medical care but often rudimentary cleanliness. Such people, as Michael Harrington pointed out in an unforgettable term, were "invisible" in the 1950s. In part this meant that they were physically shut away: in hospitals, on reservations, in migrant workers' camps, on the other side of freeways, or in inner cities abandoned by the middle class. But they were also politically invisible, without organized groups among themselves or representation through any other group, such as the Democratic party fixed to its institutional base in the unions. The fifties lacked an intellectual as well as a workers' Left; and this means not so much that the country was deprived of the specific policies such a Left might have achieved but that the conservative administration was able to be much more conservative, having no articulate opponent able to compel concessions from it.

John Kennedy knew his times well and believed he could cope with their problems. His near success in winning the vice-presidential nomination in 1956, and his enormous victory in the 1958 Massachusetts Senate race, made him a serious candidate for the presidency in 1960. The absence of other strong Democratic candidates was another advantage for Kennedy. Some party professionals thought he alone might pull back into the Democratic party the many Catholic voters who had deserted it in 1952 and 1956. Nevertheless, the party's leaders worried about his religion and his youthfulness. Since Al Smith's crushing defeat in 1928 still haunted the party, Kennedy would first have to show in the primaries that he could attract solid support from Protestants. His unimpressive victory over Hubert Humphrey in the early Wisconsin primary did not prove the point, for that state had too many Catholic voters. West Virginia, where he was scheduled to contest the persistent Humphrey on May 10, would be the crucial field of the preconvention campaign.

Kennedy's advisers told him to play down the religious issue in West Virginia. But average West Virginians, Kennedy instinctively believed, knew they were being tested and that their vote, above all else, would be interpreted by the nation at large as a repudiation or an endorsement of bigotry. Humphrey vehemently attacked the candidate's wealth, but West Virginians, like other Americans, admire wealth; and besides, Kennedy appeared moved by what he saw of poverty in the state. Kennedy himself repeatedly drew attention to his religion; he used the issue in a way that his opponent could not, managing to make it a matter of sportsmanship. West Virginia, a state 95 percent Protestant and only 4 percent black, cast 61 percent of its Democratic primary vote for Kennedy.

The victory in West Virginia carried Kennedy to a first-ballot nomination in Los Angeles. The Democratic Convention in that city was graced by Senator Eugene McCarthy's eloquent plea for the nomination of Adlai E. Stevenson, twice defeated as the party's presidential candidate: "Do not reject this man who made us all proud to be called Democrats. . . ." But Stevenson's candidacy, which he suspected was engineered by the Johnson people in an effort to head off the main contender, irritated Kennedy. When a close election seemed in the offing, why did Stevenson let liberals rally in an impossible drive against the front-runner? For him and for Eleanor Roosevelt the reason was to keep Kennedy aware that his record needed to be more daring. But the Senator believed Stevenson's bid to be a hopeless and egotistical gesture certain to endanger party unity, and the venture by the Stevenson forces did not stop Kennedy from offering the vice-presidency to a man unpopular among northern liberals—Lyndon Baines Johnson.

Much has been written about the selection of Johnson, who had held second place in the presidential balloting. Most of the accounts treat the offer and the acceptance as spontaneous and even impulsive; this may be true but both men, who respected each other considerably, must also have been calculating the likelihood for months: such a ticket would certainly be the strongest one imaginable. The Republican candidate, Richard Nixon, knowing this, had anticipated the ticket. The least measurable issue of the campaign, Kennedy's religion, presented the worst handicap in the South, where the Texas Protestant Johnson would greatly aid the ticket. Johnson was well regarded among farmers, businessmen, and conservative independents in the rest of the country many of whom might have been expected to lean toward Nixon. Such voters would be attracted by Johnson's prudent legislative record, his willingness to cooperate with Eisenhower, and his universally acknowledged political skill at leading the Democratic party in the Senate. True, Johnson's candidacy would not be good news to labor and the liberals— but where else could they go? Nixon, they had decided long ago, was beyond redemption. Apparently the vice-presidency also suited the ambitions of Johnson, who had offered to run with Stevenson in 1956; the office would lift him above a confining Southern identity, which had stood in the way of the presidential nomination.

Johnson went on to conduct a superbly professional campaign. Kennedy, in Norman Mailer's image, was a young professor whose manner was adequate for the classroom, but whose mind was off in some intricacy of the Ph.D. thesis he was writing; the man was always a touch too aloof from the candidate. Johnson, on the other hand, gave all of himself: he was "a political animal, he breathed like an animal, sweated like one, you knew his mind was entirely absorbed with the compendium of political fact and maneuver." On his brilliant campaign trips through the South, Johnson demanded order and precision: the rostrum had to be exactly 52 inches high when he spoke, the band must blast the first note of "The Yellow Rose of Texas" the second he finished speaking, the train must pull away from the station at the syllable of farewell. The content of Johnson's message as he sped from one small town to another—"God bless yuh, Rocky Bottom. Ah wish ah could stay an' do a little sippin' an' whittlin' with yuh. . . . God bless yuh, Gaffney"— seemed to clash oddly with the technical skill of the performance and the abrupt manners of the candidate among his advisers but apparently spoke to his audience.

Kennedy's Republican opponent, Vice-President Nixon, was a strong candidate. Much more attuned to the country's politics than Dwight Eisenhower, he had been an active and partisan Vice-President, urging his administration to take a more progressive view on civil rights, the economy, and public education. He was effective on television and welcomed the chance to debate Kennedy. Newspaper editors and publishers generally favored Nixon, and his campaign chest more than matched Kennedy's. His greatest fault was one that John Kennedy spotted easily: Nixon lacked taste. He fabricated sentimentality and sought a level of communication much below his capacity.

Nixon's campaign was fated to a series of misfortunes. His running mate, Henry Cabot Lodge, proved to be an unenthusiastic campaigner. A preconvention meeting at Governor Nelson Rockefeller's New York apartment was interpreted by many Republican conservatives as a capitulation to Rocky's liberal domestic views. Early in the campaign, Nixon suffered an infected knee and was hospitalized for two weeks; later, still underweight and in a weakened condition, he caught a bad case of the flu. Despite the loss in time, he insisted on fulfilling a pledge to visit all fifty states, spending valuable hours in Alaska when he should have been barnstorming downstate Illinois. Instead of benefiting from Eisenhower's projected meeting with Khrushchev at Paris in the spring of 1960, Nixon shared with the administration the embarrassment of being caught in the act of espionage; a short time before, an American U-2 high-altitude reconnaissance plane had been shot down deep in Russian territory. Thereby the Republican slogan of peace and prosperity, already in doubt because of the continuing recession, suffered a further loss of credibility. In August, Eisenhower was none too helpful when he carelessly told a reporter who had asked him what major administration decisions Nixon had participated in: "If you give me a week, I might think of one." And Nixon could not make good use of Eisenhower in the closing weeks of the campaign, for the President's doctors advised against it. When the Reverend Norman Vincent Peale, Nixon's New York pastor, condemned Kennedy on religious grounds, the minister in fact lent strength to the argument that a vote for a Catholic was a vote for freeing politics of the sterile religious issue. The incident gave Kennedy an opportunity dramatically to convince an audience of Houston ministers that they had no call to fear him. Worst of all, a series of television debates demolished the myth of Kennedy's youthful inexperience and placed the haggard Nixon in the role of defending a passive administration. The Vice-President had counted on his ability: there was the effective "kitchen debate" of 1959 with Khrushchev in Moscow; and in a television speech of the 1952 campaign, when Nixon defended himself against dubious allegations of financial misconduct and evoked the name of his dog, Checkers, he had proved his mastery of television. He could not strike hard, since he thought it unwise to evoke memories of his ruthlessness in anti-Communist investigation during the McCarthy era, and in any case Kennedy kept him off balance.

Once Eisenhower had set the depression psychosis to rest, the nation was ready to venture beyond tranquillity to a more exciting economics of expansion, and this the young Kennedy offered it. Economic experiment came to seem not only possible but necessary if America was to maintain a position of world leadership. The Cold War, which for so long had hampered experimentation, now encouraged it, for Russia was embarked on a phase of economic competition with the United States. Khrushchev's threat "We will bury you," by which he signified economic triumph, illustrates that the Cold War was shifting from direct confrontation to a struggle for the Third World, whose need for development meant that the United States and Russia had to compete as models of productivity. Kennedy, by shrewdly emphasizing a missile gap and Castro's victory in Cuba, and by linking the issues of national prestige and economic growth, implied that Nixon—part of a well-intentioned but ineffective administration—could not solve these difficulties. The two party platforms, an aggressive Democratic document and a defensive Republican one, seemed to restate the difference between the candidates.

During the campaign Kennedy rarely attacked the substance of the Eisenhower foreign policies. But citing a supposed missile gap, he urged that we catch up with Russia technologically, particularly in space. With problems like Cuba and Laos in mind, Kennedy also called for a new look for the army. A one-sided reliance on nuclear weapons—the "bigger bang for the buck" philosophy of Eisenhower's Defense Secretary Charles E. Wilson—denied us any flexibility of choice, Kennedy argued. Faced with a war of national liberation, we were restricted to the alternatives of doing nothing or threatening a nuclear strike, and that threat could not be carried out except at a catastrophic price. Perhaps, of course, Eisenhower and Dulles never really thought nuclear war to be an option. Conceivably they believed that no aggressive military move by Russia was likely and that our opposition to localized revolts would have to take nonmilitary form. Eisenhower himself talked of peace and offered his "open skies" disarmament proposal; his own enormous prestige enabled him stubbornly to resist enlarged military appropriations and to criticize influential generals and admirals as "parochial." Kennedy, on the other hand, proposed that the nation complement its nuclear arsenal with a well-financed, innovative armed force and an improved stock of conventional weapons. He was capitalizing on a debate in the Pentagon itself; for such army leaders as Maxwell Taylor and Matthew Ridgway were calling for a more mobile and sophisticated force capable of fighting in limited kinds of unrest such as that in Laos and the Congo. Kennedy's kinetic charm (he talked too fast for most people to grasp his arguments) and his confidence in fathoming the complexity of public problems cast him as a man with a more sophisticated, more dashing, and more effective response to the familiar problems of the fifties. He defeated Nixon by 303 to 219 electoral votes and by a hairsbreadth in the popular vote. Even the electoral vote in truth should have been closer: alleged fraud in counting the close returns in Illinois and Texas cast deep suspicion on the Kennedy victory in those states. Any Democrat should have won easily given the recession and the strength of his party. It is puzzling that Kennedy did not do better. Whether his religion helped or harmed him is questionable. The Survey Research Center of the University of Michigan, and other similar organizations, found that the issue cost him 2 percent of the popular vote but helped him in crucial states with substantial Catholic blocs and large electoral votes.

In the course of his presidency, Kennedy would eventually articulate a foreign policy of restraint and accommodation, and bring the Cold War almost to the point of its terminating in explicit agreements and implicit understandings. Yet he came to the office with a remarkable bellicosity. John Kennedy, Congressman and Senator from 1947 to 1960, was a product and, like almost everyone of that era, a prisoner to some extent of the Cold War. He had matured from its earlier rhetoric—he apologized for blaming the loss of China on the Truman administration —he had profited from its growing sophistication, and he hoped, with Eisenhower, for an eventual accommodation with Russia. But he was of two minds, for he also appeared to believe that communism would continue to be America's implacable foe. In Kennedy's years in the House of Representatives, that body had habitually voted overwhelmingly for resolutions calling on the peoples of eastern Europe to revolt against their Communist rulers; and Kennedy had joined in these votes. Anticommunism, moreover, was a strong tradition of Kennedy's own family and church. In the first television debate with Nixon he endorsed a devil theory of communism.

President Kennedy's selection of advisers like Dean Rusk for State, Robert McNamara for Defense, and Walt Rostow and McGeorge Bundy as White House aides showed he was not ready for a foreign policy like that of Adlai Stevenson, who had been almost alone in believing, as early as 1956, that the Cold War might conceivably be liquidated. Kennedy chose his staff from organization men who held positions demanding great technical competence in government, business, or university bureaucracies. He finally rejected independent figures like Senator William Fulbright, his own initial favorite for the post of State. Rusk, who became a strong, and stubborn, Secretary of State, failed at first to provide leadership. McNamara, a man of some genius, talked of "cost-effectiveness" and "flexible response," but rarely if ever disagreed with a unanimous decision of the Joint Chiefs of Staff. Hawkish former Secretary of State Dean Acheson gave his approval to the Kennedy appointments, recommending Rusk after warning that the selection of

Stevenson for State would be a "terrible disaster" and that of Fulbright a "mistake." If the year 1960 had a tone in foreign policy, it was set by the publication of Herman Kahn's *On Thermonuclear War,* which Kennedy studied closely. Kahn, who thought war likely and described how we could survive, argued that if Russia braced for a nuclear attack and America did not, our world position would be weakened.

The beliefs on foreign policy that Kennedy carried with him into office are caught for history in the Bay of Pigs fiasco. The Eisenhower administration, to be sure, had prepared the way for anti-Communist guerrillas to invade Cuba. More than a thousand Cuban refugees, trained by America's Central Intelligence Agency, awaited commands at a coffee plantation high in the Guatemalan mountains. To cancel the planned invasion and disperse the men, who would tell tales, might say to the world that the new administration in Washington was weak. To some degree, events generated their own momentum, and Kennedy received misinformation and bad advice from the CIA. He had also seen that the increasingly dictatorial Castro had deceived many liberals, and he had his own jingoistic campaign rhetoric to live with. Finally, the bureaucracies of government, during the Bay of Pigs and later in the Vietnam escalations, discouraged criticism and "rocking the boat"; here Kennedy might have been saved by the visceral liberals his temperament could not abide. Still, it was absurd to suppose that the well-entrenched Castro could be overthrown without the active support of the United States Air Force, Army, and Navy; and to make an abortive attempt would be disastrous. Cuba, as Senator Fulbright observed, was after all a thorn in the flesh, not a dagger in the heart. The important creditable part of the President's role came in restraining the militarists who wanted an all-out attack when it was plain that the landing had failed.

How could a hardheaded pragmatist like Kennedy have been misled by advisers he hardly even knew? It was perhaps a part of his competitive temper that drove him almost to court crisis; in the inaugural, for instance, he had declaimed, "Before my term has ended we shall have to test anew whether a nation organized and governed such as ours can endure." He repeatedly declared America to be at the most critical point in its history. In those days he even gave serious thought to a planned assassination of Castro, according to a source perhaps inaccurate, Senator George Smathers. In 1962 he told the journalist Stewart Alsop that a nuclear war in the next decade stood an even chance. Some part of the decision to place our prestige on the line with the guerrilla invaders, however, must also have been based on the faulty premise that because communism was totalitarian the people who lived under it yearned for freedom and would revolt at the first opportunity. And since communism was evil, the rebels would succeed. They failed miserably. Their CIA-directed strategy included every blunder imaginable: the wrong landing place, inadequate air cover, munitions and equipment piled in a single boat, and an underestimation of the enemy's strength.

In the short term, the Bay of Pigs possibly taught Kennedy the wrong lesson: it firmed his resolve to expect and be prepared for future encounters, and he redoubled his efforts to increase military spending. Though he also pushed the Alliance for Progress, seeking to reconstruct Latin America economically, he discounted arguments that building up an arsenal of conventional weapons would itself be a provocative act demanding a like response from the Soviets.

The first years of the Kennedy administration were a brief but dangerous period in international relations. During these times the old policy of threatening a massive nuclear retaliation existed perilously alongside a new problem, the national liberation movements. In Asia, in Africa, and in Latin America, in countries like Laos, the Congo, and Cuba, dynamic revolutionary forces were challenging the world balance of power. In the fresh context of the sixties, irresponsible third powers might precipitate the ultimate conflict between Russia and the United States.

In the long, tense confrontation over Berlin that lasted throughout 1961, Kennedy seemed to believe that an actual war could break out, that Russian determination might force war. Such was his impression from talking with Khrushchev at the summit meeting held in Vienna in June 1961; the Russian leader said that before the end of the year his country would sign a treaty with East Germany banning us from West Berlin. The encounter deeply troubled Kennedy, and shortly afterward he spurred fallout shelter construction, increased draft quotas, and called up military reserve units. For some years Russia had appeared to be ahead in space, in industrial growth, in long-range missiles; and it seemed that Communist imperialism was making progress almost everywhere in the world except Western Europe, where, since NATO and the Marshall Plan, communism had stopped its advance. At Vienna Khrushchev sharply challenged Kennedy even in Europe, demanding that the West sign a German peace treaty or quit Berlin. Stiffened by the hard-line opinion of Dean Acheson that Berlin was a "simple conflict of wills," Kennedy saw Khrushchev's "ultimatum" as an audacious effort to upset the one area of the world where America was incontestably ahead.

Khrushchev eventually compromised on Western Europe, constructing the Berlin wall and withdrawing the deadline of January 1, 1962, for western acquiescence. In the long run, the wall was a propaganda triumph for the West. But international tension continued to tighten in 1962. The previous summer and fall Kennedy had sped his plan for building fallout shelters. America's increased defense spending provoked a comparable rise in Russia. In response to Khrushchev's resumption of atmospheric nuclear testing in the fall of 1961, Kennedy followed suit the next April. In Africa, Russia and Communist China slipped from the toehold they had gained around the turn of the decade. The United Nations was instrumental in preserving the new Congo nation and in blocking a Soviet-American clash there; and Kennedy scored a coup by an order denying arms to South Africa as long as it should practice hard racial separation. On the other hand, although Khrushchev managed to effect a neutralization of Laos, indigenous Communist movements were gaining ground in South Vietnam, Cambodia, and the Philippines. In reaction, Kennedy, appealing to American pride, competitiveness, anticommunism, and respect for technology, secured enormous congressional appropriations for military purposes and for the race to the moon, which the President promised to reach before the end of the decade.

Then in the autumn of 1962 the world came as close as it ever has come to destruction. During the preceding summer Khrushchev had decided to place long-range nuclear missiles in Cuba. Once again, the Central Intelligence Agency failed Kennedy on Cuba; Senator Kenneth Keating of New York, using Cuban refugees as his source, seemed to be able to guess more about the missiles than the administration. Not until mid-October was it known definitely in Washington that Russian missiles in Cuba were aimed at principal American cities. The immediate reaction was one of astonishment. Nowhere else in the world outside its own borders had Russia set up such missiles. The tactical advantage was slight; Russian submarines equipped with similar weapons had been passing close to American shores for many years. But from a diplomatic standpoint the interference in an area so patently within America's sphere of influence was flagrant.

At first Kennedy's advisers considered every alternative course of action, but soon two groups coalesced, one advising an air strike and the other some kind of blockade. The Joint Chiefs favored the more warlike course, even though it would probably kill Soviet technicians. Robert Kennedy persuasively argued against a surprise air attack on the grounds that it conflicted with our national traditions and brought to mind Pearl Harbor. Eventually the view prevailed that the less risky course, the quarantine, should be pursued initially; stronger actions could be commenced later should they become necessary. Kennedy moved the blockade as close to Cuba as he dared so that Khrushchev would have time to consider all the implications it presented. After some indecision the Kremlin decided to respect the blockade, as soon as the first ship with launching equipment turned away, the world was safe—for a time. Kennedy had heightened the confrontation by refusing Khrushchev's offer to remove the missiles if we would dismantle our own obsolete ones in Turkey. A diplomatic settlement was worked out whereby Russia removed all missiles from Cuba, and America promised to respect that country's territorial integrity. Some critics have faulted Kennedy for making the missile confrontation a public affair. He might have given Khrushchev a private ultimatum. Public exposure gave the Russian leader an opportunity to appear temperate in the face of world opinion. But Kennedy had grown beyond the Bay of Pigs affair, gaining courage and restraint.

It is said that the missile crisis scared Khrushchev; in the condescending vocabulary of the Chief of Staff Maxwell Taylor, it made him "tractable." It undoubtedly scared Kennedy, too. But the missile crisis, which might have blown up the world, instead cleared the air.

A sudden realization dawned that in an age of national revolutionary movements such as Castro's Cuba, direct nuclear confrontation was no longer thinkable. Nineteen sixty-three was to be the year of the great international thaw. The United States and the Soviet Union, locked in nuclear stalemate, established a "hot line" to guard against future misunderstandings. In June the President delivered a moving speech at American University, calling for a new era of harmony and mutual progress with Russia. The Test Ban Treaty of 1963, which Kennedy drove through the Senate in face of stiff opposition from the Pentagon, was his one great positive accomplishment in foreign policy. The Soviets broke with the Chinese on the issue of peaceful coexistence and publicly stressed the need to avoid nuclear war, while the United States made arrangements to sell wheat to Russia. Kennedy himself was said to be tiring of Dean Rusk's clichéd rhetoric and hard-line ideas. In the long run, the missile crisis perhaps simply quickened the shift of the Cold War from confrontation between the superpowers to less cataclysmic "wars of national liberation," but the immediate effect was a loosening of tension.

On other issues as well, Kennedy began his presidential years unimpressively, and matured only as experience and circumstances compelled. Sobered by his meager margin of victory in 1960, he had arranged harmony meetings with Nixon and Eisenhower even before taking office, and he gave continuity to government (and continued conservative policies) by keeping on officials such as J. Edgar Hoover of the FBI and Allen Dulles of the CIA. After Congress convened in 1961 Kennedy forced a change in the size of the House Rules Committee, and thereby opened up the possibility that controversial legislation might at least reach the floor. But again his margin of victory was so slight that in the months ahead he rarely challenged Congress on important issues: federal aid to education floundered on religious controversy; a new cabinet department of urban affairs failed to win approval; foreign aid was cut drastically, owing to successive administration blunders. The Trade Expansion Act of 1962 was the one early achievement, but it was not of major importance, despite the publicity given it. Kennedy, it seemed, would endorse Jefferson's dictum: "Great innovations should not be forced on slender majorities."

The lack of programs of Kennedy's first year in the presidency is especially to be noted with respect to the great domestic issue of the sixties, the one for which he is honored most—that of civil rights. Actually, the President entered office with an undistinguished record on the question of race. Twice he had voted with the South on the Civil Rights Bill of 1957: on the abortive effort to return the bill to Mississippi Senator James Eastland's Judiciary Committee; and on the successful O'Mahoney amendment guaranteeing jury trials in criminal contempt cases—and so ensuring, in effect, that southern white defendants in civil rights cases would be tried by southern white juries. In the vice-presidential balloting of 1956 Kennedy had received support from such sources as Arkansas Governor Orville Faubus, and in the late fifties the governors of Alabama and Mississippi had urged his presidency. At a time when Kennedy was giving no more account of himself than this, Richard Nixon was calling for a strong civil rights bill and speaking against discrimination in jobs and housing.

Kennedy's campaign of 1960 was also unpromising on the question. When in January he listed the "real issues of 1960," he omitted civil rights—and this from a candidate who during the campaign declared, quoting Franklin D. Roosevelt, that the presidency is "above all, a place of moral leadership." Along with Nixon he did make many campaign promises to the cause of racial equality, and he even phoned a message of consolation to Mrs. Martin Luther King, whose husband had been imprisoned in an Atlanta jail. Dr. King's early release was probably attributable to a phone call from Robert Kennedy to an Atlanta judge. But in his inaugural President Kennedy mentioned civil rights only briefly and in the most general terms.

Fearing loss of support for other programs, Kennedy sponsored virtually no new rights legislation in 1961 and 1962, relying instead on executive action. He did not appear to sense the explosive potential of the racial situation. Had he understood it better, he would never have appointed his brother Attorney General, for that office bore the responsibility of enforcing civil rights laws and it would have been politically astute to choose for it a man of independent reputation.

Yet the Department of Justice brought about much of the concrete gains the Kennedy administration achieved on racial matters. Believing that once southern Negroes voted, their political power would secure other rights, Bobby Kennedy introduced many new federal lawsuits in behalf of the Negro franchise. The Justice Department also saw to it that transportation facilities became almost entirely desegregated in the South. (In 1962, however, the Federal Aviation Agency awarded a $2 million grant to build an airport with segregated restaurants and rest rooms in Jackson, Mississippi.) Though he had earlier urged the Negro leader Ralph Abernathy to hold back the freedom riders, the Attorney General in May 1961 dispatched 600 federal marshals to Alabama to protect them. Vice-President Lyndon Johnson, who chaired the Committee on Equal Employment, took another approach: intimate with the art of persuasion, he urged government contractors to hire more Negro workers. But Johnson came to realize that coercion would be needed, and in 1963 the Vice-President delivered strong civil rights speeches in Gettysburg and Detroit.

President Kennedy avoided the ultimate sanction, that of forcing desegregation by the withholding of federal funds. In the fall of 1962, two years after criticizing Eisenhower for failing, "by a stroke of the presidential pen," to eliminate discrimination in federally assisted housing, the President did issue such an order, sandwiching it between major news releases so that it received minimal publicity; but administrative interpretations then softened even this forward step. President Kennedy decried "straight-from-the-shoulder platitudes" on civil rights, not comprehending that this was a place where presidential exhortation might be of some value. Whatever progress the Justice Department made in 1961 and in 1962, the President wiped out some of it by appointing several segregationists to lifetime positions on southern district courts; they exhibited little enthusiasm for enforcing the Supreme Court school desegregation decision of 1954.

Then, in the last year of his life, Kennedy—and the churches and much of the nation—awakened to the moral crisis that the civil rights movement had long been seeking to publicize. Events compelled him to act, but he acted in a manner that brought credit to his presidency. In the fall of 1962 he had enforced with federal troops the enrollment of James Meredith at the University of Mississippi, employing radio and television to call on southerners to obey the law. The following spring, when Governor George Wallace attempted to prevent the court-ordered entrance of Vivian Malone and James Hood into the University of Alabama, the President's pronouncement went beyond the issue of obedience to law, where federal declarations in crises of illegal resistance to integration had typically placed themselves, and spoke to the moral question. (Earlier, Kennedy had borrowed Lincoln's birthday from the Republicans by inviting several hundred Negro leaders to the White House.) In May of 1963 Kennedy moved in troops to quell brutal repression in Birmingham, Alabama, where police had used dogs, fire hoses, and electric cattle prods against Negroes. In June he gave a moving speech on civil rights and he finally sent new legislation to Congress. The President proposed a limited ban on discrimination in public places, asked for powers enabling the Justice Department to sue for school desegregation where an aggrieved citizen asked its help, and urged a broad provision authorizing the government to withhold funds for federally assisted programs where discrimination occurred. But it contained no proposal for mandatory fair employment practices and failed to resurrect the unsuccessful Part III of the 1957 bill giving the Justice Department power to intervene in all civil rights cases. Kennedy also took a step backward when he gave tax reform priority over civil rights legislation, reasoning that a stronger economy would help the Negro more than anything else. And certainly the President feared southern congressional power. Some critics even charged that there was an unstated agreement with the South, gaining votes on other bills in exchange for stalling on civil rights. But just before he was killed the President secured an agreement from congressional leaders that would probably have assured passage of a strong civil rights act early in 1964.

Kennedy's claim to be celebrated as a champion of Negro rights is precarious. Though the great Negro leader, the Reverend Martin Luther King, Jr., granted in June 1963 that Kennedy had perhaps done "a little more" than Eisenhower, King added that "the plight of the vast majority of Negroes remains the same." The following August 250,000 people participated in the March on Washington to be counted in favor of civil rights legislation and to hear King speak: "I have a dream that one day on the red hills of Georgia the sons of former slaves and the sons of former slaveowners will be able to sit together at the table of brotherhood. . . . I have a dream that one day even the State of Mississippi, a desert state sweltering with the heat of injustice and oppression, will be transformed into an oasis of freedom and justice. . . . I have a dream that one day the State of Alabama . . . will be transformed into a situation where little black boys and black girls will be able to join hands with little white boys and girls and walk together as sisters and brothers." Despite Kennedy's failure to share King's vision, in few places did his death arouse such sorrow as in the Negro communities. And subsequent efforts to pass effective legislation gained from being construed as a memorial to the martyred President; the first law easily went through Congress early in 1964 and soon others followed.

The pattern of initiative in race relations during the Kennedy years generally repeated itself in the President's handling of the economy. Kennedy in the 1960 campaign had criticized the Republicans for not maintaining a high rate of economic growth and for lapsing into recessions from fear of employing advanced economic policies. In office, however, the new President at first proceeded cautiously, endorsing in practice the economic policies he had earlier condemned. Unemployment remained substantial in 1961 and 1962. Certainly many real obstacles held Kennedy back from economic experimentation: the adverse balance of payments discouraged expansive policies; a severe break in the stock market in May 1962 evoked distrust of the President in the economic community; he was wary of the image of "reckless spender" that the Republicans had tried to fix on the Democrats; and the congressional seniority system rewarded conservatives of long service. Kennedy did succeed in holding down the cost of living, and in 1961 he supported a boost in Social Security payments and the minimum wage to end the "Eisenhower recession" of 1960–1961. These techniques were similar to those Eisenhower himself had used when the economy faltered.

Kennedy evidently believed in such tools as deficit spending, a tax cut, and easy credit, but he thought the powerful and independent Federal Reserve Board might rebel at a novel program. But when the economy later in 1962 ceased its recovery from the earlier recession, the President and his able Republican Treasury Secretary, Douglas Dillon, decided to follow a truly radical economic policy. For the first relatively prosperous time in American history an administration proposed the deliberate unbalancing of the budget through tax reduction as a means of stimulating growth. It was a great victory for the university economists who had sought to influence the President. According to Ted Sorenson, Kennedy became convinced by a speech they prepared for him to deliver at the Economic Club of New York in December. He also believed that a tax cut was an indirect means of helping the poor, the black, and the cities—and the stock market, which had moved downward the preceding spring. If the tax policy should give new life to the economy, Congress might do something to redress the imbalance between public squalor and private affluence. Early in 1963 Kennedy proposed a $10 billion tax cut, despite a record-breaking peacetime deficit. The unbalanced budget troubled the business community, but it disliked high taxes even more and supported the President. After the Kennedy recommendations became law early in 1964, the pace of economic growth quickened, and before our extensive involvement in Vietnam, prosperity without serious inflation briefly seemed within reach. In a sense, then, it was Kennedy's tax policy, which led to a $30 billion enlargement of Gross National Product that made possible the harvest of Great Society legislation.

Businessmen generally responded well to the economic policies of the Kennedy-Johnson years, though many of them continued to distrust the government's sympathy toward labor. Kennedy obtained tax credits and a liberal depreciation allowance for business in 1962, and reduced corporate income taxes by 20 percent in 1963. But he soon found himself in a confrontation with a powerful segment of business. Early in the Kennedy administration, which had vigorously pursued an anti-inflation policy, the steel industry attempted to raise prices. The act was a major embarrassment for the government, for when Labor Secretary Arthur Goldberg, anxious to avoid a critical strike that might delay economic recovery, had employed his experience in negotiation to persuade labor to keep its wage demands down, he had repeated an assurance given by industry leaders that prices would be held steady. When Roger Blough, President of U.S. Steel, appeared at the White House at 5:45 P.M. on April 10, 1962, to announce that press releases of an industry-wide price rise were just then being distributed, the President was furious. He quoted his father as having said that steelmen were "sons of bitches," and then launched an almost unprecedented attack on a major American industry. The President withdrew defense contracts and threatened antitrust action and new antitrust laws; he used every major branch of the government to bring the steel companies into line. Secretary of Commerce Luther Hodges, himself a businessman, gave Kennedy full support. The President addressed the people bluntly: "In this serious hour in our nation's history, when we are confronted with grave crises in Berlin and Southeast Asia . . . , the American public will find it hard, as I do, to accept a situation in which a tiny handful of steel executives whose pursuit of private power and profit exceeds their sense of public responsibility can show such utter contempt of the interests of 185 million Americans." Kennedy over-played by having the FBI take some uncertain role, but by and large it was a handsome demonstration of presidential power in the service of the public interest. Big Steel, following the lead of some smaller companies, rescinded the price increase. Arthur Krock observed afterward that presidential anger "must be reserved for those rare occasions when the office and the nation as well as the man are basically offended"; the steel episode was such an occasion.

Made confident by successes in foreign affairs and hopeful of improving domestic life, Kennedy gave promise by 1963 of fashioning a stronger presidency. Then Kennedy, two years and ten months after becoming President, went to Dallas. In a typical but foolish gesture, the President sat in an open car moving slowly through the streets of the hostile southern city. In the previous presidential campaign, even Lyndon Johnson had been spat upon in Dallas, and a woman had hit

Ladybird on the head with a placard. And only weeks before, Adlai Stevenson had been physically abused there. The man who almost certainly shot and killed Kennedy, Lee Harvey Oswald, was a refugee of the political Left; but he might easily have been a right-wing fanatic or any lunatic with a grudge against the government. The President's body was flown home to Washington, where the next day, November 23, 1963, a Roman Catholic mass was held in the White House for the first time —something bigots had feared. Chief Justice Earl Warren, reporting swiftly for an investigation panel of eminent but busy men, uncovered no evidence of a conspiracy, and subsequent efforts to find one have proved unconvincing.

A summary view of the Kennedy administration would be out of focus if it concentrated heavily on how much legislation passed through Congress. Such a view could not take into account the times and the might-have-beens—or the possibility that the death of Kennedy provided the national temper needed for the passage of the Kennedy program. This is not to say that the domestic achievements of the thousand days were unimpressive. When Kennedy promised in the presidential campaign to get the country moving again he was referring principally to the economy. As a result of Kennedy's recommendations, the national economy became brilliantly active. Kennedy's belated leadership in the civil rights movement must not be discounted. But the President also made the White House a home for the arts, and he even promised that America would reach the moon before the decade was finished. Important legislation surmounted the Congressional deadlock of the early sixties, including the Peace Corps and drug labeling; and critical beginnings were made on problems of water and air pollution, area redevelopment, and manpower training. Finally, Kennedy acted intelligently in crises: Ole Miss, the University of Alabama, Birmingham, the steel episode, the Cuban missile crisis, and—at least by refusing to compound errors—the Bay of Pigs.

What made the Kennedy years most memorable, besides the event that brought them to a premature conclusion, was something quite intangible. The ambiance of the administration was more significant than its actual legislative record. In attempting to answer various social needs that the New Deal had failed to meet and that had enlarged and multiplied in twenty years of political stasis during hot and cold war, President Kennedy implied that the country could no longer simply go its ordinary way. It required a more intense and faster pace, and a call to moral arms—in the rhetoric of the campaign, a "new frontier." John and Jacqueline Kennedy placed a high and racy fashion of living before a people of growing affluence. It can be granted that much of the Kennedy style fed upon glittering, banal values, that the President's record displays naïveté as often as sophistication, that Kennedy's own taste was often trivial and dull, and that estimates of him are colored by his romance with the intellectuals. But the Kennedy manner gave sharper edge to American life, created expectations still unfulfilled, gave encouragement to civil rights workers, and contributed something to an awakening among America's youth.

Certain forces of the Kennedy era were moving toward a fundamental reconsideration of American society. The issues here are hard to characterize: broadly speaking, they are cultural rather than economic; they relate to race, education, health, the environment, public safety, attitudes toward youth and the quality of life. They are founded, most of them, in the economic and social concern that American liberalism has carried down from the New Deal. The emergence of the racial question in the Kennedy years, however, would bring radical acts of civil disobedience and militant protest by the young, as well as new strivings for social reconstructions and innovative conceptions of community. A cultural politics, which the President scarcely intended, was spawned in the Kennedy years.

The Port Huron Statement

STUDENTS FOR A DEMOCRATIC SOCIETY

The radical tradition in America is a series of episodes, not a continuous story. Where conservatives and liberals never cease reaching back for real or imaginary forbears, radicals have generally insisted on forgetting the history of radicalism as the first act in any new beginning. In the early 1960's, when the Students for a Democratic Society spread from campus to campus, drawing together activists in the civil rights and peace movements, the group received compliments for precisely this tendency to forget the radical past. It was "pragmatic," "non-ideological," and "non-programmatic." The movement worried little about its intellectual underpinnings; its main concern was action. The Port Huron Statement, drawn up at the first SDS convention in 1962, achieved wide circulation on the campuses as an "agenda for a generation."

The document, written principally by Tom Hayden, is impressive in surprising ways. Its tentative assertions, social science language, and generally nationalistic and cooperative stance contrast sharply with the image of campus militancy of the later 1960's. In its quiet way, however, it states the main themes of the youth political movement: rejection of bureaucracy, anti-communism, alienation, and the lack of community. It is clearly the beginning of a quest, not a set of final answers. Where that quest led was one of the fascinating subjects of the decade. It raises the inevitable question—to what extent did the young radicals relive the experience of earlier radicals because they began by rejecting its lessons?

INTRODUCTION: AGENDA FOR A GENERATION

We are people of this generation, bred in at least modest comfort, housed now in universities, looking uncomfortably to the world we inherit.

When we were kids the United States was the wealthiest and strongest country in the world; the only one with the atom bomb, the least scarred by modern war, an initiator of the United Nations that we thought would distribute Western influence throughout the world. Freedom and equality for each individual, government of, by, and for the people—these American values we found good, principles by which we could live as men. Many of us began maturing in complacency.

As we grew, however, our comfort was penetrated by events too troubling to dismiss. First, the permeating and victimizing fact of human degradation, symbolized by the Southern struggle against racial bigotry, compelled most of us from silence to activism. Second, the enclosing fact of the Cold War, symbolized by the presence of the Bomb, brought awareness that we ourselves, and our friends, and millions of abstract "others" we knew more directly because of our common peril, might die at any time. We might deliberately ignore, or avoid, or fail to feel all other human problems, but not these two, for these were too immediate and crushing in their impact, too challenging in the demand that we as individuals take the responsibility for encounter and resolution.

While these and other problems either directly oppressed us or rankled our consciences and became our own subjective concerns, we began to see complicated and disturbing paradoxes in our surrounding America. The declaration "all men are created equal . . ." rang hollow before the facts of Negro life in the South and the big cities of the North. The proclaimed peaceful intentions of the United States contradicted its economic and military investments in the Cold War status quo.

We witnessed, and continue to witness, other paradoxes. With nuclear energy whole cities can easily be powered, yet the dominant nation-states seem more likely to unleash destruction greater than that incurred in all wars of human history. Although our own technology is destroying old and creating new forms of social organization, men still tolerate meaningless work and idleness. While two-thirds of mankind suffers undernourishment, our own upper classes revel amidst superfluous abundance. Although world population is expected to double in forty years, the nations still tolerate anarchy as a major principle of international conduct and uncontrolled exploitation governs the sapping of the earth's physical resources. Although mankind desperately needs revolutionary leadership, America rests in national stalemate, its goals ambiguous and tradition-bound instead of informed and clear, its democratic system apathetic and manipulated rather than "of, by, and for the people."

Not only did tarnish appear on our image of American virtue, not only did disillusion occur when the hypocrisy of American ideals was discovered, but we began to sense that what we had originally seen as the American Golden Age was actually the decline of an era. The worldwide outbreak of revolution against colonialism and imperialism, the entrenchment of totalitarian states, the menace of war, overpopulation, international disorder, supertechnology—these trends were testing the tenacity of our own commitment to democracy and freedom and our abilities to visualize their application to a world in upheaval.

Our work is guided by the sense that we may be the last generation in the experiment with living. But we are a minority—the vast majority of our people regard the temporary equilibriums of our society and world as eternally-functional parts. In this is perhaps the outstanding paradox: we ourselves are imbued with urgency, yet the message of our society is that there is no viable alternative to the present. Beneath the reassuring tones of the politicians, beneath the common opinion that America will "muddle through," beneath the stagnation of those who have closed their minds to the future, is the pervading feeling that there simply are no alternatives, that our times have witnessed the exhaustion not only of Utopias, but of any new departures as well.

Feeling the press of complexity upon the emptiness of life, people are fearful of the thought that at any moment things might be thrust out of control. They fear change itself, since change might smash whatever invisible framework seems to hold back chaos for them now. For most Americans, all crusades are suspect, threatening. The fact that each individual sees apathy in his fellows perpetuates the common reluctance to organize for change. The dominant institutions are complex enough to blunt the minds of their potential critics, and entrenched enough to swiftly dissipate or entirely repel the energies of protest and reform, thus limiting human expectancies. Then, too, we are a materially improved society, and by our own improvements we seem to have weakened the case for further change.

Some would have us believe that Americans feel contentment amidst prosperity—but might it not be better be called a glaze above deeply-felt anxieties about their role in the new world? And if these anxieties produce a developed indifference to human affairs, do they not as well produce a yearning to believe there *is* an alternative to the present, that something *can* be done to change circumstances in the school, the workplaces, the bureaucracies, the government? It is to this latter yearning, at once the spark and engine of change, that we direct our present appeal. The search for truly democratic alternatives to the present, and a commitment to social experimentation with them, is a worthy and fulfilling human enterprise, one which moves us and, we hope, others today. On such a basis do we offer this document of our convictions and analysis: as an effort in understanding and changing the conditions of humanity in the late twentieth century, an effort rooted in the ancient, still unfulfilled conception of man attaining determining influence over his circumstances of life. . . .

THE STUDENTS

In the last few years, thousands of American students demonstrated that they at least felt the urgency of the times. They moved actively and directly against racial injustices, the threat of war, violations of individual rights of conscience and, less frequently, against economic manipulation. They suceeded in restoring a small measure of controversy to the campuses after the stillness of the McCarthy period. They succeeded, too, in gaining some concessions from the people and institutions they opposed, especially in the fight against racial bigotry.

The significance of these scattered movements lies not in their success or failure in gaining objectives—at least not yet. Nor does the significance lie in the intellectual "competence" or "maturity" of the students involved—as some pedantic elders allege. The significance is in the fact the students are breaking the crust of apathy and overcoming the inner alienation that remain the defining characteristics of American college life.

If student movements for change are still rareties on the campus scene, what is commonplace there? The real campus, the familiar campus, is a place of private people, engaged in their notorious "inner emigration." It is a place of commitment to business-as-usual, getting ahead, playing it cool. It is a place of mass affirmation of the Twist, but mass reluctance toward the controversial public stance. Rules are accepted as "inevitable," bureaucracy as "just circumstances," irrelevance as "scholarship," selflessness as "martyrdom," politics as "just another way to make people, and an unprofitable one, too."

Almost no students value activity as citizens. Passive in public, they are hardly more idealistic in arranging their private lives: Gallup concludes they will settle for "low success, and won't risk high failure." There is not much willingness to take risks (not even in business), no settling of dangerous goals, no real conception of personal identity except one manufactured in the image of others, no real urge for personal fulfillment except to be almost as successful as the very successful people. Attention is being paid to social status (the quality of shirt collars, meeting people, getting wives or husbands, making solid contacts for later on); much, too, is paid to academic status (grades, honors, the med school rat race). But neglected generally is real intellectual status, the personal cultivation of the mind.

"Students don't even give a damn about the apathy," one has said. Apathy toward apathy begets a privately-constructed universe, a place of systematic study schedules, two nights each week for beer, a girl or two, and early marriage; a framework infused with personality, warmth, and under control, no matter how unsatisfying otherwise.

Under these conditions university life loses all relevance to some. Four hundred thousand of our classmates leave college every year.

But apathy is not simply an attitude; it is a product of social institutions, and of the structure and organization of higher education itself. The extracurricular life is ordered according to *in loco parentis* theory, which ratifies the Administration as the moral guardian of the young.

The accompanying "let's pretend" theory of student extracurricular affairs validates student government as a training center for those who want to spend their lives in political pretense, and discourages initiative from the more articulate, honest, and sensitive students. The bounds and style of controversy are delimited before controversy begins. The university "prepares" the student for "citizenship" through perpetual rehearsals and, usually, through emasculation of what creative spirit there is in the individual.

The academic life contains reinforcing counterparts to the way in which extracurricular life is organized. The academic world is founded on a teacher-student relation analogous to the parent-child relation which characterizes *in loco parentis*. Further, academia includes a radical separation of the student from the material of study. That which is studied, the social reality, is "objectified" to sterility, dividing the student from life—just as he is restrained in active involvement by the deans controlling student government. The specialization of function and knowledge, admittedly necessary to our complex technological and social structure, has produced an exaggerated compartmentalization of study and understanding. This has contributed to an overly parochial view, by faculty, of the role of its research and scholarship, to a discontinuous and truncated understanding, by students, of the surrounding social order; and to a loss of personal attachment, by nearly all, to the worth of study as a humanistic enterprise.

There is, finally, the cumbersome academic bureaucracy extending throughout the academic as well as the extracurricular structures, contributing to the sense of outer complexity and inner powerlessness that transforms the honest searching of many students to a ratification of convention and, worse, to a numbness to present and future catastrophes. The size and financing systems of the university enhance the permanent trusteeship of the administrative bureaucracy, their power leading to a shift within the university toward the value standards of business and the administrative mentality. Huge foundations and other private financial interests shape the under-financed colleges and universities, not only making them more commercial, but less disposed to diagnose society critically, less open to dissent. Many social and physical scientists, neglecting the liberating heritage of higher learning, develop "human relations" or "morale-producing" techniques for the corporate economy, while others exercise their intellectual skills to accelerate the arms race.

Tragically, the university could serve as a significant source of social criticism and an initiator of new modes and molders of attitudes. But the actual intellectual effect of the college experience is hardly distinguishable from that of any other communications channel—say, a television set—passing on the stock truths of the day. Students leave college somewhat more "tolerant" than when they arrived, but basically unchallenged in their values and political orientations. With administrators ordering the institution, and faculty the curriculum, the student learns by his isolation to accept elite rule within the university, which prepares him to accept later forms of minority control. The real function of the educational system—as opposed to its more rhetorical function of "searching for truth"—is to impart the key information and styles that will help the student get by, modestly but comfortably, in the big society beyond.

THE SOCIETY BEYOND

Look beyond the campus, to America itself. That student life is more intellectual, and perhaps more comfortable, does not obscure the fact that the fundamental qualities of life on the campus reflect the habits of society at large. The fraternity president is seen at the junior manager levels; the sorority queen has gone to Grosse Pointe; the serious poet burns for a place, any place, to work; the once-serious and never-serious poets work at the advertising agencies. The desperation of people threatened by forces about which they know little and of which they can say less; the cheerful emptiness of people "giving up" all hope of changing things; the faceless ones polled by Gallup who listed "international affairs" fourteenth on their list of "problems" but who also expected thermonuclear war in the next few years; in these and other forms, Americans are in withdrawal from public life, from any collective effort at directing their own affairs.

Some regard these national doldrums as a sign of healthy approval of the established order—but is it approval by consent or manipulated acquiescence? Others declare that the people are withdrawn because compelling issues are fast disappearing—perhaps there are fewer bread-lines in America, but is Jim Crow gone, is there enough work and work more fulfilling, is world war a diminishing threat, and what of the revolutionary new peoples? Still others think the national quietude is a necessary consequence of the need for elites to resolve complex and specialized problems of modern industrial society—but, then, why should *business* elites help decide foreign policy, and who controls the elites anyway, and are they solving mankind's problems? Others, finally, shrug knowingly and announce that full democracy never worked anywhere in the past—but why lump qualitatively different civilizations together, and how can a social order work well if its best thinkers are skeptics, and is man really doomed forever to the domination of today?

There are no convincing apologies for the contemporary malaise. While the world tumbles toward final war, while men in other nations are trying desperately to alter events, while the very future qua future is uncertain—America is without community, impulse, without the inner momentum necessary for an age when societies cannot successfully perpetuate themselves by their military weapons, when democracy must be viable because of the quality of life, not its quantity of rockets.

The apathy here is, first *subjective*—the felt powerlessness of ordinary people, the resignation before the enormity of events. But subjective apathy is encouraged by the *objective* American situation—the actual structural separation of people from power, from relevant knowledge, from pinnacles of decision-making. Just as the university influences the student way of life, so do major social institutions create the circumstances in which the isolated citizen will try hopelessly to understand his world and himself.

The very isolation of the individual—from power and community and ability to aspire—means the rise of a democracy without publics. With the great mass of people structurally remote and psychologically hesitant with respect to democratic institutions, those institutions themselves attenuate and become, in the fashion of the vicious circle, progressively less accessible to those few who aspire to serious participation in social affairs. The vital democratic connection between community and leadership, between the mass and the several elites, has been so wrenched and perverted that disastrous policies go unchallenged time and again.

POLITICS WITHOUT PUBLICS

The American political system is not the democratic model of which its glorifiers speak. In actuality it frustrates democracy by confusing the individual citizen, paralyzing policy discussion, and consolidating the irresponsible power of military and business interests.

A crucial feature of the political apparatus in America is that greater differences are harbored within each major party than the differences existing between them. Instead of two parties presenting distinctive and significant differences of approach, what dominates the system is a natural interlocking of Democrats from Southern states with the more conservative elements of the Republican party. This arrangement of forces is blessed by the seniority system of Congress which guarantees congressional committee domination by conservatives—ten of 17 committees in the Senate and 13 of 21 in the House of Representatives are chaired currently by Dixiecrats.

The party overlap, however, is not the only structural antagonist of democracy in politics. First, the localized nature of the party system does not encourage discussion of national and international issues: thus problems are not raised by and for people, and political representatives usually are unfettered from any responsibilities to the general public except those regarding parochial matters. Second, whole constituencies are divested of the full political power they might have: many Negroes in the South are prevented from voting, migrant workers are disenfranchised by various residence requirements, some urban and suburban dwellers are victimized by gerrymandering, and poor people are too often without the power to obtain political representation. Third, the focus of political attention is significantly distorted by the enormous lobby force, composed predominantly of business interests, spending hundreds of millions each year in an attempt to conform facts about productivity, agriculture, defense, and social services, to the wants of private economic groupings.

What emerges from the party contradiction and insulation of privately-held power is the organized political stalemate: calcification dominates flexibility as the principle of parliamentary organization, frustration is the expectancy of legislators intending liberal reform, and Congress becomes less and less central to national decision-making especially in the area of foreign policy. In this context, confusion and blurring is built into the formulation of issues, long-range priorities are not discussed in the rational manner needed for policy-making, the politics of personality and "image" become a more important mechanism than the construction of issues in a way that affords each voter a challenging and real option. The American voter is buffeted from all directions by pseudo-problems, by the structurally-initiated sense that nothing political is subject to human mastery. Worried by his mundane problems which never get solved, but constrained by the common belief that politics is an agonizingly slow accommodation of views, he quits all pretense of bothering.

A most alarming fact is that few, if any, politicians are calling for changes in these conditions. Only a handful even are calling on the President to "live up to" platform pledges; no one is demanding structural changes, such as the shuttling of Southern Democrats out of the Democratic Party. Rather than protesting the state of politics, most politicians are reinforcing and aggravating that state. While in practice they rig public opinion to suit their own interests, in word and ritual they enshrine "the sovereign public" and call for more and more letters. Their speeches and campaign actions are banal, based on a degrading conception of what people want to hear. They respond not to dialogue, but to pressure: and knowing this, the ordinary citizen sees even greater inclination to shun the political sphere. The politician is usually a trumpeter to "citizenship" and "service to the nation," but since he is unwilling to seriously rearrange power relationships, his trumpetings only increase apathy by creating no outlets. Much of the time the call to "service" is justified not in idealistic terms, but in the crasser terms of "defending the free world from communism"—thus making future idealistic impulses harder to justify in anything but Cold War terms.

In such a setting of status quo politics, where most if not all government activity is rationalized in Cold War anti-communist terms, it is somewhat natural that discontented, super-patriotic groups would emerge through political channels and explain their ultra-conservatism as the best means of Victory over Communism. They have become a politically influential force within the Republican Party, at a national level through Senator Goldwater, and at a local level through their important social and economic roles. Their political views are defined generally as the opposite of the supposed views of communists: complete individual freedom in the economic sphere, non-participation by the government in the machinery of production. But actually "anti-communism" becomes an umbrella by which to protest liberalism, internationalism, welfareism, the active civil rights and labor movements. It is to the disgrace of the United States that such a movement should become a prominent kind of public participation in the modern world—but, ironically, it is somewhat to the interests of the United States that such a movement should be a public constituency pointed toward realignment of the political parties, demanding a conservative Republican Party in the South and an exclusion of the "leftist" elements of the national GOP.

THE ECONOMY

American capitalism today advertises itself as the Welfare State. Many of us comfortably expect pensions, medical care, unemployment compensation, and other social services in our lifetimes. Even with one-fourth of our productive capacity unused, the majority of Americans are living in relative comfort—although their nagging incentive to "keep up" makes them continually dissatisfied with their possessions. In many places, unrestrained bosses, uncontrolled machines, and sweatshop conditions have been reformed or abolished and suffering tremendously relieved. But in spite of the benign yet obscuring effects of the New Deal reforms and the reassuring phrases of government economists and politicians, the paradoxes and myths of the economy are sufficient to irritate our complacency and reveal to us some essential causes of the American malaise.

We live amidst a national celebration of economic prosperity while poverty and deprivation remain an unbreakable way of life for millions in the "affluent society," including many of our own generation. We hear glib references to the "welfare state," "free enterprise," and "shareholder's democracy" while military defense is the main item of "public" spending and obvious oligopoly and other forms of minority rule defy real individual initiative or popular control. Work, too, is often unfulfilling and victimizing, accepted as a channel to status or plenty, if not a way to pay the bills, rarely as a means of understanding and controlling self and events. In work and leisure the individual is regulated as part of the system, a consuming unit, bombarded by hard-sell, soft-sell, lies and semi-true appeals to his basest drives. He is always told that he is a "free" man because of "free enterprise." . . .

THE MILITARY-INDUSTRIAL COMPLEX

The most spectacular and important creation of the authoritarian and oligopolistic structure of economic decision-making in America is the institution called "the military-industrial complex" by former President Eisenhower—the powerful congruence of interest and structure among military and business elites which affects so much of our development and destiny. Not only is ours the first generation to live with the possibility of world-wide cataclysm—it is the first to experience the actual social preparation for cataclysm, the general militarization of American society. In 1948 Congress established Universal Military Training, the first peacetime conscription. The military became a permanent institution. Four years earlier, General Motors' Charles E. Wilson had heralded the creation of what he called the "permanent war economy," the continuous use of military spending as a solution to economic problems unsolved before the post-war boom, most notably the problem of the seventeen million jobless after eight years of the New Deal. This has left a "hidden crisis" in the allocation of resources by the American economy.

Since our childhood these two trends—the rise of the military and the installation of a defense-based economy—have grown fantastically. The Department of Defense, ironically the world's largest single organization, is worth $160 billion, owns 32 million acres of America and employs half the 7.5 million persons directly dependent on the military for subsistence, has an $11 billion payroll which is larger than the net annual income of all American corporations. Defense spending in the Eisenhower era totaled $350 billions and President Kennedy entered office pledged to go even beyond the present defense allocation of 60 cents from every public dollar spent. Except for a war-induced boom immediately after "our side" bombed Hiroshima, American economic prosperity has coincided with a growing dependence on military outlay—from 1941 to 1959 America's Gross National Product of $5.25 trillion included $700 billion in goods and services purchased for the defense effort, about one-seventh of the accumulated GNP. This pattern has included the steady concentration of military spending among a few corporations. In 1961, 86 percent of Defense Department contracts were awarded without competition. The ordnance industry of 100,000 people is completely engaged in military work; in the aircraft industry, 94 percent of 750,000 workers are linked to the war economy; shipbuilding, radio and communications equipment industries commit 40 percent of their work to defense; iron and steel, petroleum, metal-stamping and machine shop products, motors and generators, tools and hardware, copper, aluminum and machine tools industries all devote at least 10 percent of their work to the same cause.

The intermingling of Big Military and Big Industry is evidenced in the 1,400 former officers working for the 100 corporations who received nearly all the $21 billion spent in procurement by the Defense Department in 1961. The overlap is most poignantly clear in the case of General Dynamics, the company which received the best 1961 contracts, employed the most retired officers (187), and is directed by a former Secretary of the Army. A *Fortune* magazine profile of General Dynamics said: "The unique group of men who run Dynamics are only incidentally in rivalry with other U.S. manufacturers, with many of whom they actually act in concert. Their chief competitor is the USSR. The core of General Dynamics' corporate philosophy is the conviction that national defense is a more or less permanent business." Little has changed since Wilson's proud declaration of the Permanent War Economy back in the 1944 days when the top 200 corporations possessed 80 percent of all active prime war-supply contracts.

MILITARY-INDUSTRIAL POLITICS

The military and its supporting business foundation have found numerous forms of political expression, and we have heard their din endlessly. There has not been a major Congressional split on the issue of continued defense spending spirals in our lifetime. The triangular relations of the business, military, and political arenas cannot be better expressed than in Dixiecrat Carl Vinson's remarks as his House Armed Services Committee reported out a military construction bill of $808 million throughout the 50 states, for 1960-61: "There is something in this bill for everyone," he announced. President Kennedy had earlier acknowledged the valuable anti-recession features of the bill.

Imagine, on the other hand, $808 million suggested as an anti-recession measure, but being poured into programs of social welfare: the impossibility of receiving support for such a measure identifies a crucial feature of defense spending—it is beneficial to private enterprise, while welfare spending is not. Defense spending does not "compete" with the private sector; it contains a natural obsolescence; its "confidential" nature permits easier boondoggling; the tax burdens to which it leads can be shunted from corporation to consumer as a "cost of production." Welfare spending, however, involves the government in competition with private corporations and contractors; it conflicts with immediate interests of private pressure groups; it leads to taxes on business. Think of the opposition of private power companies to current proposals for river and valley development, or the hostility of the real estate lobby to urban renewal; or the attitude of the American Medical

Association to a paltry medical care bill; or of all business lobbyists to foreign aid; these are the pressures leading to the schizophrenic public-military, private-civilian economy of our epoch. The politicians, of course, take the line of least resistance and thickest support: warfare, instead of welfare, is easiest to stand up for: after all, the Free World is at stake (and our constituency's investments, too). . . .

THE STANCE OF LABOR

Amidst all this, what of organized labor, the historic institutional representative of the exploited, the presumed "countervailing power" against the excesses of Big Business? The contemporary social assault on the labor movement is of crisis proportions. To the average American, "big labor" is a growing cancer equal in impact to Big Business—nothing could be more distorted, even granting a sizeable union bureaucracy. But in addition to public exaggerations, the labor crisis can be measured in several ways. First, the high expectations of the newborn AFL-CIO of 30 million members by 1965 are suffering a reverse unimaginable five years ago. The demise of the dream of "organizing the unorganized" is dramatically reflected in the AFL-CIO decision, just two years after its creation, to slash its organizing staff in half. From 15 million members when the AFL and CIO merged, the total has slipped to 13.5 million. During the post-war generation, union membership nationally has increased by four million—but the total number of workers has jumped by 13 million. Today only 40 percent of all non-agricultural workers are protected by any form of organization. Second, organizing conditions are going to worsen. Where labor now is strongest—in industries—automation is leading to an attrition of available work. As the number of jobs dwindles, so does labor's power of bargaining, since management can handle a strike in an automated plant more easily than the older mass-operated ones.

More important, perhaps, the American economy has changed radically in the last decade, as suddenly the number of workers producing goods became fewer than the number in "nonproductive" areas—government, trade, finance, services, utilities, transportation. Since World War II "white collar" and "service" jobs have grown twice as fast as have "blue collar" production jobs. Labor has almost no organization in the expanding occupational areas of the new economy, but almost all of its entrenched strength in contracting areas. As big government hires more, as business seeks more office workers and skilled technicians, and as growing commercial America demands new hotels, service stations and the like, the conditions will become graver still. Further, there is continuing hostility to labor by the Southern states and their industrial interests—meaning "runaway" plants, cheap labor threatening the organized trade union movement, and opposition from Dixiecrats to favorable labor legislation in Congress. Finally, there is indication that Big Business, for the sake of public relations if nothing more, has acknowledged labor's "right" to exist, but has deliberately tried to contain labor at its present strength, preventing strong unions from helping weaker ones or from spreading to unorganized sectors of the economy. Business is aided in its efforts by proliferation of "right-to-work" laws at state levels (especially in areas where labor is without organizing strength to begin with), and anti-labor legislation in Congress.

In the midst of these besetting crises, labor itself faces its own problems of vision and program. Historically, there can be no doubt as to its worth in American politics—what progress there has been in meeting human needs in this century rests greatly with the labor movement. And to a considerable extent the social democracy for which labor has fought externally is reflected in its own essentially democratic character: representing millions of people, not millions of dollars; demanding their welfare, not eternal profit.

Today labor remains the most liberal "mainstream" institution—but often its liberalism represents vestigial commitments, self-interestedness, unradicalism. In some measure labor has succumbed to institutionalization, its social idealism waning under the tendencies of bureaucracy, materialism, business ethics. The successes of the last generation perhaps have braked, rather than accelerated labor's zeal for change. Even the House of Labor has bay windows: not only is this true of the labor elites, but as well of some of the rank-and-file. Many of the latter are indifferent unionists, uninterested in meetings, alienated from the complexities of the labor-management negotiating apparatus, lulled to comfort by the accessibility of luxury and the opportunity of long-term contracts. "Union democracy" is not simply inhibited by labor-leader elitism, but by the related problem of rank-and-file apathy to the tradition of unionism. The crisis of labor is reflected in the co-existence within the unions of militant Negro discontents and discriminatory locals, sweeping critics of the obscuring "public interest" marginal tinkering of government and willing handmaidens of conservative political leadership, austere sacrificers and business-like operators, visionaries and anachronisms—tensions between extremes that keep alive the possibilities for a more militant unionism. Too there are seeds of rebirth in the "organizational crisis" itself: the technologically unemployed, the unorganized white collar men and women, the migrants and farm workers, the unprotected Negroes, the poor, all of whom are isolated now from the power structure of the economy, but who are the potential base for a broader and more forceful unionism.

HORIZON

In summary: a more reformed, more human capitalism, functioning at three-fourths capacity while one-third of America and two-thirds of the world goes needy, domination of politics and the economy by fantastically rich elites, accommodation and limited effectiveness by the labor movement, hard-core poverty and unemployment, automation confirming the dark ascension of machine over man instead of shared abundance, technological change being introduced into the economy by the criteria of profitability—this has been our inheritance. However inadequate, it has instilled quiescence in liberal hearts—partly reflecting the extent to which misery has been overcome, but also the eclipse of social ideals. Though many of us are "affluent," poverty, waste, elitism, manipulation are too manifest to go unnoticed, too clearly unnecessary to go accepted. To change the Cold War status quo and other social evils, concern with the challenges to the American economic machine must expand. Now, as a truly better social state becomes visible, a new poverty impends: a poverty of vision, and a poverty of political action to make that vision reality. Without new vision, the failure to achieve our potentialities will spell the inability of our society to endure in a world of obvious, crying needs and rapid change. . . .

TOWARDS AMERICAN DEMOCRACY

Every effort to end the Cold War and expand the process of world industrialization is an effort hostile to people and institutions whose interests lie in perpetuation of the East-West military threat and the postponement of change in the "have not" nations of the world. Every such effort, too, is bound to establish greater democracy in America. The major goals of a domestic effort would be:

1 *America must abolish its political party stalemate.*

Two genuine parties, centered around issues and essential values, demanding allegiance to party principles shall supplant the current system of organized stalemate which is seriously inadequate to a world in flux. . . . What is desirable is sufficient party disagreement to dramatize major issues, yet sufficient party overlap to guarantee stable transitions from administration to administration.

Every time the President criticizes a recalcitrant Congress, we must ask that he no longer tolerate the Southern conservatives in the Democratic Party. Every time a liberal representative complains that "we can't expect everything at once" we must ask if we received much of anything from Congress in the last generation. Every time he refers to "circumstances beyond control" we must ask why he fraternizes with racist scoundrels. Every time he speaks of the "unpleasantness of personal and party fighting" we should insist that pleasantry with Dixiecrats is inexcusable when the dark peoples of the world call for American support.

2 *Mechanisms of voluntary association must be created through which political information can be imparted and political participation encouraged.*

Political parties, even if realigned, would not provide adequate outlets for popular involvement. Institutions should be created that engage people with issues and express political preference, not as now with huge business lobbies which exercise undemocratic *power* but which carry political *influence* (appropriate to private, rather than public, groupings) in national decision-making enterprise. Private in nature, these should be organized around single issues (medical care, transportation systems reform, etc.), concrete interest (labor and minority group organizations); multiple issues or general issues. These do not exist in America in quantity today. If they did exist, they would be a significant politicizing and educative force bringing people into touch with public life and affording them means of expression and action. Today, giant lobby representatives of business interests are dominant, but not educative. The Federal government itself should counter the latter forces whose intent is often public deceit for private gain, by subsidizing the preparation and decentralized distribution of objective materials on all public issues facing government.

3 Institutions and practices which stifle dissent should be abolished, and the promotion of peaceful dissent should be actively promoted.

The First Amendment freedoms of speech, assembly, thought, religion and press should be seen as guarantees, not threats, to national security. While society has the right to prevent active subversion of its laws and institutions, it has the duty as well to promote open discussion of all issues—otherwise it will be in fact promoting real subversion as the only means of implementing ideas. To eliminate the fears and apathy from national life it is necessary that the institutions bred by fear and apathy be rooted out: the House Un-American Activities Committee, the Senate Internal Security Committee, the loyalty oaths on Federal loans, the Attorney General's list of subversive organizations, the Smith and McCarran Acts. The process of eliminating the blighting institutions is the process of restoring democratic participation. Their existence is a sign of the decomposition and atrophy of participation.

4 Corporations must be made publicly responsible.

It is not possible to believe that true democracy can exist where a minority utterly controls enormous wealth and power. The influence of corporate elites on foreign policy is neither reliable nor democratic; a way must be found to subordinate private American foreign investment to a democratically-constructed foreign policy. . . .

Labor and government as presently constituted are not sufficient to "regulate" corporations. A new re-ordering, a new calling of responsibility is necessary: more than changing "work rules" we must consider changes in the rules of society by challenging the unchallenged politics of American corporations. Before the government can really begin to control business in a "public interest," the public must gain more substantial control of government: this demands a movement for political as well as economic realignments. We are aware that simple government "regulation," if achieved, would be inadequate without increased worker participation in management decision-making, strengthened and independent regulatory power, balances of partial and/or complete public ownership, various means of humanizing the conditions and types of work itself, sweeping welfare programs and regional *public* development authorities. These are examples of measures to re-balance the economy toward public—and individual—control.

5 *The allocation of resources must be based on social needs. A truly "public sector" must be established, and its nature debated and planned.*

At present the majority of America's "public sector," the largest part of our public spending, is for the military. When great social needs are so pressing, our concept of "government spending" is wrapped up in the "permanent war economy." . . .

The main *private* forces of economic expansion cannot guarantee a steady rate of growth, nor acceptable recovery from recession—especially in a demilitarizing world. Government participation will inevitably expand enormously, because the stable growth of the economy demands increasing "public" investments yearly. Our present outpour of more than $500 billion might double in a generation, irreversibly involving government solutions. And in future recessions, the compensatory fiscal action by the government will be the only means of avoiding the twin disasters of greater unemployment and a slackening rate of growth. Furthermore, a close relationship with the European Common Market will involve competition with numerous planned economies and may aggravate American unemployment unless the economy here is expanding swiftly enough to create new jobs.

All these tendencies suggest that not only solutions to our present social needs but our future expansion rests upon our willingness to enlarge the "public sector" greatly. Unless we choose war as an economic solvent, future public spending will be of non-military nature— a major intervention into civilian production by the government. . . .

6 *America should concentrate on its genuine social priorities: abolish squalor, terminate neglect, and establish an environment for people to live in with dignity and creativeness.*

A. A program against *poverty* must be just as sweeping as the nature of poverty itself. It must not be just palliative, but directed to the abolition of the structural circumstances of poverty. At a bare minimum it should include a *housing* act far larger than the one supported by the Kennedy Administration, but one that is geared more to low- and middle-income needs than to the windfall aspirations of small and large private entrepreneurs, one that is more sympathetic to the quality of communal life than to the efficiency of city-split highways. Second, *medical care* must become recognized as a lifetime human right just as vital as food, shelter and clothing—the Federal government should guarantee health insurance as a basic social service turning medical treatment into a social habit, not just an occasion of crisis, fighting sickness among the aged, not just by making medical care financially feasible but by reducing sickness among children and younger people. Third, existing institutions should be expanded so the Welfare State cares for *everyone's* welfare according to need. *Social Security* payments should be extended to everyone and should be proportionately greater for the poorest. A *minimum wage* of at least $1.50 should be extended to all workers (including the 16 million currently not covered at all). Programs for equal *educational opportunity* are as important a part of the battle against poverty.

B. A full-scale public initiative for civil rights should be undertaken despite the clamor among conservatives (and liberals) about gradualism, property rights, and law and order. The executive and legislative branches of the Federal government should work by enforcement *and* enactment against any form of exploitation of minority groups. No Federal cooperation with racism is tolerable—from financing of schools, to the development of Federally-supported industry, to the social gatherings of the President. Laws hastening school desegregation, voting rights, and economic protection for Negroes are needed right now. The moral force of the Executive Office should be exerted against the Dixiecrats specifically, and the national complacency about the race question generally. Especially in the North, where one-half of the country's Negro people now live, civil rights is not a problem to be solved in isolation from other problems. The fight against poverty, against slums, against the stalemated Congress, against McCarthyism, are all fights against the discrimination that is nearly endemic to all areas of American life.

C. The promise and problems of long-range *Federal economic development* should be studied more constructively. It is an embarrassing paradox that the Tennessee Valley Authority is a wonder to most foreign visitors but a "radical" and barely influential project to most Americans. The Kennedy decision to permit private facilities to transmit power from the $1 billion Colorado River Storage Project is a disastrous one, interposing privately-owned transmitters between publicly-owned generators and their publicly (and cooperatively) owned distributors. The contrary trend, to public ownership of power, should be generated in an experimental way.

The Area Redevelopment Act of 1961 is a first step in recognizing the underdeveloped areas of the United States. It is only a drop in the bucket financially and is not keyed to public planning and public works on a broad scale. It consists only of a few loan programs to lure industries and some grants to improve public facilities to lure these industries. The current public works bill in Congress is needed—and a more sweeping, higher-priced program of regional development with a proliferation of "TVAs" in such areas as the Appalachian region are needed desperately. However, it has been rejected already by Mississippi because the improvement it bodes for the unskilled Negro worker. This program should be enlarged, given teeth, and pursued rigorously by Federal authorities.

D. We must meet the growing complex of "city" problems; over 90 percent of Americans will live in urban areas within two decades. Juvenile delinquency, untended mental illness, crime increase, slums, urban tenantry and non-rent controlled housing, the isolation of the individual in the city—all are problems of the city and are major symptoms of the present system of economic priorities and lack of public planning. Private property control (the real estate lobby and a few selfish landowners and businesses) is as devastating in the cities as corporations are on the national level. But there is no comprehensive way to deal with these problems now amidst competing units of government, dwindling tax resources, suburban escapism (saprophitic to the sick central cities), high infrastructure costs and no one to pay them.

The only solutions are national and regional. "Federalism" has thus far failed here because states are rural-dominated; the Federal government has had to operate by bootlegging and trickle-down measures dominated by private interests, with their appendages through annexation or federation. A new external challenge is needed, not just a Department of Urban Affairs but a thorough national *program* to help the cities. The *model* city must be projected—more community decision-making and participation, true integration of classes, races, vocations— provision for beauty, access to nature and the benefits of the central city as well, privacy without privatism, decentralized "units" spread horizontally with central, regional democratic control—provision for the basic facility-needs, for everyone, with units of planned *regions* and thus public, democratic control over the growth of the civic community and the allocation of resources.

E. *Mental health institutions* are in dire need; there were fewer mental hospital beds in relation to the numbers of mentally-ill in 1959 than there were in 1948. Public hospitals, too, are seriously wanting; existing structures alone need an estimated $1 billion for rehabilitation. Tremendous staff and faculty needs exist as well, and there are not enough medical students enrolled today to meet the anticipated needs of the future.

F. Our *prisons* are too often the enforcers of misery. They must be either re-oriented to rehabilitative work through public supervision or be abolished for their dehumanizing social effects. Funds are needed, too, to make possible a decent prison environment.

G. *Education* is too vital a public problem to be completely entrusted to the province of the various states and local units. In fact, there is no good reason why America should not progress now toward internationalizing rather than localizing, its education system—children and young adults studying everywhere in the world, through a United Nations program, would go far to create mutual understanding. In the meantime, the need for teachers and classrooms in America is fantastic. This is an area where "minimal" requirements should hardly be considered as a goal—there always are improvements to be made in the education system, e.g., smaller classes and many more teachers for them, programs to subsidize the education for the poor but bright, etc.

H. America should eliminate *agricultural policies* based on scarcity and pent-up surplus. In America and foreign countries there exist tremendous needs for more food and balanced diets. The Federal government should finance small farmers' cooperatives, strengthen programs of rural electrification, and expand policies for the distribution of agricultural surpluses throughout the world (by Food-for-Peace and related

UN programming). Marginal farmers must be helped to either become productive enough to survive "industrialized agriculture" or given help in making the transition out of agriculture—the current Rural Area Development program must be better coordinated with a massive national "area redevelopment" program.

I. *Science* should be employed to constructively transform the conditions of life throughout the United States and the world. Yet at the present time the Department of Health, Education, and Welfare and the National Science Foundation together spend only $300 million annually for scientific purposes in contrast to the $6 billion spent by the Defense Department and the Atomic Energy Commission. One-half of all research and development in America is directly devoted to military purposes. Two imbalances must be corrected—that of military over nonmilitary investigation, and that of biological-natural-physical science over the sciences of human behavior. Our political system must then include planning for the human use of science: by anticipating the political consequences of scientific innovation, by directing the discovery and exploration of space, by adapting science to improved production of food, to international communications systems, to technical problems of disarmament, and so on. For the newly-developing nations, American science should focus on the study of cheap sources of power, housing and building materials, mass educational techniques, etc. Further, science and scholarship should be seen less as an apparatus of conflicting power blocs, but as a bridge toward supra-national community: the International Geophysical Year is a model for continuous further cooperation between the science communities of all nations.

Building the Great Society: The Case of Equal Rights

JAMES SUNDQUIST

The reputation of Lyndon Johnson and his Great Society is at low ebb. Conservatives never honored it; many liberals have rejected it out of distaste for and fear of a strong executive and a preference for local, communal, or anti-bureaucratic means; blacks have passed beyond it to demands which its legislation could not meet. Yet this does an acute disservice to the man who, as the black novelist Ralph Ellison wrote, will "have to settle for being recognized as the greatest American President for the poor and for the Negroes. . . ." The radicals who have moved from their dissatisfaction with Johnson's domestic program to a rejection of the entire American political tradition have had logic on their side. If Johnson on civil rights is to be considered a mistake then all else in our history can only be called a scandal. The credibility of every effort to bring racial justice to America may stand or fall with the achievements of the 1960's.

James Sundquist makes clear that Johnson did what black people themselves demanded. After the Civil Rights Act of 1964, which the civil rights movement forced on the nation, Johnson was pressing farther than political expediency required. He chose to make the revolution irreversible with voting rights and housing acts breathtaking in scope and radical in long-range effects. He pressed for action far beyond the national consensus of which he endlessly spoke. While it is correct to remember Johnson as the man whose administration was politically destroyed by Vietnam, Sundquist reminds us that at least some of his popularity was eroded because of his militant support for civil rights. Apparently many white Americans feared that the Johnson program did in fact contain the possibility of revolutionary changes in race relations. The future will tell whose alarm was more justifiable: that of the militants who deprecated Johnson's program as tame and inadequate, or that of white racists who feared it had already gone too far.

"We Have Talked Long Enough." President Johnson moved at once to set at rest any doubt that a southern President was as firmly committed to civil rights as his northern predecessor. In his brief address to Congress on November 27, he listed first among "immediate tasks" the passage of the civil rights bill. "We have talked long enough in this country about equal rights," he told Congress. "We have talked for one hundred years or more. It is time now to write the next chapter, and to write it in the books of law. . . ."

Chairman Howard Smith of the House Rules Committee said a few days later that he planned no hearings. Celler then filed a discharge petition, and Johnson said he would give the petition his full support.

Smith responded by promising hearings early in January. With unanimous Republican and northern Democratic support, the measure easily cleared the Rules Committee. The "most intensive, extensive, and effective lobby assembled in Washington in many years"—as Senator Russell ruefully called it—helped the leadership and the Democratic Study Group make sure that committed congressmen were in Washington and on the floor for teller votes, and with this support Celler and McCulloch defeated every major amendment and the bill coasted to passage, 290-130. In the opposition were twenty-two Republicans and four Democrats from outside the South, but offsetting these were eleven southern Democratic votes.

In the Senate as in the House, the Republicans held the key to the final outcome—and they held it even more tightly, because a two-thirds vote to break a filibuster would require the almost solid support of senators of both parties from the North and West. Minority Leader Dirksen, who was also ranking Republican on the Judiciary Committee, occupied the central position as leader of his party's uncommitted "moderates." Initially, Dirksen had declined to support the public accommodations section of the Kennedy program, and he had never supported a fair employment practices bill that had enforcement features. For the next three months he was the pivotal figure in the civil rights debate and the focus of the most intensive pressure by the civil rights groups.

As in 1957 and 1960, the House bill was intercepted and placed directly on the Senate calendar without referral to committee. On March 9, Majority Leader Mansfield moved for the bill's consideration—and one of the longest filibusters in the history of the Senate began. The southerners were, as before, organized in teams to hold the floor as long as necessary, but the nonsoutherners were organized too. Majority Whip Hubert Humphrey was designated as floor leader, with Minority Whip Thomas H. Kuchel of California as his opposite number. Individual senators on both sides were assigned responsibility for mastering particular titles of the bill and defending them in floor debate. Floor duty was scheduled. A daily information bulletin was published. The senators and their staffs met daily with Justice Department representatives, and twice a week with spokesmen for the Leadership Conference.

The Humphrey-Kuchel strategy was to avoid a cloture motion until they could count the necessary two-thirds vote to end debate. President Johnson made clear that time did not matter—all other Senate business could wait three months, if necessary, to get the civil rights bill passed. The leadership held Saturday sessions, and met morning and afternoon, but avoided the all-night sessions that might irritate potential supporters. Once the southerners had had unquestionably ample time to present their case—and as the civil rights groups did their work on the uncommitted senators—the votes for cloture grew.

By all accounts the work of the churches was decisive. "Washington has not seen such a gigantic and well-organized lobby since the legislative days of Volstead and the Prohibition amendment," complained Georgia's Senator Russell early in the debate. "Groups of ministers from all over the nation arrive in relays. . . ." Three months later he compared "the philosophy of coercion by the men of the cloth" to the doctrines of the Spanish inquisition and observed: "We have seen cardinals, bishops, elders, stated clerks, common preachers, priests, and rabbis come to Washington to press for passage of the bill. They have sought to make its passage a great moral issue. . . . They have encouraged and prompted thousands of good citizens to sign petitions supporting the bill. . . ." Douglas said "the active participation of the church people . . . is . . . the decisive venture in the civil rights struggle. Religious bodies of many faiths organized in large part the historic nonviolent March on Washington that was televised to the nation in August 1963. Clergymen were prominent in demonstrations everywhere; they were among the jailed and the killed. The chief executive of the United Presbyterian Church, Eugene Carson Blake, was arrested for trying to integrate a Baltimore amusement park. The churches supplied a civil rights constituency, for the first time, to senators from the Rocky Mountain and Great Plains states where Negroes are few and civil rights sentiment had in the past been weak—and whose senators had traditionally voted against cloture motions. And despite the "white backlash" that was apparent in some primaries, there was no organized opposition to the bill in the North to offset the church influence.

Meanwhile, Humphrey and his colleagues and the Justice Department negotiated intensively with Dirksen; President Johnson "never let him alone for thirty minutes," as one White House staff member put it. The Kuchel bloc of Republican activists kept him under pressure—and also kept Humphrey under pressure not to concede too much. Mc-Culloch and other House Republicans let Dirksen know they were not abandoning their bill. Public opinion polls showed overwhelming support for action. And Dirksen moved steadily toward a compromise. In mid-May, when the compromise was announced, it was clear that he had come far more than halfway. He accepted an enforceable title on employment practices, with relatively minor modifications: Suits would be brought by the attorney general, rather than the equal employment opportunity commission, and only in cases where he found a "pattern" of discrimination; and an aggrieved individual could not sue until he had exhausted state or local remedies. The minority leader accepted the public accommodations title with those same limitations on the attorney general and individual complaints. Explicit language was written into the school desegregation section making clear that it did not affect the de facto segregation that had become an issue in northern cities. All of these provisions, taken together, enabled senators from northern states that had already enacted civil rights legislation to tell their constituents that the bill would not affect their states. The "compromise," introduced jointly by Mansfield and Dirksen, made seventy other changes in the House bill, but most were technical and minor. The House bill remained basically intact.

"An Idea Whose Time Has Come." The show of negotiations with Dirksen and the concessions made to him, however minor, won the entire center bloc of uncommitted Republicans, and the leaders were now ready to try for cloture. Now it was too late for the southerners to seek

concessions. The cloture petition was filed June 6, with Dirksen's name leading its thirty-seven signatures, and the vote was taken four days later. For the second time in twenty-nine years—and for the first time ever on a civil rights bill—the Senate voted cloture. The tally was 71-29. The opponents included twenty-one southerners, and three Democrats and five Republicans from outside the South, including Barry Goldwater. As pending amendments were then voted upon, only a few minor changes were accepted; ninety-nine amendments were defeated on successive roll call votes in six days. A motion to strike each title was defeated in turn, the highwater mark for the opposition being thirty-three votes against the fair employment title. The bill then passed, 73-27. This time, only one nonsouthern Democrat (Robert C. Byrd of West Virginia) and Goldwater and four other nonsouthern Republicans voted in the negative. Goldwater said he found "no constitutional basis for the exercise of federal regulatory authority" over employment practices and public accommodations. "To give genuine effect to the prohibitions of the bill," he added, "will require the creation of a federal police force of mammoth proportions."

George Smathers, Democrat of Florida, said the bill was being passed in an "emotional binge," powered by "the propaganda of police dogs, bully sticks and mass jailings." Dirksen quoted words attributed to Victor Hugo: "Stronger than all the armies is an idea whose time has come." "America grows, America changes," said Dirksen. "In the history of mankind there is an inexorable moral force that carries us forward." To Douglas the act was "a substantial measure of atonement for three and a half centuries of wrongs."

When the bill was accepted without change in the House, one more southern voice was added to the eleven who had voted for civil rights in February. Charles L. Weltner, Atlanta Democrat, told the House: "Change, swift and certain, is upon us, and we in the South face some difficult decisions. We can offer resistance and defiance, with their harvest of strife and tumult. We can suffer continued demonstrations, with their wake of violence and disorder. Or, we can acknowledge this measure as the law of the land. We can accept the verdict of the Nation. Already, the responsible elements of my community are counseling this latter course. . . . I shall cast my lot with the leadership of my community. . . . And finally, I would urge that we at home now move on to the unfinished task of building a new South. We must not remain forever bound to another lost cause."

Jacob Javits, in his closing speech, had expressed a wishful thought: "It is now clear that the mainstream of my party is in support of civil rights legislation, and, particularly, support of this bill." But his party nominated for president one of the half dozen Republican senators who stood outside the mainstream in the Senate voting, while Lyndon Johnson underlined his own unflagging support of the strongest civil rights bill in a century by taking as his running mate the senator who had been the Democrats' floor leader in the long struggle, Hubert Humphrey.

After a victory like the Civil Rights Act of 1964, some men might rest. But Lyndon Johnson's style was otherwise. "Great social change tends to come rapidly in periods of intense activity before the impulse slows," he told the National Urban League in December 1964. "I believe we are in the midst of such a period of change. Now, the lights are still on in the White House tonight—preparing programs that will keep our country up with the times."

He had asked the Justice Department what more could be done for civil rights before the impulse slowed. They responded that in the field of voting rights—the one section of the Kennedy bill that had been weakened by Congress—new law was needed. The provision of the 1960 act authorizing federal judges to appoint referees to enroll Negro voters had not been utilized, except in one minor instance, and Negro applicants were still encountering the procedural obstacles described in elaborate detail in the Civil Rights Commission's first report. Accordingly, the President inserted in his State of the Union message of January 1965 a general sentence urging "elimination of barriers to the right to vote," and the Justice Department proceeded to consider specific legislation.

Thus, when Martin Luther King, Jr., began his voting rights demonstrations in Selma, Alabama, on January 18, the President had anticipated the crisis that would develop. By early February two thousand Negroes, including King, had been jailed for "parading without a permit" when they marched to the Dallas County courthouse demanding that eligible Negroes be registered. King failed to open the voters' rolls to Negroes in Selma, but as in Birmingham two years before, he accomplished his other purpose—he attracted national attention. Fifteen congressmen, seven of them freshman Democrats elected in the Johnson landslide, spent four days in Alabama and reported to the House their findings. In Dallas County, Negroes outnumbered whites, but the registration figures were 9,800 white voters to 325 Negroes (up from 163 in 1959)—70 percent of voting age white persons registered against only 2 percent of the Negroes. In the adjacent counties of Lowndes and Wilcox, not a single Negro had yet registered. White applicants were helped to fill out the literacy test questionnaire but Negroes were not. Six voting rights lawsuits had been filed in Dallas County beginning in April 1961, but only in February 1965 had Federal Judge Daniel H. Thomas enjoined use of some of the more complicated provisions of the literacy test. Democratic Representative Charles C. Diggs, Jr., of Detroit, leader of the delegation, quoted the mayor of Selma as stating that if outsiders would leave town, things would return to normal. "That is what we were afraid of, that things would return to normal," commented Diggs. The delegation agreed that some kind of new legislation on voting rights was needed.

President Johnson repeated his promise of new legislation when King visited the White House February 8. Republicans promised their support. As Justice Department lawyers continued to ponder the terms of an administration bill, a group of Republican leaders—five governors, four senators, and twenty-two representatives—prodded the President: "How long will Congress and the American people be asked to wait while this administration studies and restudies Dr. King's request for

new federal legislation? The need is apparent. The time is now. . . .
Despite abuse, threats, and beatings, Dr. King and his people walk the
streets of Selma in protest. Republicans march with them." This time
the unpredictable Dirksen was out in front; he announced that he was
drafting a bill, and Attorney General Nicholas deB. Katzenbach,
through Majority Leader Mansfield, entered into negotiations in the
hope of producing the "consensus" bill, this time, before it was introduced.

King meanwhile assembled his forces for a Sunday march from
Selma to Montgomery. Governor Wallace ordered the march halted. At
the end of the long bridge over the Alabama river leading out of
Selma, reported *The Washington Post*, "state troopers and mounted
deputies bombarded 600 praying Negroes with tear gas . . . and then
waded into them with clubs, whips, and ropes, injuring scores." Then
they "chased the screaming, bleeding marchers nearly a mile back to
their church, clubbing them as they ran." The scene "resembled that
in a police state," said *The New York Times*. The next day a white
Unitarian minister from Boston, the Reverend James J. Reeb, was
beaten to death by white men in Selma.

Once again, through television and news pictures, the nation became an eye-witness to southern violence, and the outrage was instantaneous. "Telegrams from horrified citizens—neighbors of mine—pour
in to me," Democrat John O. Pastore of Rhode Island told the Senate.
"The citizens of Minnesota . . . can no longer tolerate the trampling
of human rights by southern law enforcement officers," said Democratic
Senator Walter F. Mondale. "Shame on you, George Wallace," cried
Senator Ralph W. Yarborough, Texas Democrat, "for the wet ropes
that bruised the muscles, for the bullwhips which cut the flesh, for the
clubs that broke the bones, for the tear gas that blinded, burned, and
choked into insensibility." Yarborough called on Wallace "to atone for
the shame he has brought . . . to my beloved Southland."

On March 15, when the Katzenbach-Dirksen-Mansfield consensus
bill was ready, the President went before an extraordinary evening session of the two houses of Congress so that all the nation could see and
hear. Listing Selma with Lexington, Concord, and Appomattox as
places where "history and fate" had met "to shape a turning point in
man's unending search for freedom," he climaxed his address by utter-
ing as his own the refrain of the civil rights marchers' hymn, "We Shall
Overcome."

The bill he presented made the voting provisions of the three previous acts look like pale compromises. It was a frankly regional measure.
It singled out seven southern states for attention by limiting its application to areas where literacy tests were used and where fewer than 50
percent of the voting-age population voted in a presidential election.
In those areas, it provided for federal registration of voters, not through
"tedious, unnecessary lawsuits" but by examiners appointed by the
executive branch. It did not merely propose to stop the abuse of literacy
tests but swept such tests away. It covered state and local as well as
federal elections. It protected not just the right to register but the right

to vote itself. In short, it removed from state to federal control the effective supervision of elections and provided a simple and uniform national standard the attorney general could enforce.

Said the President:

Every American citizen must have an equal right to vote. There is no reason which can excuse the denial of that right.

Yet . . . every device of which human ingenuity is capable has been used to deny this right. . . . The fact is that the only way to pass these barriers is to show a white skin.

. . . No law that we now have on the books—and I have helped to put three of them there—can insure the right to vote when local officials are determined to deny it.

In such a case our duty must be clear to all of us. . . .

And we ought not and we cannot and we must not wait another 8 months before we get a bill. We have already waited a hundred years or more, and the time for waiting is gone.

Their cause must be our cause too, because it is not just Negroes but really it is all of us, who must overcome the crippling legacy of bigotry and injustice. And we shall overcome.

The President did not have to wait eight months for his bill—or twelve months, as in 1963–64. It was passed in five. From March to August the civil rights forces never lost momentum. The Leadership Conference and its member organizations pressed to strengthen the bill at every point where they could detect a compromise. When the bill reached the President's desk, they could hail it as stronger than the one originally proposed.

Much of the legislative struggle centered on the poll tax. Although outlawed by the Twenty-fourth Amendment for use in federal elections, poll taxes remained as a barrier to voting in state and local elections in four southern states. The administration opposed, on constitutional grounds, trying to remove these barriers by statute, but the House voted to do so anyway, and the Senate, on an amendment offered by Edward M. Kennedy, Massachusetts Democrat, came within four votes of doing likewise. In a compromise solution, Congress approved a congressional declaration that poll taxes abridged the right to vote and a directive to the attorney general to bring suit to test their constitutionality. The suits were filed immediately after the act was signed, and the poll taxes were outlawed by the courts.

Yielding to criticism from House Republicans, the Congress also extended the impact of the act beyond the states originally affected to include "pockets of discrimination" anywhere the attorney general demonstrated their existence to a federal court. The final bill also contained a provision, inserted by committees in both houses, authorizing poll watchers in any subdivision where examiners had been assigned.

The two parties shared the credit, although the Republicans were embarrassed when southern opponents embraced their substitute measure as "relatively moderate" and "far preferable" to the bill that was finally approved. The vote in the House was 333–85. Among those voting for it were eight representatives from Texas, six from Florida, four from Tennessee, two each from Georgia and Louisiana, and one from Virginia. In the Senate, cloture was voted, 70–30, after twenty-five days of debate, and then the bill passed, 77–19. Two days after the bill became law, federal examiners assumed their voter registration duties in Selma, Alabama, and eight other counties in three southern states.

"They came in darkness and they came in chains," said the President on signing the bill. "Today we strike away the last major shackle of those fierce and ancient bonds." And a year later federal examiners had certified 124,000 new voters in forty-two counties in four states, and Negro registration in the six southern states wholly covered by the act had risen from 30 to 46 percent of those eligible. Negro voters defeated Sheriff James G. Clark, Jr., of Dallas County, Alabama, in the Democratic primary.

"BLACK POWER"—AND THE BILL THAT FAILED (1965–66)

But there were yet other shackles. Foremost among the areas of discrimination still untouched by federal legislation was housing. As early as 1959, the Civil Rights Commission had devoted more than a third of its first report to housing discrimination, which it found resulted in "high rates of disease, fire, juvenile delinquency, crime and social demoralization" among those confined to ghetto slums.

In November 1962, after a long delay, President Kennedy issued the "stroke of a pen" executive order that the commission had recommended, but the order was by no means all-inclusive. It was limited to housing guaranteed or insured by the Federal Housing Administration (FHA) and the Veterans Administration (VA), and it contained no retroactive feature. Thus, it excluded all existing homes and about 80 percent of new housing. To enforce the order and to encourage voluntary fair practices in the sale or rental of housing not covered, Kennedy established the President's Committee on Equal Opportunity in Housing under the chairmanship of former Governor David L. Lawrence of Pennsylvania. At its second meeting the committee concluded that the order that established it was too limited. It was supported by builders using FHA insurance, who complained at being covered while their competitors were not.

As long as the 1964 civil rights act was pending, the committee did not press its demand for a broader order. But after that act was signed, and after the 1964 election, it made a formal recommendation to President Johnson. The President asked Vice President Humphrey to review it and to consider, with Attorney General Katzenbach, the legal problems involved. While this review was underway, the President and Humphrey were faced with a danger—reported in a newspaper column —that several of the committee's members, including its Negro members, would resign if the President rejected its recommendations. This, said the columnists, would mean "the virtual dissolution of the Law-rence committee" and "would trigger recriminations from responsible civil rights leaders."

Counsels of Boldness. Perhaps the President's decision was never in doubt, but when he made it he went all the way. Instead of issuing a new executive order—which at best could only cover new housing and would be on dubious legal grounds for some of that—he would ask for legislation. That course would plunge him into one more fight on Capi-tol Hill and one more Senate filibuster, but if it were successful he would have covered *all* housing, on a secure and permanent legal foun-dation, with suitable enforcement machinery, and with the superior moral suasion that attaches to a solemn congressional enactment as distinct from a presidential decree.

In the South the right most forcefully demanded was the right to protection of life itself—specifically, protection of the lives of persons asserting other rights. In 1964, at Philadelphia, Mississippi, three civil rights workers had been slain upon their release from jail, but state and local officials apprehended no one for the crime, and when the Federal Bureau of Investigation arrested a score of suspects—including the sheriff and deputy sheriff who had custody of the civil rights workers before their release—Federal District Judge Harold Cox dismissed the case against them on the ground that murder was not a federal crime. A similar case was dismissed, for the same reason, in Georgia. The accused killers of two northerners who had participated in civil rights demonstrations in Alabama were quickly acquitted by all-white juries in October 1965. In that state not one conviction had been obtained in twelve recent civil rights slayings, either because nobody had been arrested or because of what northern newspapers called "sham" and "mock" trials.

In November 1965 the Civil Rights Commission, in a 188-page re-port on law enforcement in the South, charged that violence was used in that region "with implicit legal sanction . . . to maintain and reinforce the traditional subservient position of the Negro." In Mississippi alone, the commission found, more than 150 serious incidents of racial violence had occurred between 1961 and 1964, including at least six murders, but "in only a few cases were those responsible arrested or prosecuted by local authorities."

The Justice Department was already publicly committed to request legislation to attack discrimination in jury selection, and the President went on record on this subject in November. Civil rights groups, in drafting legislation for the coming session of Congress, made clear that physical protection for southern Negroes and civil rights workers would be a major objective. The planning session for the White House con-ference on civil rights, meeting in November, urged a broad "civil rights protection act of 1966."

In his State of the Union message in January, the President asked for action in three areas—juries, physical security, and housing. By late April the specific proposals were ready, and they left little for civil rights groups to criticize. The housing recommendations were all-embracing, covering all sales and rental transactions. The recommendations relating to juries covered state and federal juries alike. The physical security provisions made it a federal crime for any person to interfere, by threats or force, with the exercise by others of their fundamental rights—and voting, education, housing, employment, jury service, and travel were enumerated among those rights. At last, racial murder would be a federal offense. The President added two other recommendations. He proposed to remove the limitations in the 1964 act upon the powers of the attorney general to initiate suits to enforce desegregation of schools or other public facilities. He also endorsed a measure, already passed by the House, to grant enforcement powers to the Equal Employment Opportunity Commission created by the Civil Rights Act of 1964.

On those provisions aimed at segregation and violence in the South, the consensus of 1964 and 1965 held firm. The House Republican Policy Committe endorsed those titles. The House Judiciary Committee added, with no discernible struggle, the entire Part III authority, which had been debated and enacted in bits and pieces over the past decade. All of these titles went through the House with ease. When a motion was made to strike the title setting federal standards for state jury selection, only thirteen votes were mustered to defend states' rights.

Housing, however, was another story. Here for the first time in the long history of five proposed civil rights acts, northerners were asked to strike at practices of discrimination that were all but universal in the North itself. The 1964 act had been amended in the Senate to enable northern senators to assure their constituents that the act would not affect their states. But the 1966 bill would destroy the sanctity of the all-white suburb, an institution more characteristically northern than southern. Only seventeen states had fair housing laws, and few covered all housing. Such large states as Illinois and Michigan had no legislation, and California voted overwhelmingly to repeal its law in a referendum in 1964.

Under these circumstances, the 1966 debate proceeded in an atmosphere dramatically altered from that of 1964 and 1965. The impact of mail from home upon northern and western congressmen was reversed. The National Association of Real Estate Boards rallied its 83,000 member firms and their business allies to "generate an immediate wave of indignation" against the bill's alleged threat to property values and free enterprise, and took credit for arousing what they reported was the heaviest flow of mail on a single issue in the memory of "many senior members of Congress." In contrast, the Leadership Conference on Civil Rights deplored the absence of mail on behalf of equal housing opportunity. Negro demonstrations, too, had a different impact. When Martin Luther King, Jr., led a band of Negroes into a white residential area of Chicago and engaged a white mob, he stirred up indignation in the North not unlike that aroused by Birmingham and Selma—but this time directed against, not for, his cause. "I have never seen such hatred—not in Mississippi or Alabama," said King. The church delegations so conspicuous in Washington in 1964 stayed home in 1966. "The music has gone out of the movement," wrote Mary McGrory. Emanuel Celler was led to remark upon the hypocrisy of "some northern civil libertarians" whose ardor for civil rights paled when it was their own institutions that were challenged.

The Chicago riots, subsequent bloodier clashes in Cleveland, the memory of last summer's Watts and the previous summer's Harlem, the ominous slogan of "black power" that appeared in 1966, overhung the debate. Roy Wilkins of the NAACP said that an uncompromised open housing title was necessary to prevent further "heartbreaking developments that could be ugly as well." Southerners repeatedly expressed the opposite view—that violence in the North was the direct result of civil rights acts already passed. "We tremble in our seats and yield to the fear of the Negro revolution," said Howard Smith of Virginia in opening the House debate for the opposition. "If that is the kind of spirit that has come to this country and we are going to operate in the Congress on the theory of fear, on the theory of violence, on the theory of mobs, and so forth, then this is not the place to which I was first elected." Responded Charles McC. Mathias, Jr., Maryland Republican: "We are not yielding to threats. Rather, we are responding to conditions—conditions which have been forced to our attention convulsively and dramatically, perhaps because we failed to apprehend dangers expressed in more placid ways. . . . We are not responding, essentially, to protests, but to the causes of those protests. . . ."

By only the narrowest of margins did the housing title survive the House. It cleared the Judiciary Committee by two votes, 17–15, after a "Mrs. Murphy" clause had been inserted exempting small apartment houses where the owner occupied one of the apartments and after an amendment by Mathias, backed by McCulloch and several Democrats, exempting sales by homeowners of their own homes. On the floor the test came on an amendment by Mathias to his own amendment to make clear that it exempted sales by homeowners of their homes through brokers. The administration and the Republican leadership saw the parliamentary situation in the same way—without the clarified Mathias amendment the title as a whole would be defeated. The administration therefore supported the amendment, which weakened its bill; and a large majority of Republicans, whose policy committee had gone on record against any fair housing title, joined southern Democrats in opposing the exemptions. They were joined by a few last-ditch supporters of the original administration bill who contended that the Mathias exemptions were, in effect, a "codification of prejudice." The amendment carried on a teller vote, 180–179. Once the amendment was adopted, the title as a whole was preserved by a more decisive margin, 198–179 on a teller vote and 222–190 on the roll call vote. On the latter tally it received only eight southern votes—all from urban centers—compared to the thirty-one cast for the Voting Rights Act of 1965, and thirty-one northern and border state Democrats defected. Nonsouthern Republicans barely supported the title, 62–61. Then the act was passed, 259–157.

"Some People Are in an Undue Hurry." As in 1964 and 1965, the

key to Senate cloture was held by Everett Dirksen. Northern and western Democrats could be counted on to vote for cloture, southern Democrats against; therefore, if two-thirds of the Senate were again to be mustered to shut off debate, northern and western Republicans would again have to provide the margin, and Dirksen's influence was crucial.

As in 1964, too, Dirksen took an initial stance of outright opposition to one feature of the bill, this time to the open housing section—"absolutely unconstitutional," he called it. But as the 1966 bill moved along its course, he found no reason to alter his position. No tidal wave of public opinion arose this time to overwhelm him. Indeed, the trend of opinion *against* the bill that had developed during House consideration intensified, if anything, in the weeks after the House acted in early August. New riots broke out—in Atlanta, Omaha, and a dozen other places. The image of the Negro in 1966 was no longer that of the praying, long-suffering, nonviolent victim of southern sheriffs; it was of a defiant young hoodlum shouting "black power" and hurling "Molotov cocktails" in an urban slum. And the white neighborhoods that might have opened their doors to a Martin Luther King of 1964 would only bar and shutter them at the thought of Stokely Carmichael as a neighbor. A survey by the Louis Harris organization, published in *Newsweek* in August, showed that 46 percent of the entire white population would object to having a Negro family next door and 70 percent thought the Negroes were "trying to move too fast." Another Harris poll, in September, listed civil rights violence among the factors that had brought President Johnson's popularity to the lowest point since he entered office. The *Wall Street Journal* reported a "heavy preponderance" of congressional mail against the bill. And just before the cloture vote, on September 13, George P. Mahoney rode to an upset victory in the Democratic primary for governor of Maryland on the single issue of "Your home is your castle—protect it." The message was clear.

Supporters of the civil rights bill did little more than go through the motions of a Senate debate, and opponents did not need to. What counted were the backstage appeals to Dirksen, and these were unavailing. "I think some people are in an undue hurry," Dirksen told the Senate, and added, "we have been talking a long time about color, when in fact we should also be talking about conduct." It was a "frightening argument," responded Edward Kennedy, that "because the actions of some Negroes deserve condemnation," all should be denied the full rights of citizenship.

After a week of dispirited discussion, which was cut short on three occasions when the Senate could not maintain a quorum, Majority Leader Mansfield scheduled the vote on cloture. A majority of the body voted to shut off debate, but not two-thirds. The vote was 54–42. Of those opposed, nineteen were southerners, four were nonsouthern Democrats, and nineteen were nonsouthern Republicans. Twelve Republicans, led by Dirksen, and one Democrat (Frank Lausche of Ohio) who had supported cloture on the 1964 and 1965 civil rights acts opposed it in 1966. A week later, Mansfield again attempted cloture but not a single vote was changed. The bill was shelved. If the prospects for civil rights legislation were to be improved, said Mansfield, "the question of riotings, marches, shootings, and inflammatory statements . . . will have to be faced frankly and bluntly."

"The problem is not going away," was Roy Wilkins' comment. "The Negro is not going away. . . . We will be back in this or another Congress." Paul Douglas and others noted that the will of the Senate majority was thwarted by rule 22 and promised to continue their fight on the filibuster issue. Lyndon Johnson told his press conference he was happy that a majority of both houses supported the bill—"in a democracy where majority rules should prevail." It is ironic that, had Lyndon Johnson spoken those words a decade earlier, majority rule would almost surely have come to prevail in the Senate.

BEYOND OPPORTUNITY TO ACHIEVEMENT

Before the 1966 setback to the cause of civil rights, the President had already announced the next stage of the struggle—"the more profound stage," he called it—in an address to the 1965 graduating class of the leading American university founded for Negroes, Howard University in Washington, D.C.

Said the President:

The voting rights bill . . . as Winston Churchill said of another triumph of freedom—"is not the end; it is not even the beginning of the end. But it is, perhaps, the end of the beginning."

That beginning is freedom. . . . But freedom is not enough. . . . it is not enough just to open the gates of opportunity. All our citizens must have the ability to walk through those gates. This is the next and the more profound stage of the battle for civil rights.

. . . the great majority of Negro Americans—the poor, the unemployed, the uprooted and the dispossessed— . . . still, as we meet here tonight, are another nation. Despite the court orders and the laws, despite the legislative victories and the speeches, for them the walls are rising and the gulf is widening.

For Negro poverty is not white poverty. Many of its causes and many of its cures are the same but there are differences—deep, corrosive, obstinate differences—radiating painful roots into the community, and into the family, and the nature of the individual.

These differences are not racial differences. They are solely and simply the consequences of ancient brutality, past injustice and present prejudice.

Perhaps most important—its influence radiating to every part of life—is the breakdown of the Negro family structure.

Part of the answer, said the President, lay in jobs, in welfare and social programs, in the poverty program, in education, training, and medical care. "But there are other answers that are still to be found, nor do we fully understand even all of the problems," he went on. To define the problems, and find the answers, he announced a White House conference of scholars and experts, officials and Negro leaders, to be held in the fall of 1965. Its theme would be "to fulfill these rights," and its objective to help the Negro move "beyond opportunity to achievement."

It was unique, observed two scholars who have studied the origin and consequences of the Howard University speech, to find the product of three decades of social science research so central to a major presidential address. It was equally remarkable, they might have added, that echoed in the speech, too, was the anguish expressed by a generation of Negro novelists, essayists, and poets. As in his "We Shall Overcome" speech, the President again, and even more deeply, committed himself to the Negro cause—but in a context of far more conceptual complexity and practical difficulty.

In the first stage of the civil rights battle, the problem and the remedies could at least be readily defined. Constitutional rights, while they evolve, are at all times written in the language of statutes and judicial interpretations. When the people of the North and West, watching the events of Birmingham and Selma on their television screens, resolved to make real in the South the Negroes' constitutional rights, the statutes could be drafted handily—though their effect through enforcement might, in many cases, be slow and gradual. But when the same people, watching the events of Watts and Cleveland on the same television sets, were stirred to demand action, there was no body of settled doctrine to which to turn. The two major parties, building upon their separate traditions, responded with quite different remedies.

Democratic leaders saw the solution in expensive programs to relieve the sordid conditions of the slums. When the Hough area of Cleveland exploded in violence, Democratic Senator Stephen M. Young of that city demanded "federal action on a large scale. . . . The housing program is too small. The poverty program is too small. The program for slum schools is too small. . . . It is clear that the elimination of slum misery will require new programs and much money." Vice President Humphrey a week earlier had been more graphic. He said "the National Guard is no answer to the problems of the slums" and—while not condoning lawlessness—predicted "open violence in every major city and county in America" as long as people were forced to "live like animals . . . in . . . filthy, rotten housing . . . with rats nibbling on the kids' toes . . . with garbage uncollected . . . with no swimming pools, with little or no recreation. . . ." If he lived in such conditions, he "could lead a mighty good revolt" himself, he added. Said the administration's top-ranking Negro, Secretary of Housing and Urban Development Robert Weaver: "Society has to act effectively to redress the deprivations of the environment that occasion despair. We must diagnose the ills of our ghettos and move to heal their sickness before they explode."

The White House conference that the President heralded at Howard University reached the same conclusion. Meeting in June 1966 (after a postponement from the previous fall), it endorsed in general the recommendations of its preparatory council, headed by Ben W. Heineman, which proposed low-cost housing construction at the rate of a million units a year, public works, guaranteed jobs for all workers, free junior colleges, improvement of slum schools, higher welfare benefits, and the strengthening of a host of other services. The council did not put a price tag on its recommendations, but a group subsequently convened by A. Philip Randolph, honorary chairman of the conference, and other civil rights leaders proposed a "freedom budget" of $185 billion over a ten-year period.

Republicans, preparing to exploit both "crime in the streets" and inflation-spending as central issues in the off-year elections, could hardly advance spending as the solution to riots. Their demand was for "law and order." To Barry Goldwater the solution to racial unrest lay not in legislation but in better police forces and stronger public support for their efforts. "How long," asked House Republican Leader Gerald Ford of Michigan, "are we going to abdicate law and order—the backbone of any civilization—in favor of a soft social theory that the man who heaves a brick through your window or tosses a fire bomb into your car is simply the misunderstood and underprivileged product of a broken home?" A Republican-sponsored amendment to the civil rights bill would have made it a crime to cross state lines or use interstate facilities with intent to incite or participate in riots. The Republican Coordinating Committee pointed out that under the Kennedy and Johnson administrations the number of crimes had increased 46 percent and, in an obvious reference to Humphrey's statement, charged that "high officials of this administration have condoned and encouraged disrespect for law and order."

The "law and order" issue unquestionably contributed to the Republican landslide of 1966. The election added forty-seven Republicans to Ford's minority in the House. And the defeat of such southern liberals as James A. Mackay of Atlanta and George W. Grider of Memphis gave civil rights supporters no cause to expect reinforcements from the Democratic south. Yet, in Roy Wilkins' simple phrase, the problem was not going away and the Negro was not going away. As the Negro's aspirations rose, his frustrations—if jobs, housing, and opportunity for full participation in American life were not open to him—would mount, and the ghettos would become ever more explosive. And each explosion, as the experience of 1966 made clear, would increase the demand for "law and order" and the resistance to the use of tax money for any program that might seem to reward the rioters. In the words of Tom Wicker of *The New York Times*, "There is at work a tragic cycle."

The urban ghetto had become, indeed, the crucial testing ground of the President's conception of his "Great Society." There all of the programs devised by the activists to cope with unemployment, with poverty, with delinquency, with the shortcomings of educational systems, would undergo their trial by ordeal and succeed or finally fail. The urban ghetto had become the central challenge, in the nation's domestic affairs, to every element of the political community—to the intellectuals, who must analyze the problems and develop the solutions; to the government administrators at all levels, who must overcome incredible obstacles to make their programs effective; but most of all to the politicians whose job it was to select appropriate measures, organize the consensus for their enactment, and raise the money to finance them. At the end of 1966 no one could say that the country's political institutions were responding on a scale and with a tempo that matched the magnitude of the challenge that confronted them.

Lyndon Johnson and Vietnam: 1968

TOWNSEND HOOPES

Americans have historically liked their wars simple. War should pit "democratic" peoples against "aggressors," it should call for "unconditional surrender," and it should be fought "all out." If the Korean war brought such narrow assumptions into question, Vietnam destroyed them completely. Here was a twilight conflict—undeclared and misunderstood at home, an enigma to our friends and allies abroad—fought in limited ways against an enemy who could not always be identified. The war clearly could not end all wars, and few believed that it could even make the nation in which it was fought safe for democracy. Bitterest note of all, there was no possibility of victory. American policy, reversing General MacArthur's arrogant dictum "there is no substitute for victory," became a search for a substitute for defeat.

The Limits of Intervention by Townsend Hoopes is one of the first insider's accounts of the American decision to cease escalating the American military presence and to seek some means of withdrawing from our untenable position in Southeast Asia. The turning point came with the Tet offensive of early 1968. This event destroyed most remaining illusions about what a campaign of firepower from the air and "search and destroy" missions on the ground might accomplish toward defeating the Viet Cong and their northern allies. The new Secretary of Defense Clark Clifford and President Truman's Secretary of State Dean Acheson argued against deeper involvement in March 1968. Tet, perhaps combined with political pressures at home, produced the great decision to begin the agonizing and protracted movement toward acknowledging the failure of American policy in Vietnam. Whatever his critics might say, Johnson had at least taken the first step.

> ARVN—The Army of the Republic of [South] Vietnam
> GVN—The Government of [South] Vietnam
> JCS—Joint Chiefs of Staff

On January 31 [1968] in a surprise offensive that burst with the suddenness of a giant bombshell all over South Vietnam, the enemy launched a wide range of powerful, simultaneous attacks against dozens of key cities and towns. A commando unit of nineteen Viet Cong infiltrated the compound of the U.S. Embassy, made their way into several buildings, but were unable to get into the Embassy itself. After six hours of fighting with Embassy guards and reinforcements, including thirty-six U.S. paratroopers landed by helicopter on the Embassy roof, the entire Viet Cong unit was wiped out.

But the Embassy raid was only the political spearhead of a massive political–military assault on the entire U.S.-GVN structure. Saigon was attacked and partially occupied by several thousand enemy troops who had arrived in civilian disguise on bicycles and public buses. There were 1,000 enemy soldiers in Hue, 2,500 in Ben Tre. NVN forces seized large sections of Kontum in the central highlands, and of Mytho, Cantho, and Soc Trang in the Mekong Delta. In Washington the first reports were confused and fragmentary, but even these gave unmistakable shape to the truth that South Vietnam was experiencing a spreading disaster.

[General] Westmoreland [the commander of allied troops] was quick to conclude that "the enemy's well laid plans went afoul." He and his spokesmen dismissed the enemy's tactics as suicidal, and pressed the suggestion that we were witnessing a "last desperate push," a final NVN effort to redress a military balance that had been moving inexorably against Hanoi by reason of the great weight of the U.S. effort. . . . In fact, [such] words were premature and optimistic in the extreme, for even the first phase of the Tet offensive swept on for another two weeks with mounting casualties, destruction, and irreversible political consequences for the allied war effort.

The enemy was carrying out a carefully calculated three-pronged drive—one prong directed against Saigon and the major cities and a second against U.S. forces at Khesanh and other outlying posts; the third was designed to fill the vacuum left in the countryside by government troops who were drawn back to defend the cities. By occupying large rural sections abandoned by the government, the NVN-VC not only dealt the whole pacification program a grievous blow, but threatened to strangle the towns by cutting them off from normal sources of supply. Three to four weeks later, a number of towns were still surrounded and dependent on airlift. Very heavy fighting continued in Saigon and its suburbs through February 20, with action centering in the Cholon district. An estimated 11,000 U.S. and ARVN forces were committed to battle against 1,000 Viet Cong. In an effort to dislodge the enemy, artillery and air strikes were repeatedly used against densely populated areas of the city, causing heavy civilian casualties. An additional 4,000 U.S. troops were brought in on February 9, part of them being helicoptered to the Pho Tho racetrack where a large Viet Cong force was entrenched. On February 11, two ARVN battalions were locked in battle with 400 VC near an ammo dump along the Ben Cat River.

Everywhere, the U.S.-ARVN forces mounted counterattacks of great severity. In the delta region below Saigon, half of the city of Mytho, with a population of 70,000, was destroyed by artillery and air strikes in an effort to eject a strong VC force. In Ben Tre on February 7, at least 1,000 civilians were killed and 1,500 wounded in an effort to dislodge 2,500 VC.

The effort to recapture Hue, the cultural and religious center of Vietnam, met fierce resistance from the 1,000 NVN troops who had captured it on January 31. After ten days of bitter street fighting, U.S.

Marines finally penetrated the inner city, an area of two square miles known as the Citadel, to which the enemy force had withdrawn. On that same day, the Mayor of Hue found the bodies of three hundred local officials and prominent citizens in a common grave several miles from the city, slain en masse by the enemy. The fierce house-to-house fighting gradually exhausted the small contingent of Marines, and reinforcements were called for on February 21 "because the steam has gone out." Not until February 24 did U.S. forces achieve reoccupation of the city as a whole and ARVN forces capture the Imperial Palace. The enemy had gradually been driven to the southern part of the Citadel. There he did not put up a last-ditch resistance, but slipped away one night to the southwest, with a sizable part of his men and equipment. The guns fell silent on a devastated and prostrate city. Eighty percent of the buildings had been reduced to rubble, and in the smashed ruins lay 2,000 dead civilians (apparently more civilians died than soldiers). Three-quarters of the city's people were rendered homeless and looting was widespread, members of the ARVN being the worst offenders.

David Douglas Duncan, a famous combat photographer who had covered all of the world's major battlefronts since World War II, including Korea, Algeria, and the French struggle to keep Vietnam, was appalled by the U.S.-ARVN method of freeing Hue. He said, "The Americans pounded the Citadel and surrounding city almost to dust with air strikes, napalm runs, artillery and naval gunfire, and the direct cannon fire from tanks and recoilless rifles—a total effort to root out and kill every enemy soldier. The mind reels at the carnage, cost, and ruthlessness of it all. Wouldn't a siege-blockade have been a more effective and less wasteful military tactic?" He contrasted this response with Henry Stimson's intervention in World War II to save Kyoto, the religious heart of Japan, which had been marked for destruction by allied airforces, and with John J. McCloy's similar rescue of classic Rothenburg in Germany. "Poor Hue, it had no friends or protectors. Now it is gone." . . .

One thing was clear to us all: the Tet offensive was the eloquent counterpoint to the effusive optimism [that had held sway the previous November]. It showed conclusively that the U.S. did not in fact control the situation, that it was not in fact winning, that the enemy retained enormous strength and vitality—certainly enough to extinguish the notion of a clear-cut allied victory in the minds of all objective men. Nor could we take seriously the view that the Vietnamese were stepping up their operations out of despair, out of a certain knowledge that time worked against them. On the contrary, the Tet offensive seemed to proceed from an NVN assessment that the situation presented a number of ripe opportunities: the garrison at Khesanh was surrounded and under increasing pressure; another sizable portion of U.S. combat forces in northern I Corps was pinned down by heavy Communist artillery fire from across the DMZ; the cities were vulnerable to attack and the surrounding countryside to recapture. In general, the doctrine of search-and-destroy had resulted in scattering U.S. combat forces all over uninhabited border lands; the Tet offensive had made blindingly clear the fatuousness of Westmoreland's ground strategy. What seemed imperative now was a shift that would deemphasize search-and-destroy, concentrate on the protection of population centers, and curtail American casualties; otherwise, I thought, domestic support for any form of long-continued effort could not be assured. Even the staunch and conservative *Wall Street Journal* was saying in mid-February, "We think the American people should be getting ready to accept, if they haven't already, the prospect that the whole Vietnam effort may be doomed, that it may be falling apart beneath our feet."

But modifications of strategy ran counter to Westmoreland's every instinct, and there was no will in Washington to bell that particular cat. It is quite possible that the idea of a strategy change never occurred to the President; that is, that either he never understood the incompatibility of Westmoreland's ground strategy with his own stated political objective, i.e., to gain the political allegiance of the people of South Vietnam—or that he regarded the political aim as mere words and the need for military victory as the only governing reality. McNamara, though he complained privately of the error and waste inherent in search-and-destroy operations, could not get his hands on the levers without explicit presidential support; and the Joint Chiefs of Staff, although some of them were disquieted by the attrition strategy, were unwilling to *direct* changes. In the particular circumstances, continued JCS deference to Westmoreland seemed an extreme form of professional courtesy, but it was a cold fact that in February 1968 the men and the means did not exist in Washington to change our military strategy in Vietnam.

The President's basic reaction to the Tet offensive was to convince himself anew that the war was a test of wills between parties of equal interest. While pressure rose on every side for a reexamination of America's prospects and strategy, he and his closest advisers gave the unmistakable impression that all the big questions had been long since resolved—and that the answer was to plunge onward. He spent much time in February visiting U.S. military bases. He announced to the world he was in no mood to compromise. He defended Westmoreland. He urged total firmness on the war. . . .

The chances of producing any dramatic change of policy seemed remote in mid-February. Control of the war effort remained tightly held by the inner group, and they were, with the exception of McNamara, united both in their conviction about the rightness of present policy and in the fact that all were implicated in the major decisions since 1964. Worse still, as it seemed, McNamara's designated successor [as Secretary of Defense] was not only a close friend of LBJ, but an eloquent hawk with no doubts about the war. In all respects, Clark Clifford seemed to fit the President's temperamental requirement for harmony within the inner group. *Newsweek* called him "loyal, well-seasoned and, more important, determined to hold the line in Vietnam." Still, I was not without hope. . . .

I had known Clifford over a number of years, particularly during the Truman period when he was at the White House, and had been impressed, then and later, by the steely independence beneath the velvet charm. He was, I thought, above all his own man. Moreover, he was too intelligent, too much the trained lawyer, with too firm a sense of proportion and too strong a passion for reasoned answers, not to grasp the galloping distortions that now dominated the conduct of Vietnam policy. I did not foresee the full measure of his courage and tenacity that the ensuing months would reveal, but I was encouraged. In any event, Clifford was the only remaining hope for restoring some sense of proportion to our national position at home and abroad. . . .

The reappraisal of Vietnam policy began on February 26 with the arrival of a cable from General Wheeler sent from Saigon. He had been dispatched by the President about February 20 "to find out what else Westmoreland might need." For three days he conferred with Westmoreland and inspected the battle areas. Then he sent a cable for McNamara, Rusk, Rostow, and Helms setting forth his assessment of the situation and of the additional "force requirements" that he and Westmoreland considered necessary or at least very desirable. . . .

Since his Senate confirmation in January, Clifford had of course been preparing himself for his new responsibilities by conferring frequently with McNamara, Nitze, and the Joint Chiefs of Staff. On February 28, two days before the swearing-in ceremony, the President named [an] Ad Hoc Task Force on Vietnam with Clifford as chairman. Its purpose was to examine the Wheeler-Westmoreland request for more forces and to determine the domestic implications. As the principals understood it, the assignment from the President was a fairly narrow one—how to give Westmoreland what he said he needed, with acceptable domestic consequences.

Clifford moved immediately to broaden the inquiry's frame of reference by stating that, to him, the basic question was whether the U.S. should continue to follow the same course in Vietnam. What was likely to happen if we put in another 200,000 men? Would that bring us any closer to our objectives? Perhaps Westmoreland did need 200,000 additional troops under his present strategic concept, but was that a sensible concept? McNamara said Westmoreland's forces had been asked to carry more of the burden of achieving U.S. political objectives in Vietnam than could be borne by military power; we could not, he said, "by limited military means" force North Vietnam to quit, but neither could they drive us out of South Vietnam; the time had therefore come to recognize the necessity for negotiations and a compromise political settlement. Nitze argued the need to reexamine the involvement in Vietnam in the wider context of U.S. interests and commitments elsewhere in the world; he said that, whatever the result in Vietnam itself, we would have failed in our purposes if the war should spread to the point of direct military confrontation with China or Russia, or to the point where our resources were so heavily committed in Vietnam as to put our other commitments in serious doubt. He thought a less ambitious strategy should be devised, in order to buy time for strengthening ARVN and for getting out. Habib, who was William Bundy's deputy and a specialist on Vietnamese affairs, thought any alternative course would be preferable to sending more U.S. troops, because that would simply take the pressure off the GVN and ARVN to stand on their own feet.

Rostow, Wheeler, and Taylor expounded the hard line, arguing that the Tet offensive was in reality a new and unexpected opportunity. The guerrilla enemy, so long elusive and unwilling to give battle under conditions that favored America's superior firepower, had suddenly exposed himself all over the country. He had come into the open in large numbers, in a desperate attempt to seize cities and promote popular uprisings. This dramatic shift of strategy indicated he could no longer stand the relentless pressure of U.S. military power in a protracted war. Therefore, the prompt and substantial reinforcing of Westmoreland could open the way to victories that would decimate the enemy force and bring Hanoi, much more quickly than otherwise, to the conference table under conditions favorable to our side. Speaking for the JCS, Wheeler said the full 206,000 men were needed, and that to provide less would be taken by Westmoreland as a vote of no confidence. Taylor doubted whether sending even the full 206,000 would enable Westmoreland "to do what he is trying to do."

Nitze and Warnke, supported by Katzenbach, sought to counter these arguments. There was, they argued, no very convincing evidence that the enemy's attack was motivated by desperation or that his immediate aims were as ambitious as a popular uprising against the GVN and the wholesale desertion of ARVN. It seemed more likely, they argued, that the enemy had decided the time was ripe for a major effort to achieve several very important, but still limited, purposes: to capture one or more major cities, to cause large-scale panic in the ARVN, to recapture large parts of the countryside in order to destroy the pacification program and gain access to new recruits; above all, to show public opinion in America that, contrary to the optimistic projections of November, the U.S. was not winning the war and in fact could not seriously attempt to win it without undermining its domestic and global interests. . . .

These various countermovements notwithstanding, the Task Force ended its seven-day effort by drafting a set of recommendations which in all essential respects confirmed existing policy. In a short, unsigned memorandum for the President, it recommended an immediate deployment of about 20,000 additional troops and the prompt approval of reserve call-ups, larger draft calls, and lengthened duty tours in Vietnam sufficient both to provide the remaining 186,000 men requested by Westmoreland and to restore a strategic reserve force adequate to meet contingencies that might arise elsewhere in the world. There was to be a reiteration of the San Antonio formula, but no new initiative toward negotiations or peace. There was also to be a step-up in the bombing, with Wheeler, Taylor, and Rostow advocating measures beyond those acceptable to the other members of the Task Force, i.e., to expand the targets around Hanoi and Haiphong, and to mine Haiphong harbor. These were the central recommendations. . . .

Clifford, although he passed along the report, was uneasy about it, for the Task Force deliberations had deepened his doubts as to the wisdom and practicality of existing policy. Moreover, in separate meetings with the Joint Chiefs of Staff, he had probed for their professional assessment of the battlefield effect of adding 206,000 troops, but had received only "vague and unsatisfactory" answers. They could not promise victory; at most, they could say that more troops would add to the cumulative weight of our pressure on the enemy. . . .

But by far the most serious deficiency of the Task Force report was its failure to gauge the horrendous political implications of its basic recommendation that the military manpower request be met. For this involved a reserve mobilization on the order of 250,000 men as well as increased draft calls. Together, these measures would add 450,000 men to U.S. active duty forces, bringing the total strength to about 8.9 million. With his sensitive journalistic antennae quivering, Goulding hastily dictated an appendix which Clifford circulated within the Task Force, but which did not go forward to the President. Goulding's appendix noted that there had been absolutely no preparation of public opinion for such a large-scale mobilization. The official line had stressed our ability to fight in Vietnam and at the same time to meet commitments elsewhere without undue strain; it had held that we were winning the war and, specifically, that we had emerged victorious from the Tet offensive; it insisted that ARVN was improving every day. Now suddenly 250,000 American reservists were to be separated from their families and careers and another 200,000 men drafted—all in the absence of any new or palpable national crisis.

Goulding argued that the shock wave would run through the entire American body politic. The doves would say the President was destroying the country by pouring its finest men and resources into a bottomless pit. The hawks would cry that the Administration had no moral right to disrupt the lives of all these young men and still insist on waging a war of limited objectives, limited geographical boundaries, and limited weapons. They would demand, Goulding wrote, that the Administration "unleash . . . hit the sanctuaries . . . if necessary invade." The antiwar demonstrations and resistance to the draft would rise to new crescendos, reinforced by civil rights groups who would feel the President had once again revealed his inner conviction that the war in Vietnam was more important than the war on poverty. It would be quite unavailing for the Administration to say that only 20,000 more men were being committed to Vietnam. That might or might not prove to be true; in the larger sense the claim would be irrelevant for, in the context of steady escalation over the past three years, it simply would not be believed. Moreover, the major political damage would be done by the increased mobilization itself, for it was this that would bring the defense budget to rise by $2.5 billion in 1968 and by $10 billion in 1969. The actual deployment of the other 186,000 to Vietnam would be, as the saying went, a "secondary explosion."

Goulding's appendix made clear that the Administration had trapped itself in repeated expressions of overblown optimism and could thus carry into effect the recommendations of the Task Force only if it were ready to accept the gravest domestic political risks. Clifford was deeply impressed by its unanswerable logic; others were equally taken aback. Fowler, who had concluded that a formal war mobilization was the only sure way to obtain the higher taxes and controls that he felt were necessary for a successful defense of the dollar, was apparently chastened by the chilling implications of the Goulding analysis.

The Task Force recommendations were sent to the President on March 7. The following day, Clifford went to the White House to discuss the proposed actions and their implications, and also to lay before the President some of the fundamental questions which had formed in his own thinking about Vietnam. The recommendations, he explained, were responsive to instructions and represented actions that the President could take "if that is the way you wish to go."

He felt obliged to add, however, that, while not yet agreeing or disagreeing with the thrust of the Task Force report, he had developed "doubts" about the efficacy of the ground strategy, the effectiveness of the bombing campaign, and what could really be accomplished by a further large infusion of American troops. He acknowledged that his doubts did not appear to be shared by the other principals on the Task Force, namely, Rusk, Rostow, Wheeler, Taylor, and Fowler. . . .

The session on March 3 ended with Clifford emphasizing the tentative nature of his own judgments and expressing the hope that there would be time for further study. Wheeler and the JCS were anxious to move ahead on the Task Force recommendations, but Rusk and Rostow were prepared to have the issues studied further, in part because the domestic implications, political and economic, seemed to grow more ominous with each passing day. Some reasonable delay appeared to meet the President's preferences. . . .

March 12 was the day of the Democratic primary in New Hampshire. While President Johnson won as a write-in candidate with 49.4 percent of the vote, Senator Eugene McCarthy polled 42.2 percent. The shock to Johnson and his supporters was very real, for the voting proved beyond denial that the reports of deep divisiveness in the country were more than newspaper talk. One Democratic politician, reflecting on New Hampshire and watching the storm clouds gather over Wisconsin, where the primary voting would take place on April 2, said "The Democratic Party is on the edge of rebellion."

On Saturday, March 16, Robert Kennedy announced for the Presidency and embarked immediately on a whirlwind campaign beginning with two speeches that produced the largest political crowds in the history of Kansas—15,000 at Kansas State University, and 17,000 at the University of Kansas. Clifford was uncertain whether Kennedy would have stayed out of the race even if the President had accepted the essential elements of his proposal, but he regarded the President's reasons for refusal as entirely cogent. He also drew the inference from this episode that the President definitely intended to run for reelection. . . .

Despite strident declarations which reflected the visceral Johnson, the President was privately troubled and uneasy during February and early March. Whatever his strong instinctive preferences, he could not responsibly ignore the hard realities of the human and financial cost of the war, the fading support for it in the country, the malaise in the foreign-military bureaucracy, and the galloping deterioration of the Democratic party. However unpalatable, these were facts that could not be wished away.

In late Febraury he had consulted Dean Acheson whom he held in the highest regard as a brilliant mind, a courageous and distinguished former Secretary of State, and the toughest of Cold Warriors. When the President asked him his opinion of the current situation in Vietnam, Acheson replied he wasn't sure he had a useful view because he was finding it impossible, on the basis of occasional official briefings given him, to discover what was really happening. He had lost faith in the objectivity of the briefers: "With all due respect, Mr. President, the Joint Chiefs of Staff don't know what they're talking about." The President said that was a shocking statement. Acheson replied that, if such it was, then perhaps the President ought to be shocked. The President said he wanted Acheson's considered judgment; Acheson replied he could give this only if he were free to make his own inquiry into the facts so that he would not be dependent on "canned briefings" from the JCS, Rostow, and the CIA. The President agreed he should have the necessary resources for an independent study.

Acheson thereupon assembled a small group of knowledgeable people at the second and third levels and worked with them over a two-week period, holding meetings at his home where he cross-examined them at length. The group included Philip Habib of State, George Carver of CIA, and Major General William DuPuy of the Joint Chiefs of Staff organization. On March 15, Acheson gave the President his findings, at a luncheon where the two men were completely alone. Acheson told the President he was being led down a garden path by the JCS, that what Westmoreland was attempting in Vietnam was simply not possible—without the application of totally unlimited resources "and maybe five years." He told the President that his recent speeches were quite unrealistic and believed by no one, either at home or abroad. He added the judgment that the country was no longer supporting the war. This was tough, unvarnished advice in the Acheson manner, though served with the customary polish and elegance. The President obviously did not like it, but he greatly respected the purveyor.

The luncheon with Acheson took place just three days after the New Hampshire primary, on the same day that Ambassador Goldberg's bombing memorandum arrived from New York, and one day before Robert Kennedy entered the presidential race. In the face of these unpalatable new pressures and of unwanted but unignorable advice, Lyndon Johnson began to feel "crowded"; his immediate reaction was to lash out in a kind of emotional tantrum. On March 17, he flew to the Middle West to deliver two thoroughly truculent speeches—to the National Alliance of Businessmen and the National Farmers Union—in the drafting of which Rostow and Fortas had a major hand. . . .

By March 20, the President appeared to have passed through his first explosive reaction to the mounting pressures and to have recovered a measure of calm. . . . Two days later, on March 22, he announced that Westmoreland would be relieved of his command and come home to be Army Chief of Staff. No successor was immediately named and no date fixed for the return. In light of his major decisions several days later, it seemed that by these acts President Johnson was tentatively clearing away the accumulated underbrush and preparing the site for the construction of a possibly different policy. Neither act was conclusive, or committed him to substantive change. Those who knew him very well thought in retrospect that the process was largely subconscious, but it did seem that, in a mysterious way peculiar to the U.S. Presidency, something was stirring and changing. Clifford continued to see hope in the mere fact that the debate went on, that the President remained willing to hear him out, rather than turning him off "which he was perfectly capable of doing." . . .

The Senior Advisory Group on Vietnam met in the White House on March 25 and 26. Those present were: Dean Acheson, Secretary of State under President Truman; George Ball, Under Secretary of State in the Kennedy-Johnson period; McGeorge Bundy, Special Assistant to Presidents Kennedy and Johnson; Douglas Dillon, Ambassador to France under President Eisenhower and Secretary of the Treasury under President Kennedy; Cyrus Vance, Deputy Secretary of Defense under McNamara and a diplomatic troubleshooter for President Johnson; Arthur Dean, chief Korean War negotiator; John J. McCloy, High Commissioner to West Germany under President Truman and Assistant Secretary of War during World War II; General Omar Bradley, World War II Commander and the first JCS Chairman; General Matthew Ridgway, Korean War Commander and later NATO Commander; General Maxwell Taylor, JCS Chairman under President Kennedy and later Ambassador to Saigon; Robert Murphy, a senior career Ambassador of the Truman-Eisenhower period; Henry Cabot Lodge, former U.S. Senator and twice Ambassador to Saigon; Abe Fortas, a sitting Associate Justice of the Supreme Court and a personal adviser to President Johnson; and Arthur Goldberg, Ambassador to the United Nations and a former Secretary of Labor and Supreme Court Justice.

They assembled in the afternoon to read a number of background papers, and then went on to dinner with the principal cabinet officers plus Rostow, Harriman, and William Bundy whom they questioned at length. After dinner, the entire group heard briefings from Habib of the State Department, Carver of the CIA, and Major General DuPuy. The discussion continued late into the evening and resumed at a session the next morning preparatory to luncheon with the President. It was apparent at an early stage that the unanimity of October had evaporated and that a majority was now deeply troubled. . . .

Two days later, on March 28, Clifford met in Rusk's office together with Rostow, William Bundy, and McPherson. He was unaccompanied by anyone from the Pentagon. The announced purpose of the meeting was to "polish the draft" of the speech the President was now scheduled to make just three days later. . . . It was still essentially a defiant, bellicose speech written to be delivered between clenched teeth. . . .

After reading the draft, Clifford said, "The President cannot give that speech! It would be a disaster! What seems not to be understood is that major elements of the national constituency—the business community, the press, the churches, professional groups, college presidents, students, and most of the intellectual community—have turned against this war. What the President needs is not a war speech, but a peace speech." This opening comment seemed to place his main argument on the grounds of domestic considerations, but in the course of a comprehensive presentation he dealt fully with the military situation in Vietnam and elsewhere in the world. For the first hour or so, Clifford still appeared to be alone, meeting only silent patience from Rusk and Rostow, and with Bundy and McPherson "not taking substantive positions, but simply sitting in as aides." But significantly Rusk did not attempt to cut him off, as he might have, with the comment, "I know your views, but let's get on with the reading." As he talked on, Clifford began to feel he was making progress with Rusk who was "troubled and sincerely anxious to find some way to the negotiating table." The Clifford manner is deliberate, sonorous, eloquent, and quite uninterruptable. It gathers momentum as it proceeds, and soon achieves a certain mesmerizing effect; the perfection of the grammar is uncanny. During the course of several hours, speaking slowly, his fingertips pressed together, and glancing occasionally at an envelope on which he had scribbled a series of points, Clifford mustered every available argument in the powerful arsenal of reasons why it was not in the United States' interest to go on pouring military resources into South Vietnam; he drew heavily on the earlier analyses provided by Nitze, Warnke, Goulding, and myself. When the meeting finally broke up at 5 P.M., the group had inadvertently reviewed not only the speech draft, but the whole of Vietnam policy. Moreover, Rusk had agreed that McPherson should prepare an alternative draft, in order that the President might have two speeches to consider and thus the benefit of a clear-cut choice. Rusk did not object to giving the President a choice. Clifford thought Rostow refrained from making a fuss because he considered the President had already made up his mind not to stop the bombing—which was now the central point at issue.

The occasion had a major impact on McPherson, who was deeply impressed by Clifford's "brilliant and utterly courageous performance" and who from that point forward became not merely a semi-covert dove, but an aroused and powerful ally. Working all through that night, McPherson wrote the first draft of the "peace speech," containing an unconditional bombing cut-off at the 20th parallel and a promise of total cessation if Hanoi provided assurances that it would respect the DMZ and refrain from attacking the cities. He sent this draft to the President early on Friday, March 29, with a note saying that it seemed to reflect the views of "your leading advisers." Later in the day, the President telephoned to ask about a passage "on page 3." McPherson had to compare the two texts in his own office before he discovered to his relief that the President was now working from the alternative draft, the peace speech. From then until the late afternoon of Sunday, March 31, the President worked with McPherson, Clifford, and a number of others to polish the new speech.

At 9 o'clock on Sunday evening, speaking from his office in the White House, the President said "Good evening, my fellow Americans. Tonight I want to talk to you of peace in Vietnam and Southeast Asia." He reviewed his Administration's efforts "to find a basis for peace talks," especially the San Antonio formula of the preceding September, and asserted that there was "no need to delay the talks that could bring an end to this long and this bloody war." He then moved to the principal conclusion of the reappraisal and the pivotal element of the new approach to Hanoi. He said "So, tonight . . . I am taking the first step to de-escalate the conflict. We are reducing—substantially reducing—the present level of hostilities . . . unilaterally and at once. Tonight, I have ordered our aircraft and our naval vessels to make no attacks on North Vietnam, except in the area north of the Demilitarized Zone where the continuing enemy buildup directly threatens allied forward positions. . . ." This meant stopping the bombing, he said, in areas inhabited by "almost 90 percent"of North Vietnam's population. "I call upon President Ho Chi Minh to respond positively, and favorably, to this new step toward peace."

He referred to the emergency deployment in mid-February of 10,500 Marine and airborne troops, and argued that to enable these forces to reach maximum combat effectiveness "we should prepare to send—during the next five months—support troops totaling approximately 13,500 men." He announced that President Thieu had, in the previous week, ordered the mobilization of 135,000 additional South Vietnamese, which would bring the total strength of ARVN to more than 800,000, and he pledged an effort to "accelerate the re-equipment of South Vietnam's armed forces" which "will enable them progressively to undertake a larger share of combat operations against the Communist invaders." The tentative estimate of these additional U.S. and ARVN costs was, he said, $2.5 billion in 1968 and $2.6 billion the following year. He then made a strong pitch for a ten percent surtax, saying "The passage of a tax bill now, together with expenditure control that the Congress may desire and dictate, is absolutely necessary to protect this nation's security, to continue our prosperity, and to meet the needs of our people."

Turning to "an estimate of the chances for peace," the President said, "As Hanoi considers its course, it should be in no doubt of our intentions. . . . We have no intention of widening this war. But the United States will never accept a fake solution to this long and arduous struggle and call it peace. . . . Peace will come because Asians were willing to work for it—and to sacrifice for it—and to die by the thousands for it. But let it never be forgotten: Peace will come also because America lent her sons to help secure it."

Finally, and somewhat surreptitiously, he came to his surprise withdrawal from the presidential race. Asserting that the country's "ultimate strength" lies in "the unity of our people," he acknowledged that "There is division in the American house now. There is divisiveness among us all tonight. And holding the trust that is mine, as President of all the people, I cannot disregard the peril to the progress of the American people and the hope and prospect of peace for all people. . . . With America's sons in the fields faraway, with America's future under challenge right here at home . . . I do not believe that I should devote an hour or a day of my time to any personal partisan causes. . . . Accordingly, I shall not seek, and I will not accept, the nomination of my party for another term as your President." . . .

How did the President come to these decisions? No one can be sure. He seemed finally to have grasped the seismic shift in public opinion and the absolute political temperature of yielding to it, at least temporarily. This shift was borne in upon him by the New Hampshire primary, Robert Kennedy's entrance into the presidential race, the solid congressional opposition to mobilizing larger reserves, and the almost unanimous hostility of the press. The intractable nature of the new environment was made personal by the sharply changed outlook of Acheson, McGeorge Bundy, Vance, and Dillon. Without question, Clifford played a pre-eminent—and I believe the decisive—role. He was the single most powerful and effective catalyst of change, bringing each day to the stale air of the inner circle a fresh perception of the national interest, unfettered by connection with the fateful decisions of 1965. He rallied and gave authoritative voice to the informed and restless opposition within the government, pressing the case for change with intellectual daring, high moral courage, inspired ingenuity, and sheer stubborn persistence. It was one of the great individual performances in recent American history, and achieved in the remarkably taut time span of thirty days. Moreover, it retained its luster and its central effectiveness amid all the backsliding and ambiguity of the Administration's final ten months in office. If, as later events showed, these prodigious efforts did not really change President Johnson's mind about the Vietnam war, at least they compelled him to decide—in favor of reason, restraint, and a new approach. And such decisions by the incumbent of perhaps the most powerful office on earth created a new situation that virtually precluded a return to the old.

Clifford's own view of the March 31 decisions was both modest and mystical: "Presidents have difficult decisions to make and go about making them in mysterious ways. I know only that this decision, when finally made, was the right one."

One Morning in the War

RICHARD HAMMER

Violence has become one of the great political and intellectual problems of the age. Nonviolent demonstrations have provoked uncontrolled violence against demonstrators. Cities, prisons, campuses have erupted in violence. Even the exercise of power by constituted authorities has sometimes been felt by its victims as open violence. Military operations in a war of tightly delimited strategies have degenerated into the rawest outrage. Commentators have rightly seized on the massacre of My Lai 4 as an awesome symbol of all that is wrong with what we have become. The account printed below calls for no introduction since nothing can prepare one for it. What it requires is a conclusion: some means of understanding what quickly passes beyond human comprehension.

Elsewhere Richard Hammer ascribes the slaughter at My Lai to "mass psychosis." From his description here this is hard to question. But it hardly explains anything, for what caused the psychosis he portrays? Ethnologists such as Konrad Lorenz and Robert Ardrey would trace such behavior back to man's biological inheritance, the millions of years he spent evolving from a beast that hunted for its food. Others prefer cultural explanations—the moral sicknesses induced by war or the sicknesses of a society out of control. Historians will one day link My Lai (March 1968) with the fears aroused by the Tet offensive of late January 1968. A few people may be able to dismiss it as mere aberration, an accident of war. But for most Americans it is part of a vast puzzle whose pieces include fire hoses, police dogs, mace, bombs, assassins, snipers, police brutality, riots, napalm, and the careful decisions that lead to such dreadful mornings in the war as that of March 16, 1968.

For Nguyen Van Danh, the deputy sub-hamlet chief of My Hoi, it had been a night of such pleasurable excitement that he had had trouble going to sleep. For the first time in four years he had seen his own house, had slept under his own roof, and he had luxuriated in the feeling of being home again. His neighbors who had stayed in the sub-hamlet all those years had come to welcome him back with the others who had returned the previous night. They had sat under the stars and talked long before going to bed. Some of what they had said had left him with an uneasy feeling. The government's claim that the village was now pacified, that the VC had departed, had been driven out, was rejected by those who had stayed. ARVN troops had patrolled the area on a few occasions, fought minor skirmishes with the VC, but VC were still only a little over a klick to the north in My Khe, and the VC still came to My Hoi whenever it wanted to, with little opposition.

But, still, it was good to be home. As he woke that bright sunny morning, Danh realized that it was late; he had finally gone to sleep very late and had slept longer than he planned. He had meant to be up early and just walk through the village and the paddies, walk down to the river, just enjoy being back.

Danh is uncertain exactly what woke him. Perhaps it was the sound. For in the distance, a little way to the west, he thought he heard the concussion of bombs and rockets, the sound of machine gun fire. At first he thought it was just his imagination. He went to the door and outside, peering toward the sounds in the west. And he could make out, hovering, helicopters. And he could see smoke and sudden bright flashes of shells exploding.

Nguyen To was at work in his rice paddy just outside Xom Lang before seven that morning. He was worried and the feel of soil and grain in his hands, the sun on his back, alleviated his concerns for the moment. He had gone early to the paddy just for that purpose, so he would not have to think about his troubles and to enjoy the paddy and the earth and the sun, for he was sure that he did not have much longer to enjoy them.

Two of his sons were off somewhere, he did not know where, fighting with the VC. His other three sons, younger, were still at home, but one of them was talking about leaving, not to join his brothers in the VC but to go west to Quang Ngai and join the ARVN. His two younger sons were still too small—only ten and fourteen—for politics and the war.

Just a few days before some ARVN had come into the hamlet during the day. They had come to his home to talk to him about his sons, about his own feelings. And from their manner toward him, from the tone of their voices, he knew he was suspected of harboring VC sympathies, of being a secret VC. And he was certain that even though he was sixty-two, he would be arrested by the government soon and taken to prison. "I did not like the government," he insists today, after having spent most of the two years since that March day in a government prison as a VC sympathizer, "but I was not VC. My two sons were VC, but I had no interest in politics."

As he worked, To thought he heard sharp clattering sounds overhead. He looked up and saw an American helicopter hovering over Xom Lang. It circled the settlement two or three times and then turned north and disappeared. A few moments later he heard a loud thud, a KAPLOW that shook the ground. The first shells had fallen on Xom Lang.

Breakfast was just being served at Mr. Sam's brick house. The immediate family and relatives and in-laws had crowded into the house and Mr. Sam's wife was spooning the morning rice from the cooking pot into each bowl. Ngo Ngo Thininh, Mr. Sam's nineteen-year-old daughter-in-law, her husband away fighting for the ARVN, remembers that her four-year-old brother was standing near the pot. His bowl had just been filled and he was about to dip his spoon into the rice.

The first shells hit just outside the house and everything shook and reverberated. She saw the bowl and the spoon drop from her brother's hands and shatter on the floor. Mr. Sam immediately ordered everyone into the bunkers outside for shelter until the shelling stopped.

For Nguyen Chi this Saturday was to have been market day. With many things to do at home, she rose early, intending to get to the market at Chau Thanh quickly and be back home with her husband and three young children before noon. They were just rising when she left the house and started down the road toward the market. Moving rapidly along the side of the road she paid little attention to what was happening above and around her until suddenly she heard a bomb explode with a loud thud behind her, from the direction of Xom Lang.

"I turned around," she remembers. "I saw them exploding in my hamlet. So I ran to a near house. It was right near the main road where I was walking. The people in the house took me down to the bunker and we all hid there. As we were going into the bunker, we saw the choppers coming overhead. One of them landed in a rice paddy near the road about one klick from where I was."

Later, when the sound of the bombs had stopped, she came out of the bunker, but quickly ducked back in when she saw American soldiers moving toward the hamlet, shooting. She stayed out just long enough, however, to look in the direction of her home which was in the first row of houses. She saw "GI burning my house and my cow house, too."

It was just about seven in the morning when the first shells began to rain on Xom Lang that March 16th. Those who were still at home—most of the people in the sub-hamlet, for it was still early and many of them were just beginning breakfast—quickly sought shelter in their family bunkers. Almost every house had its bunker dug into the ground nearby. The VC when they had arrived had forced the people to build them, and from friends in other hamlets they had heard enough tales to know that in case of a bombardment, a bunker was one of the few hopes of survival. So each family dug its own.

The shells continued to thud into the ground and explode, destroying houses and gouging deep craters for about twenty minutes. The artillery barrage marched up and down the hamlet and the area around it, preparing the landing zone for the troop-carrying helicopters. Overhead, helicopter gunships hovered without any opposition, pounding the hamlet and the ground around it with rockets and machine gun fire.

When the artillery finally stopped, there was a momentary silence, made louder by the sudden absence of exploding high-explosives, and then the air filled with the ear-shattering clatter of the helicopters beginning to settle into the rice paddies and fields at the western edge of Xom Lang.

Captain Ernest Medina was in the lead chopper, watching the artillery and the gunships level Xom Lang. He "could see the smoke and flash of artillery" as the settlement was ripped apart. Then his helicopter settled into a paddy about a hundred and fifty meters west. Immediately the door gunners strafed the surrounding countryside with machine gun fire in case there happened to be VC waiting among the growing rice and brush.

As far as Medina could tell there was no return fire. "My instant impression," he says, "was that I didn't hear the familiar crackle of rifle bullets zinging over my head."

Accompanied by his radio operator and other company aides, Medina clambered down from the helicopter and rushed across the paddy to the edge of a small graveyard just at the edge of Xom Lang. Still there was no return fire, and all around him the other choppers were settling to the ground and the men of Company C were pouring through the doors, firing toward the houses as they emerged. It seemed to have occurred to no one at that moment that the lack of return fire might mean that this was not the hamlet where the VC was centered, that this was not "Pinkville."

But Medina did note the lack of armed resistance. He radioed back to the tactical operations center at LZ Dottie that the landing had been smooth and that his men had come under no fire. "I reported the LZ is cold. Immediately thereafter the helicopter pilot broke in and reported, 'Negative, negative, negative. LZ is hot. You are receiving small arms fire.' "

This was the only report that morning of opposition. And it is more than likely that the pilot thought the firing of the American troops moving in toward Xom Lang indicated that small arms were being shot back from the settlement.

Though Medina could neither see nor hear any return fire from the houses, he quickly passed the word to the leaders of his three platoons, two of them blocking access to Xom Lang, or My Lai (4) as the Americans had it on their maps, and to Calley's first platoon advancing on the settlement itself. "I told them to move with extreme caution and to return any fire."

Moving with that extreme caution and deliberation toward Xom Lang, the thirty-odd men of Calley's first platoon expected at any moment to come under intense fire they had been warned they would receive. They were tense, as though girding themselves to repel the bullets which would hit them. But there was only silence from Xom Lang.

As they approached the first houses, they broke into smaller units —squads and even smaller, just a few men separating and advancing on different targets. And from that moment on, no man saw all the action, saw all that happened. Each man's knowledge of the events of the next few hours that morning—as was the knowledge of those inside the settlement waiting for the Americans to arrive—was limited by his own immediate area of combat and vision, to his own particular ground inside and around Xom Lang and nearby Binh Dong. The events of those next hours, and particularly that next forty minutes, then, were necessarily episodic and chaotic; there was no order, no sequence, merely action and reaction, here and there and everywhere.

Any attempt, then, to describe what happened—on the basis of the recollections of the American soldiers as related to this reporter and others, and of Vietnamese reliving the carnage in conversations with me —can only, at best, attempt to reveal the chaos of the whole and the separateness of the small individual scenes.

With Sergeant Mitchell in the lead, five men of Charley Company descended from their chopper right outside the hamlet. They began moving toward the houses in a single line, Mitchell in the lead. Paul Meadlo remembers that "there was one man, a gook in a shelter, all huddled down in there, and the soldier called out and said there's a gook over here." Sergeant Mitchell brusquely gave the orders to shoot. "And so then the man was shot. So we moved on into the village."

"When the attack started," Sergeant Charles West recalls, "it couldn't have been stopped by anyone. We were mad and we had been told that the enemy was there and we were going in there to give them a fight for what they had done to our dead buddies."

Approaching Xom Lang, "we went in shooting," West says. "We'd shoot into the hootches and there were people running around. There were big craters in the village from the bombing. When I got there I saw some of the people, some of the women and kids all torn up."

"I was just coming to the first row of houses, with five or six other guys," says another member of the platoon, "when we heard this noise behind us. Everybody was scared and on edge, and keyed up, too, to kill, and somebody turned quick and snapped off a shot. We all turned and shot. And there was this big old water buffalo, I guess that's what it was, standing in the middle of this field behind us. Everybody was shooting at it and you could see little puffs jumping out where the bullets hit. It was like something in slow motion, and finally that cow just slumped down and collapsed." His face contorted by the remembrance, he adds, "Now it seems kind of funny, but it didn't then. And once the shooting started, I guess it affected everyone. From then on it was like nobody could stop. Everyone was just shooting at everything and anything, like the ammo wouldn't ever give out."

The contagion of slaughter was spreading throughout the platoon.

Combat photographer Ronald Haeberle and Army Correspondent Jay Roberts had requested permission to accompany a combat mission in order to get both pictures and a story of American soldiers in action. They had been assigned to Charley Company and to Calley's platoon. Leaving their helicopter with about ten or fifteen other soldiers, they came upon a cow being slaughtered, and then the picture turned sickeningly grisly. "Off to the right," Haeberle said, "a woman's form, a head appeared from some brush. All the other GI's started firing at her, aiming at her, firing at her over and over again."

The bullets riddled the woman's body. She slumped against a well pump in the middle of the rice paddy, her head caught between two of its poles. She was obviously already dead, but the infection, the hysteria was now ascendant. The men were oblivious to everything but slaughter. "They just kept shooting at her. You could see the bones flying in the air, chip by chip."

There were the sounds: the shots running into and over each other from inside the hamlet; it sounded as though everyone had his rifle on automatic, no one bothering to save ammunition by switching to single shot. And not drowned by the sharp bark of the rifles and duller thuds of grenades were screams; they sounded like women and children, but how can anyone tell in that kind of moment from a distance who is screaming?

Four or five Americans were outside the hamlet, moving along its perimeter. The job of their platoon was to seal it off and so prevent the VC inside from fleeing from Calley's men, to catch them in a pincer and slaughter them. Vernardo Simpson and these other soldiers were probing the bushes on the outskirts, delicately, searching for mines and booby traps. As they neared the first group of houses, a man dressed in black pajamas—the dress convinced Simpson that he must be a VC even though black pajamas were traditional peasant dress—suddenly appeared from nowhere, from some bushes and began running toward the hamlet. A woman and child popped up from the same underbrush and started "running away from us toward some huts."

"Dong lai! Dong lai!" The Americans shouted after the Vietnamese. But they kept on running. Lieutenant Brooks, the leader of this second platoon, gave the orders to shoot. If these people did not stop on command, then they must necessarily be VC. "This is what I did," Simpson says. "I shot them, the lady and the little boy. He was about two years old."

A woman and a child? Why?

"I was reluctant, but I was following a direct order. If I didn't do this I could stand court martial for not following a direct order."

Before the day was over, Simpson says, he would have killed at least ten Vietnamese in Xom Lang.

With the number killed there, his total was about the average for each soldier.

When the shelling stopped, Pham Phon crept from the bunker near his hootch. About fifty meters away, he saw a small group of American soldiers. Poking his head back into the bunker, he told his wife and three children—two sons aged nine and four, and a seven-year-old daughter—to come up and walk slowly toward the Americans.

Like almost all Vietnamese in the hamlets around the country, Phon and his family had learned from the three previous American visits and from the tales told by refugees who had come to Xom Lang to seek shelter after their hamlets had been turned into battlegrounds and from tales carried by others from far away, just how to act when American troops arrived.

It was imperative not to run, either toward the Americans or away from them. If you ran, the Americans would think that you were VC, running away from them or running toward them with a grenade, and they would shoot.

It was imperative not to stay inside the house or the bunker. If you did, then the Americans would think you were VC hiding in ambush, and they would shoot or throw grenades into the house or bunker.

It was imperative to walk slowly toward the Americans, with hands in plain view, or to gather in small groups in some central spot and wait for the Americans to arrive—but never to gather in large groups, for then the Americans would think the group was VC waiting to fire. It was absolutely imperative to show only servility so that the Americans would know that you were not VC and had only peaceful intent.

So Phon and his family walked slowly toward the soldiers. The three children smiled and shouted, "Hello! Hello! Okay! Okay!"

Only this time, unlike the three previous American visitations, there were no answering grins, no gifts of candy and rations. The Americans pointed their rifles at the family and sternly ordered them to walk to the canal about a hundred meters away.

Inside the hamlet, the men of the first platoon were racing from house to house. They planted dynamite and explosive to the brick ones and blew them into dust. They set fires with their lighters to the thatched roofs and to the hootches, watched them flare into a ritual bonfire and then raced on to the next hootch. Some soldiers were pulling people from bunkers and out of the houses and herding them into groups. Some of the Vietnamese tried to run and were immediately shot. Others didn't seem to know what was happening, didn't understand what the Americans were doing or why. But most of them behaved as they had learned they must behave. Meekly they followed any order given.

Some of the groups were marched away in the direction of the canal, and those who straggled behind, could not keep up, were promptly shot.

There were soldiers standing outside the hootches, watching them burn, and as Vietnamese suddenly emerged from the pyres, would shoot them.

And through everything, through the sound of gunfire and through the crackling of flames, through the smoke that had begun to cover everything like a pall, came high-pitched screams of pain and terror, bewildered cries, pleading cries. All were ignored.

Michael Bernhardt remembers coming into the hamlet and seeing his fellow soldiers "doing a whole lot of shooting up. But none of it was incoming. I'd been around enough to tell that. I figured we were advancing on the village with fire power."

Inside the hamlet, Bernhardt "saw these guys doing strange things. They were doing it in three ways. They were setting fire to the hootches and huts and waiting for the people to come out and then shooting them. They were going in to the hootches and shooting them up. They were gathering people in groups and shooting them."

The raging fever in the other members of his platoon stunned and shocked Bernhardt. He watched one soldier shooting at everything he saw, blazing away indiscriminately and laughing hysterically as he kept pulling the trigger, kept his finger on the trigger until all the bullets in a clip were gone, then throwing away the clip and reloading and starting again. And laughing all the time. "He just couldn't stop. He thought it was funny, funny, funny."

Bernhardt says that he was sickened and appalled by what he was seeing, yet he felt helpless to do anything about it, helpless to do anything but stand and watch. "I found out," he told one reporter, "that an act like that, you know, murder for no reason, that could be done by just about anybody."

All through that bloody hour, Bernhardt kept his rifle in its sling, pointing toward the ground. He felt he had no reason to unsling it, no reason to aim it at anybody.

For Private Herbert Carter it was too much, a nightmare from where there seemed no awakening. "People began coming out of their hootches and the guys shot them and burned the hootches—or burned the hootches and then shot the people when they came out. Sometimes they would round up a bunch and shoot them together. It went on like that for what seemed like all day. Some of the guys seemed to be having a lot of fun. They were wisecracking and yelling, 'Chalk that one up for me.' "

When he could stand the sight no longer, Carter turned and stumbled out of the hamlet. He sat down under a tree and shot himself in the foot.

He was Charley Company's only casualty that morning.

When the first shells hurled their way into Xom Lang, Nguyen Thi Nien and her family took shelter in their bunker adjacent to their house. In the bunker with her were her eighty-year-old father-in-law, her sister and her sister's seven-year-old daughter, her own husband and their three children. They cowered in the bunker for a considerable length of time. Finally they heard steady rifle fire around them and American voices yelling: "VC di ra! VC di ra!"—VC, get out! VC, get out!

The family crawled slowly and carefully out of the bunker, making every effort to display no hostility. But once they were out they noticed that the Americans were still some distance away. Taking her youngest child, still a baby, in one arm and holding her second youngest by the hand, Nguyen Thi Nien started away, toward the rice paddies. She did not run, but walked on steadily. Her husband and the oldest child started to follow her. But her sister and her sister's daughter hung back, then started in another direction. And her father-in-law turned and . started back to the house.

"I am too old," she remembers him calling after her. "I can not keep up. You get out and I will stay here to keep the house."

There was almost no argument. "We told him," Nguyen Thi Nien says, "all right, you are too old. So you stay here and if the GI's arrive you ask them not to shoot you and not to burn the house."

The old man called that that was exactly what he intended to do. He would stand guard over the family home. But then Nguyen Thi Nien's husband decided that he could not leave his father alone in the house. He turned, sending the oldest child after his wife and the other children, and went back to his father. They stood outside the house for a brief moment arguing. The son trying to convince the old man to get out of the house and go with them to the paddies before the Americans arrived. The Americans were approaching and they could hear the clatter of shots, they could see the flames licking around other houses, and the smoke.

But the old man remained adamant. He was too old, he kept insisting. He could not make it to the paddy. He refused to leave, turning from his son and starting into the house.

The Americans were almost on them; the firing was all around them now. Nien realized that he could wait no longer. If he were to escape the approaching Americans—he realized by then that this was not a friendly visit, that the Americans were hostile this time and were shooting at everything—he would have to flee immediately.

About four hundred meters away, he saw his wife and three children just ducking into the rice paddies, safe. He started after them. Ahead of him, just a few feet, was an old woman, a nearby neighbor.

But suddenly [he says], five GI's were in front of me, about a hundred meters or so from me. The GI's saw us and started to shoot and the lady was killed. I was hit and so I lay down. Then I saw blood coming from my stomach and so I took a handkerchief and put it over my wound. I lay on the ground there for a little while and then I tried to get back to my house, to my old father and my sister-in-law and her child who must still be there. I could not walk very well and so I was crawling. On the way back to my house I saw five children and one father lying dead on the ground. When I reached my house, I saw it was on fire. Through the fire I could see the bodies of my old father, my sister-in-law and her child inside the house. Then I lost consciousness and I do not know anything more of what happened.

All around there was burning and explosions, shooting and the dead, the screams of the living and, beginning, the sweet smell of burning flesh in the hootches turned into funeral pyres. And, now and again, there was the awful hysterical laughter of one soldier or another. Some of the American faces had expressions which frightened and shocked their friends, those friends at least who emerged from the mass hysteria, which seemed to fill the entire company, long enough to look around them.

I was just coming into the middle of that ville (remembers one soldier, refusing to look around or to meet his questioner's eyes as he talks), and I saw this guy. He was one of my best friends in the company. But honest to Christ, at first I didn't even recognize him. He was kneeling on the ground, this absolutely incredible . . . I don't know what you'd call it, a smile or a snarl or something, but anyway, his whole face was distorted. He was covered with smoke, his face streaked with it, and it looked like there was blood on him, too. You couldn't tell, but there was blood everywhere. Anyway, he was kneeling there holding this grenade launcher, and he was launching grenades at the hootches. A couple of times he launched grenades at groups of people. The grenades would explode, you know, KAPLOW, and then you'd see pieces of bodies flying around. Some of the groups were just piles of bodies. But I remember there was this one group a little distance away. Maybe there was ten people, most of them women and little kids, huddled all together and you could see they were really scared, they just couldn't seem to move. Anyway, he turns around toward them and lets fly with a grenade. It landed right in the middle of them. You could hear the screams and then the sound and then see the pieces of bodies scatter out, and the whole area just suddenly turned red like somebody had turned on a faucet. . . .

There is a well-documented theory of many psychiatrists that sex and violence are two aspects of the same emotion. And that sometimes violence will set loose uncontrollable erotic desires. It has happened often enough in civilized society during peacetime: the incidence of well-publicized sex murders is too well-known to even bother to comment on. If violence during peace can let loose erotic behavior, violence during war seems often to make such desires even less controllable. There had been evidence of this on patrols before. And there was evidence of it again in Xom Lang. The killing, the indiscriminate slaughter all around brought such emotions to the surface in some of the men in the platoon.

Jay Roberts and Ronlad Haeberle moved about the havoc taking pictures. They came upon one group of Americans surrounding a small group of women, children and a teen-age girl. She was perhaps twelve or thirteen and was wearing the traditional peasant black pajamas. One of the Americans grabbed her by the shoulders while another began to try to strip the pajamas off her, pulling at the top of the blouse to undo it.

"Let's see what she's made of," one of the soldiers laughed.

Another moved close to her, laughing and pointing at her. "VC, boom-boom," he said. He was telling her in the GI patois that she was a whore for the VC, and indicating that if she did it for them why not for the Americans.

A third soldier examined her carefully and then turned to the others. "Jesus," he said, "I'm horny."

All around there were burning buildings and bodies and the sounds of firing and screams. But the Americans seemed totally oblivious to anything but the girl. They had almost stripped her when her mother rushed over and tried to help her escape. She clutched at the American soldiers, scratched them, clawed at their faces, screaming invectives at them. They pushed her off. One soldier slapped her across the face; another hit her in the stomach with his fist; a third kicked her in the behind, knocking her sprawling to the ground.

But the mother's actions had given the girl a chance to escape a little. She took shelter behind some of the other women in the group and tried to button the top of her blouse. Haeberle stepped in, knelt and took a picture of the scene.

Roberts remembers that at that moment, "when they noticed Ron, they left off and turned away as if everything was normal. Then a soldier asked, "Well, what'll we do with 'em?'

" 'Kill 'em,' another answered.

"I heard an M-60 go off, a light machine gun, and when we turned all of them and the kids with them were dead."

Somewhere else in the hamlet another soldier says that he saw a buddy suddenly pull a small child out of a group of women. "She was just a little thing," he says. "She couldn't have been more than five or six."

What happened?

"He dragged her into one of these brick houses that hadn't been blown up yet."

And?

"I don't know. I didn't go inside with him. And I don't like to talk about it." He pauses for a few moments, looking away, and then he speaks in a muffled voice, toward the table. "He was in there maybe five, ten minutes. Then he comes out, turns around and throws a grenade into the house."

Another soldier says he saw a teen-age girl running across a rice paddy, trying to hide from an American who was chasing her. As he watched, he saw this American soldier aim with his rifle and shoot. The girl gave a cry and fell down. The soldier went after her and vanished into the paddy. A few minutes later there was another shot from the area and then the soldier walked back from the field into the hamlet.

Nguyen Thi Doc is over seventy, an ancient, stooped peasant woman with a stoic, expressionless face. Today she squats in misery in the doorway of the hootch she shares with a small grandson and a small granddaughter in the refugee camp across from Xom Lang.

On that March morning she was just beginning to make breakfast for her husband, her son, two daughters and nine grandchildren from three to sixteen. They were all gathered around her waiting for their rice. When the bombardment started, all took shelter in the bunker just outside the door. When the shells ceased, they emerged and went back into the house to eat.

A few minutes later Nguyen Thi Doc "heard the Americans come down from the sky." Within minutes they were at her doorway. Without saying a word, they began spraying the inside of the house with machine gun fire. Her husband, her son, her two daughters and seven of her grandchildren—the oldest seven—were killed immediately. Nguyen Thi Doc was shot in the arm; her five-year-old granddaughter was shot in the foot. Today it is scarred and shriveled and the child limps through the camp, often hiding from others. Only the youngest child, a little boy, escaped unharmed.

The Americans then set fire to the house. Somehow, Nguyen Thi Doc managed to get outside, taking her granddaughter and grandson with her, and from the yard they watched the house burn, inside of it the rest of her family.

Now she sits in the refugee camp, asking no questions why it happened. "I am too old," she says. "I have no idea why the GI's come and do this thing. The thing I must do is to make money to take care of these children. They have no one else. And I am too old. I just want to die."

Just outside the village there was a big pile of bodies. Jay Roberts sees this "really tiny kid—he only had a shirt on—nothing else. He came over to the people and held the hand of one of the dead. One of the GI's behind me dropped into a kneeling position thirty meters from this kid and killed him with a single shot."

Haeberle sees two small children, maybe four or five years old. "A guy with an M-16 fired at the first boy and the older boy fell over him to protect the smaller one. Then they fired six more shots. It was done very businesslike."

A small boy, three or four, suddenly appears from nowhere on the trail in front of a group of Americans. He is wounded in the arm. Michael Terry sees "the boy clutching his wounded arm with his other hand while the blood trickled between his fingers. He was staring around himself in shock and disbelief at what he saw. He just stood there with big eyes staring around like he didn't understand what was happening. Then the captain's radio operator put a burst of 16 into him."

When Paul Meadlo came into Xom Lang, Lieutenant Calley set him and some of the other men to work gathering the people together in groups in a central location. "There was about forty, forty-five people that we gathered in the center of the village," Meadlo told an interviewer. "And we placed them in there, and it was like a little island, right there in the center of the village."

The soldiers forced the people in the group to squat on the ground. "Lieutenant Calley came over and said, 'You know what to do with them, don't you?' And I said, 'Yes.' So I took it for granted he just wanted us to watch them. And he left and came back about ten or fifteen minutes later, and said, 'How come you ain't killed them yet?' And I told him that I didn't think he wanted us to kill them, that you just wanted us to guard them. He said, 'No, I want them dead.' "

At first Meadlo was surprised by the order—not shocked or horrified, but surprised. "But three, four guys heard it and then he stepped back about ten, fifteen feet, and he started shooting them. And he told me to start shooting. I poured about four clips into the group."

A clip is seventeen rounds. Meadlo fired sixty-eight rounds into this group of people. "I fired them on automatic," he said, "so you can't . . . you just spray the area on them and so you can't know how many you killed 'cause they were going fast. So I might have killed ten or fifteen of them."

One slaughter was over, but there was more to come, and the thirst for blood had become so contagious that no one thought anything about what he was doing. "We started to gather them up, more people," Meadlo says, "and we had about seven or eight people that we was gonna put into a hootch and we dropped a hand grenade in there with them."

Then Meadlo and several other soldiers took a group of civilians—almost exclusively women and children, some of the children still too young to walk—toward one of the two canals on the outskirts of Xom Lang. "They had about seventy, seventy-five people all gathered up. So we threw ours in with them and Lieutenant Calley told me, he said, 'Meadlo, we got another job to do.' And so he walked over to the people and started pushing them off and started shooting."

Taking his cue from Calley, Meadlo and then the other members of this squad "started pushing them off and we started shooting them. So altogether we just pushed them all off and just started using automatics on them. And somebody told us to switch off to single shot so that we could save ammo. So we switched off to single shot and shot a few more rounds."

And all the time the Vietnamese at the canal were screaming and pleading with the Americans for mercy. . . .

Just as the slaughter at the canal began, Michael Terry happened to be passing by. "They had them in a group, standing over a ditch—just like a Nazi-type thing," he remembers. "One officer ordered a kid to machine gun everybody down. But the kid couldn't do it. He threw the machine gun down and the officer picked it up. I don't remember seeing any men in the ditch. Mostly women and kids."

Terry left for another part of the hamlet. Later he returned. Calley and his men had left by then and only a small group had stayed behind. Terry was at the canal, sitting on a mound eating some chow with William Doherty. As they were eating, the two noticed that "some of them were still breathing. They were pretty badly shot up. They weren't going to get any medical help, and so we shot them, shot maybe five of them."

In another part of Xom Lang, James Bergthold was moving just behind another soldier carrying a light machine gun. This soldier was moving from house to house, spraying in through the doors, not even looking where he was shooting. He came to one hootch, opened up and then strolled away. Bergthold stopped and looked in. An old man was writhing on the floor in pain, screaming, with large pieces of his legs shot away. Bergthold took his rifle and shot the old man. "Just to put him out of his misery."

All through Xom Lang and around it, the slaughter and the destruction continued endlessly, senselessly. Houses were blown apart and burned. Dead bodies were tossed into the pyres which had once been their homes, or they were left where they had fallen. Animals were slaughtered. Haeberle remembers one scene of a GI stabbing a cow over and over again with his bayonet while the blood spurted in all directions and other soldiers stood around watching and laughing and commenting on his technique. Dead animals and dead bodies were thrown down wells to pollute the water supply. And everywhere, it seemed, was Lieutenant Calley.

But for some Americans, at least, there was no joy in what was happening in Xom Lang, no glory and no victory. Haeberle saw one GI go over to a little boy who had been badly torn apart by a fusillade and with infinite tenderness cover him with a blanket.

And that night, when Nguyen Chi returned to the hamlet to seek her family, she found her three young sons still alive. When the first shells had fallen, the boys had taken their buffalo from the barn into the fields to hide it. At one point they raised their heads to see what was happening. Near them was an American soldier. He stared at them for a moment, then with great urgency motioned for them to duck again. No one is certain who this American was, but he may have been Pvt. Olson—like Bernhardt, he refused to shoot anyone that morning.

This chaotic dance of death was not enacted before an empty auditorium. There were spectators, an audience viewing the drama like ancient Romans at the martyrdom of the Christians. These spectators had a panoramic view.

There were the helicopters circling back and forth, hovering over Xom Lang, reconnoitering the area for signs of the VC and for information on what was going on below. The pilot of one of these choppers was Warrant Officer Hugh C. Thompson of Decatur, Georgia.

The gunner in this helicopter, Specialist Fourth Class Larry Colburn, says that as they were hovering low over one part of the hamlet, they "noticed people dead and wounded along the road and all through the village. There was an irrigation ditch full of bodies. We noticed that some people were still alive. We didn't know what had happened."

Thompson decided to drop down and evacuate some of the wounded. But the helicopter was already pretty full with his own crew, and so he radioed for the gunships to return and help lift the wounded civilians, mainly children, to safety. Then he spotted a group of about fifteen or a dozen children in the midst of the dead and the dying. "We went down," Colburn says, "and our crew chief brought out a little boy about two years old. He seemed in shock."

Huddled in a bunker a short distance away were about a dozen more children. Once again Thompson's radio operator called for the gunships to come in and help the children, ferry them to the nearest field hospital. As Thompson's helicopter lifted off, Colburn noticed that "there must have been about seventy-five or eighty people in a ditch—some dead, some wounded. I had never seen so many people dead in one place before." . . .

Violence in Chicago, 1968: The Walker Report

The eminent novelist Phillip Roth complained early in the 1960's that it was becoming increasingly difficult to satirize American society because so much of it seemed a satire of itself. By 1968 it had also become difficult to dramatize America in any imaginative way because the reality of our lives had become so melodramatic. American society, always cross-grained by a heterogeneous population, seemed finally to fragment in 1968. The street fighting at the Democratic Convention in Chicago that summer climaxed a half-decade of violence in the form of assassinations and rioting at home and warfare half a world away. The official record of all this disorder—the Warren Commission, the McCone Commission, the Kerner Commission, and the rest—had become our ritual efforts at understanding what we were. Most of these reports were thorough and useful, but their recommendations were largely ignored.

The report that the Chicago study team under Daniel Walker prepared for the National Commission on the Causes and Prevention of Violence does not deserve oblivion. In addition to its solid research and its arresting conclusion—that a "police riot" occurred in Chicago in 1968—it is a thrilling book, alive wih the language of the crisis, a vivid portrait which has not lost its capacity to shock. Nineteen sixty-eight was one of the great historic years of American history, and the events here recorded seem its climax, bringing together questions of war and peace, of stability and revolution, and of conflicting cultural styles, symbols of the struggle.

CONFRONTATION AT THE CONRAD HILTON

The U.S. Attorney's report says about 2,000 persons, "mostly normally dressed," had already assembled at the Hilton. Many of these were demonstrators who had tired of waiting out the negotiations and had broken off from the marchers and made their way to the hotel. It appears that police already were having some difficulty keeping order at that location. Says the U.S. Attorney's report: "A large crowd had assembled behind the police line along the east wall of the Hilton. This crowd was heavily infiltrated with 'Yippie' types and was spitting and screaming obscene insults at the police."

A policeman on duty in front of the hotel later said that it seemed to him that the obscene abuses shouted by "women hippies" outnumbered those called out by male demonstrators "four to one." A common epithet shouted by the females, he said, was "Fuck you, pig." Others included references to policemen as "cock suckers" and "mother fuckers."

During this time, he said, the officers did and said nothing in retaliation. At one point, he recalled, a policeman made a retort to a "hippie" and "was immediately told to remain silent." All the while, he said, the policemen were "constantly being photographed by hippies with cameras."

According to his statement, "an Assistant U.S. Attorney and a policeman were sprayed in the face with oven cleaner. . . ." The police reporter mentioned earlier recalls that persons in the crowd were chanting, "Hump sucks" and "Daley sucks Hump."

A short time later the reporter noticed a lot of debris being hurled from one of the upper floors of the Hilton. He climbed into a police squad car parked in the area and with the aid of police binoculars saw that rolls of toilet paper were coming from the 15th floor, a location he pinpointed by counting down from the top of the building. He then went to the 15th floor and found that the section the paper was coming from was rented by Senator McCarthy campaigners. He was not admitted to the suite. . . .

Police in the area were in a far from cheerful mood. A neatly dressed sociology student from Minnesota says he stepped off the sidewalk onto the grass and two policemen pulled their billy clubs back as though ready to swing. One of them said, "You'd better get your fucking ass off that grass or I'll put a beautiful god dam crease in your fucking queer head." The student overheard another policeman say to a "hippie-looking girl of 14 or 15, 'You better get your fucking dirty cunt out of here.'" Another witness recalls that while he was seeking an exit from the park, a young policeman "walked up to me and just looked at me and said, 'Fuck you, you son-of-a-bitch!'" The witness was getting scared and moved rapidly on. The growing feeling of entrapment was intensified and some witnesses noticed that police were letting people into the park but not out. The marshals referred to the situation as a "trap."

As the crowd moved north, an Assistant U.S. Attorney saw one demonstrator with long sideburns and hippie garb pause to break up a large piece of concrete, wrapping the pieces in a striped T-shirt. . . .

Before the march formally disbanded, an early contingent of demonstrators, numbering about 30 to 50, arrived at the spot where Congress Plaza bridges the IC tracks at approximately the same time as a squad of 40 National Guardsmen. The Guard hurriedly spread out about three feet apart across Congress with rifles at the ready, gas masks on, bayonets fixed.

There was a lot of heckling. Some demonstrators tapped Guardsmen's helmets, urging the Guard to join them.

A medic who was in the Guard line says that several "leaders" assembled at the northeast edge of the bridge and with bullhorns "attempted to incite the crowd to break through the line." He says they addressed the crowd with such comments as, "They're more afraid of you than you are of them" and "They're one of us," implying, he felt, that the Guardsmen were draft dodgers.

The medic recalls that he tried to render medical aid to another youth who was "hit across the forehead by a rifle butt while attempting to grab it away from its owner. The downed man was lying just inside the south edge of the line. I went over. I was surrounded, pushed, punched and kicked by a group of demonstrators." The attack did not cease until the Guardsman finally identified himself as a medic.

As the crowd swelled, it surged periodically towards the Guard line, sometimes yelling, "Freedom, freedom." On one of these surges a Guardsman hurled two tear gas canisters. Later a National Guard official, Brigadier General John Phipps, exclaimed that the commander of the 40-man platoon on the bridge had a few more people on the scene than he could control and used "a little tear gas" to push them back. Guard reinforcements arrived, and gas was freely dispensed from CA-3 back-pack sprayers (converted flame throwers). One witness says: "A Guardsman stepped in front [of the Guard line] and walked the width of the bridge laying down a stream of tear gas. . . . As cars came up, the ranks of troops closed and the man sprayed more gas." The wind was then from the northeast and the gas was generally blown back into the Guard lines and southwest towards the Hilton and the Blackstone.

Some of the tear gas was fired directly into the faces of demonstrators. "We came across a guy really badly gassed," a college coed says. "We were choking, but we could still see. But this guy we saw was standing there helpless with mucous-type stuff on his face, obviously in pain. There was a medic near us with water and we washed this guy's eyes out and helped him along until he could see."

An Assistant U.S. Attorney says he saw "hundreds of people running, crying, coughing, vomiting, screaming." Some women ran blindly to Buckingham Fountain and leaped into the water to bathe their faces. The Guard medic quoted earlier says he was again assaulted by demonstrators when he went into the crowd to treat a man felled by "a particularly heavy dose of tear gas."

On a stiff breeze off Lake Michigan, the gas swept west through the Guard line, over the blockaded bridge and into Michigan Avenue. Startled businessmen, office workers, late shoppers on the street held their faces and ran into stores and buildings to get away from the stinging fumes. Because of the wind, says one onlooker, the demonstrators in the park on the whole got less gas than "the Michigan Avenue crowd, the conventioneers, strollers, hotel residents, what I call the coat-and-tie-set. They were the hardest hit."

By 7 P.M., the gas was reported "heavy" at Congress and Michigan, two blocks north of the Hilton. A little later when the observer entered the Hilton, he noticed vomit stains on the lobby carpet "from persons who could not hold their gas." A rotten stench pervaded the hotel. There is a good chance that what the reporter smelled was not, in fact, vomit. Throughout the convention week, a putrid odor permeated the Hilton and other hotels where convention visitors were staying. On Friday, police arrested three young women from New Jersey who had allegedly dropped "stench bombs" (made of acid-soaked tissues) on carpets and furniture in several hotels. Vials of the acid were found in the women's purses, police said, and a gallon jug of the acid was found in a locker of a Loop bus station. One of the women had a key to the locker. The three were charged with criminal damage to property.

At the McCarthy headquarters on the 15th floor, young campaign workers were administering first aid treatment to persons who had been gassed. Another first aid station was set up in the Pick-Congress Hotel further north on Michigan.

"In Grant Park, the gassed crowd was angered . . . more aggressive," says [a college] history professor. Shortly after the gassing, says the Guard medic quoted earlier, "two forces of police arrived, one from the Michigan Avenue side of the bridge and one from the south on the east side of the bridge. They immediately waded into the crowd with clubs swinging indiscriminately, driving them off the bridge and away from the area." Once more, the Guardsman said, he was assaulted by demonstrators—this time when he tried "to treat an individual who received a severe head injury from the police."

One of the demonstration marshals says that the "primary motivation" of the crowd was to "get out of the park before dark because there was fear of being beaten out of view of the cameras if it got dark before we reached Michigan Avenue."

Surging north from Congress Plaza to a footbridge leading from the park, the crowd encountered more Guardsmen. More tear gas was dispensed. Surging north from the site of the gassings, the crowd found the Jackson Boulevard bridge unguarded. Word was quickly passed back by loud-speaker "Two blocks north, there's an open bridge; no gas." As dusk was settling, hundreds poured from the park into Michigan Avenue.

THE CROWD ON MICHIGAN AVENUE

At 7:14 P.M., as the first groups of demonstrators crossed the bridge toward Michigan Avenue, they noticed that the mule train of the Poor People's Campaign was just entering the intersection of Michigan and Jackson, headed south. The train consisted of three wagons, each drawn by two mules, and was accompanied by a number of SCLC blacks in fieldwork attire. The wagons were painted, "Jobs & Food for All." The train had a permit to parade within the Loop and south on Michigan Avenue.

The train was accompanied by 24 policemen on foot, five on three-wheelers, and four in two squadrols. A police official was in front with the caravan's leaders. The sight of the train seemed to galvanize the disorganized Grant Park crowd and those streaming over the bridge broke into cheers and shouts. "Peace now!" bellowed the demonstrators. "Dump the Hump!" This unexpected enthusiastic horde in turn stimulated the mule train marchers. Drivers of the wagons stood and waved to the crowd, shouting: "Join us! Join us!" To a young man watching from the 23rd floor of the Hilton Hotel, "the caravan seemed like a magnet to demonstrators leaving the park."

A medic accompanying the march reports that "at this time it appeared that the marshals had lost control and the group was moving more or less under mob psychology."

At this the exodus from Grant Park swelled to a torrent and Michigan rapidly filled out with now revitalized, shouting demonstrators. The two squadrols, driving at the rear of the train, were unable to move to the front because of the crush of the crowd.

Led by Viet Cong red and black flags, and the loud-speaker, and constantly joined by more people escaping from Grant Park, all came slowly south on Michigan with the mule train in the middle of this sea of people. The crowd, estimated at "several thousand" by a police official, filled out an entire city block and chanted "We want peace." As the demonstrators marched, says an Assistant U.S. Attorney, "four or five policemen ran into the crowd swinging nightsticks. I saw a couple of policemen strike some of the individuals." Few policemen were, however, present on the street.

THE BALBO-MICHIGAN CROWD BUILDS UP

When the crowd's first rank reached the intersection of Balbo and Michigan, the northeast corner of the Hilton, it was close to the approximately 2,000 to 3,000 demonstrators and spectators massed east of a police line along the two blocks of Grant Park opposite the Hilton and 500 others contained between another police line and the hotel's east face.

An additional single line of police was formed diagonally across Michigan at the south line of Balbo to divert the new oncoming crowd off the street and into Grant Park. A portion of the crowd had spilled west on Balbo toward Wabash, a block west of Michigan, where there was another police line across Balbo.

The police were armed with riot helmets, batons, mace, an aerosol tear gas can and their service revolvers (which they always carry).

Behind the police lines, parked in front of the Hilton, was a fire department high pressure pumper truck hooked up to a hydrant. Pairs of uniformed firemen were also in the vicinity.

The growing crowds, according to the U.S. Attorney's report, were a blend of "young and old, hippies, Yippies, straights, newsmen and cameramen," even two mobile TV units. TV cameras also were situated on an entrance canopy jutting out from the north side of the Hilton. The smell of tear gas from the Congress bridge encounter still hung heavy in the air.

When the line of march reached the police line across Michigan, it stopped and the crowd began to bunch up in the intersection. It quickly overflowed into all available adjacent areas. All traffic was immobilized, both on Michigan and the cross streets. The forces that would clash at 7:57 P.M. in the unreal glow of TV lights were in final deployment.

Some in the crowd were equipped with helmets and gas masks and armed with rocks, sticks, bottles and other weapons. Volunteer "medic" teams were on hand among the demonstrators.

While the crowd was not organized in any traditional sense, it had leaders—some self-appointed, some the marshals. Dellinger and other demonstration leaders had disappeared after the dispersal of the line of march at Balbo and Columbus. Among other things, these "leaders" had exhorted the marchers by loudspeaker, while the crowd was pushing south on Michigan with the mule train, to sit down on the pavement if the police tried to prevent their eventual passage to the Amphitheatre.

Facing this vast, virtually encircling congregation of 4,000 to 4,500 people were 300 police. One demonstrator says that when three policemen on three-wheel motorcycles tried to get through the crowd, the throng surrounded them and covered the cycles with Yippie posters, such as "Vote the Pig Vote." The officers finally were let through when they said they were off duty and on their way home.

A police officer recalls that shortly after 7 P.M. he attempted to clear the intersection by saying, "Get up on the curb, please" and "Clear the streets, please." Initially, he said, "there was compliance with this request" until a tall, slender youth, about 20 years old, "appeared on the scene and told the people to disregard the police request and come back into the street." They obeyed.

The police officer approached the youth and asked him to cooperate with the police. According to the officer, the young man pushed him with both hands. Quickly the two were "surrounded by a large group." Two of them knocked the officer to the ground. In his opinion, he was in danger of being "stomped." Other officers quickly rescued him, but his ankle was badly injured in the scuffle.

From within the crowd were rising the usual shouts from some of the demonstrators: "Hell no, we won't go!" . . . "Fuck these Nazis!" . . . "Fuck you, L.B.J.!" . . . "No more war!" . . . "Pigs, pigs, pigs." . . . "The streets belong to the people!" . . . "Let's go to the Amphitheatre!" . . . "Move on, Move on!" . . . "You can't stop us." . . . "From the hotel," recalls a student, "people who sympathized were throwing confetti and pieces of paper out of the windows and they were blinking their room lights."

The history professor quoted earlier, standing on the northwest corner of the Balbo-Michigan intersection, said: "The police would move periodically north on Michigan, forcing the crowd back, or move east on Balbo, or would split the group north and south." But then they would return to their positions and "the crowd would flow back." . . .

BACK AT THE CONRAD HILTON

Vice President Humphrey was now inside the Conrad Hilton Hotel and the police commanders were afraid that the crowd might either attempt to storm the hotel or march south on Michigan Avenue, ultimately to the Amphitheatre. The Secret Service had received an anonymous phone call that the Amphitheatre was to be blown up. A line of police was established at 8th and Michigan at the south end of the

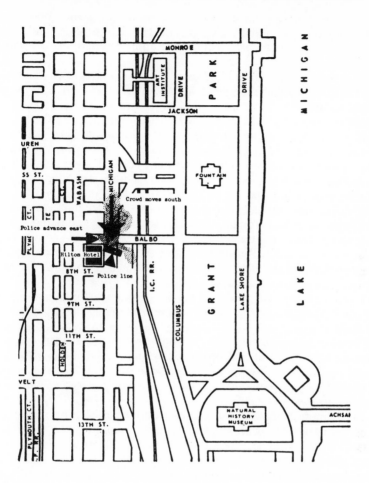

hotel and the squads of police stationed at the hotel doors began restricting access to those who could display room keys. Some hotel guests, including delegates and Senator McCarthy's wife, were turned away.

By 7:30 P.M., the SCLC people, too, were growing apprehensive. They were becoming concerned for the mule train because of the press of demonstrators and the crowd's escalating emotionalism. Also a rumor was passing around that the Blackstone Rangers and the East Side Disciples, two of Chicago's most troublesome street gangs, were on their way to the scene. (This was later proven to be untrue; neither of these South Side gangs was present in any numbers in either Lincoln Park or Grant Park.)

At this point, a Negro male was led through the police line by a police officer. He spoke to the police officer, a city official and a deputy superintendent of police. He told them that he was in charge of the mule train and that his people wanted no part of this mob. He said he had 80 people with him, that they included old people and children, and he wanted to get them out of the mob. The police officer later stated the group wanted to go past the Hilton, circle it, and return to the front of the hoel where Reverend Ralph Abernathy could address the crowd.

At this time, says the police sergeant who had thrown the smoke bomb into the bandshell crowd, and who now was on duty at the Hilton, people were screaming foul language of every type at the police and shouting, "Who's your wife with now?" . . . "Where's your wife tonight?" Some were spitting on the officers and daring them to come and hit them. "The obscenities," says an attorney who was present, "were frequently returned in kind by the police."

In response to the mule train leader's plea, the deputy superintendent of police ordered a police escort to lead the wagons through the crowd. Flying wedges of officers pushed back the resisting crowd and the train was let through the police skirmish line at Balbo. It then moved up in front of the hotel.

In a few minutes, Reverend Ralph Abernathy appeared and, according to the police officer's statement, "said he wanted to be taken out of the area as he feared for the safety of his group." The police officer directed that the train be moved south on Michigan to 11th Street and then, through a series of turns through the Loop, to the West Side.

Before the train moved out, a leader of the mule train addressed the crowd with a bullhorn provided by police. He said: "We have nothing against you joining our demonstration, and we have nothing against joining your demonstration . . . I think it was very violent for the police to tear gas you."

The demonstrators did not pay much attention to him but, instead, seemed bent on making their march to the Amphitheatre. Obscenities and vulgar epithets were shouted at the police. There were also chants of "One, two, three, four; stop this damn war"; "Dump the Hump"; "Daley must go"; "Ho, Ho, Ho Chi Minh"; "The streets belong to the people"; and "Prague, Prague, Prague!"

A policeman on Michigan later said that at about this time a "female hippie" came up to him, pulled up her skirt and said, "You haven't had a piece in a long time."

A policeman standing in front of the Hilton remembers seeing a blond female who was dressed in a short red minidress make lewd, sexual motions in front of a police line. Whenever this happened, he says, the policemen moved back to prevent any incident. The crowd, however, egged her on, the patrolman says. He thought that "she and the crowd wanted an arrest to create a riot." Earlier in the same general area a male youth had stripped bare and walked around carrying his clothes on a stick.

An attorney who was present at the intersection, a member of the ACLU, later said that "perhaps ten people were on lampposts and shoulders of other people, waving at the cameras. . . . The noise was very loud. . . . I felt this was a violent crowd that came to fight and was looking for trouble."

The intersection at Balbo and Michigan was in total chaos at this point. The street was filled with people. Darkness had fallen but the scene was lit by both police and television lights. As the mule train left, part of the group tried to follow the wagons through the police line and were stopped. According to the deputy superintendent of police, there was much pushing back and forth between the policemen and the demonstrators. He said that this is where real physical contact began. An old car bearing a sign announcing a draft card burning rally edged up to the police lines.

Continual announcements were made at this time over a police amplifier for the crowd to "clear the street and go up on the sidewalk or into the park area for their demonstrations." The broadcast said "Please gather in the park on the east side of the street. You may have your peaceful demonstration and speechmaking there." The demonstrators were also advised that if they did not heed these orders they would face arrest. The response from many in the crowd, according to a police observer, was to scream and shout obscenities. A Chicago attorney who was watching the scene recalls that when the announcements were broadcast, "No one moved."

"There was roughly a ten-yard distance between the police line and the demonstrators," recalls an Assistant U.S. Attorney. "Two policemen periodically walked across the gap, took hold of a demonstrator and walked him to a paddy wagon behind the police line. They arrested approximately ten protesters this way. We saw them hit a few with their nightsticks as they were pushing them into the paddy wagon but it appeared that none of the protesters was injured."

A police observer recalls that the deputy superintendent then made another announcement: "Will any nondemonstrators, anyone who is not a part of this group, any newsmen, please leave the group." Despite the crowd noise, the loud-speaker announcements were "loud and plainly heard," according to this officer. Police state that the messages to clear the street were repeated—officers "walked to the front of the crowd and repeated these messages to individuals all along the line, all the while pointing over to the east side of the street where we wanted them to go."

Presently, a police officer states, he glanced back and noticed that part of the crowd had moved forward and had "completely surrounded" the police car from which the announcements were being broadcast. Police rushed to the car and helped clear a path so that it could be driven slowly north through the crowd. Before it reached the north side of Balbo, according to the officer, its windshield, side windows and headlights had been pasted with McCarthy stickers. "When we finally got into the car and it began to move," said the officer, "it became apparent that the right rear tire was almost flat." The valve had been loosened. The car limped away in search of a filling station.

The deputy superintendent of police states that at this point demonstrators staged "massive sit-downs" in Michigan Avenue. While some sit-downs occurred, the films and still photographs do not show any that were "massive." But this was a tactic that had been discussed

earlier among the crowd, should the march to the Amphitheatre ultimately be thwarted. The sitters, according to the deputy, were hamper-
ing the orderly movements of his police. "People in the streets were
having face-to-face confrontations with the police officers, telling them
that they did not have to move and that they were not going to move,"
he says. As police announcements were made to leave the street, demonstrators with loud-speakers of their own shouted to the crowd, "You
don't have to go. Hell no, don't go!"

The crowd was becoming increasingly ugly. The deputy superintendent states that demonstrators were pushing police lines back,
spitting in officers' faces and pelting them with rocks, bottles, shoes,
glass and other objects.

While this was happening on Michigan Avenue, a separate police
line had begun to move east toward the crowd from the block of Balbo
that lies between Michigan and Wabash along the north side of the
Hilton.

About 7:45 P.M., the police radio had crackled with "10-1," the
emergency code for "police officer needs help." A police captain was
reporting imminent danger in front of the Hilton and, in response to
his call, a reserve platoon had been ordered to the northwest corner
of the hotel on Balbo. Shortly after that, all available vans in the
vicinity were ordered to converge on the Hilton.

The reserve platoon, numbering some 40 policemen, had arrived
by special CTA bus at Wabash and Balbo, one block west of Michigan,
at 7:55 P.M., under the command of a deputy chief of police. The men
came from a skirmish with demonstrators at 14th and Wabash, several
blocks southwest of the Hilton, where they had arrived after another
unit had broken up an attempted march on the Amphitheatre and had
rounded up a group of demonstrators. Some had also been on duty at
Columbus and Balbo in Grant Park that afternoon.

As the bus unloaded, the unit formed up building-to-building across
Balbo in four ranks of ten led by a deputy chief and a lieutenant.

At the same time, Sidney Peck with his bullhorn was urging people
to follow him west on Balbo in an effort to flee the Michigan intersection. "We saw the police approaching," Peck states. He says he called
people back and urged the police "not to move against them." Over
the loud-speaking equipment, Peck shouted, "Sit down and no violence
will happen. Don't use any violence."

The deputy chief states, on the other hand, that he saw marchers
coming toward his men. He felt that "a disorderly mob surging west
on Balbo from Michigan, taking up the whole street and sidewalks,
shouting and screaming slogans and insults [was] taking over the
Blackstone and Hilton Hotel entrances with the intention of taking
over these hotels."

The police unit moved east on Balbo toward Michigan Avenue at
a fast walk. As they did so, the throng on Balbo backed east toward the
intersection or crowded onto the sidewalk. By the time the officers
reached the west edge of Michigan, they slowed to a determined walk.

A 19-year-old boy, working as a chauffeur for Senator McGovern's staff, relates: "An officer was counting off 'Hut, two, three, four,' and several of the men were chanting along with him. . . . The policemen were walking slowly with their nightsticks extended, held in both hands. I did not see anything thrown from the demonstrators at the police at this time or any charge by the demonstrators at the police."

As a response to seeing the police phalanx, however, says a law student who was standing near the front of the mob, the chant, "Pigs . . . pigs . . . pigs" went up.

Policemen in the line of march claim that they suffered more than verbal abuse. One officer states that in the vicinity of the Haymarket, a cocktail lounge in the Hilton's northeast corner with an entrance on Balbo, a bottle shattered about 18 inches behind him. He thought it was dropped from a hotel window. When the line reached Michigan, he said, he heard someone say, "Mother fucker, I'm going to kill you." He saw a man, about 33 years old, bearded and wearing a helmet, standing with a wine bottle in his hand, . . . "ready to swing at me. I knocked the bottle out of his hand at that point, someone behind me hit me with some heavy object in the back, and I fell to one knee." While he was down, he said, the crowd surrounded him, cutting him off from other police. "People were pushing and shoving as well as throwing bottles, shoes and eggs," he said. "I was hit with an egg." He used his baton, he said, "in order to shove the crowd aside."

Another officer states that "many rocks and bottles were being thrown at [us]. . . . A house brick struck me on the side of my head after glancing off my helmet." He lost his balance and fell to the pavement. The films fail to show any barrage of missiles at this time, although some may have been thrown.

Just as the police in front of the Hilton were confronted with some sit-downs on the south side of the intersection of Balbo and Michigan, the police unit coming into the intersection on Balbo met the sitting demonstrators. What happened then is subject to dispute between the police and some other witnesses.

The Balbo police unit commander asserts that he informed the sit-downs and surrounding demonstrators that if they did not leave, they would be arrested. He repeated the order and was met with a chant of "Hell no, we won't go." Quickly a police van swung into the intersection immediately behind the police line, the officers opened the door at the rear of the wagon. The deputy chief "ordered the arrest process to start."

"Immediately upon giving this order," the deputy chief later informed his superiors, "we were pelted with rocks, bottles, cans filled with unknown liquids and other debris, which forced the officers to defend themselves from injury. . . . My communications officer was slugged from behind by one of these persons, receiving injuries to his right eye and cheekbone." That officer states: "All this debris came instantaneously, as if it was waiting for the signal of the first arrest."

A sergeant who was on the scene later said that "the hippies behind those sitting down appeared to be the ones doing most of the throwing.

. . . Police officers were constantly being hit . . . and were obviously becoming anxious to do something."

A patrolman who was in the skirmish line states that "the order was given to remain in position." But then, he says, one of his fellow officers "ran into the crowd, he was surrounded and I lost sight of him." At this point, the patrolman and other officers in the line "broke into the crowd," using their batons to "push away people who had gathered around" their fellow officer.

He claims they then returned to the line. But another patrolman states that "several police officers were being knocked down by the crowd and several policemen broke formation" to help them "because groups of rioters were attempting to kick and pummel them." At this point, he said, "everything went up for grabs."

The many films and video tapes of this time period present a picture which does not correspond completely with the police view described above. First, the films do not show a mob moving west on Balbo; they show the street as rather clean of the demonstrators and bystanders, although the sidewalks themselves on both sides of the street are crowded. Second, they show the police walking east on Balbo, stopping in formation, awaiting the arrival of the van and starting to make arrests on order. A total of 25 seconds elapses between their coming to a halt and the first arrests.

Also, a St. Louis reporter who was watching from inside the Haymarket lounge agrees that the police began making arrests "in formation," apparently as "the result of an order to clear the intersection." Then, the reporter adds, "from this apparently controlled beginning the police began beating people indiscriminately. They grabbed and beat anyone they could get hold of."

To many other witnesses, it seemed that the police swept down Balbo and charged, with clubs swinging, into the crowd without the slightest pause. What these witnesses may, in fact, have seen was a second sweep of the officers, moving east on Balbo after the first arrest. Once this second action started, the officers did run across the intersection.

"There was just enough time for a few people to sit down before the cops charged," says the law student, quoted earlier. "The guys who sat down got grabbed, and the cops really hit hard. I saw a pair of glasses busted by a billy club go flying through the air."

"The crowd tried to reverse gears," a reporter for a St. Louis paper says. "People began falling over each other. I was in the first rank between police and the crowd and was caught in the first surge. I went down as I tried to retreat. I covered my head, tried to protect my glasses which had fallen partially off, and hoped that I would not be clubbed. I tried to dig into the humanity that had fallen with me. You could hear shouting and screaming. As soon as I could, I scrambled to my feet and tried to move away from the police. I saw a youth running by me also trying to flee. A policeman clubbed him as he passed, but he kept running.

"The cops were saying, 'Move! I said, move, god dammit! Move, you bastards!'" A representative of the ACLU who was positioned among the demonstrators says the police "were cussing a lot" and were shouting, "Kill, kill, kill, kill, kill!" A reporter for the *Chicago Daily News* said after the melee that he, too, heard this cry. A demonstrator remembers the police swinging their clubs and screaming, "Get the hell out of here." . . . "Get the fuck out of here." . . . "Move your fucking ass!"

"People were trying to move but were clubbed as they did" the reporter for the St. Louis paper continued. "I fell to my knees, stumbling over somebody. . . ."

Adds the ACLU representative: "The police kept coming in. . . . The crowd kept trying to get away, but it was so thick that there were many people who seemed . . . to be stuck in the middle and unable to do anything about it. There was a great deal of screaming and yelling. A lot of people were crying and shouting for help. . . ."

The crowd frantically eddied in a halfmoon shape in an effort to escape the officers coming in from the west. A UPI reporter who was on the southern edge of the crowd on Michigan Avenue, said that the advancing police "began pushing the crowd south." A cherry bomb burst overhead. The demonstrators strained against the deputy superintendent of police's line south of the Balbo-Michigan intersection. "When I reached that line," says the UPI reporter, "I heard a voice from behind it say, 'Push them back, move them back!' I was then prodded and shoved with nightsticks back in a northerly direction, toward the still advancing line of police."

"Police were marching this way and that," a correspondent from a St. Louis paper says. "They obviously had instructions to clear the street, but apparently contradicting one another in the directions the crowd was supposed to be sent."

"At first," says the McGovern worker, "the police just pushed the demonstrators with their nightsticks. The demonstrators [nearest the police] tried to move, but couldn't because of the press of the crowd. There was no place for them to go."

The deputy superintendent of police recalls that he ordered his men to "hold your line there" . . . "stand fast" . . . "Lieutenant, hold your men steady there!" These orders, he said, were not obeyed by all.

"Two or three policemen broke formation and began swinging at everyone in sight," the McGovern worker says. The deputy superintendent states that police disregarded his order to return to the police lines—the beginning of what he says was the only instance in which he personally saw police discipline collapse. He estimates that ten to 15 officers moved off on individual forays against demonstrators. But the McGovern worker says "this became sort of spontaneous. Every few seconds more policemen would break formation and began swinging until . . . all the policemen from the original line at Balbo were just swinging through the crowd."

"I turned toward the north and was immediately struck on the back of the head from behind," says the UPI reporter. "I fell to the ground. . . ."

Thus, at 7:57 P.M., with two groups of club-wielding police converging simultaneously and independently, the battle was joined. The portions of the throng out of the immediate area of conflict largely stayed put and took up the chant, "The whole world is watching," but the intersection fragmented into a collage of violence.

Re-creating the precise chronology of the next few moments is impossible. But there is no question that a violent street battle ensued.

People ran for cover and were struck by police as they passed. Clubs were swung indiscriminately.

Two Assistant U.S. Attorneys who were on the scene characterized the police as "hostile and aggressive." Some witnesses cited particularly dramatic personal stories.

I saw squadrols of policemen coming from everywhere [a secretary said]. The crowd around me suddenly began to run. Some of us, including myself, were pushed back onto the sidewalk and then all the way up against . . . the Blackstone Hotel along Michigan Avenue. I thought the crowd had panicked.

Fearing that I would be crushed against the wall of the building . . . I somehow managed to work my way . . . to the edge of the street . . . and saw police everywhere.

As I looked up I was hit for the first time on the head from behind by what must have been a billy club. I was then knocked down and while on my hands and knees, I was hit around the shoulders. I got up again, stumbling and was hit again. As I was falling, I heard words to the effect of "move, move" and the horrible sound of cracking billy clubs.

After my second fall, I remember being kicked in the back, and I looked up and noticed that many policemen around me had no badges on. The police kept hitting me on the head.

Eventually she made her way to an alley behind the Blackstone and finally, "bleeding badly from my head wound," was driven by a friend to a hospital emergency room. Her treatment included the placing of 12 stitches.

Another young woman, who had been among those who sat down in the intersection, ran south on Michigan, a "Yippie flag" in her hand, when she saw the police. "I fell in the center of the intersection," she says. "Two policemen ran up on me, stopped and hit me on the shoulder, arm and leg about five or six times, severely. They were swearing and one of them broke my flag over his knee." By fleeing into Grant Park, she managed eventually to escape.

To my left, the police caught a man, beat him to the ground and smashed their clubs on the back of his unprotected head. I stopped to help him. He was elderly, somewhere in his mid-50's. He was kneeling and holding his bleeding head. As I stopped to help him, the police turned on me. "Get that cock sucker out of here!" This command was accompanied by four blows from clubs—one on the middle of my back, one on the bottom of my back, one on my left buttock, and one on the back of my leg. No attempt was made to

arrest me or anybody else in the vicinity. All the blows that I saw inflicted by
the police were on the backs of heads, arms, legs, etc. It was the most slow and
confused, and the least experienced people who got caught and beaten.

The police were angry. Their anger was neither disinterested nor instrumental. It was deep, expressive and personal. "Get out of here you cock suckers"
seemed to be their most common cry.

To my right, four policemen beat a young man as he lay on the ground.
They beat him and at the same time told him to "get up and get the hell out
of here." Meanwhile, I struggled with the injured man whom I had stopped to
help. . . .

One demonstrator said that several policemen were coming toward
a group in which he was standing when one of the officers yelled, "Hey,
there's a nigger over there we can get." They then are said to have
veered off and grabbed a middle-aged Negro man, whom they beat.

A lawyer says that he was in a group of demonstrators in the park
just south of Balbo when he heard a police officer shout, "Let's get 'em!"
Three policemen ran up, "singled out one girl and as she was running
away from them, beat her on the back of the head. As she fell to the
ground, she was struck by the nightsticks of these officers." A male friend
of hers then came up yelling at the police. The witness said, "He was
arrested. The girl was left in the area lying on the ground."

The beating of two other girls was witnessed from a hotel window.
The witness says, he saw one girl "trying to shield a demonstrator who
had been beaten to the ground," whereupon a policeman came up
"hitting her with a billy club." The officer also kicked the girl in the
shoulder, the witness said.

A *Milwaukee Journal* reporter says in his statement, "when the
police managed to break up groups of protesters they pursued individuals and beat them with clubs. Some police pursued individual
demonstrators as far as a block . . . and beat them. . . . In many cases
it appeared to me that when police had finished beating the protesters
they were pursuing, they then attacked, indiscriminately, any civilian
who happened to be standing nearby. Many of these were not involved
in the demonstrations."

In balance, there is no doubt that police discipline broke during
the melee. The deputy superintendent of police states that—although
this was the only time he saw discipline collapse—when he ordered his
men to stand fast, some did not respond and began to sally through
the crowd, clubbing people they came upon. An inspector-observer from
the Los Angeles Police Department stated that during this week, "The
restraint of the police both as individual members and as an organization, was beyond reason." However, he said that on this occasion:
"There is no question but that many officers acted without restraint
and exerted force beyond that necessary under the circumstances. The
leadership at the point of conflict did little to prevent such conduct and
the direct control of officers by first-line supervisors was virtually non-
existent."

The deputy superintendent of police has been described by several observers as being very upset by individual policemen who beat demonstrators. He pulled his men off the demonstrators, shouting "Stop, damn it, stop. For Christ's sake, stop it."

"It seemed to me," an observer says, "that only a saint could have swallowed the vile remarks to the officers. However, they went to extremes in clubbing the Yippies. I saw them move into the park, swatting away with clubs at girls and boys lying in the grass. More than once I witnessed two officers pulling at the arms of a Yippie until the arms almost left their sockets, then, as the officers put the Yippie in a police van, a third jabbed a riot stick into the groin of the youth being arrested. It was evident that the Yippie was not resisting arrest."

A witness adds: "I witnessed four or five instances of several officers beating demonstrators when it appeared the demonstrators could have been easily transported and confined to police vans waiting nearby."

Anyone who was in the way of some of the policemen was struck (a UPI correspondent concludes in his statement). Police continued to hit people in the back who were running away as fast as possible. I saw one man knocked to the street. . . . A policeman continued to poke his stick at the man's groin and kidney area. Several newsmen were struck. Individual incidents of violence were going on over the entire area at once, in any direction you might look.

In one incident, a young man, who apparently had been maced, staggered across Michigan . . . helped by a companion. The man collapsed. . . . Medical people from the volunteer medical organization rushed out to help him. A police officer (a sergeant, I think) came rushing forward, followed by the two other nightstick-brandishing policemen and yelled, "Get him out of here; this ain't a hospital." The medical people fled, half dragging and half carrying the young man with them. . . .

Another incident I vividly recall is two policemen dragging one protester by one leg, with his shoulders and possibly his head dragging on the pavement as they ran toward a paddy wagon. So much violence was going on at one time. . . .

A university student who was watching the melee from a hotel window says she saw one young man attempting to flee the police. "Two or three grabbed him and beat him until he fell to the ground." Then, she says, "two or three more policemen were attracted to him and continued to beat him until he was dragged into a paddy wagon."

At another moment, the girl says, she saw another youth "felled by two or three policemen." A medic "dressed all in white and wearing a white helmet" came to aid him. When police saw him giving aid to the downed boy, "they came upon the medic and began to beat him."

"I saw a well-dressed man carrying a well-dressed woman screaming in his arms," said a *Chicago Daily News* reporter. "He tried to carry her to the Hilton Hotel front door and get in. It was secured, so it certainly would have been safe to permit them in. But the police stopped him, and he then carried her back into the crowd. She was hysterical, and I can see no reason for the police treatment of this injured woman." Also during the melee, the reporter says, he saw policemen using sawhorses as "battering rams" against the crowd.

The history professor quoted earlier says, "A number of motorcycle police drove up over the curb on the east side of Michigan and into the crowd." Police also charged demonstrators and onlookers gathered around the old car with the antidraft rally sign which earlier had been taken up to the police line in front of the Hilton.

A series of arrests were made around the antidraft car, some peaceful and some with considerable force. During the course of these arrests, one girl in this group lost her skirt. Although there have been unverified reports of police ripping the clothes from female demonstrators, this is the only incident on news film of any woman being disrobed in the course of arrest.

While violence was exploding in the street, the crowd wedged, behind the police sawhorses along the northeast edge of the Hilton, was experiencing a terror all its own. Early in the evening, this group had consisted in large part of curious bystanders. But following the police surges into the demonstrators clogging the intersection, protesters had crowded the ranks behind the horses in their flight from the police.

From force of numbers, this sidewalk crowd of 150 to 200 persons was pushing down toward the Hilton's front entrance. Policemen whose orders were to keep the entrance clear were pushing with sawhorses. Other police and fleeing demonstrators were pushing from the north in the effort to clear the intersection. Thus, the crowd was wedged against the hotel, with the hotel itself on the west, sawhorses on the southeast and police on the northeast.

Films show that one policeman elbowed his way to where he could rescue a girl of about ten years of age from the viselike press of the crowd. He cradled her in his arms and carried her to a point of relative safety 20 feet away. The crowd itself "passed up" an elderly woman to a low ledge. But many who remained were subjected to what they and witnesses considered deliberate brutality by the police.

"I was crowded in with the group of screaming, frightened people," an onlooker states, "We jammed against each other, trying to press into the brick wall of the hotel. As we stood there breathing hard . . . a policeman calmly walked the length of the barricade with a can of chemical spray [evidently mace] in his hand. Unbelievably, he was spraying at us." Photos reveal several policemen using mace against the crowd.

Another witness, a graduate student, said she was on the periphery of the crowd and could see that "police sprayed mace randomly along the first line of people along the curb." A reporter who was present said a woman cried, "Oh no, not mace!" He said a youth moaned, "Stop it! We're not doing anything!" "Others," recalls another witness, "pleaded with the police to tell them where they should move and allow them to move there."

"Some of the police then turned and attacked the crowd," a Chicago reporter says. The student says she could see police clubbing persons pinned at the edge of the crowd and that there was "a great deal of screaming and pushing within the group." A reporter for a Cleveland paper said, "The police indiscriminately beat those on the periphery of the crowd." An Assistant U.S. Attorney put it, "The group on the sidewalk was charged by police using nightsticks." A young cook caught in the crowd relates that "The police began picking people off. They would pull individuals to the ground and begin beating them. A medic wearing a white coat and an armband with a red cross was grabbed, beaten and knocked to the ground. His whole face was covered with blood."

"The cops just waded into the crowd," says a law student. "There was a great deal of clubbing. People were screaming, 'Help.' "

As a result, a part of the crowd was trapped in front of the Conrad Hilton and pressed hard against a big plate glass window of the Haymarket Lounge. A reporter who was sitting inside said, "Frightened men and women banged . . . against the window. A captain of the fire department inside told us to get back from the window, that it might get knocked in. As I backed away a few feet I could see a smudge of blood on the glass outside."

With a sickening crack, the window shattered, and screaming men and women tumbled through, some cut badly by jagged glass. The police came after them.

I was pushed through by the force of large numbers of people (one victim said). I got a deep cut on my right leg, diagnosed later by Eugene McCarthy's doctor as a severed artery. . . . I fell to the floor of the bar. There were ten to 20 people who had come through . . . I could not stand on the leg. It was bleeding profusely.

A squad of policemen burst into the bar, clubbing all those who looked to them like demonstrators, at the same time screaming over and over, "We've got to clear this area." The police acted literally like mad dogs looking for objects to attack.

A patrolman ran up to where I was sitting. I protested that I was injured and could not walk, attempting to show him my leg. He screamed that he would show me I could walk. He grabbed me by the shoulder and literally hurled me through the door of the bar into the lobby. . . .

I stumbled out into what seemed to be a main lobby. The young lady I was with and I were both immediately set upon by what I can only presume were plainclothes police. . . . We were cursed by these individuals and thrown through another door into an outer lobby. (Eventually a McCarthy aide took him to the 15th floor.)

In the heat of all this, probably few were aware of the Haymarket's advertising slogan: "A place where good guys take good girls to dine in the lusty, rollicking atmosphere of fabulous Old Chicago. . . ."

During the evening, at least one other window of the Hilton was also broken by crushing crowds.

There is little doubt that during this whole period, beginning at 7:57 P.M. and lasting for nearly 20 minutes, the preponderance of violence came from the police. It was not entirely a one-way battle, however.

Firecrackers were thrown at police. Trash baskets were set on fire and rolled and thrown at them. In one case, a gun was taken from a policeman by a demonstrator.

"Some hippies," said a patrolman in his statement, "were hit by other hippies who were throwing rocks at the police." Films reveal that when police were chasing demonstrators into Grant Park, one young man upended a sawhorse and heaved it at advancing officers. At one point the deputy superintendent of police was knocked down by a thrown sawhorse. At least one police three-wheeler was tipped over. One of the demonstrators says that "people in the park were prying up cobblestones and breaking them. One person piled up cobblestones in his arms and headed toward the police." Witnesses reported that people were throwing "anything they could lay their hands on. From the windows of the Hilton and Blackstone hotels, toilet paper, wet towels, even ash trays came raining down." A police lieutenant stated that he saw policemen bombarded with "rocks, cherry bombs, jars of vaseline, jars of mayonnaise and pieces of wood torn from the yellow barricades falling in the street." He, too, noticed debris falling from the hotel windows.

A patrolman on duty during the melee states that among the objects he saw thrown at police officers were "rocks, bottles, shoes, a telephone and a garbage can cover. Rolls of toilet paper were thrown from hotel windows. I saw a number of plastic practice golf balls, studded with nails, on the street as well as plastic bags filled with what appeared to be human excrement." He said he saw two policemen, one of them wearing a soft hat, get hit with bricks.

A sergeant states that during the fracas, two men under his command had their plastic faceguards (which they pay for themselves) shattered by bricks or rocks.

A number of police officers were injured, either by flying missiles or in personal attacks. One, for example, was helping a fellow officer "pick up a hippie when another hippie gave [me] a heavy kick, aiming for my groin." The blow struck the officer partly on the leg and partly in the testicles. He went down, and the "hippie" who kicked him escaped.

An attorney who was present also told of seeing demonstrators kick policemen in the groin.

In another instance, a Chicago police reporter said in his statement, "a police officer reached down and grabbed a person who dove forward and bit the officer on the leg. . . . Three or four fellow policemen came to his aid. They had to club the demonstrator to make him break his clamp on the officer's leg." In another case, the witness saw a demonstrator "with a big mop of hair hit a police officer with an old British Army type metal helmet." The reporter said he also heard "hissing sounds from the demonstrators as if they were spraying the police." Later he found empty lacquer spray and hair spray cans on the street. Also he heard policemen cry out, "They're kicking us with knives in their shoes." Later, he said, he found that demonstrators "had actually inserted razor blades in their shoes."

Another type of police difficulty was described by a police captain and mentioned by several other officers in their statements. The captain said that when news cameramen equipped with portable flood lights turned them toward the police, this "caused temporary blindness" and reduced the police effectiveness. . . .

Youth as a Stage of Life

KENNETH KENISTON

By 1970 opinion polls showed that Americans considered the youthful counter-culture the number one public problem. A rising tide of student rebellion, beginning with civil rights and peace-movement activities in the early sixties and turning inward against the universities at Berkeley in 1964, crested in the period from 1968 to 1970 as campus after campus— San Francisco State, Harvard, Columbia, and finally Kent State—erupted in disorder, violence and, at last, fatalities. Millions of uncomprehending citizens saw before them a nation haunted by strange new breeds— "hippies," "freaks," "heads," "crazies," "flower children"—living in a strange new world of drugs, festivals, bombs, bad trips, long hair, dirty clothes, and loud incomprehensible music. Some adults were puzzled, some enraged, some even dangerously violent about the strangers in their midst. "Don't shoot," one writer quipped, "we are your children."

Kenneth Keniston, a social psychiatrist at Yale University, has been studying and writing about college youth since the 1950's—long before they became a major public concern. He has watched the dominant mood of college students change from passivity in the fifties to enthusiastic idealism in the early-to-mid sixties to desperation and nihilism by the end of the decade. His books and articles over these years come as close as anything could to being the report card on a generation. Keniston's view of an emerging new stage in life presents the youth culture as both more and less alarming than its critics' lurid portrayals suggest. It is not marked by a taste for disorder, yet it profoundly questions the current ordering of society. If Keniston's picture proves to be correct, we must perhaps reenvision the entire social contract, constructing a society in which each individual must agree with his fellow man on the terms of existence. Keniston points out that no past society has ever operated this way. The question he poses is whether our complex and rapidly changing world can survive in any other fashion.

Before the twentieth century adolescence was rarely included as a stage in the life cycle. Early life began with infancy and was followed by a period of childhood that lasted until around puberty, which occurred several years later than it does today. After puberty, most young men and women simply entered some form of apprenticeship for the adult world. Not until 1904, when G. Stanley Hall published his monumental work *Adolescence: Its Psychology and Its Relations to Physiology, Anthropology, Sociology, Sex, Crime, Religion, and Education,* was this further pre-adult stage widely recognized. Hall's work went through many editions and was much popularized; "adolescence" became a household word. Hall's classic description of the *Sturm und Drang,* turbulence, ambivalence, dangers, and possibilities of adolescence has since been echoed in almost every discussion of this stage of life.

But it would be incorrect to say that Hall "discovered" adolescence. On the contrary, from the start of the nineteenth century, there was increasing discussion of the "problem" of those past puberty but not yet adult. They were the street-gang members and delinquents who made up what one nineteenth-century writer termed the new "dangerous class"; they were also the recruits to the new public secondary schools being opened by the thousands in the late nineteenth century. And once Hall had clearly defined adolescence, it was possible to look back in history to discover men and women who had shown the hallmarks of this stage long before it was identified and named.

Nonetheless, Hall was clearly reflecting a gradual change in the nature of human development, brought about by the massive transformations of American society in the decades after the Civil War. During these decades the "working family," where children labored alongside parents in fields and factories, began to disappear; rising industrial productivity created new economic surpluses that allowed millions of teen-agers to remain outside the labor force. America changed from a rural agrarian society to an urban industrial society, and this new industrial society demanded on a mass scale not only the rudimentry literacy taught in elementary schools, but higher skills that could be guaranteed only through secondary education. What Hall's concept of adolescence reflected, then, was a real change in the human experience, a change intimately tied to the new kind of industrial society that was emerging in America and Europe.

Today, Hall's concept of adolescence is unshakably enshrined in our view of human life. To be sure, the precise nature of adolescence still remains controversial. Some observers believe that Hall, like most psychoanalytic observers, vastly overestimated the inevitability of turbulence, rebellion, and upheaval in this stage of life. But whatever the exact definition of adolescence, no one today doubts its existence. A stage of life that barely existed a century ago is now universally accepted as an inherent part of the human condition.

In the seven decades since Hall made adolescence a household word, American society has once again transformed itself. From the industrial era of the turn of the century, we have moved into a new era without an agreed-upon name—it has been called postindustrial, technological, postmodern, the age of mass consumption, the technetronic age. And a new generation, the first born in this new era of postwar affluence, television, and the bomb, raised in the cities and suburbs of America, socially and economically secure, is now coming to maturity. Since 1900, the average amount of education received by children has increased by more than six years. In 1900, only 6.4 per cent of young Americans completed high school, while today almost 80 per cent do, and more than half of them begin college. In 1900, there were only 238,000 college students; in 1970, there were more than 7 million, with 10 million projected for 1980.

These social transformations are reflected in new public anxieties. The "problem of youth," "the now generation," "troubled youth," "student dissent," and "the youth revolt" are topics of extraordinary concern to most Americans. No longer is our anxiety focused primarily upon the teen-ager, upon the adolescent of Hall's day. Today we are nervous about new "dangerous classes"—those young men and women of college- and graduate-school age who can't seem to "settle down" the way their parents did, who refuse to consider themselves adult, and who often vehemently challenge the existing social order. "Campus unrest," according to a June, 1970, Gallup Poll, was considered the nation's *main* problem.

The factors that have brought this new group into existence parallel in many ways the factors that produced adolescence: rising prosperity, the further prolongation of education, the enormously high educational demands of a postindustrial society. And behind these measurable changes lie other trends less quantitative but even more important: a rate of social change so rapid that it threatens to make obsolete all institutions, values, methodologies, and technologies within the lifetime of each generation; a technology that has created not only prosperity and longevity, but power to destroy the planet, whether through warfare or violation of nature's balance; a world of extraordinary complex social organization, instantaneous communication, and constant revolution. The "new" young men and young women emerging today both reflect and react against these trends.

But if we search among the concepts of psychology for a word to describe these young men and women, we find none that is adequate. Characteristically, they are referred to as "late adolescents and young adults"—a phrase whose very mouth-filling awkwardness attests to its inadequacy. Those who see in youthful behavior the remnants of childhood immaturity naturally incline toward the concept of "adolescence" in describing the unsettled twenty-four-year-old, for this word makes it easier to interpret his objections to war, racism, pollution, or imperialism as "nothing but" delayed adolescent rebellion. To those who are more hopeful about today's youth, "young adulthood" seems a more flattering phrase, for it suggests that maturity, responsibility, and rationality lie behind the unease and unrest of many contemporary youths.

But in the end, neither label seems fully adequate. The twenty-four-year-old seeker, political activist, or graduate student often turns out to have been *through* a period of adolescent rebellion ten years before, to be all too formed in his views, to have a stable sense of himself, and to be much further along in his psychological development than his fourteen-year-old high school brother. Yet he differs just as sharply from "young adults" of age twenty-four whose place in society is settled, who are married and perhaps parents, and who are fully committed to an occupation. What characterizes a growing minority of postadolescents today is that they have not settled the questions whose answers once defined adulthood: questions of relationship to the existing society; questions of vocation; questions of social role and life style.

Faced with this dilemma, some writers have fallen back on the concept of "protracted" or "stretched" adolescence—a concept with psychoanalytic origins that suggests that those who find it hard to "settle down" have "failed" the adolescent developmental task of abandoning narcissistic fantasies and juvenile dreams of glory. Thus, one remedy for "protracted adolescence" might be some form of therapy that would enable the young to reconcile themselves to abilities and a world that are rather less than they had hoped. Another interpretation of youthful unease blames society, not the individual, for the "prolongation of adolescence." It argues that youthful unrest springs from the unwillingness of contemporary society to allow young men and women, especially students, to exercise the adult powers of which they are biologically and intellectually capable. According to this view, the solution would be to allow young people to "enter adulthood" and do "real work in the real world" at an earlier age.

Yet neither of these interpretations seems quite to the point. For, while some young men and women are indeed victims of the psychological malady of "stretched adolescence," many others are less impelled by juvenile grandiosity than by a rather accurate analysis of the perils and injustices of the world in which they live. And plunging youth into the "adult world" at an earlier age would run directly counter to the wishes of most youths, who view adulthood with all of the enthusiasm of a condemned man for the guillotine. Far from seeking the adult prerogatives of their parents, they vehemently demand a virtually indefinite prolongation of their nonadult state.

If neither "adolescence" nor "early adulthood" quite describes the young men and women who so disturb American society today, what can we call them? My answer is to propose that *we are witnessing today the emergence on a mass scale of a previously unrecognized stage of life,* a stage that intervenes between adolescence and adulthood. I propose to call this stage of life the stage of *youth,* assigning to this venerable but vague term a new and specific meaning. Like Hall's "adolescence," "youth" is in no absolute sense new: indeed, once having defined this stage of life, we can study its historical emergence, locating individuals and groups who have had a "youth" in the past. But what is "new" is that this stage of life is today being entered not by tiny minorities of unusually creative or unusually disturbed young men and women, but by millions of young people in the advanced nations of the world.

To explain how it is possible for "new" stages of life to emerge under changed historical conditions would require a lengthy excursion into the theory of psychological development. It should suffice here to emphasize that the direction and extent of human development—indeed the entire nature of the human life cycle—is by no means predetermined by man's biological constitution. Instead, psychological development results from a complex interplay of constitutional givens (including the rates and phases of biological maturation) and the changing familial, social, educational, economic, and political conditions that constitute the matrix in which children develop. Human development can be obstructed by the absence of the necessary matrix, just as it can be stimulated by other kinds of environments. Some social and historical conditions demonstrably slow, retard, or block development, while others stimulate, speed, and encourage it. A prolongation and extension of development, then, including the emergence of "new" stages of life, can result from altered social, economic, and historical conditions.

Like all stages, youth is a stage of transition rather than of completion or accomplishment. To begin to define youth involves three related tasks. First, we need to describe the major *themes* or issues that dominate consciousness, development, and behavior during this stage. But human development rarely if ever proceeds on all fronts simultaneously: instead, we must think of development as consisting of a series of sectors, or "developmental lines," each of which may be in or out of phase with the others. Thus we must also describe the more specific *transformations* or changes in thought and behavior that can be observed in each of several "lines" of development (moral, sexual, intellectual, interpersonal, and so on) during youth. Finally, we can try to make clear what youth is *not*. What follows is a preliminary sketch of some of the themes and transformations that seem crucial to defining youth as a stage of life.

MAJOR THEMES IN YOUTH

Perhaps the central conscious issue during youth is the *tension between self and society*. In adolescence, young men and women tend to accept their society's definitions of them as rebels, truants, conformists, athletes, or achievers. But in youth, the relationship between socially assigned labels and the "real self" becomes more problematic and constitutes a focus of central concern. The awareness of actual or potential conflict, disparity, lack of congruence between what one is (one's identity, values, integrity) and the resources and demands of the existing society increases. The adolescent is struggling to define who he is; the youth begins to sense who he is and thus to recognize the possibility of conflict and disparity between his emerging selfhood and his social order.

In youth, *pervasive ambivalence* toward both self and society is the rule; the question of how the two can be made more congruent is often experienced as a central problem of youth. This ambivalence is not the same as definitive rejection of society, nor does it necessarily lead to political activism. For ambivalence may also entail intense self-rejection, including major efforts at self-transformation employing the methodologies of personal transformation that are culturally available in any historical era: monasticism, meditation, psychoanalysis, prayer, hallucinogenic drugs, hard work, religious conversion, introspection, and so forth. In youth, then, the potential and ambivalent conflicts between autonomous selfhood and social involvement—between the maintenance of personal integrity and the achievement of effectiveness in society—are fully experienced for the first time.

The effort to reconcile and accommodate these two poles involves a characteristic stance vis-à-vis both self and world, perhaps best described by the concept of the *wary probe*. For the youthful relationship to the social order consists not merely in the experimentation more characteristic of adolescence, but with now more serious forays into the adult world, through which its vulnerability, strength, integrity, and possibilities are assayed. Adolescent experimentation is more concerned with self-definition than are the probes of youth, which may lead to more lasting commitments. This testing, exacting, challenging attitude may be applied to all representatives and aspects of the existing social order, sometimes in anger and expectation of disappointment, sometimes in the urgent hope of finding honor, fidelity, and decency in society, and often in both anger and hope. With regard to the self, too, there is constant self-probing in search of strength, weakness, vulnerability, and resiliency, constant self-scrutiny designed to test the individual's capacity to withstand or use what his society would make of him, ask of him, and allow him.

Phenomenologically, youth is a time of alternating *estrangement* and *omnipotentiality*. The estrangement of youth entails feelings of isolation, unreality, absurdity, and disconnectedness from the interpersonal, social, and phenomenological world. Such feelings are probably more intense during youth than in any other period of life. In part they spring from the actual disengagement of youth from society; in part they grow out of the psychological sense of incongruence between self and world. Much of the psychopathology of youth involves such feelings, experienced as the depersonalization of the self or the derealization of the world.

Omnipotentiality is the opposite but secretly related pole of estrangement. It is the feeling of absolute freedom, of living in a world of pure possibilities, of being able to change or achieve anything. There may be times when complete self-transformation seems possible, when the self is experienced as putty in one's own hands. At other times, or for other youths, it is the nonself that becomes totally malleable, then one feels capable of totally transforming another's life; or creating a new society with no roots whatsoever in the mire of the past. Omnipotentiality and estrangement are obviously related: the same sense of freedom and possibility that may come from casting off old inhibitions, values, and constraints may also lead directly to a feeling of absurdity, disconnectedness, and estrangement.

Another characteristic of youth is the *refusal of socialization* and acculturation. In keeping with the intense and wary probing of youth, the individual characteristically begins to become aware of the deep effects upon his personality of his society and his culture. At times he may attempt to break out of his prescribed roles, out of his culture, out of history, and even out of his own skin. Youth is a time, then, when earlier socialization and acculturation is self-critically analyzed, and massive efforts may be made to uproot the now alien traces of historicity, social membership, and culture. Needless to say, these efforts are invariably accomplished within a social, cultural, and historical context, using historically available methods. Youth's relationship to history is therefore paradoxical. Although it may try to reject history altogether, youth does so in a way defined by its historical era, and these rejections may even come to define that era.

In youth we also observe the emergence of *youth-specific identities* and roles. These contrast both with the more ephemeral enthusiasms of the adolescent and with the more established commitments of the adult. They may last for months, years, or a decade, and they inspire deep commitment in those who adopt them. Yet they are inherently temporary and specific to youth: today's youthful hippies, radicals, and seekers recognize full well that, however, reluctantly, they will eventually become older; and that aging itself will change their status. Some such youth-specific identities may provide the foundation for later commitments; but others must be viewed in retrospect as experiments that failed or as probes of the existing society that achieved their purpose, which was to permit the individual to move on in other directions.

Another special issue during youth is the enormous value placed upon change, transformation, and *movement,* and the consequent abhorrence of *stasis.* To change, to stay on the road, to retain a sense of inner development and/or outer momentum is essential to many youths' sense of active vitality. The psychological problems of youth are experienced as most overwhelming when they seem to block change: thus, youth grows panicky when confronted with the feeling of "getting nowhere," of "being stuck in a rut," or of "not moving."

At times the focus of change may be upon the self, and the goal is then to *be moved.* Thus, during youth we see the most strenuous, self-conscious, and even frenzied efforts at self-transformation, using whatever religious, cultural, therapeutic, or chemical means are available. At other times, the goal may be to create movement in the outer world, to *move others:* then we may see efforts at social and political change that in other stages of life rarely possess the same single-minded determination. And on other occasions, the goal is to *move through* the world, and we witness a frantic geographic restlessness, wild swings of upward or downward social mobility, or a compelling psychological need to identify with the highest and the lowest, the most distant and apparently alien.

The need for movement and terror of stasis are often a part of a heightened *valuation of development* itself, however development may be defined by the individual and his culture. In all stages of life, of course, all individuals often wish to change in specific ways: to become more witty, more attractive, more sociable, or more wealthy. But in youth, specific changes are often subsumed in the devotion to change itself—to "keep putting myself through the changes," "not to bail out," "to keep moving." This valuation of change need not be fully conscious. Indeed it often surfaces only in its inverse form, as the panic or depression that accompanies a sense of "being caught in a rut," "getting nowhere," "not being able to change." But for other youths, change becomes a conscious goal in itself, and elaborate ideologies of the techniques of transformation and the *telos* of human life may be developed.

In youth, as in all other stages of life, *the fear of death* takes a special form. For the infant, to be deprived of maternal support, responsiveness, and care is not to exist; for the four-year-old, nonbeing means loss of body intactness (dismemberment, mutilation, castration); for the adolescent, to cease to be is to fall apart, to fragment, splinter, or diffuse into nothingness. For the youth, however, to lose one's essential vitality is merely *to stop.* For some, even self-inflicted death or psychosis may seem preferable to loss of movement; and suicidal attempts in youth often spring from the failure of efforts to change and the resulting sense of being forever trapped in an unmoving present.

The youthful *view of adulthood* is strongly affected by these feelings. Compared to youth, adulthood has traditionally been a stage of slower transformation, when as Erik H. Erikson has noted, the relative developmental stability of parents enables them to nurture the rapid growth of their children. This adult deceleration of personal change is often seen from a youthful vantage point as concretely embodied in apparently unchanging parents. It leads frequently to the conscious identification of adulthood with stasis, and to its unconscious equation with death or nonbeing. Although greatly magnified today by the specific political disillusionments of many youths with the "older generation," the adulthood = stasis (= death) equation is inherent in the youthful situation itself. The desire to prolong youth indefinitely springs not only from an accurate perception of the real disadvantages of adult status in any historical era, but from the less conscious and less accurate assumption that to "grow up" is in some ultimate sense to cease to be really alive.

Finally, youths tend to band together with other youths in *youthful countercultures,* characterized by their deliberate cultural distance from the existing social order, but *not* always by active political or other opposition to it. It is a mistake to identify youth as a developmental stage with any one social group, role, or organization. But youth *is* a time when solidarity with other youths is especially important, whether the solidarity be achieved in pairs, small groups, or formal organizations. And the groups dominated by those in this stage of life reflect not only the special configurations of each historical era, but also the shared developmental positions and problems of youth. Much of what has traditionally been referred to as "youth culture" is, in the terms here used, adolescent culture; but there are also groups, societies, and associations that are truly youthful. In our own time, with the enormous increase in the number of those who are entering youth as a stage of life, the variety and importance of these youthful countercultures is steadily growing.

This compressed summary of themes in youth is schematic and interpretive. It omits many of the qualifications necessary to a fuller discussion, and it neglects the enormous complexity of development in any one person in favor of a highly schematic account. Specifically, for example, I do not discuss the ways the infantile, the childish, the adolescent, and the truly youthful interact in all real lives. And perhaps most important, my account is highly interpretive, in that it points to themes that underlie diverse acts and feelings, to issues and tensions that unite the often scattered experiences of real individuals. The themes, issues, and conflicts here discussed are rarely conscious as such; indeed, if they all were fully conscious, there would probably be something seriously awry. Different youths experience each of the issues here considered with different intensity. What is a central conflict for one may be peripheral or unimportant for another. These remarks, then, should be taken as a first effort to summarize some of the underlying issues that characterize youth as an ideal type.

TRANSFORMATION OF YOUTH

A second way of describing youth is by attempting to trace out the various psychological and interpersonal transformations that may occur during this stage. Once again, only the most preliminary sketch of youthful development can be attempted here. Somewhat arbitrarily, I will distinguish between development in several sectors or areas of life, here noting only that, in fact, changes in one sector invariably interact with those in other sectors.

In pointing to the *self-society relationship* as a central issue in youth, I also mean to suggest its importance as an area of potential change. The late adolescent is only beginning to challenge his society definition of him, only starting to compare his emerging sense of himself with his culture's possibilities and with the temptations and opportunities offered by his environment. Adolescent struggles for emancipation from external familial control and internal dependency on the family take a variety of forms, including displacement of the conflict onto other "authority figures." But in adolescence itself, the "real" focus of conflict is on the family and all of its internal psychic residues. In youth, however, the "real" focus begins to shift: increasingly, the family becomes more paradigmatic of society than vice versa. As relatively greater emancipation from the family is achieved, the tension between self and society, with ambivalent probing of both, comes to constitute a major area of developmental "work" and change. Through this work, young people can sometimes arrive at a synthesis whereby both self and society are affirmed, in the sense that the autonomous reality, relatedness, yet separateness of both is firmly established.

There is no adequate term to describe this "resolution" or the tension between self and society, but C. G. Jung's concept of *"individuation"* comes close. For Jung, the individuated man is a man who acknowledges and can cope with social reality, whether accepting it or opposing it with revolutionary fervor. But he can do this without feeling his central selfhood overwhelmed. Even when most fully engaged in social role and societal action, he can preserve a sense of himself as intact, whole, and distinct from society. Thus the "resolution" of the self-society tension in no way necessarily entails "adjusting" to the society, much less "selling out"—although many youths see it this way. On the contrary, individuation refers partly to a psychological process whereby self and society are differentiated internally. But the actual conflicts between men and women and their societies remain, and indeed may become even more intense.

The meaning of individuation may be clarified by considering the special dangers of youth, which can be defined as extremes of *alienation, whether from self or from society*. At one extreme is that total alienation from self that involves abject submission to society, "joining the rat race," "selling out." Here society is affirmed but selfhood denied.

The other extreme is a total alienation from society that leads not so much to the rejection of society, as to its existence being ignored, denied, and blocked out. The result is a kind of self-absorption, and enforced interiority and subjectivity, in which only the self and its extensions are granted live reality, while all the rest is relegated to a limbo of insignificance. Here the integrity of the self is purchased at the price of a determined denial of social reality and the loss of social effectiveness. In youth both forms of alienation are often assayed, sometimes for lengthy periods. And for some whose further development is blocked, they become the basis for lifelong adaptations—the self-alienation of the marketing personality, the social alienation of the perpetual dropout. In terms of the polarities of Erikson, we can define the central developmental possibilities of youth as individuation vs. alienation.

Sexual development continues in important ways during youth. In modern Western societies, as in many others, the commencement of actual sexual relationships is generally deferred by middle-class adolescents until their late teens or early twenties: the modal age of first intercourse for American college males today is around twenty, for females about twenty-one. Thus, despite the enormous importance of adolescent sexuality and sexual development, actual sexual intercourse often awaits youth. In youth, there may occur a major shift from masturbation and sexual fantasy to interpersonal sexual behavior, including the gradual integration of sexual feelings with intimacy with a real person. And as sexual behavior with real people commences, one sees a further working-through, now in behavior, of vestigial fears and prohibitions whose origin lies in earlier childhood—specifically, of Oedipal feelings of sexual inferiority and of Oedipal prohibitions against sex with one's closest intimates. During youth, when these fears and prohibitions can be gradually worked through, they yield a capacity for genitality, that is, for mutually satisfying sexual relationships with another whom one loves.

The transition to genitality is closely related to a more general pattern of *interpersonal development*. I will term this the shift from *identicality* to mutuality. This development begins with adolescence and continues through youth: it involves a progressive expansion of the early-adolescent assumption that the interpersonal world is divided into only two categories: first, me-and-those-who-are-identical-to-me (potential soulmates, doubles, and hypothetical people who "automatically understand everything"); and second, all others. This conceptualization gradually yields to a capacity for close relationships with those on an approximate level of *parity* or similarity with the individual.

The phase of parity in turn gives way to a phase of *complementarity*, in which the individual can relate warmly to others who are different from him, valuing them for their dissimilarities from himself. Finally, the phase of complementarity may yield in youth to a phase of *mutuality*, in which issues of identicality, parity, and complementarity are subsumed in an overriding concern with the other *as other*. Mutuality entails a simultaneous awareness of the ways in which others are identical to oneself, the ways in which they are similar and dissimilar, and the ways in which they are absolutely unique. Only in the stage of mutuality can the individual begin to conceive of others as separate and unique selves and relate to them as such. And only with this stage can the concept of mankind assume a concrete significance as pointing to a human universe of unique and irreplaceable selves.

Relationships with elders may also undergo characteristic youthful changes. By the end of adolescence, the hero worship or demonology of the middle adolescent has generally given way to an attitude of more selective emulation and rejection of admired or disliked older persons. In youth, new kinds of relationships with elders become possible: psychological apprenticeships, then a more complex relationship of mentorship, then sponsorship, and eventually peership. Without attempting to describe each of these substages in detail, the overall transition can be described as one in which the older person becomes progressively more real and three-dimensional to the younger one, whose individuality is appreciated, validated, and confirmed by the elder. The sponsor, for example, is one who supports and confirms in the youth that which is best in the youth, without exacting an excessive price in terms of submission, imitation, emulation, or even gratitude.

Comparable changes continue to occur during youth with regard to *parents*. Adolescents commonly discover that their parents have feet of clay and recognize their flaws with great acuity. Childish hero worship of parents gives way to a more complex and often negative view of them. But it is generally not until youth that the individual discovers his parents as themselves complex, three-dimensional historical personages whose destinies are partly formed by their own wishes, conscious and unconscious, and by their historical situations. Similarly, it is only during youth that the questions of family tradition, family destiny, family fate, family culture, and family curse arise with full force. In youth, the question of whether to live one's parents' life, or to what extent to do so, becomes a real and active question. In youth, one often sees what Ernst Prelinger has called a "telescoped re-enactment" of the life of a parent—a compulsive need to live out for oneself the destiny of a parent, as if to test its possibilities and limits, experience it from the inside, and (perhaps) free oneself of it. In the end, the youth may learn to see himself and his parents as multidimensional persons, to view them with compassion and understanding, to feel less threatened by their fate and failings, and to be able, if he chooses, to move beyond them.

In beginning by discussing affective and interpersonal changes in youth, I begin where our accounts of development are least precise and most tentative. Turning to more cognitive matters, we stand on somewhat firmer ground. Lawrence Kohlberg's work on *moral development*, especially on the attainment of the highest levels of moral reasoning, provides a paradigmatic description of developments that occur only in youth, if they occur at all. . . .

Kohlberg's research suggests that most contemporary Americans, young or old, do not pass beyond the conventional stage of moral reasoning. But some do, and they are most likely to be found today among those who are young and educated. Such young men and women may develop moral principles that can lead them to challenge the existing moral order and the existing society. And Kohlberg finds that the achievement of his highest level, the stage of personal principles, occurs in the twenties, if it occurs at all. Moral development of this type can thus be identified with youth, as can the special moral "regressions" that Kohlberg finds a frequent concomitant of moral development. Here the arbitrariness of distinguishing between sectors of development becomes clear, for the individual can begin to experience the tension between self and society only as he begins to question the absolutism of conventional moral judgments. Unless he has begun such questioning, it is doubtful whether we can correctly term him "a youth."

In no other sector of development do we have so complete, accurate, and convincing a description of a "development line" that demonstrably characterizes youth. But in the area of *intellectual development,* William Perry has provided an invaluable description of the stages through which college students may pass. Perry's work emphasizes the complex transition from epistemological dualism to an awareness of multiplicity and to the realization of relativism. Relativism in turn gives way to a more "existential" sense of truth, culminating in what Perry terms "commitment within relativism." Thus, in youth we expect to see a passage beyond simple views of right and wrong, truth and falsehood, good and evil, to a more complex and relativistic view; and as youth proceeds, we look for the development of commitments within a universe that remains epistemologically relativistic. Once again, intellectual development is only analytically separable from a variety of other sectors—moral, self-society, and interpersonal, to mention only three.

In his work on *cognitive development,* Jean Piaget has emphasized the importance of the transition from concrete to formal operations, which in middle-class Western children usually occurs at about the age of puberty. For Piaget the attainment of formal operations (whereby the concrete world of the real becomes a subset of the hypothetical world of the possible) is the highest cognitive stage possible. But in some youths, there seems to occur further stages of cognitive development that are not understandable with the concept of formal operations. Jerome Bruner has suggested that beyond the formal stage of thought there lies a further stage of "thinking about thinking." This ability to think about thinking involves a new level of consciousness—consciousness of consciousness, awareness of awareness, and a breaking-away of the phenomenological "I" from the contents of consciousness. This breaking-away of the phenomenological ego during youth permits phenomenological games, intellectual tricks, and kinds of creativity that are rarely possible in adolescence itself. It provides the cognitive underpinning for many of the characteristics and special disturbances of youth, for example, youth's hyperawareness of inner processes, the focus upon states of consciousness as objects to be controlled and altered, and the frightening disappearance of the phenomenological ego in an endless regress of awarenesses of awarenesses.

Having emphasized that these analytically separated "lines" of development are in fact linked in the individual's experience, it is equally important to add that they are never linked in perfect synchronicity. If we could precisely label one specific level within each developmental line as distinctively youthful, we would find that few people were "youthful" in all lines at the same time. In general, human development proceeds unevenly, with lags in some areas and precocities in others. One young woman may be at a truly adolescent level in her relationship with her parents, but at a much later level in moral development; a young man may be capable of extraordinary mutuality with his peers, but still be struggling intellectually with the dim awareness of relativism. Analysis of any one person in terms of specific sectors of development will generally show a simultaneous mixture of adolescent, youthful, and adult features. The point, once again, is that the concept of youth here proposed is an ideal type, a model that may help understand real experience but can never fully describe or capture it.

WHAT YOUTH IS NOT

A final way to clarify the meaning of youth as a stage of life is to make clear what it is not. For one thing, youth is not the end of development. I have described the belief that it is—the conviction that beyond youth lie only stasis, decline, foreclosure, and death—as a characteristically youthful way of viewing development, consistent with the observation that it is impossible truly to understand stages of development beyond one's own. On the contrary, youth is but a preface for further transformations that may (or may not) occur in later life. Many of these center around such issues as the relationship to work and to the next generation. In youth, the question of vocation is crucial, but the issue of work—of productivity, creativity, and the more general sense of fruitfulness that Erikson calls generativity—awaits adulthood. The youthful attainment of mutuality with peers and of peerhood with elders can lead on to further adult interpersonal developments by which one comes to be able to accept the dependency of others, as in parenthood. In later life, too, the relations between the generations are reversed, with the younger now assuming responsibility for the elder. Like all stages of life, youth is transitional. And although some lines of development, such as moral development, may be "completed" during youth, many others continue throughout adulthood.

It is also a mistake to identify youth with any one social group, role, class, organization, or position in society. Youth is a *psychological* stage; and those who are in this stage do not necessarily join together in identifiable groups, nor do they share a common social position. Not all college students, for example, are in this stage of life: some students are psychological adolescents, while others are young adults—essentially apprentices to the existing society. Nor can the experience of youth as a stage of life be identified with any one class, nation, or other social grouping. Affluence and education can provide a freedom from economic need and an intellectual stimulation that may underlie and promote the transformations of youth. But there are poor and uneducated young men and women, from Abraham Lincoln to Malcolm X, who have had a youth, and rich, educated ones who have moved straightaway from adolescence to adulthood. And although the experience of youth is probably more likely to occur in the economically advanced nations, some of the factors that facilitate youth also exist in the less advanced nations, where comparable youthful issues and transformations are expressed in different cultural idioms.

Nor should youth be identified with the rejection of the *status quo* or specifically with student radicalism. Indeed, anyone who has more or less definitively defined himself as a misanthrope or a revolutionary has moved beyond youthful probing into an "adult" commitment to a position vis-à-vis society. To repeat: what characterizes youth is not a definitive rejection of the existing "system," but an ambivalent tension over the relationship between self and society. This tension may take the form of avid efforts at self-reform that spring from acceptance of the *status quo,* coupled with a sense of one's own inadequacy vis-à-vis it. In youth the relationship between self and society is indeed problematical, but rejection of the existing society is not a necessary characteristic of youth.

Youth obviously cannot be equated with any particular age-range. In practice, most young Americans who enter this stage of life tend to be between the ages of eighteen and thirty. But they constitute a minority of the whole age-grade. Youth as a developmental stage is emergent; it is an "optional" stage, not a universal one. If we take Kohlberg's studies of the development of postconventional moral reasoning as a rough index of the "incidence" of youth, less than 40 per cent of middle-class (college-educated) men and a smaller proportion of working-class men have developed beyond the conventional level by the age of twenty-four. Thus, "youths" constitute but a minority of their age group. But those who are in this stage of life today largely determine the public image of their generation.

Admirers and romanticizers of youth tend to identify youth with virtue, morality, and mental health. But to do so is to overlook the special youthful possibilities for viciousness, immorality, and psychopathology. Every time of human life, each level of development, has its characteristic vices and weaknesses, and youth is no exception. Youth is a stage, for example, when the potentials for zealotry and fanaticism, for reckless action in the name of the highest principles, for self-absorption, and for special arrogance are all at a peak. Furthermore, the fact that youth is a time of psychological change also inevitably means that it is a stage of constant recapitulation, re-enactment, and reworking of the past. This reworking can rarely occur without real regression, whereby the buried past is reexperienced as present and, one hopes, incorporated into it. Most youthful transformation occurs *through* brief or prolonged regression, which, however benignly it may eventually be resolved, constitutes part of the psychopathology of youth. And the special compulsions and inner states of youth—the euphoria of omnipotentiality and the dysphoria of estrangement, the hyperconsciousness of consciousness, the need for constant motion, and the terror of stasis—may generate youthful pathologies with a special virulence and obstinacy. In one sense those who have the luxury of a youth may be said to be "more developed" than those who do not have (or do not take) this opportunity. But no level of development and no stage of life should be identified either with virtue or with health.

Finally, youth is not the same as the adoption of youthful causes, fashions, rhetoric, or postures. Especially in a time like our own, when youthful behavior is watched with ambivalent fascination by adults, the positions of youth become part of the cultural stock-in-trade. There thus develops the phenomenon of *pseudo youth*—preadolescents, adolescents, and frustrated adults masquerade as youths, adopt youthful manners, and disguise (even to themselves) their real concerns by the use of youthful rhetoric. Many a contemporary adolescent, whether of college or high school age, finds it convenient to displace and express his battles with his parents in a pseudo-youthful railing at the injustices, oppression, and hypocrisy of the Establishment. And many an adult, unable to accept his years, may adopt pseudo-youthful postures to express the despairs of his adulthood.

To differentiate between "real" and pseudo youth is a tricky, subtle, and unrewarding enterprise. For, as I have earlier emphasized, the concept of youth as here defined is an ideal type, an abstraction from the concrete experience of many different individuals. Furthermore, given the unevenness of human development and the persistence throughout life of active remnants of earlier developmental levels, conflicts, and stages, no one can ever be said to be completely "in" one stage of life in all areas of behavior and at all times. No issue can ever be said to be finally "resolved"; no earlier conflict is completely "overcome." Any real person, even though on balance we may consider him a "youth," will also contain some persistent childishness, some not-outgrown adolescence, and some precocious adulthood in his makeup. All we can say is that, for some, adolescent themes and levels of development are *relatively* outgrown, while adult concerns have not yet assumed full prominence. It is such people whom one might term "youths."

THE IMPLICATIONS OF YOUTH

I have sketched with broad and careless strokes the rough outlines of a stage of life I believe to characterize a growing, although still small, set of young men and women. This sketch, although presented dogmatically, is clearly preliminary; it will doubtless require revision and correction after further study. Yet let us for the moment assume that, whatever the limitations of this outline, the concept of a post-adolescent stage of life has some merit. What might be the implications of the emergency of youth?

To most Americans, the chief anxieties raised by youth are over social stability and historical continuity. In every past and present society, including our own, the great majority of men and women seem to be, in Kohlberg's terms, "conventional" in moral judgment and, in Perry's terms, "dualistic" in their intellectual outlook. Such men and women accept with little question the existing moral codes of the community, just as they endorse their culture's traditional view of the world. It is arguable that both cultural continuity and social stability have traditionally rested on the moral and epistemological conventionality of most men and women, and on the secure transmission of these conventional views to the next generation.

What, then, would it mean if our particular era were producing millions of postconventional, nondualistic, postrelativistic youth? What would happen if millions of young men and women developed to the point that they "made up their own minds" about most value, ideological, social, and philosophical questions, often rejecting the conventional and traditional answers? Would they not threaten the stability of their societies?

Today it seems clear that most youths are considered nuisances or worse by the established order, to which they have not finally pledged their allegiance. Indeed, many of the major stresses in contemporary American society spring from or are aggravated by those in this stage of life. One aspect of the deep polarization in our society may be characterized psychologically as a struggle between conventionals and postconventionals, between those who have not had a youth and those who have. The answer of the majority of the public seems clear: we already have too many "youths" in our society; youth as a developmental stage should be stamped out.

A more moderate answer to the questions I am raising is also possible. We might recognize the importance of having a *few* postconventional individuals (an occasional Socrates, Christ, Luther, or Gandhi to provide society with new ideas and moral inspiration) but nonetheless establish a firm top limit on the proportion of postconventional, youth-scarred adults our society could tolerate. If social stability requires human inertia—that is, unreflective acceptance of most social, cultural, and political norms—perhaps we should discourage "youth as a stage of life" in any but a select minority.

A third response, toward which I incline, seems to me more radical. To the argument of social stability and cultural continuity, one might reply by pointing to the enormous *in*stabilities and gross cultural *dis*continuities that characterize the modern world. Older forms of stability and continuity have *already* been lost in the postindustrial era. Today it is simply impossible to return to a bygone age when massive inertia guaranteed social stability (if there really was such an age). The cake of customs crumbled long ago. The only hope is to learn to live without it.

In searching for a way to do this, we might harken back to certain strands in socialist thought that see new forms of social organization possible for men and women who are more "evolved." I do not wish to equate my views on development with revolutionary socialism or anarchism, much less with a Rousseauistic faith in the goodness of the essential man. But if there is anything to the hypothesis that different historical conditions alter the nature of the life cycle, then men with different kinds of development may require or be capable of living in different kinds of social institutions. On the one hand, this means that merely throwing off institutional shackles, as envisioned by some socialist and anarchist thinkers, would not automatically change the nature of men, although it may be desirable on other grounds. "New men" cannot be created by institutional transformations alone, although institutional changes may, over the very long run, affect the possibilities for continuing development by changing the matrix in which development occurs.

But on the other hand, men and women who have attained higher developmental levels may be capable of different kinds of association and cooperation from those at lower levels. Relativism, for example, brings not only skepticism but also tolerance of the viewpoints of others and a probable reduction in moralistic self-righteousness. Attaining the stage of personal principles in moral development in no way prevents the individual from conforming to a just social order or even, for that matter, from obeying unreasonable traffic laws. Men and women who are capable of interpersonal mutuality are not for that reason worse citizens; on the contrary, their capacity to be concerned with others as unique individuals might even make them better citizens. Examples could be multiplied, but the general point is obvious: higher levels of development, including the emergence on a mass scale of "new" stages of life, may permit new forms of human cooperation and social organization.

It may be true that all past societies have been built upon the unquestioning inertia of the vast majority of their citizens. And this inertia may have provided the psychological ballast that prevented most revolutions from doing more than reinstating the *ancien régime* in new guise. But it does not follow that this need always continue to be true. If new developmental stages are emerging that lead growing minorities to more autonomous positions vis-à-vis their societies, the result need not be anarchy or social chaos. The result might instead be the possibility of new forms of social organization based less upon unreflexive acceptance of the *status quo* than upon thoughtful and self-conscious loyalty and cooperation. But whether or not these new forms can emerge depends not only upon the psychological factors I have discussed here, but even more upon political, social, economic, and international conditions.

3 4 5 6 7 8 9 10 11 12 13 14 15   88 87 86 85 84 83 82 81 80 79 78 77 76 75